COLUMBIA COLLEGE CHICAGO

DATE DUE

Demco, Inc. 38-293

MAY 25 2011

The Power of Song

*Music and Dance in the Mission Communities of
Northern New Spain, 1590–1810*

The Power of Song

Music and Dance in the Mission Communities of Northern New Spain, 1590–1810

Kristin Dutcher Mann

Stanford University Press
Stanford, California

and

The Academy of American Franciscan History
Berkeley, California
2010

Library of Congress Cataloging-in-Publication Data

Mann, Kristin Dutcher, 1972–
 The power of song : music and dance in the mission communities of northern New Spain, 1590–1810 / Kristin Dutcher Mann.
   p. cm.
 Includes bibliographical references and index.
 ISBN 978-0-8047-7086-6 (alk. paper)
  1. Music—Social aspects—United States—History. 2. Music—Social aspects—Mexico—History. 3. Music—Religious aspects—United States—History. 4. Music—Religious aspects—Mexico—History. 5. Indians of North America—Colonization—United States. 6. Indians of North America—Colonization—Mexico. 7. Missionaries—United States—History. 8. Missionaries—Mexico—History. I. Title.
 ML3916.M35 2010
 780.972—dc22
                                                            2009045117

Parts of Chapters 2, 3, and 4 were previously published in *Religion in New Spain*, Susan Schroeder and Stafford Poole, editors, 2007, University of New Mexico Press. Published with permission.

© 2010 by the Board of Trustees of the
Leland Stanford Junior University

No part of this book may be reproduced or transmitted in any form or by any means, electronic or mechanical, including photocopying and recording, or in any information storage or retrieval system without the prior written permission of Stanford University Press.

Contents

Introduction   1

Part I. Musical Traditions   17

Chapter 1.   Reconstructing Indigenous Music and Dance   19
Chapter 2.   Liturgical and Religious Music in Europe, 1500–1800   43

Part II. Mission Music   67

Chapter 3.   Musical Cultures Meet   69
Chapter 4.   Music, Dance, and Community, 1680–1767   101
Chapter 5.   Changing Communities, 1768–1810   133

Part III. Song, Time, and Space   177

Chapter 6.   Music and the Restructuring of Time   179
Chapter 7.   Music and the Restructuring of Physical and Social Space   213

Conclusions   253

Bibliography   261

Index   293

Acknowledgments

As far back as I can remember, my parents ended our days by singing—lullabies from my mother, and when I was older, prayers with my father. As I grew, I sang with my father, and now, I sing to my own two sons. The power of melodies to soothe, establish routines, teach, and impact our psychological states fascinates me, much as it must have interested Indians and missionaries centuries ago. The soundscapes of our world today are increasingly complex, and music often provides an escape from the multiple stimuli and pressures of our daily lives. The proliferation of personal portable electronic musical devices has allowed consumers to access music from other places and times more easily than ever before. Although I study the power of song hundreds of years in the past, we can see the same force at work today.

I first became fascinated by the history of the Spanish borderlands by growing up in Texas, taking short trips to visit the San Antonio Missions with my parents, brother, and sister, and visiting extended family in the Rio Grande Valley. An unforgettable high school history teacher, Nancy Graves, inspired critical thinking and writing about history. As an undergraduate student at Trinity University in San Antonio, Allan Kownslar and Alida Metcalf guided my curiosity about Latin America and Texas. Some of the first lesson plans I wrote and taught to my high school students at the International School of the Americas in San Antonio were about cultural encounters and their legacies.

During the decade in which I have been researching and writing this book, I have received immeasurable support from family, friends, and colleagues. I could not have asked for a better graduate educational experience than the broad, thematic training that I engaged in with the history faculty at Northern Arizona University, especially my advisor, Susan Deeds, who encouraged me to travel with her to conferences, and spent countless hours mentoring me. Classes from Susan, Karen Vieira Powers, and Sanjay Joshi gave me practical tools to succeed as an historian. A summer in Seville with Karen at the AGI, and shorter trips to Mexico with Susan introduced me to archival research. I am grateful for the financial support I received while at Northern Arizona University, in the form of graduate assistantships and the McAllister Transition Fellowship. The staff at the Cline Library Special Collections and Archives, where I worked part-time, as well as dissertation committee member Linda Curcio-Nagy, were also invaluable resources. Fellow graduate student and friend Tracy Goode has read drafts of this project since 1999, and I appreciate her wide knowledge of theory and historiography. A dissertation fellowship from the Academy of American Franciscan History, and support from the Texas State Historical Association, allowed me to complete my research and writing in the spring of 2002.

A semester of half-time leave from the University of Arkansas at Little Rock (UALR) in the spring of 2006 enabled me to focus entirely on research. I am thankful to Francisco Morales, of the Centro de Estudios Históricos Fray Bernardino de Sahagún at the Biblioteca Franciscana in San Pedro, Cholula, for helping to arrange a visiting professorship with the Universidad de las Americas in Puebla, so that my family and I could live in Cholula while I worked with materials at the Biblioteca. Deans Deborah Baldwin and Daryl Rice, and department chair Charlie Bolton, helped make that leave possible. My colleagues at UALR have provided feedback on various portions of this manuscript, particularly Laura Smoller, Moira Maguire, and Jim Ross, who share research interests in the intersections of religion, ethnicity, and social control. I also appreciate travel support from the University of Arkansas at Little Rock, and the Academy of American Franciscan History. Because of this support, I have been able to engage in meaningful dialogue with musicologists and ethnohistorians about music and missions in colonial Latin America. Research staff at the AGI, AGN, Biblioteca Franciscana, Arizona State Museum, the University of Texas and University of New Mexico libraries, and Our Lady of the Lake University, as well as interlibrary loan staff at UALR, have been helpful and efficient.

Doing interdisciplinary research is fraught with difficulties, and I am immensely grateful to John Koegel for his careful reading of my manuscript in 2008, and his willingness to share his musical expertise. C.T. Aufdemberge, Bill Summers, Craig Russell, and my father-in-law Robert Mann have also provided guidance about musical and liturgical terms. Historians Francisco Morales, Fritz Schwaller, Susan Schroeder, Cynthia Radding, Amy Turner Bushnell, Robert Senkewicz, Rose Marie Beebe, and Susan Kellogg have encouraged my research, commented on my work, answered questions, and invited me to participate in conferences or publications. Jeffrey Burns of the Academy of American Franciscan History has supported the project of turning my original dissertation into this book for the last seven years, and I am immensely thankful for his guidance. Erin Pennington provided copy editing support, and Stanford University Press worked quickly to move the publishing process along.

Most of all, I am thankful for my family for helping to keep me grounded, and my life balanced. My parents, grandparents, siblings, niece and nephews, and close family friends have supported me at every point in this process. I regret that my father, Don, my mother-in-law, Mary Jane, and Grandpa Sam are not here to see the return on their investments of confidence in me. My husband David, the most giving person I know, has had unshakable faith in my ability to see this book through, and his sacrifices of time, listening, and assistance with maps and photographs, were tremendous assets. Our sons Aaron and Adam daily remind me of the important things in life, and their curiosity about the world reminds me why I became interested in history in the first place.

The wide geographic scope and time frame of this work were dictated by the fragmentary nature of historical evidence. I have tried to gain a glimpse of the daily rhythms of life, song, and dance in the northern frontier spaces of New Spain, a project that can, and will, last a lifetime.

INTRODUCTION

In the 1986 movie, *The Mission*, a stirring scene portrays the initial contact between a Jesuit missionary, Father Gabriel (Jeremy Irons), and the Guaraní people of central South America.[1] Father Gabriel plays an intriguing tune on his small wooden recorder as he treads through the dense foliage atop a spectacular waterfall. Several indigenous men appear from behind the trees and, instead of attacking the solitary figure, they are enraptured by the sound of the melody he makes, and invite him to their settlement. Throughout the film, music reappears as a central element in the conversion of the Guaraní. Ennio Morricone's notable score imagines the music of the Guaraní missions. As the film concludes, although the mission and many native lives have been destroyed in a fierce battle with the colonial troops, surviving Indian children paddle a canoe down the river away from the mission community. The background music swells, and one boy retrieves a broken violin from the river and continues paddling into the wilderness. While the film's romanticized illustration of mission life has been justly criticized by historians,[2] its portrayal of the use of music as an evangelization tool is grounded in the extensive musical culture of the Jesuit Guaraní missions. For me, the prominence of music in the movie prompted questions about the historical presence of music in the missions of Spain's American colonies. To what degree was music utilized in frontier missions? How was it involved in the imposition of colonial rule, particularly conversion and Hispanicization efforts? Was the film's portrayal of the power of music and its lasting importance in indigenous society accurate throughout the Spanish American colonies? What story would the Guaraní tell, if given the opportunity to describe their encounters with European liturgical music?

Some time after first watching *The Mission*, I was given a recording of music entitled *Native Angels* performed by the San Antonio Vocal Ensemble

---

[1] *The Mission*, produced by Fernando Ghia and David Puttnam, directed by Roland Joffé (Enigma Productions, 1986).

[2] See James S. Saeger, "*The Mission* and Historical Missions: Film and the Writing of History," *The Americas* 51:3 (January 1995), 393-415.

(SAVAE).³ As I listened to their recreations of colonial music from the cathedrals and parishes of New Spain and read the liner notes describing the fusion of European and indigenous forms of religious music, I again questioned the role played by music in the colonization and conversion of the indigenous peoples of the Americas. Was the music performed by SAVAE the same as that performed in the missions I had visited on family vacations as a child? Did this type of music truly represent a union between Catholic and indigenous sacred music? I searched for other recordings of mission music and found that sacred music from the Spanish colonies had been recently recorded by musical ensembles, such as Chanticleer and Boston Camerata, as the quincentenary of the Columbian exchange renewed interest and discussion in cultural contacts.

My initial research examined the use of music as an evangelization tool in central New Spain and in the missions of the north. I discovered that music and dance filled many functions beyond attracting Indians to a mission and teaching them doctrine. It was an integral part of the colonial encounters, involved in cultural accommodation and exchange. Indigenous peoples were able to influence the type of music and dance performed for Catholic functions in mission communities. In some cases, they used music to gain advantages or control in the context of the power relations that shaped their lives under colonial rule.

This study examines sacred music in mission communities throughout northern New Spain from founding the northern missions in the late sixteenth century until the end of Spanish colonial rule. During this period, northern New Spain encompassed the territories of Baja and Alta California, Sinaloa, Sonora, Nueva Vizcaya, Nuevo León, Nuevo México, Nuevo Santander, Coahuila, Texas, Louisiana, and Florida.⁴ Missions were the initial religious institutions in frontier communities, distinct from more fully developed parish churches, or

---

³ San Antonio Vocal Arts Ensemble, *Native Angels: Musical Miracles from the New World* (Iago CD204, 1996), compact disc.

⁴ Louisiana was handed by the French to the Spanish empire in 1763, and remained under Spanish control until the Louisiana Purchase of 1803. French missionary presence in the territory prior to 1763 was much more extensive than Spanish missionary activity in the latter half of the eighteenth century. See Jean Delanglez, *The French Jesuits in Lower Louisiana, 1700–1763* (Washington, DC: Catholic University of America, 1935); and *Hennepin's Description of Louisiana: A Critical Essay* (Chicago: Institute of Jesuit History, 1941). On music in New France, see Élisabeth Gallat-Morin and Jean Pierre Pinson, *La Vie Musicale en Nouvelle-France* (Sillery, Québec: Septentrion, 2003), and Paul-André Dubois, *De l'oreille au coeur: Naissance du chant religieux en langues amérindiennes dans les missions de Nouvelle-France 1600–1650* (Sillery, Québec: Septentrion, 1997); and John Koegel, "Rural Musical Life in the French Villages in Upper Louisiana," in Paul Laird and William Everett, eds., *On Bunker's Hill: Essays on Music in Honor of J. Bunker Clark* (Warren, MI: Harmonie Park Press, 2007), 13-25.

parroquias. They were organized by the regular clergy (Jesuits and Franciscans in this region), politically controlled by missionaries, and subsidized by the Spanish Crown. As Spanish soldiers and settlers moved into frontier areas, many communities centered around the missions, which were secularized or handed over to diocesan control, after their congregated populations were instructed in the faith and economically self-sufficient.

Compared with records about mission finances, economic activity, presidial activity, revolts, and mission registers, information on music and dance is relatively scarce. As part of daily life, musical activity was generally not remarkable enough to note in written correspondence unless a missionary was requesting supplies, supplying an inventory of mission contents, or describing a special celebration. Thus, I have cast my net wide both chronologically and geographically to gain a sense of how song and dance intersected with the daily lives of Indians and missionaries. In the decades after the conquest of the peoples of central Mesoamerica, the Spanish Crown and the Catholic Church turned their attention northward. Expansion in this area was undertaken by Franciscan and Jesuit missionaries with scattered support from the military and groups of civilian and Hispanicized indigenous settlers. Missionaries and Spanish officials relied heavily on establishing control through persuasion and demonstration in their attempts to colonize and convert such a vast territory populated by diverse indigenous groups.[5]

Music—performed, structured sound—was an important instrument in the processes of conquest, persuasion, and identity and community formation. It was an integral part of the cultures of the ethnic groups in the mountains, deserts, and oases of the north, and it provided a starting point for intercultural communication. Song and European-style musical instruments helped attract potential converts to the missions. Once missionaries had piqued the curiosity of the Indians, many tried to teach Catholic doctrine by using music as a mnemonic device. Repetition of important prayers set to familiar tunes and the use of bells and spiritual songs to structure daily activities helped to establish social control over the population within range of their sound. Liturgical rites and ceremonies for special occasions reinforced authority, but also opened up a space for resettled and reconfigured indigenous groups to invent and reshape cultural practices. Some groups responded to the music of the mission communities by refashioning ceremonies, particularly those involving dance, to delineate group boundaries and re-create community identity.

---

[5] Edward Spicer, *Cycles of Conquest: The Impact of Spain, Mexico, and the United States on the Indians of the Southwest, 1533–1960* (Tucson: University of Arizona Press, 1962), 324.

Refusal to congregate in the missions and indigenous revolts were longtime elements of life in northern New Spain. In some areas, Indians determined the conditions and outcomes of their interactions with Spaniards, while in others, colonial power structures enforced compliance or strategic accommodation occurred more readily. By the end of the colonial period, however, the north was more fully incorporated into the Spanish state and its peoples were familiar with the liturgy and rituals of the Catholic Church, even if their interpretations of meaning behind these ceremonies differed. After over two hundred years of interaction (less in some areas), the contact between indigenous and missionary cultures produced unique and changed religious music such as the *alabado*, *matachines*, and portions of the sung liturgy for the mass and Divine Office, as well as performances for special occasions.[6] These forms reveal a great deal of accommodation, transformation, and syncretism in the cultural encounters of mission communities.

The central themes of this work reveal the importance of music and dance in New Spain's north. First, music creates and marks collective identity in ongoing cultural processes. Music, especially that considered "traditional," delineates boundaries of inclusion in social groups. Group performance of song and dance reinforces shared history and values, enforcing cooperation and coordination.[7] From the singing of alma mater fight songs to work songs and spirituals, the role of music and dance in forging group identity is clear. In my study, Franciscans and Jesuits articulated their purpose and calling through liturgical chants sung in unison. Christianized Indians, mestizos, and Spaniards living in mission communities expressed collective identity through the singing of devotional songs, folk dances, and performances for special occasions. These identities were fluid, changing as political, economic, and social conditions in the northern mission communities changed.

Second, music is an agent of social control, heavily involved in the exercise of power. Music is employed today to influence consumer behavior, increase task performance, and change emotional mood.[8] In colonial Latin

---

[6] The alabado is an extraliturgical spiritual song, while matachines are dance-dramas re-enacting the conversion of indigenous populations to Christianity. Music as part of the Catholic liturgy (in Latin) included sung and instrumental portions of the Mass and antiphons, hymns, and psalms, which were part of the liturgy of the Divine Office. Performances for special occasions included elements such as dance-dramas and spiritual songs used in processions.

[7] Brown, "Introduction," in Steven Brown and Ulrick Volgsten, eds., *Music and Manipulation: On the Social Uses and Social Control of Music* (New York: Berghahn Books, 2006), 2.

[8] See the essays in Brown and Volgsten, *op. cit.*, particularly, "The Effectiveness of Music in Television Commercials: A Comparison of Theoretical Approaches," by Claudia Bullerjahn, and "Music in Business Environments," by Adrian C. North and David J. Hargreaves.

America, Franciscans and Jesuits used song to reshape time and teach Catholic doctrine. Then, as now, rhythm, repetition, melody, and harmony worked together to increase the meaning and memorability of linguistic messages.[9] Music's power is accessible to all and it has been used to challenge authority. From reggae, to the music of the Civil Rights Movement in the United States, to songs used to protest war and colonial rule, this function has been widely studied in the twentieth century.[10] In the colonial period music and dance were also used to challenge hierarchy. Puebloans in New Mexico challenged the authority of the friars by dancing on the roof of the church, and women challenged the patriarchy of Catholicism and Hispanic society by participating in mission choirs and singing solos in front of important visitors. Song and dance were conduits through which spiritual power could be accessed and channeled, for both indigenous groups and the missionaries who worked among them.

A third recurring theme is that music is a language with potent communicative powers. Within groups, it promotes cooperation and helps to resolve conflict.[11] Conformity to societal norms is emphasized in ritual music, such as patriotic anthems, liturgical chants, or dance-dramas. Songs and ritual gestures help transmit cultural knowledge from one generation to another. Music in both contemporary and historical times has functioned as an educational aid, mnemonic device, and a way to engage students in learning. Today, children learn their alphabet by singing their ABCs. Cultural values are passed on through nursery rhymes and games. Children in indigenous societies learned cultural fundamentals through songs and dances in much the same way.

In addition, music communicates differences within a group. Sound preference can sort people into groups within a society, and it often carries ethnic and gendered stereotypes.[12] Song and dance can separate a group into performers and observers, different voice and instrumental parts, and gendered choruses. Proficiency in music and movement affords special status within groups, and this status can overcome ethnic, religious, and gendered barriers.

---

[9] Brown, "Introduction," 4. See also Bruce Richmann, "How Music Fixed 'Nonsense' into Significant Formulas: On Rhythm, Repetition, and Meaning," in Nils Lennart Wallin, Björn Merker, and Steven Brown, eds., *The Origins of Music* (Cambridge, MA: MIT Press, 2000).

[10] Reebee Garofalo, ed., *Rockin' the Boat: Mass Music and Mass Movements* (Boston: South End Press, 1992); Ron Eyerman and Andrew Jamison, *Music and Social Movements: Mobilizing Traditions in the Twentieth Century* (New York: Cambridge University Press, 1998).

[11] See Veit Erlmann, *Music, Modernity, and the Global Imagination: South Africa and the West* (New York: Oxford University Press, 1999), 6.

[12] David Samuels, *Putting a Song on Top of It: Expression and Identity on the San Carlos Apache Reservation* (Tucson: University of Arizona Press, 1994), 102-103.

Furthermore, the language of music facilitates communication between groups. Today this is overwhelmingly evident in the prevalence of music in global popular culture. In my study, music as language carried the meaning of important spiritual concepts between missionaries and Indians. Dance and location in processions communicated social hierarchy. Song and dance were used, as they are today, to communicate with the spirit world, access power, receive messages, and honor deities.

While the forms and functions of music and dance within the framework of colonial religious encounters are subjects that have received little attention by historians of colonial Latin America, recent literature on the cultural encounters between missionaries and indigenous peoples in Latin America has caused researchers to move far beyond the traditional interpretation of the mission as an institution of frontier civilization. This understanding, which emphasized the paternal benevolence of missionaries and the uncivilized ways of the Indians, was propagated by Herbert Eugene Bolton and his students.[13] They placed the mission at the center of the frontier to the exclusion of other frontier peoples, processes, and institutions. The "new mission history" instead emphasizes the degrees to which indigenous peoples participated in the missionization process as historical actors.[14] Mission communities are examined as places of intercul-

---

[13] See in particular, Bolton, *The Mission as a Frontier Institution in the Spanish-American Colonies* (El Paso: Texas Western College Press for Academic Reprints, 1960); *The Spanish Borderlands: A Chronicle of Old Florida and the Southwest* (New Haven, CT: Yale University Press, 1921); and *Rim of Christendom: A Biography of Eusebio Francisco Kino, Pacific Coast Pioneer* (New York: The Macmillan Company, 1936). Others wrote in the Boltonian tradition about missions and missionaries, including John Francis Bannon and Peter Masten Dunne.

[14] See the essays in Erick Langer and Robert H. Jackson, eds., *The New Latin American Mission History* (Lincoln: University of Nebraska Press, 1995), as well as the essays in Robert H. Jackson, ed., *New Views of Borderlands History* (Albuquerque: University of New Mexico Press, 1998). Specific case studies of indigenous people in northern missions include Amy Turner Bushnell, *Situado and Sabana Spain's Support System for the Presidio and Mission Provinces of Florida*, Anthropological Papers of the American Museum of Natural History, no. 74 (New York: American Museum of Natural History, 1994); Susan M. Deeds, *Defiance and Deference in Mexico's Colonial North: Indians Under Spanish Rule in Nueva Vizcaya* (Austin: University of Texas Press, 2003); Cynthia Radding, *Wandering Peoples: Colonialism, Ethnic Spaces, and Ecological Frontiers in Northwestern Mexico, 1700–1850* (Durham: Duke University Press, 1997); Cecilia Sheridan, *Anónimos y Desterrados: La contienda por el "sitio que llaman de Quauyla," siglos XVI–XVIII* (Mexico City: Porrúa, 2000); Juliana Barr, *Peace Came in the Form of a Woman: Indians and Spaniards in the Texas Borderlands* (Chapel Hill: University of North Carolina Press, 2007); Ignacio del Río, *El regimen jesuítico de la Antigua California* (Mexico City: Universidad Autónoma de México, 2003); Harry Crosby, *Antigua California: Mission and Colony on the Peninsular Frontier, 1697–1768* (Albuquerque: University of New Mexico Press, 1994); Steven W. Hackel, *Children of Coyote, Missionaries of Saint Francis: Indian–Spanish Relations in Colonial California, 1769–1850* (Chapel Hill: University of North Carolina Press, 2005); and for South

tural contact in which Spanish and Catholic power was negotiated, in some cases dominating, in others, rejected by indigenous inhabitants. Economic and political factors, revolts and other forms of resistance, as well as cultural processes of accommodation and compromise, figure largely in these works. In addition, the new mission literature takes into account the importance of disease, depopulation, ecological change, gender, and violence in shaping the frontier landscape.[15] It is important to situate any study of life in the missions of northern New Spain in the complex circumstances surrounding colonial rule in frontier areas.

Within mission communities, there was a range of reactions to Spanish attempts to impose colonial rule. A wide literature on indigenous responses to colonialism, greatly stimulated by the quincentenary of Columbus's voyages to the Americas, examines the ways in which Indians reacted to the conquerors.[16] Much of this literature centers around groups, such as the Nahua, Maya, and Inca who left records of their encounters.[17] These monographs address the

---

America, James S. Saeger, *The Chaco Mission Frontier: The Guaycuran Experience* (Tucson: University of Arizona Press, 2000); and Barbara Ganson, *The Guaraní under Spanish Rule in the Río de la Plata* (Stanford, CA: Stanford University Press, 2003).

[15] For more on frontier conditions, see the essays in Donna J. Guy and Thomas Sheridan, eds., *Contested Ground: Comparative Frontiers on the Northern and Southern Edges of the Spanish Empire* (Tucson: University of Arizona Press, 1998); and David J. Weber and Jane M. Rausch, eds., *Where Cultures Meet: Frontiers in Latin American History* (Wilmington, DE: Scholarly Resources, 1994). For northern New Spain, in particular, see Miguel Léon Portilla, "The Norteño Variety of Mexican Culture: An Ethnohistorical Approach," in Edward H. Spicer and Raymond H. Thompson, eds., *Plural Society in the Southwest* (New York: Interbook, 1972), 109-114; Susan M. Deeds, "New Spain's Far North: A Changing Historiographical Frontier?" *Latin American Research Review* 25:1 (1990), 226-235; and Manuel Ceballos Ramirez, *De historia e historiografía de la frontera norte* (Nuevo Laredo: Universidad Autónoma de Tamaulipas, 1996); and Jesús F. de la Teja and Ross Frank, eds., *Choice, Persuasion, and Coercion: Social Control on Spain's North American Frontier* (Albuquerque: University of New Mexico Press, 2005).

[16] For example, see Charles Gibson, *The Aztecs under Spanish Rule* (Stanford, CA: Stanford University Press, 1964); Nancy M. Farriss, *Maya Society and Colonial Rule: The Collective Enterprise of Survival* (Princeton, NJ: Princeton University Press, 1984); Grant D. Jones, *Maya Resistance to Spanish Rule: Time and History on a Colonial Frontier* (Albuquerque: University of New Mexico Press, 1989); Robert W. Patch, *Maya and Spaniard in Yucatan, 1648–1812* (Stanford, CA: Stanford University Press, 1993); and William B. Taylor, *Landlord and Peasant in Colonial Oaxaca* (Stanford, CA: Stanford University Press, 1972). For South America, see Karen Spalding, *Huarochirí: An Andean Society under Inca and Spanish Rule* (Stanford, CA: Stanford University Press, 1984); Steve J. Stern, *Peru's Indian Peoples and the Challenge of Spanish Conquest: Huamanga to 1640* (Madison: University of Wisconsin Press, 1982); Karen Vieira Powers, *Andean Journeys: Migration, Ethnogenesis, and the State in Colonial Quito* (Albuquerque: University of New Mexico Press, 1995); and Susan Ramírez, *The World Upside Down: Cross-Cultural Contact and Conflict in Sixteenth-Century Peru* (Stanford, CA: Stanford University Press, 1997).

[17] Native language sources have been used to document indigenous perspectives, particularly for the people of central Mesoamerica. See, among others, James Lockhart, *The Nahuas after the*

resistance, accommodation, adaptation, and cultural transformations that took place in Indian territories as a result of incorporation into the Spanish state, sometimes after prolonged struggles. Fewer monographs examine responses to colonial rule in the more sparsely populated areas of Spain's vast American empire due to the paucity of source material, absence of native-language sources, and because many of these peoples have ceased to exist as distinct indigenous groups.[18]

Approaches and models used by scholars writing about the colonial encounter in the religious sphere are also useful for investigating indigenous responses to colonial rule.[19] For example, Louise Burkhart showed not only how missionaries attempted to Christianize the Nahua by converting indigenous rhetoric to the expression of Christian moral concerns, but also how Christian rhetoric was made indigenous by its adoption in Nahua form. This process was similar to the use of music for evangelization purposes in the north, including the appropriation of native song and dance. Like Christian rhetoric, Catholic liturgical celebrations were made indigenous through the dialogic process of accommodation in mission communities.[20]

Conquest: A Social and Cultural History of the Indians of Central Mexico, Sixteenth through Eighteenth Centuries (Stanford, CA: Stanford University Press, 1992); Susan Kellogg, *Law and the Transformation of Aztec Culture* (Norman: University of Oklahoma Press, 1995); Susan Schroeder, *Chimalpahin and the Kingdom of Chalco* (Tucson: University of Arizona Press, 1991); and Matthew Restall, *The Maya World: Yucatec Culture and Society, 1550–1850* (Stanford, CA: Stanford University Press, 1997).

[18] See Spicer, *Cycles of Conquest*; William B. Griffen, *Indian Assimilation in the Franciscan Areas of Nueva Vizcaya* (Tucson: University of Arizona Press, 1979); Evelyn Hu-Dehart, *Missionaries, Miners, and Indians: Spanish Contact and the Yaqui Nation, 1533–1820* (Tucson: University of Arizona Press, 1981); Ignacio del Río, *Conquista y aculturación en la California jesuítica* (Mexico City: Universidad Autónoma de México, 1984); Rámon Gutiérrez, *When Jesus Came, the Corn Mothers Went Away: Marriage, Sexuality and Power in New Mexico, 1500–1846* (Stanford, CA: Stanford University Press, 1991), as well as the monographs concerning northern missions listed above.

[19] Louise Burkhart, *The Slippery Earth: Nahua-Christian Dialogue in Sixteenth-Century Mexico* (Tucson: University of Arizona Press, 1989); William B. Taylor, *Magistrates of the Sacred: Priests and Parishioners in Eighteenth-Century Mexico* (Stanford, CA: Stanford University Press, 1996); Kenneth Mills, *Idolatry and Its Enemies: Colonial Andean Religion and Extirpation, 1640–1750* (Princeton, NJ: Princeton University Press, 1997); Susan Schroeder and Stafford Poole, eds., *Religion in New Spain* (Albuquerque: University of New Mexico Press, 2007).

[20] This process of accommodation is similar to that described by John and Jean Comaroff in *Ethnography and the Historical Imagination* (Boulder, CO: Westview Press, 1992), for South Africa. Historian Steven Hackel describes a similar phenomenon, which he terms "convergence," in the Franciscan mission communities of Alta California. *Children of Coyote, Missionaries of Saint Francis: Indian-Spanish Relations in Colonial California, 1769–1850* (Chapel Hill: University of North Carolina Press, 2005).

INTRODUCTION														9

In addition, others have analyzed material culture as a vehicle through which indigenous responses to colonial rule can be studied. Art, architecture, theater, music, and dance were all used in various ways by Spanish colonizers.[21] European techniques and forms blended with indigenous cultural expression and created new, hybridized forms of culture. Jeanette Peterson's study of the murals in the Augustinian convent at Malinalco, for example, was based on the idea that murals, as social texts, both recorded and helped to carry out the Church's mandate in the New World.[22] Music in the missions of northern New Spain can be examined in much the same way. Descriptions of musical events as well as lyrics to hymns in the vernacular reveal clues about the interaction between cultures. Similarly, Linda Curcio-Nagy's work on colonial spectacles such as Corpus Christi not only recounted the pageantry of these rituals, but also interpreted the descriptions of these events as social documents.[23] While cultural history provides a methodology for considering culture as text, this study also recognizes that historians must always be careful to situate cultural phenomena in their political and economic contexts.[24] Thus, music in the missions of northern New Spain is best viewed in light of the volatile and porous demographic, political, military, and economic landscape of this frontier region.

Due to its interdisciplinary nature, this project also relies on the work of music historians and musicologists who have examined the Mexican colonial period.[25] Scholars of music history have analyzed extant musical manuscripts

---

[21] The literature of colonization through culture includes Jeanette Favrot Peterson, *The Paradise Garden Murals of Malinalco: Utopia and Empire in Sixteenth-Century Mexico* (Austin: University of Texas Press, 1993); Serge Gruzinski, *Painting the Conquest: The Mexican Indians and the European Renaissance*, trans. Deke Dusinberre (Paris: Flammarion, 1992); Jaime Lara, *City, Temple, Stage* (New Haven, CT: Yale University Press, 2005); Louise M. Burkhart, *Holy Wednesday: A Nahua Drama from Early Colonial Mexico* (Philadelphia: University of Pennsylvania Press, 1996); Carol E. Robertson, ed., *Musical Repercussions of 1492: Encounters in Text and Performance* (Washington, DC: Smithsonian Institution Press, 1992); Clara Bargellini, *Misiones y Presidios de Chihuahua* (Mexico City: Gobierno del Estado de Chihuahua, 1997); and Beth K. Aracena, "Singing Salvation: Jesuit Musics in Colonial Chile, 1600–1767" (PhD diss., University of Chicago, 1999).

[22] *Paradise Garden Murals of Malinalco*, 6.

[23] Linda A. Curcio, "Saints, Sovereignty and Spectacle in Colonial Mexico" (PhD diss., Tulane University, 1993); Linda Curcio-Nagy, "Giants and Gypsies: Corpus Christi in Colonial Mexico City," in William Beezley, Cheryl English Martin, and William French, eds., *Rituals of Rule, Rituals of Resistance* (Wilmington, NC: SR Books, 1994). The other essays in this volume also look at ritual as text and use it as a vehicle through which social relations can be examined.

[24] Eric Van Young, "New Cultural History Comes to Old Mexico," *Hispanic American Historical Review* 79:2 (May 1999), 234–237.

[25] Robert Murrell Stevenson, *Music in Mexico: A Historic Survey* (New York: Thomas W. Crowell Company, 1952); and Jesús Estrada, *Música y músicos de la época virreinal* (Mexico City: Sep/Setentas, 1973).

and considered ways in which Jesuits and Franciscans utilized music as a tool of evangelization in their missions.[26] These works suggest that music functioned primarily as a tool used by the missionaries to evangelize and Hispanicize the indigenous peoples of the north. However, whereas the forms of music utilized in these settings are documented, music's power to affect social control, direct group identity, and facilitate communication is not prominently considered.

Antonio Gramsci's concept of cultural hegemony provides a point of departure for a discussion of music and social control. Instead of conquest by military force, cultural hegemony is domination based on pervasive, although often subtle, means of social control through the use of cultural institutions, such as schools, art, and the media.[27] Conquerors ensure that dominant ideologies put forth by these institutions appear natural, so that the colonized do not question their underlying assumptions. The end result is culturally induced submission to the social agenda of those in power. In some cases, the internalization of Spanish culture by subjugated peoples ensured hegemony without a great deal of physical force in Latin America. There is evidence for this form of hegemony, particularly in the daily schedules and ritual calendars imposed on neophytes by the missionaries.

Colonial processes such as the restructuring of time and impositions of behavioral norms may also be considered through the lens of post-structuralism proposed by Michel Foucault.[28] Mission communities, particularly those in

---

[26] For northern New Spain, see John Koegel, "Spanish and French Mission Music in Colonial North America," *Journal of the Royal Musical Association* 126 (2001): 1-53; Margaret Cayward, *Musical Life at Mission Santa Clara de Asís, 1777–1836* (Santa Clara, CA: Santa Clara University, 2006); Alfred E. Lemmon, "Jesuits and Music in Mexico," *Archivum Historicum Societatis Iesu* 46 (1977): 191-198; Craig Russell, *From Serra to Sancho: Music in the California Missions* (Oxford: Oxford University Press, 2009); and the scholarship of William Summers, including "New and Little Known Sources of Hispanic Music from California," *Inter-American Music Review* 11:2 (Spring–Summer 1991): 13-24, and "Orígenes hispanos de la música misional de California," *Revista Musical Chilena* 34:149–150 (January–June 1980), 34-48. For central New Spain, Pius J. Barth, *Franciscan Education and the Social Order in Spanish North America* (Chicago: N.p., 1950); George N. Heller, "Music Education in the Valley of Mexico during the Sixteenth Century" (PhD diss., University of Michigan, 1973); and Arthur J.O. Anderson, ed., *Psalmodia Christiana* (Salt Lake City: University of Utah Press, 1993). For South America, T. Frank Kennedy, "An Integrated Perspective: Music and Art in the Jesuit Reductions of Paraguay," in Christopher Chapple, ed., *The Jesuit Tradition in Education and Missions* (Scranton, PA: University of Scranton Press, 1993).

[27] Gramsci's ideas, laid out in *Prison Notebooks*, trans. Joseph A. Buttigieg and Antonio Callari (New York: Columbia University Press, 1991), have been used by many historians to help explain the colonial encounter.

[28] Foucault, *Discipline and Punish: The Birth of the Prison*, trans. Alan Sheridan (New York: Pantheon Books, 1977).

which Indians resided at the mission complex, shared many similarities with the monasteries and prisons discussed by Foucault, in which the lives and bodies of residents were disciplined through enclosure, timetables, and gestures. Power structures, reproduced and disseminated through movement and song, limited the agency of those within the sound of mission bells and were instrumental in the construction of identity. Relations among missionaries, the Spanish Crown, indigenous converts, and those who chose to reject mission life formed dense webs of power as they passed through institutions such as the colonial mission. Music and dance, including sacred and secular forms and ceremonies, were tangled in these webs, and even helped spin them, but also provided those with little room to speak more space in which to be heard.[29] Examining music within the context of colonial power relations heeds ethnomusicologist Anthony Seeger's warning that the relationship between music and identity cannot be looked at apart from the historical processes of which they are a part—particularly when relationships involve the hegemony of one group over another.[30]

Within the construct of cultural hegemony, however, there was also space for indigenous action to contest colonial rule. This contestation occurred in active forms, such as violent rebellions, flight from the missions, and refusal to attend religious services, doctrinal instruction, or required labor in mission fields or shops. In addition, more subtle responses have been documented by colonial historians. The work of James C. Scott has greatly influenced literature on indigenous responses to colonial rule; it helps scholars to search out indigenous voices in the Spanish colonial documents pertaining to the missions. Scott's analyses of "weapons of the weak" and "hidden transcripts" suggest ways in which these Spanish sources can be interrogated for the information they contain about indigenous action.[31] A rich body of literature on missions in colonial Latin America suggests that not only violent rebellion, but also flight, theft, foot

---

[29] See Gayatri Chakravorty Spivak, "Can the Subaltern Speak?," in *Colonial Discourse and Post-Colonial Theory: A Reader*, eds. Patrick Williams and Laura Chrisman (New York: Columbia University Press, 1994). I do not accept Spivak's contention that the subaltern have no space in which to be heard as historical agents—music, and particularly dance, helped to provide this space.

[30] Anthony Seeger, "Performance and Identity: Problems and Perspectives," in *Musical Repercussions of 1492*: Encounters in Text and Performance, (Washington, DC: Smithsonian Institution Press, 1992), 452-453. See also Raúl R. Romero, *Debating the Past: Music, Memory, and Identity in the Andes* (New York: Oxford University Press, 2001), 5-6; and Victoria Lindsay Levine, *Writing American Indian Music: Historic Transcriptions, Notations, and Arrangements*, Music of the United States of America, 11 (Middleton, WI: A-R Editions, Inc., 2002).

[31] Scott, *Weapons of the Weak: Everyday Forms of Peasant Resistance* (New Haven, CT: Yale University Press, 1985), and *Domination and the Arts of Resistance: Hidden Transcripts* (New Haven, CT: Yale University Press, 1990).

dragging, slander, false deference, and the appropriation of Christian symbols were among indigenous responses to the hegemony exerted in the missions. Indigenous appropriation of Christian music is evident in the northern missions. Indians could also study and perform as musicians to avoid other forms of more demanding labor or to seek advancement in the new social hierarchy of the missions. Women could challenge patriarchy through participation in music. Outward signs of conversion in the missions, such as the adoption of Hispanic forms of dress and the singing of hymns, could mask differing degrees of resistant behavior. By accepting some elements and rejecting or transforming others, Indians achieved a degree of agency under colonial rule in a process that historian Steve Stern refers to as "resistant adaptation."[32]

In other realms, particularly dance, cultural reinvention of traditional practices was more common. Through the processes of ethnogenesis, indigenous peoples under colonial rule maintained and reshaped their culture and ethnic identities in response to colonial pressures.[33] In some cases, Indians defended shifting, fluid identities based on their relationship to the land and its resources, as illustrated in Cynthia Radding's concept of social ecology.[34] In others, native groups selectively incorporated elements of European Catholicism into reinvented or new cultural practices, through the process of transculturation.[35] In her study of early colonial Nueva Vizcaya, Susan Deeds found that the ability to assert agency through ethnogenesis was mitigated by moral and biological barriers, including cultural frameworks and the impact of disease and dislocation, a framework she refers to as mediated opportunism.[36] In my understanding of ethnogenesis, where limiting factors such as disease allowed the reformation of group identity throughout the colonial period, music and dance were key elements through which identity and community were communicated. Altered forms of sacred and profane music and dance were created through transculturation, and missionaries also benefited from selective reciprocal cultural borrowing of indigenous culture.

---

[32] Stern, "New Approaches to the Study of Peasant Rebellion and Consciousness: Implications of the Andean Experience," in Stern, ed., *Resistance, Rebellion, and Consciousness in the Andean Peasant World, 18th to 20th Centuries* (Madison: University of Wisconsin Press, 1987), 3-28.

[33] On ethnogenesis, see Jonathan Hill, ed., *History, Power, and Identity: Ethnogenesis in the Americas, 1492–1992* (Iowa City: University of Iowa Press, 1996); Vieira Powers, *Andean Journeys*; and Radding, *Wandering Peoples*.

[34] Radding, *Wandering Peoples*, 1-8.

[35] Ganson, *The Guaraní under Spanish Rule in the Río de la Plata*, 12. Ganson also discusses the idea of reciprocal borrowing mentioned below.

[36] Deeds, *Defiance and Deference*, 2.

How is it possible to construct the indigenous side of the mission encounter in the north, where a body of indigenous language sources does not exist? An ethnohistorical approach is necessary for examining the incomplete record of the colonial period in northern New Spain. The works of archaeologists, anthropologists, sociologists, and ethnomusicologists have informed my research, and I have tried to read Spanish documentation critically, while understanding that it is impossible to look through the eyes of indigenous peoples to witness their encounters with colonialism. Certainly the missionary accounts of life in the missions must be carefully considered and contextualized. Ethnographic details must be gleaned from descriptions of indigenous cultural rites, and complaints of the barbarous nature of Indians read for the information they contain about cultural maintenance, reinvention, and change.

The primary question this study seeks to answer is, "How did music and dance function in mission communities?" The first part of this work looks separately at pre-Hispanic indigenous and European liturgical music cultures prior to the cultural encounters between the groups. In Chapter 1, I examine the varieties and social functions of music in the diverse indigenous societies in the territories that would become New Spain's northern frontier. For the peoples of the deserts, river valleys, mountains, and eastern pine forests, songs and dances were primary methods of communicating within and between groups, accessing the spiritual world, and transmitting history and culture. Music served important social functions, including enculturation of the young, transferring information, healing physical and psychological pain, reinforcing social identity during life transitions, and displaying resources. The problem of source material is most acute in this chapter, where anthropological upstreaming, despite its problems, helps to gain a sense of the meanings of musical performances. Chapter 2 investigates the music brought by Franciscan and Jesuit missionaries to New Spain and ultimately to the frontier missions. The ritual obligations of the liturgy, which included music, shaped the daily lives of those who entered the religious orders. Music was used by Franciscans and Jesuits to communicate with God, Mary, and the saints. In Counter-Reformation Europe, the Catholic Church carefully defined liturgical music in order to control religious expression, and thus, collective Catholic identity. Each religious order developed specific rules and practices regarding the place of music in their communities.

The second part of this work studies the way in which the varied musical cultures came into contact within the context of evangelization in mission communities. Chapter 3 begins with the role of music in the evangelization of central New Spain, and discusses the place of music in the earliest encounters of the north: *entradas* and the first Jesuit missions in the near north, and Franciscan missions in New Mexico and Florida. Early missionaries to New Spain were impressed by the fervor with which indigenous peoples learned instrumental and vocal music, and grand plans for using music to teach adults and children were developed, and in some cases, implemented. This chapter discusses the types of liturgical music present in early northern missions and describes its use as a teaching tool. It also considers the function of music, and particularly dance, in seventeenth-century revolts. Chapter 4 focuses on the 1680–1767 period, as the mission system expanded farther north and many missionaries expressed frustration with frontier conditions and the persistence of indigenous rituals and beliefs. An examination of the use of music in the Jesuit missions of Baja California, Nueva Vizcaya, and Sonora, and the Franciscan missions in New Mexico, Coahuila, and Texas, reveals that the forms and functions of music and dance in these mission communities mirrored political and economic realities of each region. A discussion of the careers of Juan María de Salvatierra and Antonio Margil de Jesús illustrates that music was an important factor in attracting Indians to the missions and facilitating the learning of Catholic doctrine and the Spanish language. The evangelization methods of these early eighteenth-century missionaries demonstrate similarities and differences in Franciscan and Jesuit uses of music. Because it was something upon which both indigenous groups and missionaries relied to communicate with the spiritual world and define collective identity, music was an instrumental part of cultural and religious encounters. Chapter 5 considers the changing mission communities in Baja California and the Pimería, when after the Jesuit expulsion in 1767, new political realities clashed with plans for evangelization. Frustration devoured Franciscans in New Mexico and Texas, where Indians were not fully integrated into growing Hispanic communities after decades of evangelization, and the threat of Apache and Comanche raids from the north wreaked havoc with the security of missionaries and converts. The foundation of an extensive chain of missions on the coast of Alta California relied heavily on music as an evangelization tool, and elaborate musical cultures developed in these missions.

The final section of the book looks thematically at the role of music and dance in reshaping time and space in northern New Spain. This part demonstrates that the hegemonic power of music as an agent of social control was used by both missionaries and Indians. In Chapter 6, I study music's ability to restructure daily and yearly concepts of time. Mission bells, the music of the liturgy, and devotional songs such as *alabados* defined daily schedules in many areas. The rotation of Catholic holy days fused with indigenous agricultural cycles and lunar phases to form new yearly calendars, largely structured by musical ritual. The study concludes in Chapter 7 with a look at the function of musical performances in restructuring space and the effects of space on musical performance. Although music was used by Franciscans and Jesuits to achieve social control, Indians were also able to access power in their responses to its use. Some Indians took advantage of the opportunities offered by performance to carve out social space. Others selectively incorporated religious music as a way of gaining material benefits. Music, particularly dance, was an agent in ethnogenesis, the continual reformation of community, in northern New Spain's mission communities. Pre-Hispanic traditions, combined with new elements from the colonial experience, were reinvented to define indigenous cultural and physical space.

Song and dance were important parts of the language of colonial encounters. *The Mission*'s Father Gabriel was able to first gain entry into Guaraní society due to his mastery of music's power, and there is evidence to suggest that missionaries in northern New Spain used music in much the same way.[37] Sound is everywhere in our world. It surrounds and envelops us, evoking strong responses, sometimes even unconscious, of the brain and nervous system.[38] Music, as performed sound, elicits emotional reactions and shapes human behavior and interaction. This book examines these forces in New Spain's northern-frontier mission communities.

---

[37] See the descriptions of the careers of Fray Antonio Margil de Jesús and Father Juan María de Salvatierra in Chapter 4.

[38] Oliver Sacks, *Musicophilia: Tales of Music and the Brain*, rev. ed. (New York: Vintage Books, 2008).

PART I
Musical Traditions

Image © The Metropolitan Museum of Art, The Crosby Brown Collection of Musical Instruments, 1889 (89.4.2631 a, b).

CHAPTER 1
Reconstructing Indigenous Music and Dance

In the beginning there was darkness. Darkness spun round upon itself and from it was born Earth Doctor. He went west, south, east, north, up, and down, looking everywhere, but there was nothing.

He created first the greasewood plant, and after that big black ants to form the gum of the greasewood. But Earth Doctor was not satisfied. . . . He created termites to live also on the greasewood. They formed dust, and he took it in his hand and shaped it into a ball. He went to a great height and placed it, but it would not remain steady. The dust blew around the earth, and the ball would not hold together. . . .

The earth was not large enough and he was not satisfied. He stood upon the top of the ball where he had placed it, holding his torch, and he sang:

The earth is spreading, spreading.
Earth Doctor made the earth,
Standing upon it he spread it in all directions.
The earth is spreading, spreading.
Earth Doctor made the earth,
The earth spread flat in all directions.

Still the earth was not large enough. He stood a second time upon it and sang. . . . He stood a third time upon it and sang. . . .
The earth became large and he was satisfied. He rested.[1]

O'odham storytellers Thomas Vanyiko and William Blackwater remembered tales passed down from their elders about Earth Doctor and the creation of the world of the ancestral Pimas and Papagos. The words and melodies of these first songs were largely responsible for the creation of the world. In this

---

[1] Donald Bahr, ed., *O'odham Creation and Related Events, as Told to Ruth Benedict in 1927 in Prose, Oratory, and Song* (Tucson: University of Arizona Press, 2001), 5-6. The song text remained the same every time Earth Doctor sang.

story, the rising and setting of the sun and moon and the physical features of the earth were all created through singing. After humans populated the earth, Earth Doctor sang to them to make them sleep, and in the darkness their spirits journeyed over the earth, while they received wisdom. Song is interwoven with the threads of O'odham identity in the past and present.[2]

These and other O'odham stories help illustrate three ways in which music functioned in indigenous societies of northern New Spain. Although recorded during early twentieth-century fieldwork, they provide a way to try to understand the place of music in native constructions of history and identity.[3] Earth Doctor's construction of the world illustrates the way in which music was tied to the act of creating and maintaining power over life: singing enlarged the earth, stopped it from shaking, governed day and night, and also played a part in the destruction of the first edenic land.[4] When the first people tried to kill Elder Brother, men and women met together at night and sang to gather strength. Humans could not kill Elder Brother by themselves, so they enlisted Buzzard. Buzzard borrowed the sun's heart and tried to kill Elder Brother with its heat, and the story climaxed in the battle between Buzzard and Elder Brother, where song is used as a weapon by each.[5] In indigenous communities across northern New Spain, like in these O'odham stories, song and dance were harnessed for purposes of gathering power or affecting social control. Furthermore, in O'odham folklore and practice, song functioned as a language for exchanges within and between groups, as well as with the spiritual world. Elder Brother taught the people songs to bring rain, he sang to them to provide instruction, and men and women learned the songs to convey to their children.[6] History and culture could not be communicated apart from song. The words of this history were inseparable from the melody, intonation, rhythm, and movement that accompanied them. Songs were passed on through oral tradition, not written down; this was something that separated the O'odham from white men. In Blackwater's recounting, Elder Brother told the people, "Whatever a white

---

[2] Ibid., 5-8, 19.

[3] Donald Bahr, in his introduction to the edited volume of Ruth Benedict's transcripts, reminds us that we need to allow for the individual creativity of authors, and not assume that one person's story is reflective of the entire culture (p. ix). The version of the genesis story collected during Benedict's fieldwork is very similar to another version, reprinted in Donald M. Bahr, ed., *The Short, Swift Time of Gods on Earth: The Hohokam Chronicles* (Berkeley: University of California Press, 1994), 46-53. In this telling, singing is also responsible for the creation of the first shamans and animals.

[4] Bahr, ed., *O'odham Creation*, 6-13.

[5] Ibid., 32.

[6] Ibid. 31, 40-41.

man hears, he can't put it into his mind. He can only remember it when he writes it down. Even when he sings, he has to sing out of a book."[7] Through the passing on of songs and stories, indigenous music of the pre-Contact and colonial era was part of the transmission and formation of group identity, as it is today. Those who knew and performed the stories and songs had the power to shape the ideologies and identities of the community. How did musical activities shape identity, structure daily and ritual experience, and communicate expectations, beliefs, and cultural norms for pre-Contact and colonial-era native groups? Stories, coupled with historical accounts, and archaeological evidence, provide a glimpse into the meanings and powers of song and dance in the diverse societies of northern New Spain.

Indigenous Music and Dance in Northern New Spain

Attempting to reconstruct the indigenous practices associated with pre-Conquest and colonial era music and dance is a daunting task. The Indians of the north, unlike those in other areas of Mesoamerica, left scant evidence of their history or encounters with Spaniards, and many of the native groups in this region were completely devastated due to disease or incorporated into other communities. Those groups who inhabit the Mexican-American borderlands region today have continually refashioned their culture throughout the past four hundred years. Surviving indigenous groups, such as the O'odham and Yaqui, have been studied by anthropologists and ethnographers, and early twentieth-century recordings of their songs exist. Ethnomusicologists who study the borderlands region have traditionally supposed that "the musical style of most of the material existed before 1492, although its geographic distribution may have been somewhat different from its present one. There seems to have been a minimum of hybridization of musical styles between the European and American Indian cultures in America."[8] This assumption fails to consider the individual power relations involved in the colonial experiences of each indigenous group.

---

[7] Ibid., 68.
[8] Bruno Nettl, *Folk and Traditional Music of the Western Continents* (Englewood Cliffs, NJ: Prentice-Hall, 1973), 4. For early recordings of indigenous music of the borderlands region, see *The Federal Cylinder Project: A Guide to Field Cylinder Collections in Federal Agencies*, 5 vols. (Washington, DC: American Folklife Center, Library of Congress, 1984–); Dorothy Sara Lee, *Native North American Music and Oral Data: A Catalogue of Sound Recordings, 1893–1976* (Bloomington: Indiana University Press, 1979); and Charlotte Johnson Frisbie, *Music and Dance Research of Southwestern United States Indians: Past Trends, Present Activities, and Suggestions for Future Research* (Detroit, MI: Information Coordinators, 1977).

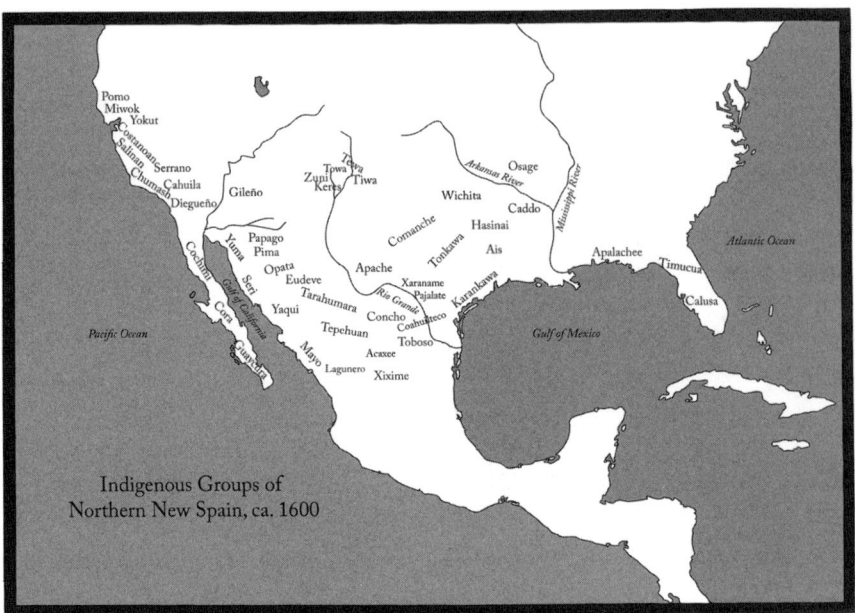

Indigenous Groups of Northern New Spain, ca. 1600

While the songs and dances of some groups, such as the Hopi, were not largely influenced by contact with Europeans, other music and dance practices were affected to a much greater degree.[9] We must carefully consider modern ethnographic data, therefore, in conjunction with the colonial and archaeological records in order to attempt to reconstruct the musical practices of indigenous groups of the north.[10]

During the colonial period, Spanish rulers claimed, but only had sporadic control over a large expanse of territory in the northern sierras, deserts, river valleys, and northeastern woodlands and coast. This vast frontier included the territories of Florida, Coahuila, Texas, Nuevo Santander, Nuevo León, Nueva Vizcaya, Sonora, Sinaloa, and Baja and Alta California, and encompassed many diverse groups of indigenous peoples with varying lifestyles and customs. In this expansive terrain, over fifty different ethnic groups speaking languages from the Hokan-Siouan, Aztec-Tanoan, Penutian, Uto-Aztecan, Athapaskan, and Hokaltecan fam-

---

[9] Joann W. Keali'Inokohomu, "Hopi and Hawaiian Music and Dance: Responses to Cultural Contact," *Musical Repercussions of 1492: Encounters in Text and Performance* (Washington, DC: Smithsonian Institution Press, 1992), 437.

[10] So-called "upstreaming" from modern anthropology is fraught with difficulties, but can help to provide context and meaning to colonial data.

ilies all made their homes.[11] Anthropologist Edward Spicer's pioneering work, *Cycles of Conquest*, classified northern Indians into four types.[12] Although he was considering a territory more limited than the area encompassed by the present study, his categories are a useful way of understanding the diversity present in the northern frontier region on the eve of Spanish encroachment.[13]

The vast majority of groups, termed *ranchería* peoples, lived in fixed settlements, spread out over large territories which sometimes shifted locations according to season and available resources. Other groups included those settled in villages, as well as agricultural and non-agricultural bands. The village peoples were well-organized societies that practiced irrigated and dryland agriculture and lived in compact villages, usually near water. In contrast, members of agricultural bands did not live in permanent settlements. Instead, they moved locations according to the seasons, engaging in small-scale farming, hunting, and gathering of native foods. These groups utilized immense areas as their homes and were often in conflict with other groups as a result. The fourth classification, small non-agricultural bands, had no fixed settlements and moved over large territories. All four types of societies possessed musical instruments, and colonial documents contain reports of singing and dancing within each of the classifications. Groups who lived in compact villages were more likely to have ritual specialists who were responsible for ceremonialism involving music, but most groups counted members who performed specialized music for healing, war, or lament. Perhaps surprisingly, the degree of economic complexity of these societies (non-agricultural band to village) did not always correspond to the importance and complexity of music in the society. The Seri, for example, although they did not have fixed settlements, ascribed a great deal of importance to music. They were one of the few groups in Spanish-claimed territory to utilize a stringed instrument, a buccal bow, prior to the arrival of the Europeans. Because sound and dance could be created without access to great resources, it was available to all.[14] Music was important

---

[11] Peter Gerhard, *A Guide to the Historical Geography of New Spain* (Cambridge: Cambridge University Press, 1972), 164, 244, 288, 305, 313, 335-336, 344; Gerhard, *The Southeast Frontier of New Spain* (Norman: University of Oklahoma Press, 1993).

[12] Spicer, *Cycles of Conquest*, 8-15.

[13] Spicer's categories have been criticized for reducing groups to their economic sustenance, but I use the categories here to demonstrate the diversity of societies, as well as to show that economic organization was not necessarily tied to musical culture in these groups.

[14] In some cases, song and dance were inseparable. A Névome vocabulary, likely compiled in the seventeenth century at Onavas, in current-day Sonora, indicated that the same word, *nuhi*, was used by these indigenous peoples of the Pimería Bajo for both song (*el canto*) and dance (*baile*). See Campbell W. Pennington, ed. and trans., *The Pima Bajo of Central Sonora, Mexico*, vol. 2 (Salt Lake City: University of Utah Press, 1980), 13, 19.

politically and culturally to northern indigenous groups, and ritual expressions became a primary means of responding to the enormous changes caused by colonialism. Colonial documentation shows that Europeans' understanding of different types of indigenous groups was framed by their social and economic complexity. While ceremonies of the village-dwelling Assinai and Puebloans were described with curiosity, rituals of the rancherías and agricultural bands were more often described as deprived or barbarous.

Music and Group Identity

Cooperative expressions of art, such as music and dance, that are involved in common life, and widely enjoyed in a community, are signs of a unified collective life. Furthermore, they are tremendous aids in the creation of such a life.[15] Music was a sign of ties among indigenous groups; as a part of culture it helped to draw boundaries between ethnic groups. For example, differences in the types of rituals most commonly performed separated northeastern groups such as the Cotoname-speakers from northwestern village-dwellers such as the Yaqui. Whereas bands in the northeast were more likely to dance in connection with war, elaborate dances with songs were more often reported in connection with fertility or seasonal harvests in the northwest. Rituals involving music and dance revealed beliefs, assumptions, and commitments that defined the communities in which they were performed. The elaborate nature of the *mitotes* and *danzas de caballeras* practiced by the Apaches and Comanches in the eighteenth century signaled the importance of military prowess in these societies. The importance of ball-game competitions between Acaxee pueblos was evidenced by the elaborate ceremonies, involving betting, singing, dancing, and honoring of the players, which were undertaken for three days and nights before the contests began.[16] When these rituals were performed, however, they further imprinted beliefs and priorities while forging group identity.

Rituals involving an entire group most often included circle dances and were characterized by unison singing and repetition. Eighteenth-century Jesuit Joseph Och provided a detailed description of a group song and dance following a hunt in Sonora:

---

[15] John Dewey, *Art as Experience*, cited in Mark Mattern, *Acting in Concert: Music, Community, and Political Action* (New Brunswick, NJ: Rutgers University Press, 1998), 15.

[16] See the Jesuit annual letter, 1604, in which Hernando de Santarén describes the Acaxees in Archivum Romanum Societatis Iesu (henceforth ARSI), Provincial Mexicana, vol. 14, 387, Vatican Film Library, St. Louis University, roll 139, as well as Andrés Pérez de Ribas, *History of the Triumphs of Our Holy Faith among the Most Barbarous and Fierce Peoples of the New World*, trans.

> *Their singing, always in monotone, is very disagreeable to the unaccustomed ear, especially because they repeat a thing twenty or thirty times. In singing, they praise the best shot of the hunt or boast about their imaginary deeds of bravery. For example: 'There runs the deer, there runs the deer, the deer runs there'—and this twenty times repeated, the words being taken up now by the youths, then by the maidens in soprano, then by the old women, and finally by everybody, and being more bellowed than sung.*[17]

From this description, we learn that the Pimas sang in a group for recreation and communicated accomplishments of group members through newly composed song lyrics. Repetition, and most likely a simple melody, characterized the song. Children, women, and men all sang, at first as individual groups (in order from highest pitch to lowest pitch), and then together to conclude the song. Through the performance of such a song, a community could come together, thus establishing and maintaining group ties and relating shared history and accomplishments.

Mourning the deaths of community members involved music for groups such as the Laguneros, Seri, and smaller northeastern bands. On such occasions the entire society came together for public expressions of grief. Andrés Pérez de Ribas described the death rites of the Laguneros:

> *The mournful verses and dirges that they composed for their dead were famous. Some mornings or evenings the relatives and acquaintances of the dead would gather at the grave, and with their faces blackened the men and women would each compose their laments. These laments celebrated or lamented the deceased and his deeds—his bravery in war, his greatness as a hunter and provider for his children, and how much they suffered due to his absence.*[18]

The performance of these songs, newly composed to honor the deceased, were an important part of maintaining community identity in the face of colonial pressures. They communicated the importance of the individual to his family and larger society, while the experience of shared grief and mourning reinforced group ties.

The amount of time spent in acquiring and preparing food for the ranchería peoples, agricultural, and non-agricultural bands was tremendous. It is no sur-

---

and ed. Daniel T. Reff, Maureen Ahren, and Richard K. Danford (Tucson: University of Arizona Press, 1999), book VIII, chapter IV, 496.

[17] Theodore Treutlein, trans. and ed., *Missionary in Sonora: The Travel Reports of Joseph Och* (San Francisco: California Historical Society, 1965), 162-163.

[18] Pérez de Ribas, *Triumphs of Our Holy Faith*, book 11, chapter 9, 667.

prise, then, that musical actions surrounding food were central to group identity. A good harvest or a successful hunt or fishing trip was cause for revelry. The aforementioned ceremonies that accompanied the ripening of cactus fruit illustrated this:

> *It has to be understood that the three month harvest season for pitahaya is like the Mardi Gras in some parts of Europe in which a good part of the men submit to an ecstasy; the natives here are so enraptured, giving themselves over to fiestas and dances at gatherings of the usually distant rancherías. They make offerings of food and buffoonery in the enjoyment of which they pass entire nights of merrymaking . . . also, these gatherings serve as times for excessive lovemaking, trading of women, and practices that maintain the customs of the tribe.*[19]

For groups such as the Cochimí of Baja California, who lived in very small bands and depended on gathering food, this harvest season defined annual cycles and drew smaller groups together for celebration. Similarly, Coahuiltecan ceremonialism was an integral part of the culture. Social pressures required attendance at revelry, and costuming or body painting was used to prepare for important dances. Shared rituals were the integrative force that held together the common culture of these smaller bands.[20]

Music has the capacity to define the borders of a community, that is, what it means to exist both inside and outside of a community.[21] Cultural markers such as religion, shared history, geographical space, language, music, art, and dance, are signs and delineators of group identification. Common songs performed in unison by an entire community evoke powerful emotions and help create bonds of shared experience. Unison singing, common in contemporary Native-American pow-wows, adds power and forcefulness to the collective affective experience of community. This physical and emotional experience is shared by musicians, dancers, and listeners in the pow-wow circle. In this forum, "shared experiences help create and sustain a common ground of memory, experience, identity, and commitment."[22]

In the colonial period, most ritual singing in the deserts and mountains of the north was performed in group settings, with men and women singing

---

[19] Constantino Bayle, *Misión de la Baja California* (Madrid: La Editorial Católica, 1946), 150-151. See also Harry W. Crosby, *Antigua California: Mission and Colony on the Peninsular Frontier, 1697–1768* (Albuquerque: University of New Mexico Press, 1994), 198-199.

[20] Frederick Ruecking, Jr., "Ceremonies of the Coahuiltecan Indians of Southern Texas and Northeastern Mexico," *Texas Journal of Science* 6:3 (1954), 336.

[21] Ibid., 140.

[22] Mattern, *Acting in Concert*, 122.

together in an octave interval. Dancers were often arranged in a circle, further reinforcing the boundaries of community. Andrés Pérez de Ribas described the dances of the Laguneros in which a throng of people "would form a circle and crown, and keeping the beat with their steps, the entire ring seemed to be one."[23] Gender boundaries were also drawn by inclusion or exclusion from a dancing circle. Dances before war, for example, sometimes excluded women (who did not participate in the fighting), whereas the celebratory dances following a battle often included women.

Performance of music and dance aids in community creation because it provides a forum through which shared ideas and values can be discovered, negotiated, and propagated. Contemporary indigenous followers of the Alleluia religion in Guyana "affirm, through daily worship, a representation of the meaning of Amerindian culture, in the recognized presence of other definitions, through [singing] hymns."[24] Similarly, through their songs and the non-verbal communication of dance movements, indigenous performers in northern New Spain promoted their shared history and values. Indigenous music is part of oral tradition, passed down through generations. Peter García, a contemporary Tewa composer, characterized the importance of dance to his culture in this manner:

> *Dance to Native Americans . . . is a central pillar of society. It means far more than socialization, the path on which a person learns to walk in the community. It is living history, a pathway to the future, and an incorporation of the Pueblo interpretation of life and the cosmos around us. . . . If there was no one here in San Juan Pueblo to carry on the songs and traditional dances, our whole society might fall apart.*[25]

In Tewa society, the performance of dance holds together elements of tribal culture. It illustrates to individuals what it means to belong to the group and functions as a record of tribal history.

Music is an important agent in ethnogenesis, the continual re-creation of group identity, particularly under stress of competition for resources and living space.[26] As later chapters will demonstrate, music was a way in which indigenous

---

[23] Pérez de Ribas, *History of the Triumphs of Our Holy Faith*, book XI, chapter 2, 657.

[24] Susan K. Staats, "Fighting in a Different Way: Indigenous Resistance through the Alleluia Religion of Guyana," in Jonathan Hill, ed., *History, Power and Identity: Ethnogenesis in the Americas, 1492-1992* (Iowa City: University of Iowa Press, 1996), 164.

[25] Julio Estrada and Peter García, "Bridging the Past and the Present," in Carol E. Robertson, ed., *Musical Repercussions of 1492: Encounters in Text and Performance* (Washington, DC: Smithsonian Institution Press, 1992), 93.

[26] Staats, "Fighting in a Different Way," and Kristin Dutcher Mann, "Music and Popular Religiosity in Northern New Spain," *Catholic Southwest* 12 (2001), 7-27.

peoples could maintain some control over their identities and respond to the extreme pressures of conquest. As groups remade themselves over time, the musical forms they used, and the contexts in which they were performed, changed.

Music and Power in Indigenous Societies

Life in the northern frontiers of New Spain revolved around the search for stable relations with the natural world and with other peoples vying for space and resources. Power was accessed and exchanged through the songs and dances associated with the living universe and war. Most groups believed that the origins of their songs were supernatural. Seri shamans participated in vision quests in isolated areas. When a quest was successful, animals appeared to a shaman and taught him songs with supernatural powers.[27] Singing released the power and provided access to resources such as rain, food, and animals. Modern ethnomusicological studies echo the idea that songs have origins in the spiritual world. Suyá people attribute many of their songs to animals, which they consider to be of divine origin.[28] Music in many contemporary South American indigenous societies is revered as the gift of a spirit.[29]

Because songs were supernatural in origin, acts of performance gave singers access to the powerful spiritual world. The O'odham sang to augment the power of medicine men as they performed ritual tasks.[30] For the Hopi, singing was considered as much work, and as important, as performing manual labor such as planting maize.[31] It helped to maintain connections with the natural world and bring rain, bountiful harvests, and balance.

Throughout the north, musicians were valued for their ability to capture musical power. Singers and instrumentalists, both male and female, served their societies as shamans, healers, or priests. Assinai instrumentalists were referred to by Franciscan Francisco Ballejo as "ministers of pipes"; other than the priests, they were the only men allowed to enter the group's ceremonial build-

---

[27] Thomas Sheridan, ed., *Empire of Sand: The Seri Indians and the Struggle for Spanish Sonora, 1645–1803* (Tucson: University of Arizona Press, 1999), 4.

[28] Anthony Seeger, *Why Suyá Sing: A Musical Anthropology of an Amazonian People* (Cambridge: Cambridge University Press, 1987).

[29] Dale A. Olsen, "Symbol and Function in South American Indian Music," in Elizabeth May, ed., *Musics of Many Cultures* (Berkeley: University of California Press, 1980), 365.

[30] Frances Densmore, *Papago Music* (Washington, DC: U.S. Government Printing Office, 1929), 169-175.

[31] Joann W. Keali' Inohomoku, "Hopi and Hawaiian Music and Dance: Responses to Cultural Contact," in Carol E. Robertson, ed., *Musical Repercussions of 1492: Encounters in Text and Performance* (Washington, DC: Smithsonian Institution, 1992), 52.

ing.[32] Among the village peoples, specialization allowed some individuals to function as ritual specialists and musicians. However, most accounts of music in the north note the participation of a large body of individuals in singing and dancing.

In contrast to Mesoamerican indigenous ceremonies, women appear prominently in the descriptions of music in societies farther north. Seri women performed the music for death rituals, which lasted for an entire day and into the night. The songs of the women consisted of unintelligible words and "a mourning melody as a sign of their pain, like the howling of cats."[33] Among many groups, laments were songs performed only by women. In Nuevo Santander, women sang the music that prepared warriors for combat; they also celebrated by singing and dancing upon the warriors' successful return.[34] In many societies, there seems to have been a clear division between women's songs and men's songs.[35]

Songs involving only men were often related to shamanism. Flawless ritual performance, however, was crucial. According to an O'odham story, "The chief medicine man was singing, and he made a mistake in his song; Coyote laughed, and the fourth company [of people] was cut in two so that half remained in the world below. The people blamed Coyote, but Coyote said, 'Why do you blame me? It is not my fault. It is the fault of the chief medicine man who made a mistake in his song.'"[36] This performance error fundamentally changed the composition of the Pima world.

Making and playing instruments was primarily a male activity. Hopi women sang as they ground corn for their families, but it was a male instrumentalist who accompanied them on a flute.[37] Male Yaqui dancers wore rattles around their ankles and wrists as they danced. In modern Tarahumara society, constructing violins is a male activity of great esteem, and virtually all men can play the

---

[32] Francisco Ballejo to King Ferdinand VI, January 17, 1750, transcribed in Benedict Leutenegger, trans., and Marion Habig, ed., *The Texas Missions of the College of Zacatecas in 1749–1750* (San Antonio, TX: Old Spanish Missions Historical Research Library, 1979), 45-46.

[33] Charles DiPeso and Daniel Matson. "The Seri Indians in 1692 as Described by Adamo Gilg, S.J." *Arizona and the West* 1, no. 7 (1961), 52.

[34] Raúl García Flóres, *¡Puro mitote! La música, el canto y la danza entre los chichimecas del noreste* (Monterrey: Fondo Editorial Nuevo León, 1993), 47.

[35] Separate women's and men's songs and dances were noted by Felipe Arroyo de la Cuesta for the Indians surrounding Mission San Juan Bautista in his response to the Interrogatorio of October 6, 1812, printed in Zephyrin Englehardt, *Mission San Juan Bautista: A School of Church Music* (Santa Barbara, CA: Schauer Printing Studio, 1931), 21. The Xixime also had some songs that were clearly delineated by gender. See also García Flores, *Puro Mitote*, 47.

[36] Bahr, ed., *O'odham Creation*, 40-41.

[37] George Peter Hammond, ed. and trans., *Narratives of the Coronado Expedition* (Albuquerque: University of New Mexico Press, 1940), 256.

violin.³⁸ Caddo men carved crane or heron bones to make small flageolets, used in healing ceremonies.³⁹ Instruments such as these were closely related to animals—made out of animal bones, skins, or antlers, they connected humans to the natural world and helped to tap into its power.

Some dances and songs were also intended to call upon the power of animals, or to honor them, especially prior to a hunt. In Alta California, Indians near Mission San Juan Bautista sang, played rattles and bone whistles, and danced in a rhythmic circle. Dancers painted their bodies and adorned themselves with feathers fastened to their hair, neck, and shoulders. They then leapt and shouted in imitation of bears, coyotes, and other animals.⁴⁰ Jesuit Ignaz Pfefferkorn, who worked among the Opatas and Eudeves in eighteenth-century Sonora, described animal imitation dances, called *toopptu*, in which the participants moved and growled like animals. On the occasions of these performances, which sometimes lasted for several days, men and women mixed freely and drinking was common.⁴¹

Dances associated with animals and seasonal harvests were often part of larger celebrations involving music, revelry, feasting, and sometimes drunkenness or the ingestion of hallucinogens such as peyote.⁴² Festivities were held in Nuevo Santander to commemorate the beginning of summer, a productive harvest of wild plants, and a young male's first successful hunting trip.⁴³ Individual males hosted the ceremonies, organized the activities, sent invitations, prepared food, drink, and peyote, and selected a suitable site.⁴⁴ Rituals involving the veneration of deer skins, heads, or antlers, originally thought to be unique to Mesoamerica, were found among the Yaqui, Mayo, and Tepehuan peoples of

---

³⁸ John G. Kennedy, *Tarahumara of the Sierra Madre: Beer, Ecology, and Social Organization* (Arlington Heights, IL: AHM Publishing Corporation, 1978), 74.

³⁹ Fray Isidro Félix de Espinosa, *Crónica de los colegios de propaganda fide de la Nueva España*, ed. Lino Gómez Canedo (Washington, DC: Academy of American Franciscan History, 1964), 161.

⁴⁰ Felipe Arroyo de la Cuesta, response to Interrogatory of 1812, transcribed in Englehardt, *Mission San Juan Bautista*, 21-22.

⁴¹ *Sonora: A Description of the Province*, 176, 181.

⁴² There are many examples in colonial documentation of such fiestas. For a simple description of a nighttime dance around a fire with drunkenness and peyote ingestion, see José Hermengildo Sánchez García, *Crónica del Nuevo Santander* (Mexico City: Colegio Regiones, 1990), 210-211. Feasting is also mentioned in many accounts, including Alonso de León, *Historia de Nuevo León* (1649), chapter X, 44-45. In "Ceremonies of the Coahuiltecan Indians" Ruecking argues that the ritual consumption of peyote originated among the Coahuiltecans prior to 1600 and spread from there to other parts of Mexico as well as to indigenous groups of the Plains (336-337).

⁴³ Fray Vicente de Santa María, *Relación histórica de la colonia del Nuevo Santander* (Mexico City: Universidad Autónoma de México, 1973), 59.

⁴⁴ Ruecking, "Ceremonies of the Coahuiltecan Indians," 332-333.

the northwest frontier during the early colonial period.[45] Deer antlers, skeletons, or skulls all appear in contemporary Tarahumara matachines and yúmari dances, as well as Yaqui deer dances.[46] Anthropologists have studied the considerable meaning in contemporary indigenous deer songs and dances. In these ritual acts, dream power is transformed into cultural potency, reinforcing ties within a group and connecting individuals to a shared history.[47]

A second type of music related to the attainment of power revolved around battle. This category included rituals in preparation for fighting as well as those to celebrate a victory. In the pre-Hispanic and colonial periods, circular dances, sometimes involving human sacrifices, military trophies (such as skulls), and loud howling, were generally held at night. Dances held before battle evoked strong bio-physiological responses, which heightened the senses of the participants and provided adrenaline and the mental state necessary for waging war. Franciscan friar Vicente de Santa María described a war incitement ceremony that was performed at night around a bonfire. One woman began to shout the record of the band's grievances against the group with which they wanted war. The crying passed from one woman to another, starting with the oldest and most respected, and lasted for hours. This noise incited the warriors, who silently prepared their bows and arrows and painted themselves for battle. At last they appeared before the group, dancing with leaps and twists to indicate their physical and emotional readiness for war.[48] In this case, music was used to heighten the passion and courage of the warriors. Women contributed to the battle through the emotional power of their songs.

Written descriptions of war dances and rituals were motivated by missionaries and soldiers seeking to justify conquest, fund missions, or boast of their conquests. Because indigenous practices were so different from the conventions of Reformation Europe, they were reported with mingled senses of fear and incredulity. The ceremonies were referred to as "diabolical" and "barbarous," and were often used to demonstrate the ferocity and heathen ways of the indige-

---

[45] García Flores, *¡Puro mitote!*, 158, n. 104.

[46] For Tarahumara dances, see Carlo Bonfiglioli, *Fariseos y matachines en la sierra Tarahumara* (Mexico City: Instituto Nacional Indigenista, 1995); and Carl Lumholtz, *Unknown Mexico* (London: Macmillan, 1903), vol. I, 333. For Yaqui deer dances, see Frances Densmore, *Yuman and Yaqui Music* (Washington, DC: Bureau of American Ethnology, Smithsonian Institution, 1932), 22-23. These dances will be discussed further in Chapters 4 and 7.

[47] Karl Kroeber, "Poem, Dream, and the Consuming of Culture," *The Georgia Review* 32 (1978), 272; and Larry Evers and Felipe S. Molina, *Yaqui Deer Songs: Maso Bwikam: A Native American Poetry* (Tucson: Sun Tracks and University of Arizona Press, 1987), 26.

[48] Santa María, *Relación histórica*, 114-117; also summarized by Ruecking, "Ceremonies of the Coahuiltecan Indians," 331.

nous participants. These dances sometimes included partaking of the flesh of enemies, ingestion of hallucinogens, and unfamiliar screaming and wailing, often for prolonged periods, at a feverish speed and pitch. None of these attributes fit European songs and dances.

Missionaries referred to communal dances as *mitotes*, from the Nahuatl verb meaning "to dance."[49] Generally, mitote was used to designate any indigenous celebration, but it particularly referred to communal dances accompanied by group singing, which the missionaries viewed as disorderly, chaotic, and sometimes even dangerous. Andrés Pérez de Ribas noted that the Devil caused Laguneros to hold their nocturnal dances, which were accompanied by the types of abuses that "the Devil promotes."[50] Fray Vicente de Santa María elaborately detailed the cannibalism involved in the Comanche mitote and argued that "this class of ferocity has no equal throughout the centuries."[51] In these cases, it was the job of the missionary to ensure that such dances did not continue under Spanish rule.

In the eighteenth century, the Apaches were a constant source of consternation for missionaries in north central New Spain. Their "diabolical rites" and "depraved customs" caused Franciscans in Texas to plead for military containment of the tribe, since their mitotes, either more attractive than the daily activities inside the missions, or generating fear of attack, were causing members of the recently converted Coahuiltecan bands to flee the missions.[52]

Following a victory, dances of celebration were common throughout the region. Dances around a pole, sometimes topped with a human scalp, were reported in Sinaloa, and among the Yaqui, Apache, and Coahuiltecan peoples. Jesuit Andrés Pérez de Ribas wrote of this practice in Sinaloa:

> *The head or the scalp of the dead enemy or some other body part such as an arm or a leg was hung on a pole in the middle of the plaza. They danced around it, unleashing a barbarous cry as they hurled insults at the dead enemy; they also sang songs that referred to the victory.*[53]

Post-victory celebrations were attacked by missionaries as being the most barbarous customs due to the dismemberment of the defeated and the mixing of members of both sexes. The Jesuit annual report of 1610 detailed a Xixime rite

---

[49] See Francisco Javier Santamaría, *Diccionario de mejicanismos*, 2nd ed. (Mexico City: Editorial Porrúa, 1974), 728.
[50] Pérez de Rivas, *History of the Triumphs of Our Holy Faith*, book XI, chapter II, 657.
[51] Santa María, *Relación histórica de la colonia del Nuevo Santander*, 117.
[52] Archivo General de Indias (hereinafter AGI), Mexico, 1933A, exp. 8, fol. 12; exp. 11, 46v.
[53] Pérez de Ribas, *History of the Triumphs of Our Holy Faith*, 89-90. Sometimes these dances are referred to as *danzas de caballeras* or *tlatoles* instead of *mitotes*.

in which a fasting virgin was released from a cave on the occasion of a military victory. Warriors brought the young girl the severed head of an opponent, which she held as she danced with men and women of the group.[54]

Fray Vicente de Santa María included a detailed description of Comanche and Apache mitotes in his *Relación histórica de la colonia del Nuevo Santander*. In these nocturnal victory celebrations, dancing and singing were interspersed with the consumption of roasted human flesh from captives of the recent battle. Women and men moved together in a circle to the rhythmic singing. Dancers alternated feet, hopping and undulating faster and faster along with the music. Those who did not participate in the dance sang as accompaniment to the dance. From time to time, dancers and singers retired to eat, drink, and consume peyote. The revelry died down as singers and dancers slipped into altered states of consciousness. At this time, an old man was given a vision and prophesied the future of the assembled group. Then the dancing and singing began again (and most likely continued until sunrise).[55] From Fray Vicente's description, it is evident that this type of dance was more than a mere post-victory celebration. It also involved the coming together of the entire community and common consumption of food and peyote, which provided strength and power over enemies. The foretelling of future successes and failures by the shaman allowed the group to connect with their gods through an esteemed intermediary in a group religious experience, which reaffirmed group identity. Over time, and in areas where groups faced intense competition for resources, missionary reports of these mitotes increased.

Healing songs constitute a third category of music used to access power. Assinai women assisted ritual healers by "howling" songs and beating jars while tending a large fire. Fray Isidro Félix de Espinosa reported that the shamans were cheered and aided by this music.[56] Participants in these healing ceremonies used music as a medium through which they could contact and petition their religious deities on behalf of the sick individual. Modern ethnography supports the idea that singing allowed shamans to access supernatural healing power. O'odham oral tradition states that healers sang melodies to cure the illnesses caused by the spirits of dead enemies.[57] Healing, a native sacrament, brought

---

[54] Anua of 1610, ARSI, México, 14, 584, as cited in Peter Masten Dunne, *Pioneer Jesuits in Northern Mexico* (Berkeley: University of California Press, 1944), 98-99.

[55] Santa María, *Relación historica*, chapter XIX, 115-117. See also W.B. Stephens Collection, 2032, f. 15 (ca. 1780), University of Texas, Nettie Lee Benson Latin American Library (henceforth UTNLB).

[56] Espinosa, *Crónica de los colegios de propaganda fide*, 703.

[57] Densmore, *Papago Music*, 169-175.

about cures through sucking, blowing, and singing.[58] Accessing the power of nature, whether for healing, victory, rain, or plentiful food, involved establishing contact with the spiritual world through song and dance. In these contexts, it is possible to analyze the communicative devices of song and dance.

Music as Ritual Communication

Music, as performed sound, has structure not unlike other language. It is able to communicate information and emotion through melody, pitch, rhythm, and tempo, in addition to words. Indigenous music in the north was performed by both singers and instrumentalists. Spanish chroniclers reported many songs in verse-refrain form, with a group repeating the chorus and individuals singing the verses. Most songs had a strong rhythmic component, and singing was often accompanied by percussive instruments such as rattles, rasping sticks, and drums. The colonial record and modern ethnography both suggest that song lyrics could be either newly composed (to tell of a war victory or the exploits of a great hunter), vocables (such as "hu-hu"), or words, sometimes unintelligible, passed down through oral tradition. Ethnographies of the Coras, Huicholes, Tepehuanes, and Yaquis suggest that the lyrics of songs considered traditional in the twentieth century come from archaic forms of native languages.[59] This type of singing was not as common in Mesoamerica, where lyrics often consisted of stylized poetry.[60]

Music was a language used for conversation with religious beings, communication within groups, and discussion between groups. In contemporary Yaqui understanding, song is a special language of the wider community of plants, animals, birds, fishes, rocks, and spring—a "lingua franca of the intelligent universe." Through song, translated as enchanted talk, experiences with the natural world are understandable and accessible to the human world.[61] As a medium, music made communication with the spiritual world possible in both contemporary and historical indigenous cultures. Ritual songs in present-day Blackfoot

---

[58] Donald M. Bahr, *The Short, Swift, Time of Gods on Earth: The Hohokam Chronicles* (Berkeley: University of California Press, 1994), 18.

[59] Fernando Nava, "Música y aspectos afines en los horizontes chichimecos y mesoamericanos," in Marie-Areti Hers, ed., *Nómadas y sedentarios en el norte de México: homenaje a Beatriz Braniff* (Mexico City: Universidad Nacional Autónoma de México, 2000), 71.

[60] See Stevenson, *Music in Mexico* and *Music in Aztec and Inca Territory*, Carol E. Robertson, "Introduction: The Dance of Conquest," in *Musical Repercussions of 1492: Encounters in Text and Performance* (Washington, DC: Smithsonian Institution Press, 1992), 17-19; and Nava, "Música y aspectos afines," 71.

[61] Evers and Molina, *Yaqui Deer Songs*, 18.

society provide a way for supernaturals to impart important ideas to humans; through these rituals, religious beliefs are validated.[62] For the colonial-era Pima, conversation with the supernatural through rituals consisting of songs and ritual speech was valued as an act of heroism for the collective good.[63]

Music could both honor and make requests of the gods. Some elaborate ceremonial songs and dances were performed as supplications to deities. According to Franciscan missionaries, the Assinai of eastern Texas venerated air, water, and fire as gods. Their ritual dances were performed as prayers to these gods. Distinguished priests heard replies from the gods in answer to these dances.[64] The dance *torom raqui*, similar to the contemporary Tarahumara *yúmari* dance, was performed by the Opatas and other northwestern groups to ask for abundant rains and harvests. Missionaries tried to eradicate this dance, which they considered diabolical and idolatrous.[65] Franciscan Gaspar José de Solís wrote of the purposes of the mitotes of the Indians served by mission Rosario in Texas: "They dedicate their mitotes to several saints; one is the god *Pichini*, another one the saint *Mel*: to these they request with these superstitious dances freedom from and triumph over their enemies, or for good events in their campaigns, or abundant harvests, or abundance of deer, bison, or bears."[66] Jesuits stationed at mission San Andrés in the early seventeenth century also wrote about their efforts to abolish indigenous dances directed to a variety of gods who appeared in animal form. Indigenous peoples of Topia performed specific dances to these gods for sickness, war, and plentiful harvests.[67] The Opata practiced a ceremony during times of drought in which young girls dressed in white danced at night to "invoke the clouds."[68] They danced a fertility ceremony, called the *torom-raqui*, to request a bountiful harvest.

Ritual communication also involved honoring the spiritual world, and restoring the sacred order of the universe during times of natural renewal, such as

---

[62] John E. Kaemmer, *Music in Human Life: Anthropological Perspectives on Music* (Austin: University of Texas Press, 1993), 61.

[63] David Leedom Shaul, "Language, Music and Dance in the Pimería Alta during the 1700s" (Tumacácori, AZ: Tumacácori National Historic Park, 1993), 108.

[64] Fray Hidalgo to the viceroy, 1716, Querétaro, leg. 1, 4-5, Catholic Archives of Texas (hereinafter CAT), 117.8; and *Relación de servicios del Colegio de Zacatecas, 1750*, Archivo San Francisco el Grande, Biblioteca Nacional, vol. 5, f. 67, UTNLB.

[65] Molina-Molina, ed., *Estado de la provincia de Sonora, 1730*, 12. See also Luís González Rodriguez, ed., *Etnología y misión en la Pimería Alta, 1715–1740* (Mexico City: Universidad Nacional Autónoma de México, 1977), 298; and "Relación sonorense de Cristóbal de Cañas," 1730, University of Arizona Special Collections, paragraph 39.

[66] Solís to Padre Guardian, 1767, AGN, Historia, 27, f. 29-30.

[67] Anua de 1600–1602, transcribed in Zubillaga, *Monumenta Mexicana*, vol. VII, 653.

[68] Juan Nentvig, as cited in Edward Spicer, *Cycles of Conquest*, 320.

spring and autumn. Timucuan ceremonies commemorating the harvest of first fruits included alms of deer skin and antlers adorned with the best fruits offered to the sun. First harvests and the first products of a hunt were offered back to the universe, carried to a prominent place, and fastened to a tree, with singing throughout, rituals that maintained the Timucuas' connection with the sacred.[69]

Music and dance were not only used for conversation with the supernatural. Members of a group communicated with each other through their music, from daily corn-grinding songs to the most elaborate ceremonial festivities. After a successful hunt, Cochimí women danced around a deerskin while a shaman recounted the hunter's success to the entire group. Musical signals, usually blown on a whistle or shell trumpet, were used by many northwestern groups to communicate over long distances. Jesuit and Franciscan missionaries to the Californias reported that singing accompanied daily tasks such as food preparation, entertaining children, fishing, and games, and storytelling within the groups that they were attempting to bring to the missions.[70] Music and dancing were forms of recreation after meals for the Pimas, and songs described familiar elements, such as the actions of animals or the prowess of hunters.[71] This type of recreation communicated the history and important traditions of a group to children and other members of the community.

Contemporary ethnomusicological fieldwork reveals communication through vocal and instrumental music in indigenous societies from both North and South America. Among the Suyá of South America, instructions for daily tasks are given in song. Songs provide a way for elders to transmit values and history to their descendants in the modern Yaqui community of Guadalupe, Arizona. Informal "jam sessions" became formalized in the mid-twentieth century as *ehkwelam*, schools to pass along songs from older to younger males in the community.[72]

The language of courtship between males and females was expressed through song and dance in colonial Sonora. Father Juan Nentvig observed that northern Pimas practiced a ritual that he likened to their idea of marriage.

---

[69] Tamara Spike, "To Make Graver This Sin: Conceptions of Purity and Pollution among the Timucua of Spanish Florida" (PhD diss., Florida State University, 2006), accessed 8/17/2007, ProQuest Digital dissertations database.

[70] See Felipe Arroyo de la Cuesta, response to Interrogatory of October 6, 1812, San Juan Bautista, Alta California, transcribed in Zephyrin Englehardt, *Mission San Juan Bautista: A School of Church Music* (Santa Barbara, CA: Schauer Printing Studio, 1931), 21; and Peter Masten Dunne, *Black Robes in Lower California* (Berkeley: University of California Press, 1952), 21, from a report about the Cochimí of Baja California.

[71] Treutlein, *Missionary in Sonora*, 162.

[72] Evers and Molina, *Yaqui Deer Songs*, 65-66.

Young girls stood in one row, and boys in another, all naked. At a given signal, the girls would scatter and the boys would chase them. Nentvig wrote,

> Upon overtaking the girl of his choice, the young man would seize her left breast. This constituted the nuptial ceremony. Dancing followed, and after a while each couple was placed between two mats made of palm leaves. The singing and dancing continued until daybreak or until the participants reached the point of exhaustion, although in these celebrations the Indians seem tireless.[73]

In this example, a dance-game facilitated courtship between males and females. This function of music applies even more universally; song and movement fill a similar role among animals, including birds and small mammals.[74]

Communicating through music was a way of publicly disseminating information between, as well as within, groups. Music and dance afford acceptable channels of communication in situations where open confrontation would be unacceptable.[75] In central Mesoamerica, mitotes called *tatol* by the Nahua scribes who accompanied conquerors seem to have been performed to provide estranged tribal heads the opportunity to engage in dialog and form alliances. Indigenous peoples may have tried to employ a similar strategy with Spaniards, as the heads of bands of Nadadores and Tobosos dressed in their mitote attire when they arrived to negotiate with the Spaniards in the seventeenth century.[76] Intertribal ceremonies surrounding welcoming, peacemaking, and mutual defense pacts included communal dancing and singing. Music and dance were also performed for the arrival of an important official or group. Indigenous groups used this form of greeting when trading or meeting for a communal celebration, and this form of music also appears in colonial documentation of Spanish military or religious expeditions. Father Gaspar José de Solís was greeted by the Ais Indians on his trip through eastern Texas with a dance of "exquisite ceremony and expression."[77] The Gálvez expedition into Alta California was greeted by indigenous women dancing and holding flowers north

---

[73] Juan Nentvig, *Rudo Ensayo: A Description of Sonora and Arizona in 1764*, trans. and ed. Alberto Francisco Pradeau and Robert Rasmussen (Tucson: University of Arizona Press, 1980), 61.

[74] Ellen Dissanayake, "Ritual and Ritualization: Musical Means of Conveying and Shaping Emotion in Humans and Other Animals," in Steven Brown and Ulrik Volgsten, eds., *Music and Manipulation: On the Social Uses and Social Control of Music* (New York: Berghahn Books, 2006), 44-47.

[75] John Kaemmer, *Music in Human Life*, 156-157.

[76] Nava, "Música y aspectos afines," 74.

[77] Solís report to Padre Guardián, 1767, on microfilm in the Old Spanish Missions Historical Research Collection, Our Lady of the Lake University (hereinafter OSMHRC), Zacatecas, reel 16, fr. 1436.

of San Diego. They were so impressed by the ceremony that they named the place *ranchería del baile de las indias*.⁷⁸ Beyond welcoming visitors, ceremonies involving song and dance helped to foster continuing goodwill. Sinaloan Indians forged alliances with other groups by smoking reed canes filled with tobacco during ritual celebrations involving singing, dancing, and consumption of food and beverages.⁷⁹

Seasonal harvests provided an opportunity for allied groups to mark time and exchange ideas and information. In Sonora and Baja California, the most elaborate celebrations occurred between April and September, when the harvests of pitahaya (prickly pear cactus fruit) and other wild plants were the most plentiful. Groups came together from throughout the region to trade, feast, and celebrate the fruitful season. More than thirty dances, all different, were performed for the entertainment of the entire assemblage.⁸⁰

The sounds made by musical instruments could communicate information with or without words or stylized movement. The use of musical instruments to accompany singing and dancing in the north was widespread. Organography of these indigenous groups did not vary widely, but certain instruments were unique to specific areas. Musical instruments were simply made and constructed of easily accessible materials, such as bone, gourds, wood, mud, or shells. By far the most common category of instrument was idiophones, including rattles, rasping sticks, clackers, and basket, log, and water drums. Idiophones were most often used to accompany ceremonies involving both song and dance, but they were also part of vocal music not accompanied by dance. Scraping or rasping sticks, made out of wood, with one stick notched, were found throughout the northwestern territory of Sonora and their use may have spread eastward.⁸¹ Rattles have been found for nearly every tribe for which archaeological work has been undertaken. The materials used to make the rattles varied according to the materials available to each group. While most northern tribes used gourd rattles to accompany singing or dancing, the articles placed inside the gourd varied from pebbles, to seeds, sand, or animal teeth. The Seris and Pimas created rattles from tortoise shells, while the Tarahumara used wood, and the Puebloan peoples used adobe. The Yaquis fashioned unique rattles referred to by the

---

⁷⁸ Miguel Costanso, Diario del Viaje, f. 1770, in the W. B. Stephens Collection 28b, 18, UTNLB).

⁷⁹ Pérez de Ribas, *History of the Triumphs of Our Holy Faith*, 90.

⁸⁰ Miguel del Barco, *Historia natural y crónica de la antigua California*, ed. Miguel León-Portilla (Mexico City: Universidad Nacional Autónoma de México, 1988), 192.

⁸¹ García Flores, *¡Puro mitote!*, 142; and Campbell Pennington, *The Tepehuan of Chihuahua: Their Material Culture* (Salt Lake City: University of Utah Press, 1969), 163.

Spaniards as *sartales de capullos*. These rattles, worn on the ankles of dancers, consisted of dried butterfly cocoons strung together. Often, concussion idiophones, instruments that resonate when their parts hit against each other, such as the previously mentioned Yaqui cocoon rattles or bracelets of small, perforated shells or animal teeth, were worn as jewelry by dancers.[82]

Membranophones, or instruments that produce sound through the vibration of a membrane, such as an animal skin, were far less common in northern New Spain than in Mesoamerica. Where present, they were usually played for social dance songs to provide a steady beat for the dancers. Most membranophones mentioned by early chroniclers or uncovered by archaeologists were found in the far northern frontier areas of Texas and New Mexico.[83] This suggests interaction with northern Plains Indians groups, for whom drums were common. A similar sound to that made by a large animal-skin drum was produced by the Miwoks of northern California by placing a large plank of redwood over a hole in the ground and stomping on the board.[84] Instead of using membranophones to provide a bass beat, groups such as the Yaqui struck baskets with the palm of their hands or used hollowed-out half-gourds played with a stick.[85]

Chordophones, or stringed instruments, were not found among indigenous societies in Mesoamerica, but their use is documented among a few groups in the north. The Apache, Costane, Cora, Huichol, Tepehuan, Papago, Pima, Seri, Yaqui, and Yuman peoples all used a hunting bow to produce a pitch. This category of musical bow was struck with a twig or an arrow, and did not change pitch. It was used to accompany singing.[86] A unique instrument, the musical bow, was in use by the Seri Indians at the time of their contact with Spaniards. It was placed on top of two vessels, struck with a stick, and sometimes bells were attached to the string.[87] This bow was unique due to its ability to sound more than one pitch. Its use later spread to the Yaquis and Tarahumaras.

---

[82] This practice was common in both the northeast and northwest. Women in Nuevo Santander wore bracelets and necklaces that jingled as they danced. See José Hermenegildo Sánchez García, *Crónica del Nuevo Santander* (Mexico City: Colegio Regiones, 1990); and García Flores, ¡*Puro mitote!*, 30.

[83] See Frances Densmore, *Music of Acoma, Isleta, Cochiti and Zuñi Pueblos* (Washington, DC: Bureau of American Ethnology, Smithsonian Institution, 1957), 3, 82-96; Nava, "Música y aspectos afines," 69; Ruecking, "Ceremonies of the Coahuiltecan Indians," 333.

[84] Mary Dominic Ray and Joseph H. Engbeck, Jr., *Gloria Dei: The Story of California Mission Music* (Sacramento: State of California Department of Parks and Recreation, 1974), 13.

[85] Densmore, *Yuman and Yaqui Music*, 23, 27.

[86] Nava, "Música y aspectos afines," 70-71.

[87] Ibid.

The final category of musical instruments, aerophones, were found throughout the indigenous societies of the north. Aerophones, whose sound was produced by vibrating air columns, were more often used for quotidian, not ritual, purposes. Bone, wooden, reed, or clay flutes or whistles were used to communicate with other groups. Colonial documentation mentioned their use in conjunction with battle—to sound retreat, or call men to battle—or in a procession.[88] Jesuit Father Eusebio Kino reported that the natives of Sinaloa brought the Jesuits "flutes made from reeds and which hang from their necks, but which they use only in battle."[89] In an O'odham story about the origin of the flute, reed flutes were used by mythical ancestors because of their ability to be heard over a long distance.[90] Conch shells were used in a similar manner by groups who lived near water, such as the Seri, as trumpets to signal war.[91] The sounding of particular instrumental melodies was a method by which neighboring groups could relay information.

We are left with little evidence to reconstruct the performance practices, contexts, and meanings surrounding musical instruments. Large baskets, for example, are found in many archaeological sites. Whether they were turned over and played with the palm of the hand as drums, in what contexts, or on what occasions they might have had different functions, is more difficult to determine. Pitch, melody, rhythm, volume, and tempo—all of these elements of instrumental music contained symbolic meaning, communicating information and emotion to those within hearing range.

Conclusions

Instrumental music, songs, and dance, then, were much more than music, words, and movement to the indigenous peoples of northern New Spain. They provided access to the spiritual world not possible with conventional speech, transmitted information and culture within groups, and facilitated interaction and alliances between groups. These processes were agents in the constant re-creation of culture and identity.

---

[88] See, for example, Joseph Neumann, *Historia de las sublevaciones indias en la Tarahumara*, ed., Bohumír Roedl (Prague: Universidad Carolinga, 1994), 113; and Ballejo to King Ferdinand, *The Texas Missions*, VI, 45.

[89] Eusebio Francisco Kino to Francisco de Castro, July 27, 1683, transcribed in Ernest J. Burrus, ed., *Kino escribe a la duquesa* (Rome: Jesuit Historical Institute, 1965).

[90] Frances Densmore, *Papago Music* (Washington DC: U.S. Government Printing Office, 1929), 63.

[91] Dane Coolidge and Mary Roberts Coolidge, *The Last of the Seris* (New York: E. Dutton and Company, 1939), 211.

Whether for entertainment or sacred purposes, music and dance were important elements of culture throughout northern New Spain. Ceremonies brought smaller bands together to interact, trade, and secure alliances in the rapidly changing political climate of the north. Mitotes, feasting, and the general chaos that accompanied them were also ways of marking time and ordering the yearly experiences of the participants.

Music was both politically important (e.g., in forging alliances) and culturally important (in the preservation of a group's history and identity). Performances occurred in a wide variety of contexts, including quotidian and ritual purposes. Nearly all members of indigenous groups in the north participated, not merely as observers, but by singing and dancing, in communal celebrations, although there were some ceremonies that were limited to specific groups (by age, profession, or gender). This heightens the importance of music and dance in the constant re-creation and maintenance of ethnic ties and group identity. Music was one of the primary means through which indigenous peoples communicated with the supernatural, and songs and dances were powerful weapons in preparing for combat. Communication within and among tribes was also facilitated by singing and dancing.

With the arrival of European missionaries, military personnel, and settlers, the indigenous music of the north was substantially altered, more in some areas than others. Both indigenous music and the music of the Franciscans and Jesuits who attempted to evangelize the territory (discussed in the next chapter) shared many important characteristics, despite their seeming dissimilarity. For both, it was the primary conduit for accessing the supernatural. Unison group singing was the most common form of expression, and songs were predominantly responsive and repetitive. Music was also an important part of cultural identity for both Indians and missionaries. In all, it was the language of conversion and response.

CHAPTER 2
Liturgical and Religious Music in Europe, 1500–1800

> *Shout with joy to God, all the earth! Sing the glory of his name; make his praise glorious! Say to God, 'How awesome are your deeds! So great is your power that your enemies cringe before you. All the earth bows down to you; they sing praise to you, they sing praise to your name.'*[1]

The Bible, Christian sacred scripture, is full of songs and poems composed for the purpose of communicating praise and supplications to God, as well as accessing spiritual power for healing, success in battle, and righteous living. Christian identity, from its start, was closely tied to singing. Paul encouraged the Ephesians to "sing the words and tunes of the psalms and hymns when you are together, and go on singing and chanting to the Lord in your hearts."[2] This music forged ties between members of the fledgling church community, and provided individual encouragement and strength outside of communal worship.

Just as music was a component of the sacred rituals and daily experiences of indigenous peoples in northern New Spain, it was also central to Christian belief and the ceremonies of the Roman Catholic liturgy. Music and liturgy structured communication with God through sung prayers, spiritual songs, and chanted masses. Christians had obligations to participate in liturgy, the formal rites of the Church, but religious song was not limited to liturgical contexts. The early Church used songs, pantomimes, and plays to communicate the tenets of Christianity to a largely illiterate population. Over time, the body of extra-liturgical performances associated with doctrine increased. Popular religious observance incorporated music, dances, and drama—expressions that heightened the presence of the body and mind in religious devotion. Struggles over the appropriate meanings and uses of music drew boundaries among religious groups in early modern Europe.

[1] Psalm 66: 1-4, New International Version.
[2] Ephesians 5:19.

This chapter traces the musical traditions of the Franciscan and Jesuit missionaries who evangelized the northern frontier of New Spain, including their relationship to the larger European body of liturgical music in the sixteenth through eighteenth centuries. The sacred music of the liturgy helped to foster group identity among believers, as well as missionaries. Musical devotion was an outward sign of inner piety and a restatement of personal belief. While the obligations of the liturgy were the primary force shaping the daily lives of those who entered religious orders, Franciscans and Jesuits were not only influenced by the liturgical music of their orders. Popular religious celebrations, processions, folk songs, and dance-dramas of the regions from which they came shaped their understanding of the power of music. In response to the challenges of the Reformation, members of the regular clergy used music to attract people to Catholicism and teach them doctrine, and in this work they found folk songs and liturgical drama to be invaluable. Thus, although initial musical practice in the religious orders was limited, it developed over time in response to the demands of evangelization, becoming an important component of the spread of Christianity to indigenous peoples throughout the Americas. The themes of music and the formation of identity, music and social control, and music as communication are significant in this study of liturgical and popular religious music. Although the forms and performance contexts of liturgical music are substantially different from those found within the pre- and post-Contact indigenous groups of northern New Spain, music served similar functions in missionary societies.

Music and Religious Identity

Defining oneself as a member of a particular religious group involved drawing boundaries between and within other groups. For missionaries, Catholicism and membership in religious orders were not only sets of theological beliefs and practices, but also social and cultural processes that structured their daily lives. Religious identity was historically produced in institutions such as the colleges and houses of the regular orders. It was constructed and transformed through performances of the rites of the church. Music aided in the construction of these religious identities and categories by helping to define boundaries between and within imagined religious communities; Christian liturgy was born singing, and it has never ceased to sing.[3] Singing held an even more prominent position; it

---

[3] J. Gelineau, "Music and Singing in the Liturgy," in Cheslyn Jones, Geoffrey Wainwright, Edward Yarnold, and Paul Bradshaw, eds., *The Study of Liturgy*, rev. ed. (New York: Oxford University Press, 1992), 494.

was through song that revealed scripture was combined with musical expression in a way that allowed time for contemplation and reassertion of religious belief.[4] For the missionaries, music was a catalyst in the formation of religious identity, not only in the public sphere of evangelization and teaching, but also in the private sphere of daily devotions and prayer.

Whether in a private cell, in the chapel of the religious college, or on a street corner in town, singing was an articulation of spirituality. It united and identified individuals as members of the corporate body of Christ. Sacred music also delineated boundaries between and within those who identified themselves as Catholics, Anglicans, Lutherans, or Calvinists. Differing musical practices in corporate worship set the missionary orders apart from each other as well as from Catholics in other parts of the world. As part of evangelization efforts in Europe and in the Americas, music not only defined boundaries between Christian and non-Christian, it also helped to bridge those boundaries.

Roman Catholic Liturgical Music

Until the significant decisions of the Second Vatican Council in the twentieth century, Roman Catholic liturgy changed little from the practices of the thirteenth-century Church. These prayers and rites defined Catholicism for both believers and outsiders. Liturgy encompassed the beliefs, history, and teachings of the Church in its texts and gestures. Music was an integral part of the sacred services of the Church, particularly the mass. In pre-Reformation Europe, mass was commonly chanted by the priest. The choir and the congregation were drawn into worship by singing responses and psalmody. These were the most integrative and participatory portions of the mass, intended to involve all present in the corporate mystical body of Christ.[5] Chanting involved more than simply adding a melody to the words of the liturgy. It was utilized during the most significant parts of the service, such as the Eucharistic prayer, to heighten the senses and emphasize the importance of the actions that would transform bread and wine into the body and blood of Jesus Christ.

On Sundays and feast days, music often moved beyond chant with the addition of harmony or instrumentation. In the late Renaissance, falsobordone, or

---

[4] Ibid., 497. On the development of plainchant in the liturgy, see David Hiley, *Western Plainchant: A Handbook*. (Oxford: Clarendon Press, 1993).
[5] John Bossy, "The Mass as a Social Institution, 1200–1700," *Past and Present*, no. 100 (August 1983), 29-61; and James Sandos, *Converting California: Indians and Franciscans in the Missions* (New Haven, CT: Yale University Press, 2004), 130.

the harmonization of the psalm or canticle tones, became popular. It was intended to provide simple part music, which was alternated with plainsong.[6] High, or sung, mass was performed in polyphonic settings by monastery, convent, royal chapel, or cathedral choirs. The sung mass contained ten musical items: the Kyrie, Gloria, Credo, Sanctus, and Agnus Dei of the Ordinarium, in which the text remained constant regardless of liturgical season; and the Introit, Gradual, Tract, or Alleluia, Offertory, and Communion of the Properium, the text of which varied according to season. This music was typically led by one or two organs and a choir, either in plainchant or simple part singing.[7] Liturgical books, both published and hand-copied onto vellum or parchment, provided guidance for the leaders of the worship.[8] A *maestro de capilla*, or chapel master, was in charge of preparing singers and instrumentalists for sacred music making, a full-time position with enormous prestige and responsibility.

Music was not only used to communicate with God within the context of the mass. Regular clergy celebrated the Divine Office, or canonical hours, and the major services of Matins, Lauds, Vespers, and Compline often involved music. These services were primarily meditational—meant to inspire devotion and remember the work of God in the world.[9] An entire community might come together on Saturday or Sunday evenings or special occasions during the church year, such as Holy Week or Christmas, to participate in the chanting of Vespers, reinforcing the solemnity of the occasion with an additional worship service. While song conveyed Christian meanings through melody, harmony, repetition, tempo, and rhythm, concepts were further illustrated through movement and gesture. Religious dramas, many containing sung or spoken dialogues, which elaborated on the liturgy, became common in the Middle Ages as a way of explaining doctrine for illiterate congregation members. Tropes, or musical additions to chant, began as brief texts for responsive recitation or words and

---

[6] Gustave Reese, *Music in the Renaissance*, rev. ed. (New York: W.W. Norton and Company, 1959), 491.

[7] Kenneth Kreitner, "Minstrels in Spanish Churches, 1400–1600," *Early Music* 20:4 (November 1992), 533.

[8] Several types of liturgical books contained music. The missal contained both spoken and chanted sections of the mass, including lessons, prayers, and the chants of the Properium and Ordinarium. Graduals held the chants for the Properium, and antiphoners contained chants and antiphons sung by choirs and soloists during the Divine Office. See Richard F. French, "Liturgical Books," in Don Michael Randel, ed., *The New Harvard Dictionary of Music* (Cambridge, MA: Belknap Press, 1996), 453-454, as well as the entries for missal, gradual, and antiphoner in Stanley Sadie and John Tyrrell, eds., *New Grove Dictionary of Music and Musicians*, 2nd ed. (New York: Oxford University Press, 2003).

[9] Hiley, *Western Plainchant*, 251.

melody added to the liturgy to accentuate important concepts, but their use dramatically expanded into solos, choir performances, or even liturgical drama by the thirteenth century.[10] Sequences, which were added after the Gradual, elaborated on this text with prose or verse, in sung or recited forms. Both tropes and sequences allowed for musical composition and creativity beyond the confines of the structured liturgy. They were popular among all classes of people, and attracted many to worship. *Autos*, or religious plays, were more lengthy and dramatized versions of tropes, such as the story of the women at Jesus's tomb at the Resurrection, the visit of the Three Kings to the Christ Child, or the *autos sacramentales*, allegorical plays that were performed during the feast of Corpus Christi.[11] Popular in Spain, and later taken to the American colonies, they physically involved worshippers in the adoration of sacraments, reinforcing Catholic identity and communicating doctrinal meanings. In sixteenth- and seventeenth-century Spain, costumes, stringed instruments, minstrels, and dancing even found their way into churches, the entrances of which often served as markets, blurring the boundaries between sacred and profane.

Solemnity of worship gained a position of increased importance in the late Middle Ages and Renaissance, due to both spiritual and political forces. Not only was the Church interested in preserving the sanctity of the Eucharist, it also needed elaborate, highly stylized rituals to display its status as a political force.[12] The Church understood that the power of song and dance had slipped out of its control, and in 1210, Pope Innocent III issued an edict banning all that was not strictly liturgical from inside church buildings. In Spain, King Alfonso X argued that performances to illustrate the birth of Christ, the arrival and adoration of the Three Kings, and the Resurrection were edifying, and could be included in services on special occasions in large cities, under the watchful eyes of bishops and archbishops. However, he cautioned that "the Church of God is for praying, and not for mocking games: thus spoke our Lord Jesus Christ in the Gospel, that His house should be a house of prayer, not a cave of bandits."[13] Attempts to limit popular religious practices in the cathedrals and chapels of the

---

[10] See William L. Smolden, *The Music of the Medieval Church Dramas* (London: Oxford University Press, 1980); and Fernando Lázaro Carreter, *Teatro Medieval* (Valencia: Castalia, 1958).

[11] See Louise K. Stein, "Auto," in Stanley Sadie, ed., *New Grove Dictionary of Music and Musicians*, vol. 2 (London: Macmillan, 2001), 242-243.

[12] Andrew Wilson-Dickson, *The Story of Christian Music* (Minneapolis: Fortress Press, 1996), 42.

[13] Las Siete Partidas, Primera Partida, title VI, law 34 (1256–1265), in Tomás Lozano, Cantemos al Alba: *Origins of Songs, Sounds, and Liturgical Drama of Hispanic New Mexico*, trans. and ed. Rima Montoya (Albuquerque: University of New Mexico Press, 2007), 6.

elite were common; screens sealed off the choir from the larger church, and commoners were generally allowed only as far as the nave of the church.[14]

The religious experiences and knowledge of the non-elite were shaped more profoundly by popular religious practices than by formal liturgical music. Popular religious practices of the Renaissance differed by region, involving drama, dance, and song. Confraternities, lay organizations composed largely of middle-class artisans, were founded in large numbers in the fifteenth and sixteenth centuries. These organizations supported elaborate celebrations in honor of their patron saint or Marian image, with the participation of small bands of instrumentalists and singers.[15] For special occasions, such as the feast days of saints, Corpus Christi, and in honor of canonizations, large processions through the town to the church were common. Minstrels were important parts of these processions, playing songs or hymns on trumpets, shawms, drums, and tambourines. In some areas, by the late fifteenth century, musicians even entered the church to perform as part of worship services.[16] Weddings, trade fairs, and carnivals all incorporated music and dancing in the lives of the middle and lower classes. Stringed instruments such as the guitar and *vihuela* were associated with secular music and dancing, and were therefore considered largely inappropriate for use in consecrated spaces.[17] The characteristics of popular musical practice—vernacular-language songs, folk melodies, use of a variety of instruments, and celebrations beyond the confines of the church buildings (which were controlled by Church authorities and the secular elite)—allowed the participation and comprehension of a larger number of believers in worship. Shared repertoires and performances bound groups together and reinforced corporate devotion and identity.

In addition to facilitating worship in parish churches, cathedrals, and city streets, music was an important part of the daily lives of clerical orders. Their days were structured by the recitation of the canonical hours[18] and the mass; this

---

[14] Wilson-Dickson, *The Story of Christian Music*, 46.

[15] Edward E. Lowinsky, "Music in the Culture of the Renaissance," *Journal of the History of Ideas* 15:4 (October 1954), 517.

[16] Spanish churches were likely the first to incorporate popular *ministrils*, or instrumentalists, into church services, as well as special celebrations in the interior of the church, beginning in the late fifteenth century. By the late sixteenth century, this practice was widespread in larger churches. Kreitner, "Minstrels in Spanish Churches," 533, 535.

[17] Jaime Moll, "Música y representaciones en las constituciones sinodales de los Reinos de Castilla del siglo XVI," *Anuario musical* 30 (1975), 209-243.

[18] Canonical hours are divisions of time that include specific liturgies to be prayed throughout the day, using the divine, or daily, office. Matins, Lauds, Prime, Terce, Sext, None, Vespers, and Compline make up the canonical hours, and vespers was the office in which non-clergy most often participated.

practice dated from a rule established by Pope Innocent III in 1215.[19] Specific music for the chanting of the hours was contained in books called antiphoners, and the music varied by clerical order.[20] In this context, chanting the liturgy and prayers was literally the daily work, or *opus dei*, of those who observed monastic rules. Daily appropriation of time was governed by these obligations, in monastic timetables of discipline.[21] This discipline was entered into voluntarily by those who entered the orders, as a way of combating sin and worldly concerns. Still, monastery bells rang out to remind the larger communities in which the religious orders resided that all time was God's time.[22] Music governed organization of time, then, whether through the bells or the expected prayers at appointed times. Furthermore, for the regular clergy, singing heightened the presence of the body and mind in prayer, and liturgical actions performed in common vocalized shared theology and purpose.

Events of the Reformation in Europe drew clear borders between Catholic and Protestant factions, as each group attempted to control the power of music in their quest to gain followers. The body of sacred music had dramatically expanded and become more elaborate in the late Renaissance. Unadorned chant, while still used in worship, was replaced in royal chapels and cathedrals with part-singing.[23] More tropes and sequences, as well as falsobordone, were commonly added to chanted sections of the mass and daily office, and composers produced polyphonic settings of the mass, some of which even included instrumentation beyond the organ. The number of liturgical settings for mass and office, as well as the amount of music in each service increased, requiring more instrumentalists, larger choirs, and increased musical proficiency.

Reformation leaders such as Martin Luther and John Calvin recognized the power of music. Luther viewed music as a gift of God, one capable of instilling order, good manners, morality, and reason.[24] Because of this, he advocated its use in the education of children and in worship. The reformers' complaints against the Catholic Church centered on ostentatious elements of the liturgy.

---

[19] C.W. Dugmore, "Canonical Hours," in J.G. Davies, ed., *The New Westminster Dictionary of Liturgy and Worship* (Philadelphia: Westminster Press, 1986), 144.

[20] The antiphonale contained music for the canonical hours, while the graduale contained music for the mass.

[21] Foucault, *Discipline and Punish:*, 19.

[22] Barnabas Hughes, "Friars, Hourglasses and Clocks," *Collectanea Franciscana* 53, nos. 3–4 (1984), 265.

[23] Reese, *Music in the Renaissance*, 491.

[24] Joe E. Tarry, "Music in the Educational Philosophy of Martin Luther," *Journal of Research in Music Education* 21:4 (Winter 1973), 356.

Luther argued that the music of the liturgy was too vast and complicated, and that it was sung in Latin, an elite language that was not meaningful to a majority of the population. He promoted the use of chorales and hymns in the vernacular instead of the sung mass and canonical hours. John Calvin fashioned a worship service focused more on preaching than prayer, music, and the Eucharist. He believed that liturgical music had become excessive and drew attention toward musicians, and away from devotion to God. Among Calvinists, only the singing of psalms in four-part chordal harmony or in octave intervals was permitted in public worship.[25] One of the defining elements of Anglican identity was the musical culture that developed in the late sixteenth century. Because leaders of the Church of England, like Luther and Calvin, believed in using vernacular languages in worship and prayer, Anglican music and the Book of Common Prayer were written in English. However, Anglican music reflected its Catholic heritage; canticles such as the *Te Deum Laudamus* and the *Benedictus* were widely used.[26] Musical practice was a language that communicated the doctrinal emphases of Catholics, Lutherans, and Calvinists, and Anglicans, as well as other Protestant groups, during the Reformation and Catholic Counter-Reformation.

The Catholic Church responded to the charges of complexity and extravagance made by Reformation leaders. Martin Luther's concern over the use of Latin for mass was recognized, but the Church believed Latin to be a more sacred, and therefore appropriate, language for the mass. Recognizing Luther's effectiveness at reaching out to larger audiences, however, spiritual songs in the vernacular were allowed, and missionaries such as the Jesuits and Franciscans used these in evangelization. Church authorities were also anxious to incorporate appropriate popular religious practices into official practice to spread the political and spiritual power of the Church. In sixteenth-century Seville, the canons of the Church decreed that processions around the church, when accompanied with music, augmented the devotion of city residents and encouraged them to follow and participate in the Divine Office.[27] Popular religiosity greatly influenced the genre of songs known as *villancicos*, which derived from the word for "villager." Originally based on medieval dance tunes, these songs were increasingly associated with religious themes by the late sixteenth century. They

---

[25] Albert Dunning, "Jean Calvin," in Stanley Sadie, ed., *New Grove Dictionary of Music and Musicians*, vol. 4 (London: Macmillan, 2001), 844-847.

[26] On early Anglican music, see Peter le Huray, *Music and the Reformation in England, 1549-1660* (New York: Oxford University Press, 1967).

[27] Lourdes Turrent, *La conquista musical de México* (Mexico City: Fondo de Cultura Económica, 1996), 40.

were sung in the vernacular, based on popular tunes with dance-like rhythms, and contained verses with easily memorized refrains. Villancicos became important components of the celebrations on feast days such as Christmas and Epiphany, particularly during Matins, where they replaced the Latin responsories. They were sung during processions for Corpus Christi, saints' feast days, and as part of Marian devotion, and were important parts of popular religious practice throughout the Spanish empire. Some of the most important Spanish composers penned villancicos, and their spread throughout Europe and the Spanish empire made them one of the most pervasive genres of music, both sacred and secular, in the seventeenth and eighteenth centuries.[28]

The most direct response of the Catholic Church to the growing plurality of Western Christianity, including the Protestant reformers, was the Council of Trent, which was convened by Pope Paul III in 1545 and met intermittently until 1563. Discussions concerning liturgical music reform occurred at the end of the meetings in 1562, during a discussion of "abuses of the Mass." The church leaders in attendance were worried about the mixing of secular tunes, voices, and instruments in worship rites and the unintelligibility of the words of the liturgy, particularly when in polyphonic settings. Many felt that the insertion of tropes, sequences, vernacular songs, and long organ compositions obscured the sacred purpose of liturgical music.[29] The most pressing concern, however, was the intelligibility of liturgical texts. Conservative cardinals called for the Council to abolish all polyphony in the liturgy because the words in complex compositions could not be understood. The Spanish bishops advocated the continued use of a variety of musical forms, so long as they did not inspire covetousness, irreverence, and superstition.[30] Ultimately, the Council said little about music. Polyphony was not outlawed, nor were compositions based on secular tunes or instruments other than the organ. The body recognized the concerns of conservatives when it decreed in *de observandis in celebratione missae* that priests

---

[28] Not only composers, but authors like Sor Juana Inéz de la Cruz, penned villancicos. Some genres of Latin American folk songs descend directly from the villancico, which also had regional variations in the Spanish colonies. African rhythms and instruments, for example, were incorporated into *negrillos*, which were composed and sung in areas such as Veracruz. Paul R. Laird, *Towards a History of the Spanish Villancico* (Warren, MI: Harmonie Park Press, 1997), 51. See also Isabel Pope and Paul R. Laird, "Villancico," in Stanley Sadie, ed., *New Grove Dictionary of Music and Musicians* (London: Macmillan, 2001), vol. 26, 621-628.

[29] Craig A. Monson, "The Council of Trent Revisited," *Journal of the American Musicological Society*, 55:1 (Spring 2002), 7; and Robert Hayburn, "Legislation on Sacred Music," *New Catholic Encyclopedia*, vol. 10 (New York: McGraw-Hill, 1967), 130.

[30] Monson, "The Council of Trent Revisited," 10.

> ... shall banish from the churches all such music that, whether by the organ or in singing, contains things that are lascivious or impure; likewise all worldly conduct, vain and profane conversations, wandering around, noise and clamor, so that the house of God may be seen to be and may truly be called a house of prayer.[31]

The regular orders were affected by Tridentine legislation as well. In the twenty-fourth session of the Council of Trent, in November 1563, the following reforms were passed:

> Let them all be required to attend divine services and not by substitutes . . . and to praise the name of God reverently, clearly and devoutly in hymns and canticles in a choir established for psalmody. . . .[32]

The council was essential in establishing the boundaries within which the Counter-Reformation Catholic Church could operate, but it left bishops with a great deal of authority in managing local affairs related to music in worship. These important actions shaped the body of late Renaissance and Baroque religious music, but also set the stage for the wide latitude given missionaries in the Spanish colonies with regard to sacred music.

The Counter-Reformation signaled a return to simplicity and religious conformity in the liturgy and an attempt to harness the power of music. These themes became part of the foundation upon which Catholic identity was constructed in the sixteenth century. Later papal legislation upheld the spirit of the Tridentine rulings. Worldly and pagan music was frowned upon, its melodies not to be used in musical settings of the mass or office, while Christian songs and chants were appropriate devotions. Musical instruments, such as the harp and guitar, that were associated with pagan music, were excluded from Catholic worship. Women were discouraged from singing or chanting because they were thought to foster sensuality rather than piety.[33] These rules illustrate the communicative power of voices, instruments, and melodies—above and beyond the liturgical texts that accompanied them. The Church shaped its image and identity by attempting to control what type of communication was received by average church-goers. Still, there was a fine line between controlling potential excesses of music in the official liturgy (performed in cathedrals and churches)

---

[31] H.J. Schroeder, *Canons and Decrees of the Council of Trent* (St. Louis: B. Herder Book Co., 1950), 151.

[32] Canon 12, November 11, 1563, in Monson, "The Council of Trent Revisited," 18.

[33] Robert F. Hayburn, *Digest of Regulations and Rubrics of Catholic Church Music* (Boston: McLaughlin and Reilly Company, 1960), 29; and "Legislation on Sacred Music," *New Catholic Encyclopedia*, vol. 10 (New York: McGraw-Hill, 1967), 129.

and reaching out to a wider audience by using folk songs in popular religious practices such as processions and dramas (performed in public, outside church buildings).

The eighteenth century brought a second wave of legislation, both papal and provincial, regarding music and worship. This legislation reflected another expansion in the baroque forms and complexity of liturgical music in Europe and colonial empires. Pope Benedict XIII decreed that no musical instruments, including the organ, should be used for celebration of masses of the dead or during the seasons of Advent and Lent.[34] Benedict XIII's tenure as Pope (1724–1730) reaffirmed plainchant as the most proper manner in which to worship. He wrote to French Franciscans in 1727, "in every single convent under our charge, the Divine Office must be celebrated . . . in the plainchant of the church, commonly called Gregorian, especially on solemn days and feast days according to the old, praiseworthy customs of our predecessors."[35]

Pope Benedict XIV published his encyclical, *Annus qui*, in 1749. This document stated that the canonical hours should be chanted in common by members of the regular orders. The use of instrumental accompaniment to the mass and office was not to overshadow the singing. This encyclical letter specifically addressed church music in Spain's American colonies, giving a glimpse of the widespread use of elaborate music in the liturgy:

> *The use of harmonic or figurative chant and of musical instruments at Masses, at Vespers, and other church functions is now so largely spread. . . . As these new American converts are endowed with extraordinary dispositions and ability in musical chant, they will, on hearing musical instruments, quickly learn all that belongs to musical art. . . . You, Venerable Brethren, will see that, if in your churches musical instruments are introduced, you will not tolerate any musical instruments along with the organ, except [those which] . . . serve to strengthen and support the voices. You will . . . exclude the tambourines, hunting horns, trumpets, flutes, harps, guitars, and in general all instruments that give a theatrical swing to music.*[36]

Disagreements about music, and the resulting rules, revealed the tensions between the educated elite and commoners, the sacred and the profane. These disagreements, although manifested in rules governing the forms of music, were really more about the function of music in each group. Was music to be used primarily to edify spirituality and bring one into closer communion with God, or was it a

---

[34] Hayburn, *Digest*, 87.
[35] Ibid.
[36] Ibid., 92-94.

The Lord's Minstrels: Franciscans and Music

> *About 1211 they obtained a permanent foothold near Assisi. . . . The first Franciscan convent was formed by the erection of a few small huts or cells of wattle, straw, and mud, and enclosed by a hedge. From this settlement, which became the cradle of the Franciscan Order . . . the Friars Minor went forth two by two exhorting the people of the surrounding country. Like children 'careless of the day,' they wandered from place to place singing in their joy, and calling themselves the Lord's minstrels. The wide world was their cloister . . . and in a short while Francis and his companions gained an immense influence, and men of different grades of life and ways of thought flocked to the order.[37]*

Biographies of St. Francis frequently include stories of he and his companions singing spiritual songs as they preached and cared for the needy.[38] Rather than recounting the devotion with which Francis chanted the music of the liturgy, these stories tell of simple songs and hymns sung while traveling, likely set to folk melodies. It is certain that the Friars Minor upheld their liturgical obligations differently from other regular clergy, who devoted their lives to quiet contemplation, study, and communal worship, including the liturgy in choral form. Instead of chanting mass and the canonical hours in common, Franciscans were instructed to devote time each day to private prayer and meditation.[39] Initially, the Franciscan order did not have choirs, liturgical books, or a rule that required choral duties. The friars lived by begging for food and owned nothing but their habits; they were too poor to afford liturgical books and said their office as their situations allowed. They were most likely to be found traveling along roads, singing improvised hymns and songs, and preaching to curious crowds.

After St. Francis's death, the friars became increasingly attached to a monastic lifestyle at his shrine in Assisi.[40] Because they were now more sedentary, the Franciscans began to devote more time to the recitation of the Divine Office,

---

[37] Paschal Robinson, "St. Francis of Assisi," *The Catholic Encyclopedia*, vol. 6 (New York: Robert Appleton Company, 1909).

[38] See also Saint Bonaventure, Cardinal, *The Life of St. Francis*, trans. Emma Gurney Salter (J.M. Dent, 1904), 88, 91.

[39] Stephen J. Van Dijk, "The Liturgical Legislation of the Franciscan Rules," *Franciscan Studies* 12 (1952), 185.

[40] John R.H. Moorman, *A History of the Franciscan Order from Its Origins to the Year 1517* (Oxford: Clarendon Press, 1968), 14-15.

although they continued to travel extensively and perform missionary work within their home communities. The Franciscan breviary, a cropped version of the Daily Office, came into use when the Franciscan order spread throughout Europe. This style of liturgy could be adapted for use in choirs or by traveling friars, but it was different from that used by the monastic orders, stripped of excess, and better suited for missionaries with other important work besides praying the liturgy.[41]

The duty of regular clergy to pray the Divine Office daily was carried out by those who resided in the *hospicios*, colleges, and convents in Europe and New Spain throughout the colonial period. Franciscan missionary colleges in the Americas were established to facilitate evangelization work in New Spain. Similar to missionary colleges founded in Europe, they provided not only academic courses (including those in indigenous languages and customs), but also an atmosphere of rigorous discipline to prepare the friars for challenging work in the mission field. Fray Isidro Félix de Espinosa, in *Crónica de los colegios de propaganda fide en Nueva España*, provided a glimpse of a typical day for Franciscans residing at the missionary college of Santa Cruz at Querétaro. The college was founded in 1682 to train missionaries to work in northern New Spain and to provide them guidance and support. The Franciscan rules as well as local regulations dictated this daily routine. The community woke at midnight to recite the canonical hours of Matins and Lauds. This was followed by an hour of oral prayers and silent meditation. The friars could sleep again from 2:30 until 5:30 A.M. (in the summer, 6:00 A.M. in the winter), when they recited the canonical hour of Prime. Afterwards, mass was celebrated. Next was the recitation of the hour of Terce at 8:00 in the church, common chanting of the conventual mass, and recitation of the hours of Sext and None. After the hours were concluded, there was an hour of instruction in Indian languages. The morning ended with the hearing of confessions in the church. Dinner was served around 1:00, and then, on some days, the residents of the college processed to the church chanting a psalm or hymn. At the church they prayed the stations of the cross and conducted other religious exercises. The canonical hour of Vespers was either recited or sung in choir between 3:30 and 4:00 P.M., followed by time for studies and the recitation of Compline. Supper followed, and afterward, the friars heard confessions, studied privately, or sang devotions with others. The members of the college then concluded their days at 8:00 in the evening.[42]

---

[41] John Harper, *The Forms and Orders of Western Liturgy from the Tenth to the Eighteenth Century* (Oxford: Clarendon Press, 1991), 18.

[42] Espinosa, *Crónica de los colegios de propaganda fide*, 173-174.

This rigorous daily schedule was structured by the obligations of the liturgy. While the "little" canonical hours of Prime, Terce, Sext, and None likely did not involve music, the more important services of Matins, Lauds, Vespers, and Compline were chanted. On Saturdays, Vespers was followed by the singing of the Salve Regina. The church at Santa Cruz de Querétaro, like those in Europe, had an organ to provide musical accompaniment. The unison chanting of the community at mass and major services of the Divine Office was a powerful reminder of the shared beliefs and devotions of the college. It reinforced religious group identity and served as an expression of piety. Chant was an important part of the liturgical ordering of daily activity for the Franciscans. The obligations of the liturgy structured weeks, months, and years, in addition to daily time. The weekly routine, including recitation of the Psalter, was interrupted by more elaborate celebrations for saints' feast days or other celebrations in the church year. The missionary college at Zacatecas celebrated the fiesta of Nuestra Señora del Refugio every July 4 with Vespers, Terce, and a sung mass, which included a sermon. Vespers was highlighted by the singing of the Salve Regina and the Litany of Mary.[43] Similar celebrations were carried out in all of the missions sponsored by the college. Local residents surrounding both the college and its missions could come to the church to celebrate, eat, visit, say confession, and take communion. Thus, the friars brought a tradition of liturgically structured time with them when they established missions, and in varying degrees attempted to impose this structure on the people they hoped to convert.

Franciscan identity was closely tied to evangelization of the masses instead of monastic life. Their musical devotions served different purposes and took on less elaborate forms. Daily corporate recitation of the canonical hours was expected, but seldom enforced. Elaborate musical celebration was often limited to Sunday at mass and evening vespers. Franciscans in Europe celebrated the mass and office in connection with their convents. But, even in the early years of the order, their interactions with common people—preaching and caring for the needy—involved employing song as a language of communication and a teaching tool. Seventeenth-century Franciscan chronicler Agustín de Vetancurt provided evidence of the way in which song moved beyond the realm of communication and became central to missionary identity. In his menology of the friars of the provincia de Santo Evangelio, most short biographies contained reference to music or singing.[44] Devotion through musical practice emerged as one

---

[43] José Antonio Alcocer, *Bosquejo de la historia del colegio de Nuestra Señora de Guadalupe y sus misiones, año de 1788*, ed. Rafael Cervantes (Mexico City: Editorial Porrúa, 1958), 187.

[44] A menology was a book of days containing short biographies of saints, or in this case, members of the Franciscan Order, to be read in commemoration each day. Vetancurt's formed part

of the ideal attributes of effective missionaries in this collection, and these eulogies were meant to be read privately or in common, to provide inspiration and example for the friars' current work.

Franciscans were involved with education from the first century of their founding. Novices taken into the order were taught first to pray the Divine Office (spoken or in chant) and how to live the life of a friar. In one eighteenth-century Franciscan convent in Cataluña, novices were required to attend daily conferences, which explained the rule of St. Francis and the constitutions of the order. They chanted the Divine Office in choir with other community members, spent two hours a day in mental prayer, performed basic tasks such as sewing, cooking, and the upkeep of the convent, and otherwise kept a rigorous silence to discipline themselves for a life of prayer.[45] After three or four years of instruction, the more promising friars were sent to *studia generalia* to train as lectors for the convents.[46] Each provincial chapter ran a convent school for the boys of the community, and many provided a school for more advanced study where promising students could continue their education and progress to the university level. While education had previously been offered only to children of the upper classes, Franciscan schools began to emphasize basic education for a larger population.[47]

St. Francis's love of singing as he traveled and ministered continued in the order's work in Renaissance and early modern Europe. Later friars combined folk tunes with religious themes in non-liturgical songs called *laudi spirituali*, for which the Franciscans and Dominicans were known. Used throughout Europe and in worldwide missionary efforts, the lauda were simple, often spontaneous, religious songs in the vernacular that gained enormous popularity among the religious confraternities and larger urban communities. The melodies of these songs were based on local village folk songs, instead of the plainsong of the church. Lauda were paraphrases of psalms and litanies, performed during processions or celebrations for special occasions.[48] They followed in the tradi-

---

of his well known *Teatro Mexicano*, a book consistently found in mission inventories. Agustín de Vetancurt, *Menologio franciscano de los varones más senalados, que con sus vidas exemplares, perfección religiosa, ciencia, predicación evangelica en su vida, y muerte, illustraron la Provincia de el Santo Evangelio de Mexico* (Mexico City, N.p., 1697).

[45] Pedro Sanahuja, *Historia de la Seráfica Provincia de Cataluña* (Barcelona: Editorial Seráfica, 1956), 437-438.

[46] These were universities considered the most prestigious places of learning in Europe. See Moorman, *A History of the Franciscan Order*, 123.

[47] Pius J. Barth, *Franciscan Education and the Social Order in Spanish North America* (Chicago: University of Chicago Press, 1945), 7.

[48] John Caldwell, "Lauda," in Stanley Sadie, ed., *New Grove Dictionary of Music and Musicians*, vol.14 (London: Macmillan, 2001), 367.

tion of the early Franciscans' identification as "minstrels of God." The practice of Christianizing popular secular songs was used in the wider church as well; *chansons*, or French folk songs, were the bases for simple polyphony in late Renaissance masses. This technique was one of the most useful methods of educating neophytes and was used widely in Franciscan missions in New Spain.

Franciscans also extended Catholicism to the general populace through the use of religious dramas containing music. St. Francis is credited with the first organized re-creation of Christ's nativity in Bethlehem, in a cave above Greccio, Italy. Men and women of the town processed up the hillside carrying torches and raising their voices in song. A group of townspeople and animals created a tableau of the Holy Family before a manger inside the cave. Then, according to his biographer and companion, Thomas of Celano, Francis

> *sang the holy gospel in a sonorous voice. And his voice was a strong voice, a sweet voice, a clear voice, a sonorous voice, inviting all to the highest rewards. Then he preached to the people standing about and he spoke charming words concerning the nativity of the poor King, and the little town of Bethlehem.*[49]

It is not surprising, then, that Franciscans showed special devotion in their celebration of Christmas, by organizing dramas that re-created the nativity story in schools and convents throughout Europe. Christmas celebrations also had the added benefit of falling near the winter solstice, replacing pagan celebrations for this marker of time with those honoring Christ's birth.

Franciscans also showed special devotion to the passion of Christ, and used passion plays containing music both to commemorate the occasion, and to appeal to all classes of people. A focus on the suffering Christ, as opposed to the triumphant Christ of the Last Supper, Resurrection, and Pentecost in both images and performances grew in the thirteenth century, in part due to Franciscan influence.[50] St. Francis had a special relationship with the crucified Christ; stigmata representing the wounds suffered by Jesus appeared on Francis's body while he was in prayer in La Verna. Devotion to the passion of Christ was central to the order he founded, and it spread among those evangelized by the friars. When coupled with public penitential rites practiced during Lent, it became a powerful representation of individual and collective piety.

---

[49] Thomas of Celano, *St. Francis of Assisi: First and Second Life of St. Francis, with Selections from Treatise on the Miracles of Blessed Francis*, ed. and trans. Placid Hermann (Chicago: Franciscan Herald Press, 1963), 42-44.

[50] See Anne Derbes, *Picturing the Passion in Late Medieval Italy: Narrative Painting, Franciscan Ideologies, and the Levant* (New York: Cambridge University Press, 1996).

Franciscan music, then, incorporated acceptable elements of popular daily life with Christian teachings from the start. Franciscan daily life was structured according to the obligations of the liturgy. However, the obligations of evangelizing and teaching, particularly among the middle and lower classes, took precedence as the order expanded its evangelization efforts.

JESUITS AND MUSIC

The Society of Jesus was founded by Ignatius of Loyola in 1540 against the backdrop of the Counter-Reformation. Jesuits crafted their identity apart from other monastic and mendicant orders because of their apostolic focus, a fervent concern with saving souls. Their evangelization methods, unlike those of the Franciscans, focused on converting elite and powerful members of non-Catholic communities to accomplish a "trickle-down" conversion effect. They worked to convert and return the European middle and upper classes to Catholicism through education by establishing institutions of higher education on the European continent. The Jesuits found favor with the pope during their early years, and as a result, they were sent on important diplomatic missions and given positions of prominence in the Church.[51]

Jesuit superiors developed musical guidelines more restrictive than those of the Council of Trent. Like John Calvin, Ignatius of Loyola was concerned that rehearsal and performance of elaborate music posed the danger of distracting clergy from their apostolic duties. When writing the constitution of the Society of Jesus, Ignatius wrestled with the place of music in the new order:

> *If I were to follow my taste and inclination, I would put choir and singing in the Society; but I do not do it because God our Lord has given me to understand that it is not his will—nor does he wish to be served by us in choir, but in other matters of his service.*[52]

The constitutions required that members refrain from holding choir for the canonical hours, singing masses or offices, or using organ accompaniment, instead focusing on pastoral care.[53] In addition, novices were not allowed to

---

[51] On the foundation and early history of the Society of Jesus, see John W. O'Malley, *The First Jesuits* (Cambridge, MA: Harvard University Press, 1993).

[52] Thomas D. Culley and Clement J. McNaspy, "The Place of Art in the Old Society," *Archivum Historicum Societatis Iesu* 40 (1971), 218.

[53] Ignatius of Loyola, *The Constitutions of the Society of Jesus*, trans. George E. Ganss (St. Louis: Institute of Jesuit Sources, 1970), 261.

keep instruments in the residences out of fear that they would be used for "vain purposes."[54] These regulations caused controversy between the order and local elites, in whose chapels the Jesuits often served. Resistance was also offered by some members of the order. In response to complaints, Ignatius allowed sung Vespers during Holy Week, provided that it was chanted in falsobordone.[55] Local Jesuit leaders also had some discretion in their application of the constitution. Francisco Borgia, for example, was a superior in Spain, a region known for polyphonic works by well-known composers and chapel masters Francisco Guerrero at the cathedral in Seville and Cristóbal de Morales in the Toledo cathedral. Borgia wrote to Ignatius in 1556 with suggestions about the use of music in his jurisdiction:

> *The president of the Royal Council . . . does not disagree in any other thing than in this business of choir. And here all the gentlemen keep saying that it would be good to sing and so forth; only in this area do they find a discrepancy in thinking well of our mode of proceeding. . . . Regarding the tone, in as much as there must be singing, it should be plainchant rather than any other kind of singing; because beyond being very devout, it is more brief. . . . I will represent the conditions with which I would be glad that it be done. 1) That no preacher, nor professed father, nor confessor go to choir, 2) that they celebrate [sung] Mass and Vespers only on Sundays and feast days, 3) that all be in plainchant, and thus the thing would seem more justified.*[56]

Borgia deviated from the prescriptions of the constitution because he was concerned about deterioration of apostolic effectiveness due to an uncompromising stand on the issue of music in worship. Ignatius later backed off strict instructions outlawing music and permitted sung mass and Vespers on Sundays and feast days out of fear that Paul IV would require singing in choir on all occasions. Above all, Ignatius's concern with singing was that it would draw the society's members away from their professed duties of confession, teaching, and pastoral care. If music functioned only to enhance spiritual experience and educate, Ignatius approved, but the line between education and entertainment must be drawn.

Throughout the sixteenth century, Jesuit fathers general (heads of the order) continued to issue strict guidelines regarding music. Everard Mercurian

---

[54] Ibid., 159-160.

[55] *Chronicon Polanci VI*, Monumenta Historica Societatis Iesu 36 (Madrid: Excudebat Typographorum Societatis Jesu, 1898), 8-9, as cited in T. Frank Kennedy, "Jesuits and Music: Reconsidering the Early Years," *Studi Musicali* 17 (1988), 78.

[56] Sanctus Franciscus Borgia quartus Gandiae dux et Societatis Iesu praepositus generalis tertius, III (1539–1665), in *Monumenta Historica Societatis Iesu*, 10 (Madrid: Gabrielis Lopez del Horno, 1908), 262-264, cited in Kennedy, "Jesuits and Music," 77-78.

forbade novices from singing in 1578 because, in his opinion, it only gave rise to diversion. In 1590, Claudio Aquaviva outlawed the use of organ in church services. The First General Congregation of the Society of Jesus, held in 1558, reflected the prevailing attitudes of members when it legislated against music and the sung liturgy.[57] Early Jesuits believed that because music was strongly connected to emotions, it was a threat to Jesuit spirituality.[58] However, due to the popularity of the sung liturgy among the population the Jesuits served, not all of these rules were strictly observed, particularly with regard to the musical life of the Jesuit colleges.

A notable music life had developed by the end of the sixteenth century in many Jesuit colleges, and the use of music in daily worship expanded in the first decade of the seventeenth century throughout Jesuit establishments in Europe.[59] The changing attitudes regarding music were closely related to the need for the Catholic Church to recruit and retain its membership in the face of the Reformation. Polyphonic and instrumental music enticed crowds to attend mass, evening vespers, or special celebrations. If music could lure onlookers to religious functions, priests and lay brothers could begin to instruct them in the tenets of Catholicism. When seen as a necessary component of evangelization, music was looked upon more favorably by Jesuit superiors. Even Ignatius had not objected to the singing of Vespers in plainchant for the purpose of attracting the people to more regular attendance at the confessions, sermons, and lectures sponsored by the Society.[60] Like the Franciscans, Jesuits discovered the assistance that melodies and rhythm provided in the memorization of doctrine. In 1562, Father Nadal sent instructions to the Jesuit College at Billom, which read, "If it could be done for greater edification, let the boys teach Christian doctrine composed in rhythm, by singing it."[61]

Still, some were disturbed by the increasing presence of music in the Society's work. At the first general congregation of the Society of Jesus in 1558,

---

[57] Dietmar von Huebner, "Jesuiten," in Ludwig Finscher, ed., *Die Musik in Geschichte und Gegenwart*, 2nd abbrev. ed., vol. 4 (Kassel: Bärenreiter, 1994), 1462.

[58] Thomas Frank Kennedy, "Jesuits and Music: The European Tradition, 1547–1622" (PhD diss., University of California at Santa Barbara, 1982), 20.

[59] Ricardo García Villoslada, "Algunos documentos sobre la música en el Antigua seminario romano," *Archivum Historicum Societatis Iesu* 31 (1962), 107-108; and Thomas D. Culley, *Jesuits and Music: A Study of the Musicians Connected with the German College in Rome during the Seventeenth Century and of Their Activities in Northern Europe* (Rome: Jesuit Historical Institute, 1970).

[60] Ignatius of Loyola, *Constitutions*, 262.

[61] Monumenta Nadal IV, *Monumenta Historicum Societatis Iesu*, 495, cited in Kennedy, "Jesuits and Music," 39.

Father General Diego Laynez was asked, "Is it appropriate to teach Christian doctrine in song, for experience teaches that children are more easily attracted to it that way and that greater success results?" He replied that the use of music was appropriate in missionary work wherever it seemed effective.[62] Laynez recognized the power of music to stir the emotions and senses, and the effectiveness of devices such as repetition and melody to aid instruction, and silenced the critics of these methods.

Musical training for missionaries was further supported when Jesuits in Brazil reported their successes with using music to teach doctrine and aid conversion. Jesuits in Spain followed their examples. Father Juan Alfonso Polanco described missionary work in Gandía in this way:

> *A certain one of our brothers went around parts of the town at fixed times every day with a bell, inviting children to sacred learning. Two boys went along with him, and they taught doctrine to the rest by way of pleasant song. . . . Throughout the town the only thing that was heard sung, by young or old, day or night, was Christian doctrine. Indeed, workers in the city and farmers in the field eased their labor with this singing; and mothers at home who did not know it, unashamedly learned it from their children.*[63]

By the late sixteenth century, Jesuits and laypersons with musical backgrounds were hired to instruct students at the Jesuit colleges in instrumental and vocal music.[64] Because liturgical music was a necessary part of the re-education of the Counter-Reformation, novices had to be trained to perform the sung mass and certain of the offices. Time for musical practice was set aside in the daily schedules of the colleges.[65] Many Jesuit colleges even allowed their students to sing and play instruments during recreation periods. The humanistic curriculum of the colleges birthed dialogues, and then dramas, which were originally intended to engage students in reason and debate over moral issues. Jesuit drama expanded in the colleges during the 1560s, and by the end of the sixteenth century, rhetoric and poetry professors were publishing the plays that had been created for use in the colleges, making them available to a wider audience.[66]

---

[62] O'Malley, *The First Jesuits*, 122.
[63] Chronicle, Polcanci IV, *Monumenta Historica Societatis Iesu*, 350-351, cited in Culley and McNaspy, "The Place of Art in the Old Society," 222.
[64] Culley and McNaspy, "The Place of Art in the Old Society," 213-245.
[65] Kennedy, "Jesuits and Music," 73.
[66] Louis J. Oldani and Victor R. Yanitelli, "Jesuit Theater in Italy: Its Entrances and Exit," *Italica* 76:1 (Spring 1999), 18.

In their apostolic work in Europe, the society used music and drama to attract community members to churches, where they could be taught and confessed. Liturical drama was an important component of outreach, a "living catechism of Christian doctrine."[67] By the mid-seventeenth century, Jesuit drama flourished and consistently attracted large crowds to colleges and churches. These productions, based on biblical stories, were written and performed in Latin with plot summaries in the vernacular. The moral dramas often included elaborate scenery, special effects, and choral music, all designed to teach students and the public. Academic assemblies made use of sacred choral and instrumental music as well. Student compositions were performed as part of liturgical drama and academic assemblies.[68] A public thesis defense at a college, for example, included entertainment before the presentation and afterwards. The choral works presented related to the text or themes being defended. This practice communicated doctrine and scholarship, making it more understandable and accessible to a wider audience.

Devotion to the Virgin Mary was an essential feature of the Counter-Reformation Catholicism that had given birth to the Society of Jesus.[69] Congregations formed within Jesuit colleges for the purpose of honoring the Virgin. They hosted Saturday-evening Vespers for the benefit of surrounding communities. The high point of the liturgy of Vespers was the singing of the *Magnificat*, a Marian antiphon, which often included polyphonic singing and instrumentation. These performances were permitted as a form of apostolic outreach. Members of Marian congregations also composed hymns venerating the Virgin. These songs were spread throughout Jesuit establishments in Europe and worldwide through missionary activity, and tied Marian devotion and song to corporate Catholic identity.

In practice, if not in Ignatius's original constitutions, the Jesuits were attracted to sacred music, and it formed an important part of their communal devotions beginning in the late sixteenth century. Drawing boundaries between music that was sacred versus profane, permitting songs and elaborations of the liturgy that were meant for edification and education, while controlling exces-

---

[67] Kennedy, "Jesuits and Music," 46.

[68] Ibid., 38-60; Thomas D. Culley, "Musical Activity in Some Sixteenth Century Jesuit Colleges with Special Reference to the Venerable English College in Rome from 1579 to 1589," *Analecta Musicologia* 19 (1980), 1-29.

[69] On the importance of Marian devotion in the sixteenth- and seventeenth-century Church, see Anthony M. Stevens-Arroyo, "The Evolution of Marian Devotionalism within Christianity and the Ibero-Mediterranean Polity," *Journal for the Scientific Study of Religion* 37:1 (March 1998), 50-73.

sive entertainment—these were the concerns of sixteenth-century Jesuits. Instead of withdrawing completely from religious musical devotion, Jesuits instead sought to shape its character. Seventeenth- and eighteenth-century European Jesuits were involved in writing and editing hymnals, producing liturgical dramas for the public, and building instruments,[70] skills that proved to be assets in the Society's worldwide evangelization efforts.

Conclusions

Music pervaded religious life in Europe, whether it was the rote chanting of the liturgy in choir at the colleges, doctrine set to music for teaching purposes, or an elaborate celebration for a religious festival. All clergy were familiar with the plainsong used in mass and the major offices. Despite early Jesuit rules limiting singing, members of both orders participated in a wide variety of music, both instrumental and vocal, within the liturgy and in more informal hymns or spiritual songs sung in the sixteenth through eighteenth centuries. Music was employed both for drawing potential converts to the Church and for teaching. The degree to which it figured in evangelization depended on the background and exposure to music of each missionary, as well as the receptiveness of the targeted audience. Although liturgical legislation from the popes, the Council of Trent, and the superiors of both orders defined the official boundaries of musical use, in practice these rules were superceded by the interest of bringing souls to God.

For the religious, music was a form of structured ritual communication with God. In daily interactions between missionaries and the peoples they hoped to convert, song and dance also became forms of communication. As such, ideas and emotions could be conveyed even when spoken languages failed. In this way, music served as a bridge between the cultural boundaries that separated literate and non-literate society, Europeans and non-Europeans. It provided an opportunity for missionaries to explore and begin to understand aspects of folk culture. The connection of special musical performances, processions, and vernacular hymns with material culture, such as food, gifts, and elaborate costumes, provided a similar opportunity for the "other" to experience Catholic and European cultures.

Music was a catalyst in the construction of religious identity in early modern Europe. It distinguished Catholics from Lutherans, Calvinists, and other reli-

---

[70] Culley and McNaspy, "The Place of Art in the Old Society," 215.

gious groups, as well as the non-religious. Special popular religious celebrations and communal duties of the canonical hours forged and maintained bonds among group members. The bonds would later become important community links for Jesuits and Franciscans who traveled to the frontier of northern New Spain, often working in isolated conditions. Transplanting the liturgical music culture of Europe to the Americas helped to provide a familiar, rigid structure of daily obligations for the missionaries who worked in unfamiliar territory. From their colleges and convents in Europe, to New Spain and the northern frontier, missionaries accompanied military expeditions or occasionally traveled alone to establish Spanish Catholic presence. Like the conquistadors, who were armed with weaponry, the missionaries were armed with religious rites as they claimed indigenous territory in the Americas for God and the King, his representative on Earth. It is to these *entradas*, and the use of music in New Spain, that we now turn.

PART II
Mission Music

Reconstructed kiva and mission church ruins at Pecos, New Mexico. Photograph by David R. Mann.

CHAPTER 3
Musical Cultures Meet[1]

As trumpets blared and drums rolled, banners bearing the emblems of the King and the Cross rippled in the breeze. Hernán Cortés announced to the gathered assembly that he would undertake a voyage to the newly discovered lands to conquer and settle them in the name of His Majesty. Weeks later, the volunteers gathered before their vessels, chanted mass, and sailed for the land that would be called New Spain.[2] Music was linked to colonialism before the conquest of the indigenous peoples of Mexico was even underway. The performance of the liturgy was a common element of the Spanish entradas, or expeditions, to new territory. Before boarding ships or beginning a march, the entire company participated in the chanting of the mass. The passage of time was marked by Sundays and feast days, upon which the expedition's clergy chanted mass, prayed the liturgy, and preached sermons. Participation in Catholic liturgy and music was one of the most familiar parts of the fantastic journeys of soldiers and missionaries to the Americas, and it was linked to conquest and evangelization throughout the Spanish empire.

This chapter examines how music was involved in the evangelization of New Spain, from the ritual acts of entradas to doctrinal instruction in the Valley of Mexico and the northern missions. It analyzes the types and functions of music in the mission communities of the late sixteenth and early seventeenth centuries. Music was a language of cultural communication and transmission recognized by both missionaries and indigenous societies; thus, it became key to the teaching of doctrine in the missions of Nueva Vizcaya, Florida, and New Mexico. Furthermore, music was crucial to the construction of Christian identity among

---

[1] Earlier portions of this chapter appear in my essay, "*Opus Dei*—'The Work of God': Franciscan and Jesuit Music," in Schroeder and Poole, *Religion in New Spain*, 266-278. Thank you to the University of New Mexico Press for permission to reprint sections of this work.

[2] Bernal Díaz, *The Conquest of New Spain*, trans. J.M. Cohen (London: Penguin Books, 1963), 47.

early converts, and evidence suggests that indigenous peoples selectively appropriated Christian forms and concepts into their cosmology and practice. In response, Jesuits and Franciscans also selectively appropriated native forms and concepts for teaching purposes in both central and northern New Spain. Doctrine took on complex meanings when Christian texts, characters, or feast days were layered upon indigenous melodies, ceremonies, or circle dances.

Forms of song and dance communicated indigenous responses to missionization, and served as markers of and elements in the formation of group identity. As in Counter-Reformation Europe, struggles to exert control over music marked the first century of evangelization in New Spain. In particular, regulations regarding the use of music in New Spain demonstrated concern over the purity of Catholic music and liturgy in light of the syncretic practices that developed when musical cultures met. Jesuit and Franciscan missionaries closely followed these regulations only when they did not interfere with their goals of fostering Christian identity in new converts. Indians also struggled to control the musical landscape of the north. Revolts and conflicts over dancing and games in the north revealed power struggles over cultural practices, both between Spaniards and natives, and within native groups, some of whom accepted new practices over old ones, and some who decried them. In post-rebellion dancing, Indians exercised the power of song and dance as a way of re-creating a world in which the Spaniards were marginalized or even absent.

ENTRADAS: COMMUNICATING INTENTIONS

Territory was claimed by the Spaniards through a combination of military victories and ceremonial acts. In the minds of those associated with the church and state, these actions were crucial to gaining possession over land and peoples, and they included the ritual speech of the *requerimiento* and mass, displays of banners and armaments, and the erection of altars or crosses.[3] In central Mexico, Bernal Díaz del Castillo reported that on Easter Sunday, 1519, Fray Bartolomé de Olmedo, "who was a fine singer, chanted mass with the assistance of Padre Juan Díaz, while the two governors and the other caciques who were with them looked on."[4] The meal and the exchange of gifts were further rites of possession practiced by the Spaniards in their conquest of new lands. Coronado's

---

[3] For more on Spanish ceremonies of possession, see Patricia Seed, *Ceremonies of Possession in Europe's Conquest of the New World, 1492–1640* (Cambridge: Cambridge University Press, 1995).

[4] Díaz, *The Conquest of New Spain*, 89.

1540–1542 expedition into the pueblos of modern-day New Mexico used a combination of ritual speech, Christian symbols, and gifts in its initial cross-cultural contacts. The requerimiento was read three times, as required by law, and friars and expedition leaders used crosses, rosaries, and gifts of clothing to convey their intentions to those they met.[5] Entrada ceremonies not only claimed territory for God and King, but also demonstrated military power, when volleys from the Spanish guns rang out in chorus with ritual speech and song.

Franciscan priests and lay brothers participated in many of the early explorations of coastal and interior North America. They provided spiritual counsel and direction for the soldiers, administrators, Indian allies, and slaves who made up the expeditions' companies.[6] In camp, they ministered to the wounded and sick, performed burials, said mass when conditions allowed, and fulfilled liturgical obligations using the breviary. Friars generally accompanied the advanced guard of an expedition upon entry to an indigenous settlement. They attempted to communicate peaceful intentions and demonstrate their status as servants of God. Likewise, *principales* headed the delegations of Indians who met the Spanish expeditions, accompanied by shamans and warriors.

Entrada ceremonies were reproduced in different contexts in the latter half of the sixteenth century, farther north. Despite their failure to find rich civilizations laden with precious metals, the amazing tales of the travels of the Soto and Coronado expeditions, and the remarkable stories of Alvar Nuñez Cabeza de Vaca's journey through the vast north country served as inspiration for regular clergy. Eager to follow the Church's mandate to convert the Indians through preaching and examples of good and holy charity, they applied for permission to work among the diverse peoples reported to reside in the vast north.[7] Expeditions designed to explore and colonize New Spain's northern frontier were accompanied by members of the regular clergy. Jesuits gained permission to travel from Culiacán farther north into the territory inhabited by the Laguneros,

---

[5] Vazquez de Coronado to the viceroy, August 3, 1540, in Richard Flint and Shirley Cushing Flint, eds. and trans., *Documents of the Coronado Expedition, 1539–1542* (Dallas, TX: Southern Methodist University Press, 2005), 256. References to these practices are found throughout the narratives of the expedition.

[6] In the case of the Coronado expedition, it is estimated that Indian allies likely outnumbered Spaniards on the expedition by a margin of three to one. Large numbers of servants and slaves, and a much smaller number of women served in capacities of support to the huge companies. See the introduction to "Muster Roll of the Expedition, Compostela, February 22, 1540," in ibid., 135-138.

[7] Millenarianism, or the belief in the impending coming of the end of the world, shaped many of the regular clergy's views about the necessity of evangelizing the many indigenous peoples of the Americas. See John Leddy Phelan, *The Millennial Kingdom of the Franciscans in the New World*, rev. 2nd ed. (Berkeley: University of California Press, 1970).

Acaxee, Xixime, Tepehuan, Tarahumara, and Yaqui in the late sixteenth century, eventually establishing missions and schools. Franciscans traveled with soldiers engaged in the colonization of Florida (settled from Cuba) and Nuevo México (settled from Mexico City). Gaspar Pérez de Villagrá recounted, in epic form, the rites performed by Don Juan de Oñate and his company upon arrival in 1598 at the Río del Norte (Rio Grande) in Nuevo México:

> And, ordering us to make proper return,
> He then did cause to be made there,
> Within a pleasant, leafy wood,
> A graceful church, one with a nave
> Of such a size that all the camp at once
> Might be contained in it without crowding.
> Within whose shelter, holy and religious,
> They sang a very solemn Mass
> And the learned Commissary, with wisdom,
> Did speak a famous sermon, well thought out.
> And when the services were done
> They did present a great drama
> The noble Captain Farfán had composed,
> Whose argument was but to show us
> The great reception of the Church
> That all New Mexico did give . . .
> Wherefore his standard then was given
> To Diego Núñez. And with that we then
> Did take possession of that land
> In your famous, heroic, lofty name . . .

The trumpet sounded, soldiers fired their muskets, and the company's scribe ensured that the writ of possession was signed by all Franciscans present.[8] Actions, including the construction of a temporary church, the chanting of mass, an improvised drama, the display of the royal banner, and the erection of a cross, culminated in the clamor created by a trumpet and gunshots. Music's power was pressed into the service of Crown and God, and the Spanish proclaimed that they had officially taken possession of the territory.

Following possession rituals, missionaries attempted to contact indigenous groups and secure their interest in congregating in mission communities. For

---

[8] Gaspar Pérez de Villagrá, *Historia de la Nueva México, 1610*, trans. and eds. Miguel Encinias, Alfred Rodríguez, and Joseph P. Sánchez (Albuquerque: University of New Mexico Press, 1992), 130-131, 138 (canto XIV).

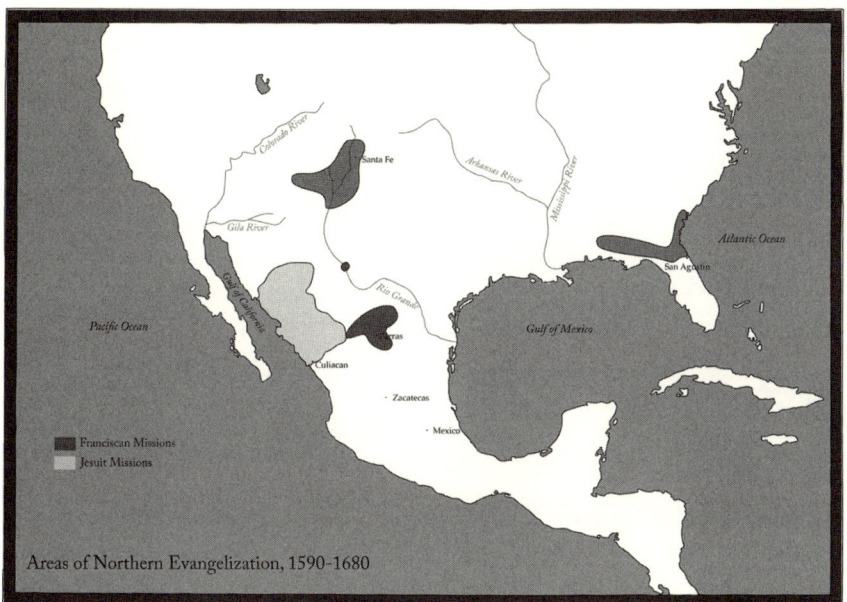

Areas of Northern Evangelization, 1590-1680

the regular clergy, the goal of an entrada was to persuade Indians to submit to the Church, congregate in villages or pueblos, and construct a mission, which would become the activity center of a new Hispanic-style community. Sixteenth-century Jesuits found some groups living in villages, but a large majority of peoples in the near north lived in rancherías, with seasonal movements. In contrast, Franciscans in the early colonial period helped to colonize areas in which Indians lived in settled villages, with more complex socioeconomic systems—areas more similar to the circumstances they encountered in central New Spain. In the entradas, the performance of music—whether the chanting of mass, singing of spiritual songs and hymns, or playing of instruments—reinforced the shared purposes and beliefs of the Company.

Spanish entrada ceremonies were paralleled by indigenous practices associated with communicating intentions to a new group. When the Coronado expedition traveled toward Cíbola, Indians on the route used a shell trumpet to announce the Spanish presence.[9] When the expedition arrived at Cíbola, the Spanish attempts at reading the requerimiento triggered a volley of arrows.[10]

---

[9] Richard Flint and Shirley Cushing Flint, eds., *Documents of the Coronado Expedition*, 256.
[10] Ibid., 257. Flint and Cushing Flint note that similar interactions took place at Hawikku (along the Zuni River) and Tiguex (on the Río Grande). See notes 52 and 53, p. 654.

Near the modern pueblo of Laguna, a smaller contingent of expeditionaries, including Hernando de Alvarado and Fray Juan de Padilla, sent a party of Christian Indians, bearing crosses, ahead to announce their presence. The next day, leaders from twelve pueblos filed around the Spanish encampment while playing flutes, as an older man spoke. The Puebloans presented the Spaniards with gifts, which Alvarado reciprocated. At Cíbola, the interaction of welcoming rituals resulted in the Spaniards violently overtaking the city. Near Laguna, more peaceful contact followed.[11] Both instances involved music and ritual speech. For both Europeans and Indians, these actions signaled the tenor of intercultural contact, and indicated the prominence of music in the ritual use of each group.

COMMUNICATING CULTURE AND BELIEF: MUSIC AND EDUCATION IN CENTRAL NEW SPAIN

Beyond communicating the intentions of each party upon initial contact, music became one of the primary vehicles through which spiritual beliefs were conveyed. Once their presence was established, both in central Mesoamerica and territories farther north, regular clergy devised methods to achieve their purpose: saving the souls of those who did not know God. Converting indigenous peoples to Christianity was a daunting, but exciting, prospect for members of the regular orders. The first missionaries to arrive in New Spain began to learn indigenous languages and attempted to translate Christian concepts into native terms. Even with the aid of translators, Franciscans quickly realized that simply preaching Catholic doctrine was not an effective means of evangelization. Instead, if the friars set the catechism to music and invited the natives to sing and dance, or put on a Christian pageant with native actors in costume, then Indians flocked to the church. It was through Christian pageantry and ritual, then, that Franciscan missionaries achieved large numbers of baptisms, an important step in converting Nahuas to Christianity.[12] Within the constraints of Spanish hegemony, the Nahuas selectively responded to the ceremonies and religious practices introduced by the friars, and ultimately exerted considerable authority over the formation of their church.[13] Just like European Christians,

---

[11] Relación de Hernando de Alvarado, 1540, in Flint and Cushing Flint, eds., *Documents of the Coronado Expedition*, 305-306.

[12] Louise Burkhart, *The Slippery Earth* (Tucson: University of Arizona Press, 1989), and "Pious Performances: Christian Pageantry and Native Identity in Early Colonial Mexico," in Elizabeth Hill Boone and Tom Cummins, eds., *Native Traditions in the Postconquest World* (Washington, DC: Dumbarton Oaks Research Library and Collection, 1992), 361-381.

[13] Burkhart, "Pious Performances," 362.

who were attracted to the church by medieval and Renaissance religious drama and instrumental and vocal music with roots in the secular sphere, Indians in the Valley of Mexico were captivated by the pageantry and material culture of ceremonies. Their positive responses ensured that the use of evangelization through music and drama spread to frontier territories. The use of these techniques in Spain's colonies, when reported in effusive terms back in Europe, ensured that villancicos, religious dramas, and instrumentalists became fixtures of worship in sixteenth- and seventeenth-century Europe as well.

One of the first examples of musical instruction is found in the evangelization methods of Fray Pedro de Gante, who arrived to New Spain shortly after the Spanish conquest of the Aztec empire. Fray Pedro founded a school at Texcoco before moving to Mexico City and establishing the school at the Convento de San Francisco, where he taught music. Joining him were friars Arnaldo de Bassacio and Juan Caro, who organized a *schola cantorum*, or singing school, in the chapel of San José to enhance the celebration of the mass and other services with chant and simple polyphonic music.[14] All learned Nahuatl and used music in their teaching of reading, writing, and Christian doctrine. The doctrina of Fray Alonso de Molina was taught to both children and adults, and all candidates for baptism were required to recite the prayers Pater Noster, Ave Maria, and Salve Regina, the texts of which were commonly taught to neophytes by translating them into the native language and then setting them to music.[15] Doctrine and prayers were learned in a call-and-response manner, with a missionary or *temastián* (catechist) asking a question, and the students repeating a standard answer. Missionaries sometimes set the questions to familiar melodies; a later training manual from the Franciscan College at Zacatecas, for example, instructed friars to teach children by singing the doctrina.[16] The communicative properties of song and rhythm were such that even if students did not fully understand or adhere to the beliefs in these prayers, they were still repeating the teachings of the church through ritual speech, song, and gesture. Whereas rituals did not automatically create com-

---

[14] Barth, *Franciscan Education*, 208.

[15] Robert Ricard, *The Spiritual Conquest of Mexico*, trans. Lesley Byrd Simpson (Berkeley: University of California Press, 1966), 101. The doctrina, or catechism, was required learning for converts before they could receive baptism. It consisted of the following items: the sign of the cross, the prayers Pater Noster, Ave Maria, and Salve Regina, the Apostle's Creed, the fourteen articles of faith, the ten commandments, the commandments of the Church, the sacraments, the spiritual and corporal works of mercy, theological virtues, cardinal virtues, seven deadly sins, enemies of the soul, and the four last things.

[16] Undated training manual, Colegio de Nuestra Señora de Guadalupe de Zacatecas, microfilmed in OSMHRC, Zacatecas, reel 13, fr. 1011.

munity or signify an interior state of belief, repetition over time communicated meaning and significance. It is difficult to know exactly how the Indians of central New Spain understood the songs and texts they sang and chanted, but the meanings they acquired were permeated with Nahua cosmology and musical practice.[17]

The arts were often used as a way to teach doctrine, particularly for those who came from cultures that relied heavily on oral and visual representations of history. Whether it was a liturgical drama, painting, drawing, mural, or song, these media made the lessons more comprehensible and more effectively piqued the curiosity of students.[18] Fray Pedro encouraged the spread of Catholic rituals among the Indians by drawing on their talents in painting and dance and by layering Christian meanings and words on top of Nahua songs and dances. Like many missionaries who followed him, he encouraged dancing and singing of spiritual songs, antiphons, and hymns on special occasions, such as Holy Week, saints' feast days, Christmas, and Corpus Christi.[19] Religious dramas for Easter and Christmas involved hundreds of men and boys, and by the seventeenth century, even some women, in all aspects of production—from writing scripts to creating costumes and performing. These dramas, often based on Spanish plays, were transmitted orally throughout Nahua society. Between Spanish secular influence and the translation of doctrine into Nahua ideas and practices, Church authorities considered some heretical and tried to curb their use.[20] But the music, drama, and festivities brought communities to the Church, and involved a larger population than those boys educated at Franciscan schools, so Franciscans such as Fray Pedro de Gante and Agustín de Vetancurt celebrated the successes of teaching through the arts and believed their impact to be tremendous. Fray Pedro wrote to his Flemish Franciscan brothers to report that after one Christmas dance festival, "the churches and their courtyards have continued [to be filled] with more people than they can

---

[17] See Serge Gruzinski, *The Conquest of Mexico: The Incorporation of Indian Societies into the Western World, 16th–18th Centuries*, trans. Eileen Corrigan (Cambridge: Polity Press; Oxford, UK, and Cambridge, MA: Blackwell Publishers, 1993), especially chapters 5 and 6.

[18] See Burkhart, "Pious Performances," as well as *Holy Wednesday: A Nahua Drama from Early Colonial Mexico* (Philadelphia: University of Pennsylvania Press, 1996); and Othón Arróniz, *Teatro de evangelización en Nueva España* (Mexico City: Universidad Nacional Autónoma de México, 1979), concerning drama. For the visual arts and evangelization, see Peterson, *The Paradise Garden Murals of Malinalco*; and Gruzinski, *Painting the Conquest*.

[19] Charles Verlinden, "Fray Pedro de Gante y su época," *Revista de historia de América* 101 (January-June 1986), 117.

[20] Jonathan Truitt, "Adopted Pedagogies: Nahua Incorporation of European Music and Theater in Colonial Mexico City," *Americas* 66:3 (January 2010), 311-330.

hold, paying honors to our Savior Jesus Christ that formerly had been paid the devils."[21] These educational techniques were praised by Toribio de Benavente (Motolinía) in his widely read history of the Indians of New Spain, and were duplicated by Franciscans in Peru and Quito.[22] In addition, Vetancurt's *Teatro Mexicano*, describing early evangelization efforts, became a common item in mission libraries throughout the Spanish empire.[23]

The arts not only helped students learn doctrine, they also introduced European culture and encouraged standards of discipline and behavior present in European colleges. Students and teachers at the San Francisco convent participated in religious celebrations and chanted the Divine Office daily in much the same way that students in Europe structured their days.[24] A report prepared by Franciscans for the visit of Licenciado Juan de Ovando, president of the Council of the Indies, expressed these sentiments:

> *The Indians themselves play . . . instruments, and their harmonious sounding together is truly a wonderful attraction to Christianity as far as the generality of the natives is concerned. The music is most necessary. The adornment of the church and all the beauty of the music lifts their spirits to God and centers their minds on spiritual things.*[25]

When engaged in performance, painting, or practice, friars believed that students' minds would not stray to material concerns—including the impact of disease and social disruptions caused by the imposition of Spanish rule. Fray Martín de Valencia reported that "[w]e devote much time to them, teaching them how to read, write, and sing both plainsong and polyphonic music. We teach them how to sing the canonical hours and how to assist at mass; and we try to encourage the highest standards of living and conduct."[26] The friars were confident that this new form of structured life would increase inward devotion and piety.

---

[21] Arthur J.O. Anderson, "Introduction," in Bernardino de Sahagún, *Psalmodia Christiana* (Salt Lake City: University of Utah Press, 1993), xix.

[22] E.A. Foster, trans. and ed., *Motolinía's History of the Indians of New Spain* (Berkeley, CA: Cortés Society, 1950), 8, 52.

[23] Agustín de Vetancurt, *Teatro mexicano: descripción breve de los sucessos exemplares, historicos, politicos, militares, y religiosos del nuevo mundo occidental de las Indias* (Mexico City: María de Benavides, 1698).

[24] Joaquín García Icazbalceta, "Fray Pedro de Gante," *Artes de México* 19:150 (1972), 100. See also Lourdes Turrent, *La conquista musical de México* (Mexico City: Fondo de Cultura Económica, 1996), 123.

[25] *Nueva Colección de Documentos para la Historia de México*, vol. II, 65-66.

[26] Martín de Valencia to Charles V, 1532, *Cartas de Indias* (Madrid: Imprenta de M.G. Hernández, 1877), 56.

Jesuits also recognized the success of using music to teach doctrine and convey expectations of appropriate behavior. In 1610, Jesuit Visitor General Rodrigo de Cabredo ordered the establishment of schools for Indian boys in the principal pueblo of each region. These schools were to teach the boys to read, write, sing, and serve in the churches so that those students could serve as examples to other Indians. Cabredo acknowledged that "this has been a very successful means of establishing Christianity and preserving peace in these nations."[27] These schools were to be modeled on those in the Valley of Mexico, where Indian students were trained in chant, polyphony, instrumental manufacture and performance, and copying music, in addition to reading, writing, and doctrine. After achieving proficiency in music, theology, or languages, students could be sent out to towns throughout Mexico to work for the Church as translators, teachers, or musicians. Music's capacity as a persuasive force was at work in these settings. The ultimate effect was that cooperative behavior within social groups, such as the students of a college, was clearly evident.[28]

Daily activities were highly structured so as to encourage conformity to European lifestyle and liturgical practice. Every Saturday at the Colegio de San Gregorio, mass was chanted in honor of Mary. Sunday evenings, after a sermon, the Salve Regina was sung to the accompaniment of organ, flutes, and shawms.[29] The school was provided with all types of instruments and good music teachers so that students could "practice every day in playing instruments, and in learning ecclesiastic chant. And thus because of their good diligence, many churches of the towns of the archdiocese have fine organists, singers, and teachers of music who grew up in San Gregorio."[30] Xacalteopan, the Indian

---

[27] Cabredo's rules appear in Pérez de Ribas, *History of the Triumphs of our Holy Faith*, book 7, chapter 14, 470; and Charles Polzer, *Rules and Precepts of the Jesuit Missions of Northwestern New Spain* (Tucson: University of Arizona Press, 1976), 68.

[28] See Steven Brown, "Introduction," in *Music and Manipulation: On the Social Uses and Social Control of Music* (New York: Berghahn Books, 2006), xiii.

[29] Shawms (*chirimías*) were double-reed instruments similar in sound to the oboe. Carta anua de la provincia de Mexico, 1599, in Felix Zubillaga, *Monumenta Mexicana*, vol. VII (Rome: Archivum Historicum Societatis Iesu, 1956), 180-181. For more on the construction of chirimías, perhaps the most important category of instruments in late sixteenth- and early seventeenth-century Latin America, see Charles McNett, "The Chirimía: A Latin American Shawm," *The Galpin Society Journal* 13 (July 1960), 44-51.

[30] Miguel Venegas, Templo mystico de la Gracia dedicado a Maria Santissima Madre de Dios, Archivo de la Provincia Mexicana de la Compañía de Jesús, f. 379-380, transcribed in Alfred E. Lemmon, "Jesuits and Music in Mexico," *Archivum Historicum Societatis Iesu* 46 (1977), 194, n. 13.

church attached to the college, was noted for its "exquisite ecclesiastical performances."[31] The Jesuit college at Tepozotlán was also recognized for its musicians. Some students played and sang so skillfully that they were offered salaries by cathedrals to play instruments such as the organ, *chirimía, bajón,* and *corneta,* and to sing in the choirs. Special liturgical activities at the school included the singing of the *Miserere* during Lent and Holy Week.[32] The music involved in celebrations for special occasions was more elaborate than the daily plainchant, with polyphonic music and the addition of brass, wind, and stringed instruments. Processions, dramas, fireworks, and festive decorations contributed to the pageantry.

While European musical practices conveyed Christian doctrine and encouraged righteous behavior, indigenous music and dance also helped communicate native cultural understandings and organization to the regular clergy. The Montezuma mitote was a mixture of graceful movement and pantomime without oral text, based on a pre-Conquest ritual in which dancers honored the Mexica emperor. It was performed as part of large, communal celebrations by trained ritual specialists.[33] For the indigenous peoples of central New Spain, dancing was an important part of communication with the gods, in supplication for successful harvests and military victories. In the late pre-Hispanic period, it increasingly carried political significance as well, communicating and reinforcing social stratification, and demonstrating increased centralization of the large Aztec empire as it incorporated other ethnic groups.[34] Dances such as the Montezuma mitote communicated native political and social hierarchies to missionaries, who could then utilize these existing structures in their conversion efforts. The gestures and movements, relationships of the performers within the story of the dance, and the corresponding melodies and rhythms in these dances

---

[31] Susan Schroeder, "Jesuits, Nahuas, and the Good Death Society in Mexico City, 1710–1767," *Hispanic American Historical Review* 80:1 (February 2000), 55.

[32] Pérez de Ribas, *History of the Triumphs,* book 12, chapter 8, 708. For more information on these sixteenth-century instruments, both Spanish and indigenous, see the entries for each in the *New Grove Dictionary of Music and Musicians,* as well as Beryl Kenyon de Pascual, "A Further Updated Review of the Dulcians (Bajón and Bajoncillo) and Their Music in Spain," *The Galpin Society Journal* 53 (April 2000), 87-116; and S. Marti, *Instrumentos Musicales Precortesianos* (Mexico City: Instituto Nacional de Antropología, 1955).

[33] For a description of four major categories of pre-Contact indigenous dance, see Robert Stevenson, *Music in Aztec and Inca Territory* (Berkeley: University of California Press, 1968).

[34] Gertrude P. Kurath and Samuel Martí described dance in the Valley of Mexico and its intense relation to religion in *Dances of Anáhuac: The Choreography and Music of Precortesian Dances* (Chicago: Aldine Publishing Company, 1964). Judith Hanna noted the importance of dance in sociopolitical perspective as well in "Dances of Anáhua—For God or Man? An Alternative Way of Thinking about Prehistory," *Dance Research Journal* 7:1 (Autumn 1974), 13-27.

allowed the clergy to better understand the worldview of the peoples they tried to convert.

In a version of the Montezuma mitote performed at the Colegio de San Gregorio shortly before Lent, the gestures of admiration and honor formerly paid to the emperor were transferred to the Eucharistic sacraments. Meanwhile, the music, rhythm, and basic structure of the original Nahua dance were relatively unchanged.[35] The dance-drama at San Gregorio involved elaborate costuming, dancers, songs performed by a double choir, and musical accompaniment. When dances such as this met European dance-dramas, such as the *moros y cristianos* dances (which celebrated the end of Moorish rule in Spain), hybrid forms evolved over time. Like Franciscans, Jesuits promoted such juxtapositions of pre-Hispanic ritual and Christian doctrine because "the Catholic faithful cannot help but be pleased to see the ancient Mexica heathenism cast down at the feet of their Redeemer."[36] The introduction of Catholic liturgical music was important, but Jesuits were also apt to look for opportunities to appropriate native cultural practices and reinterpret them for purposes of evangelization. This support of pre-Hispanic ritual in new Christian contexts concerned the Church hierarchy.

REGULATING THE POWER OF MUSIC IN CENTRAL NEW SPAIN

The popularity of European-style liturgical and popular music, and its selective appropriation by the indigenous peoples of central New Spain, was widely reported in official letters and reports and early published histories. Attempts to ensure that Catholic rites were not polluted by heathen practices led to a series of mandates in the second half of the sixteenth century. The leadership of the Mexican Church issued decrees that illustrated attempts by those in power to regulate the forms and functions of liturgical music in colonial New Spain, just as Tridentine legislation had sought to purify church music in Counter-Reformation Europe.

After the Spanish conquest, a large number of Nahuas, introduced to European instruments and singing styles in the schools run by missionaries, aimed at becoming professional church musicians. Singers and instrumentalists enjoyed prestige in their communities, valued by both indigenous and Catholic

---

[35] Arróniz, *Teatro de evangelización en Nueva España*, 140-142; and Pilar Gonzalbo Aizpuru, "La influencia de la Compañía de Jesús en la sociedad novohispana del siglo XVI," *Historia Mexicana* 32:2 (1982), 273.

[36] Perez de Ribas, *History of the Triumphs*, book 12, chapter 11, 715.

cultures. Not only did musicians enjoy social benefits, it was economically beneficial—church musicians were initially exempt from tribute obligations.[37] Instruments were valuable commodities and important signifiers of social status, and even bequeathed in wills.[38] Indigenous musicians were not simply collaborators in the reproduction of European liturgical music in the landscape of early colonial New Spain. They benefited from a system that endowed musicians with privilege, and influenced the composition and performance of music in the convents, colleges, and cathedrals of New Spain.[39] The availability of musicians, their interest in fabricating instruments and performing religious music, and the skill of early chapel masters in New Spain led to a rich musical culture in the colleges, cathedrals, and convents of the late sixteenth century. Many forms of instrumental and vocal music cluttered sacred music in Spain's American colonies in the sixteenth century—violating the spirit of Tridentine legislation to ensure the sacred nature of liturgical music. Over-supply of musicians and concerns about lack of control over religious music led directly to rulings by the first Mexican Provincial Council and Archbishop Fray Alonso de Montúfar.

The first Mexican Provincial Council met in 1555 to establish rules governing the use of music as an evangelization tool. First, although singing in the vernacular was allowed, songs sung by Indians on feast days had to be examined by a person knowledgeable in the native language to detect heathen references. Next, native songs had to be adapted to reflect Christian doctrine. Indians were to use no ornaments recalling their native religious rites, and their singing was to be censored by priests or lay translators. Dancing and liturgical drama were not permitted in public before dawn and high mass. They were only permissible during the day, and then, not inside church buildings.[40] The organ, and not other instruments, was considered appropriate for use inside the churches. In addition, Archbishop Montúfar limited numbers of musicians by requiring that all church musicians be examined to ensure that they were knowledgeable in the faith, and in good standing with the Church.[41]

---

[37] Extracto de los capítulos que Fray Francisco de Mena, de la Orden de San Francisco, y Comisario General de Indians, presentó al Rey sobre varios puntos de buen gobierno en la América, 1550, AGI, Patronato, 171, n. 2, f. 12.

[38] Truitt, "Adopted Pedagogies."

[39] See Gerard Béhague, *Music in Latin America: An Introduction* (Englewood Cliffs, NJ: Prentice-Hall, 1979); and Robert Stevenson, *Music in Aztec and Inca Territory* (Berkeley: University of California Press, 1968).

[40] *Constituciones de el Arzobispado, y provincia de la muy ynsigne, y muy leal Ciudad de Tenuxtitlan, México de la Nueva España*, Concilio I, Capítulo XXVII, 82-83, and Capítulo LXXII, 146-147 (Mexico City: Juan Pablos, 1556), UTNLB (hereinafter *Concilio I*).

[41] *Concilio I*, Capítulo LXVI, 140-142.

While limiting the types of music and ensuring the piety of musicians, the early Mexican Church recognized that mastery of song was essential to conversion efforts. The first Mexican Provincial Council also governed musical training for clergy in the viceroyalty. It required that candidates for minor orders know the fundamentals of plainsong, and be able to sight-sing proficiently. Candidates for the diaconate had to master the breviary's rules for singing, while priests were required to demonstrate an even higher level of musical ability in plainchant.[42] Theoretically, then, members of both the regular and secular clergy were well versed in the music of the liturgy.

The aims of church and state were similar: to gain control over indigenous peoples and ensure their conversion to Catholicism, Hispanic laborers who could contribute to the empire of God and King. Music was a tool used to achieve both these aims. In 1573, colonial authorities were directed to employ singers and instruments in the service of soothing, pacifying, and influencing the Indians. Otherwise, peaceful acceptance of Catholicism and Spanish rule was thought to be impossible.[43] The ability of music to influence behavior figured prominently in this directive. The Third Provincial Council of 1585 reinforced the mandates of the first council. In all, these regulations reflected the syncretic brand of liturgical music and dance that flourished in the second half of the sixteenth century. They indicate that concerns about the perseverance of gentile customs troubled authorities, even while they sought to use those customs to instill doctrine and decorum.

A large number of religious texts and scores printed in Mexico City elaborated upon the political and spiritual uses of music, and provided appropriate music for liturgical occasions.[44] Choir books and musical treatises were among the items printed for the use of clerics. Juan de Tovar, an early Jesuit missionary in Mexico, wrote a musical treatise printed in the sixteenth century.[45] Franciscan Friar Bernardino de Sahagún's book, *Psalmodia Christiana*, coauthored by four Nahuas educated at the Franciscan College in Tlatelolco, was one of the most influential books of any type printed in Mexico. It was a response to the legislation of the First Provincial Council of the Church in New Spain and attempted

---

[42] *Concilio I*, Capítulo XLV, 107-112.

[43] *Recopilación de leyes de los reynos de las Indias* (Madrid: Consejo de la Hispanidad, 1943), vol. I, título I, ley 4.

[44] Stevenson, *Music in Mexico,* 68-81. Twelve of the books printed in Mexico City in the sixteenth century were liturgical books containing music. This number is large, not only in comparison to the number of liturgical books with music printed in Spain, but also because no other musical books were published in any of Spain's other colonies.

[45] Ernest J. Burrus, "Two Lost Mexican Books of the Sixteenth Century," *Hispanic American Historical Review* 37 (1957), 310-320.

to replace the words of Nahua songs and dances with texts that taught the catechism and praised God.⁴⁶ This book provided materials that the local missionary could use in preaching, teaching, and adapting native music and dances to make them appropriate for performance in churches. The *Psalmodia Christiana*'s hymns and canticles, written in Spanish, Latin, and Nahuatl, and set to existing Nahua, chant, and Spanish melodies, were approved by New Spain's ecclesiastical authorities; in 1585 the Third Provincial Council recommended it for use in converting the Indians. This book was used widely throughout New Spain, and missionaries of all orders used its methodology throughout the Americas. Like the *laude spirituali* made popular in Europe by the Franciscans, the popular songs of the Nahua were appropriated and their texts adapted for the sake of teaching doctrine.

Music in the Missions of Northern New Spain

Beginning in the 1570s, the Spanish Crown approved and funded the expansion of the Spanish empire farther north, where native groups were more linguistically and socioeconomically diverse. From the earliest missionary efforts in northern New Spain, musical implements were considered a necessity. They were integral parts of the material culture of missions, and essential communicative devices. Bells called the faithful to structured times for worship, instruction, work, and prayer. Instruments provided music for worship. Melodies, rhythms, dances, and pantomimes all helped introduce Christian doctrine and Hispanic customs to Indians, as well as indigenous customs to missionaries. Permanent Spanish presence in these regions depended less on military might and more on cultural hegemony. Instead of simply subduing a region by military force, cultural hegemony was based on pervasive, often subtle, means of social control.⁴⁷ Through cultural and ideological leadership, missionaries and converted Indians from central Mexico (and to a much smaller degree, settlers), imposed Catholic and Hispanic practices, while presidios provided some military protection.

---

⁴⁶ Anderson, *Psalmodia Christiana*, x. See also Louise Burkhart, "A Doctrine for Dancing: The Prologue to the *Psalmodia Christiana*," *Latin American Indian Literatures Journal* 11:1 (Spring 1995), 21-33.
⁴⁷ Many scholars of New Spain have employed Antonio Gramsci's concept with respect to colonial encounters. Susan Kellogg's explanation of cultural hegemony, informed by many of these works, is useful: "Hegemony develops not because people collaborate in their own subjugation, but because a dominating power has been able to institute practices and beliefs that rational people choose to adhere to, often because of coercive threats, but that over time come to appear normal, even natural." *Law and the Transformation of Aztec Culture* (Norman: University of Oklahoma Press, 1995), xix.

Music was culturally important in the establishment and early years of the missions of northern New Spain. As part of a policy of *reducción* of rancherías, it helped convince groups to congregate in a mission-centered community. For those groups already living in villages, music provided one incentive to engage in the socioeconomic structure of mission life. Whether used to teach doctrine or celebrate important occasions in the liturgical year, music was a hegemonic device, integrally involved in the reshaping of indigenous culture. Internalization of hymns, songs, and chants of the mass helped ensure the dominance of the missionaries among some groups through the adoption of Catholicism, without the liberal use of physical force. Hegemonic processes, however, were contested by the Indians of the north, and thus there was a degree of exchange between colonizers and colonized. Within the constructs of these power relations, there was room for acceptance, negotiation, resistant adaptation, and outright rejection of the missionaries' programs. The entire range of these responses can be seen in the Franciscan missions in Nuevo México and Florida and the Jesuit missions of near northwestern New Spain, in the period from 1572 to 1680.[48]

Franciscans began missionary work in Florida in the late sixteenth century, and friars traveled with Juan de Oñate's expedition to colonize Nuevo México in 1598. Jesuits gained permission to establish missions on the northern edge of Spanish territory beginning in the late sixteenth century. Supply requests and inventories from Nueva Vizcaya, Nuevo México, and Florida contain references to instruments, liturgical books, and choir vestments. Before Father Andrés Pérez de Ribas agreed to accept the assignment of establishing the first Jesuit mission among the Yaquis, he asked for assurances that he would be given altar ornaments, church bells, and musical instruments to help in his work. He stressed the importance of cultivating a musical culture in his missions, including training choirs and orchestras.[49] His history of the early Jesuit missions in northwestern New Spain was intended to be a textbook for those new to the mission field, and it recounts the widespread use of music, both for teaching

---

[48] Although there was other, more limited missionary presence in the north during this period, I have drawn examples in this chapter from Jesuit missions in the northwest and Franciscan missions in New Mexico and Florida. Conclusions in Chapters 3 and 4 are based on my database of over three hundred Jesuit and Franciscan missions in the north, from 1572 to 1820. I collected evidence from missionary reports, letters, and diaries; reports from visiting church and state officials; and inventories and supply requests. While the scope of this project forced me to rely on some printed primary sources, I also conducted archival work in Spain, Mexico, and the United States.

[49] Edward Spicer, *The Yaquis: A Cultural History* (Tucson: University of Arizona Press, 1980), 23.

purposes, and in *casos de edificación*, in which Christian practices and beliefs were substituted for native customs.[50]

Early chroniclers such as Pérez de Ribas took care to emphasize the talents of teachers and students in the frontier regions, comparing them favorably to the larger colleges in central New Spain:

> *Feast days are celebrated with song and skillfully performed musical arrangements. The priests have gone to great efforts to introduce ecclesiastical music. Accordingly, in the pueblos on these first rivers there are church choirs that can compete with those in the great and civilized pueblos in and around Mexico City.*[51]

Indeed, evidence suggests that musical culture during the early mission period was much more elaborate than might be expected due to the difficulties of transporting liturgical items, instruments, and books on long journeys, and securing talented instructors for remote positions. Motets, masses with stringed and wind instruments, and polyphony were all reported in the early Jesuit missions.[52] On one occasion, ten students from the Colegio de San Gregorio were sent north ahead of the Jesuits to teach songs and gestures, and prepare the community to receive a mission.[53] A wide variety of instruments were transported from Mexico City or manufactured in mission workshops, including harps, flutes, trumpets, clarines, bajones, chirimías, guitars, and bells.[54] *Capillas musicales*, or musical groups, composed of indigenous musicians, flourished in some communities, including San Francisco Xavier Arivechi and Santa Cruz de Topia.[55]

Descriptions of Franciscan music in seventeenth-century New Mexico also rivaled those of music in European and Mexican schools. Converts excelled in "ecclesiastic chant, counterpoint, and plainchant, skillful in the instruments of the choir—organ, bassoon, and cornet."[56] Trained choirs traveled throughout the region, singing for early morning mass, high mass, and vespers. Indians sang the Salve Regina prior to morning Mass, and learned the alabado in Spanish

---

[50] See Daniel Reff, Maureen Ahern, and Richard Danforth's preface to Pérez de Ribas, *History of the Triumphs of Our Holy Faith*, 4-5.

[51] Pérez de Ribas, *History of the Triumphs*, book 2, chapter 36, 193.

[52] For example, the Jesuit annual letter of 1598 boasted of Mission Santa María de las Parras, where motets and figured chant were sung as part of the celebration of mass and Divine Office. *Monumenta Mexicana VI* (Rome: Societatis Iesu, 1961), 638.

[53] Carta anua de 1600, Zubillaga, *Monumenta Mexicana*, vol. VII, 246.

[54] Juan Ortíz Zapata, "Relación de las misiones" *Documentos para la historia de México*, 4th series, vol. 3 (Mexico City: N.p., 1853–1857), microfilm copy in Documentary Relations of the Southwest, Arizona State Museum, Tucson (hereinafter DRSW).

[55] Ibid.

[56] Estevan de Perea, *Verdadera relación* (1632), 579v, UTNLB.

from their friars.[57] The presence of these instruments in mission inventories and descriptions belies the assumption that frontier missions suffered from lack of resources.[58] The effort necessary to move a portable organ from Mexico City to New Mexico, generally on the back of a burro, was tremendous.[59] Where organs were not used, some missionaries compensated by substituting a choir of flutes or chirimías to provide a rich melody.[60] Still, complex instrumentation, well-trained choirs, and a variety of musical practices were present in the seventeenth century in New Spain's far north.

In the late sixteenth and early seventeenth centuries, Franciscan and Jesuit musical practices in the missions were remarkably similar. As we have seen, training for members of both orders included singing, and music was a feature of the colleges in Europe and central New Spain. Popular histories of the evangelization of natives, such as Motolinía's *History of the Indians of New Spain*, recognized the importance of music in conversion, and were widely read by members of both orders. Franciscans and Jesuits requested instruments, strings, and liturgical books for their work in Florida, New Mexico, and Nueva Vizcaya. Conversion to Christianity and indoctrination into Hispanic culture required massive social change, but missionaries did not attempt to entirely eradicate indigenous customs and lifestyles. Practices seen as contrary to Christian teachings (such as nocturnal dances, idols, polygamy, and the consumption of hallucinogens) were prohibited. However, both Jesuits and Franciscans attempted to learn local customs. They often saw the value of agricultural practices and native healing remedies, and Jesuits, in particular, attempted to learn and use indigenous languages in their religious instruction. Even those native dances and rituals not considered offensive (or which could be slightly altered to reflect Christian beliefs) were encouraged by the missionaries.[61] Mission Indians likely

---

[57] Baker H. Morrow, trans. and ed., *A Harvest of Reluctant Souls: The Memorial of Fray Alonso de Benavides, 1630* (Niwot: University of Colorado Press, 1996), chapter 20, 42.

[58] Clara Bargellini's work on northern New Spain suggests this with regard to art and material culture. See "Objetos artisticos, viajeros: cuales, como y porque llegaron al Nuevo México?" in *El camino real de tierra adentro, historia y cultura* (Chihuahua, Mexico: Instituto Nacional de Antropología e Historia, 1997).

[59] Portable organs may have been transported from Mexico City to some of the New Mexican missions. Fray García de San Francisco, a resident friar at Nuestra Señora de Guadalupe del Paso in 1659, was also an organmaker, and he may have crafted some of these instruments. See Lota Mae Spell, *Music in Texas: A Survey of One Aspect of Cultural Progress* (Austin, TX: AMS Press, 1936), 7.

[60] Joaquín García Icazbalceta, *Colección de documentos para la historia de México*, vol. I (Mexico City: Editorial Porrúa, 1971), 210.

[61] See William L. Merrill, "Conversion and Colonialism in Northern Mexico: The Tarahumara Response to the Jesuit Mission Program, 1601–1767," in Robert W. Hefner, ed.,

learned to sing songs or play instruments familiar to the individual missionaries. In the northwestern Jesuit missions, a greater degree of interaction with miners, slaves, and settlers likely led to the introduction of popular songs and dances, both religious and non-religious. Some Jesuit missions demonstrated a greater tolerance for the intermingling of indigenous elements of music and dance (such as percussion, or circular dances) with Catholic practices on special occasions such as saint feast days. However, both Franciscans and Jesuits were preoccupied with destroying the Devil, whenever he appeared to influence converts and convince them to return to their old customs.[62] In all three regions, a very limited number of missionaries worked among thousands of Indians, with the aid of imported Christian Indians, and recent converts. They relied heavily upon music, dance, and movement to convey new concepts.

Communicating Doctrine and Culture

In initial meetings between missionaries and those they hoped to convert, music could communicate a powerful impression. Musical practices, both European and indigenous, were conduits of information, sometimes more readily understood than the information conveyed through speech in translation. Alonso de Benavides described an occasion upon which he helped to broker peace between the Tewas at Santa Clara and the Navajo. After chanting mass, which provided them great cheer, a delegation of Tewas, armed with a peace arrow and a rosary, traveled to the first Navajo village. The Navajo leader accepted the gifts peacefully but desired a meeting with Benavides to determine his true intentions. Fray Alonso took the opportunity to display all the trappings of Christianity: ritual gestures, song, candles, bells, and the liturgy.

> *This was just the right time for the bells to peal and the trumpets and hornpipes to sound, and I made sure that happened. He liked the sound of all this, as it was the first time he had heard it. I hung all the arrows from the altar as trophies of the Divine Word of God, though it had come from a minister as humble as I. And that was how I presented everything to the crowd so that they might give thanks to Our Divine Majesty.*[63]

Conversion to Christianity: Historical and Anthropological Perspectives on a Great Transformation (Berkeley: University of California Press, 1993), 135.

[62] Sixteenth- and seventeenth-century Franciscans were particularly preoccupied with actions attributed to the Devil. See Fernando Cervantes, "The Devils of Querétaro: Scepticism and Credulity in Late Seventeenth-Century Mexico," *Past and Present* 130 (February 1991), 51-69.

[63] "The Conversion of the Apaches de Navajó," in Morrow, *A Harvest of Reluctant Souls*, 64-69.

Benavides' intent was to intrigue unconverted Indians with the ceremonies of the Church, deference of the converted Tewas, and gifts. Perhaps then they would agree to lasting peace, establish a mission, and form a civilized community. However, his description acknowledges that he used indigenous forms of communication as well. As the documents of the Coronado expedition illustrated, music and arrows (which indicated a group's intentions) were part of greeting rituals for the pueblos of this area. Fray Alonso intended to communicate the supremacy of the altar and God's word by hanging the arrows of war from it. Whatever the message received by the Navajo leader, it was enough to impress him of the sincerity of Benavides' peace offer and good intentions. Music continued to be a prominent part of communication between the two. The Navajo were received with bells, trumpets, and hornpipes, and treated to singing of the Salve Regina accompanied by elaborate instrumentation on a successive visit.[64]

Once a population agreed to the presence of a missionary, they participated in the construction of church buildings and living quarters, even as they were encouraged to follow Christian Indians, or nearby Spaniards in their daily routines. One of the first priorities for missionaries involved learning indigenous languages in order to facilitate instruction. Jesuit Father Gerónimo Ripalda prepared a widely used version of the catechism developed by the Council of Trent for educational use, first printed in Spanish in 1591.[65] Missionaries enlisted the aid of indigenous informants to translate this catechism into many languages. Some set the words to music to aid in memorization and to interest the Indians. Jesuit missionaries in New Spain were ordered to teach the *doctrina*, which also included biblical stories and instructions, twice daily to children. Adults were required to attend only one session, usually in the morning.[66]

Like in central New Spain, Jesuits and Franciscans in the north focused much of their educational efforts on the instruction of children, who were thought to be more malleable and receptive to new religious ideas and Hispanic customs. Children were future leaders in frontier regions, and if they were converted into pious, loyal, productive workers, the stability and profitability of these territories would be ensured. In most missions, children were required to attend daily instruction in the teachings of the Church until they reached their teenage years, while instruction at *visitas* was limited to that provided by indigenous catechists and occasional visits of the missionary. Daily instruction took

[64] Ibid., 70.
[65] Ernest J. Burrus, S.J., "The Author of the Mexican Council Catechisms," *Americas* 15 (1958), 171-181.
[66] Hernando de Cabredo, "The Regulations Made by the Visitors General for the Whole Province, and by the Provincials for the Missions, 1662," in Polzer, *Rules and Precepts,* 68.

place in the morning and afternoon, with meals provided before and after lessons. Some missions designated as administrative centers even provided a school to instruct children from the community and outlying settlements.[67] Spanish, reading, writing, singing, recitation of doctrine, and manual skills such as blacksmithing and carpentry, were emphasized in regimented daily schedules similar to those of the colleges of central New Spain and Europe.[68] Franciscans in Florida and New Mexico focused on the children of native leaders. If the children of the elite could be educated and taught to participate in the duties of worship, they could return to their pueblos to assist with religious ceremonies and identify and admonish those who strayed from the faith.[69] Throughout northern New Spain, converted and Hispanicized youth modeled appropriate customs, served as acolytes and translators, and functioned as cultural intermediaries. They were invaluable aides in planting new missions and in bringing their families into alliance with the Spaniards.

This method of doctrinal instruction reversed the order of cultural transmission in mission communities. Previously, children had learned from their elders the history and cosmology of their societies, including songs that told of the creation of the universe. In this system, missionaries empowered children to transmit knowledge of the Christian world and its meanings to their elders. The Jesuit annual letter from 1637 described such a situation:

> *In some partidos of the missions they have introduced through the children particular songs, which are sung in their language in the neighborhoods and in their houses. The mysteries of the faith are sung in couplets and these are to replace other bad songs, and gentile ones, and parents of these children also gather to sing, having entered on the path through the good example of the children.*[70]

---

[67] Regional head missions in the Jesuit northwest were called *cabeceras*, while Franciscans in New Mexico and Florida called them *doctrinas*. Missionaries (generally one in the case of Jesuits, and two in the case of Franciscans) made the head missions their residences, and established schedules for traveling to nearby settlements, called *visitas*, to provide sacraments and occasional instructions. Converts from the visitas generally traveled to the head mission on feast days, and for confession.

[68] Carta anua de 1662, AGN, Misiones, vol. 26, exp. 27, f. 160-163. Francisco Zambrano, *Diccionario bio-bibliográfica de la Compañía de Jesús en México*, vol. 6 (Mexico City: Editorial Jus, 1961), 62, mentions 35 pesos annually given to support a school for the children of Bacanora, Sahuaripa, and Arivechi.

[69] Isabel Arenas Frutos, "Al norte de la Nueva España: diversidad de experiencias evangelizadoras," in Francisco Morales, O.F.M., ed., *Franciscanos en América* (Mexico City: Curia Provincial Franciscana, 1993), 263-265; and Ramón A. Gutiérrez, *When Jesus Came, the Corn Mothers Went Away: Marriage, Sexuality, and Power in New Mexico, 1500–1846* (Stanford, CA: Stanford University Press, 1991), 75-80.

[70] Vicente de Aguilar to Padre Provincial, February 12, 1638, AGN, Misiones, vol. 25, exp. 23, f. 272v.

These songs and musical settings of the doctrina communicated ideology and behavior between European missionaries and neophyte children, but also within the larger community. Once learned by memory, they promoted corporate Christian identity as they were repeated outside mission walls and courtyards.

Because of the massive numbers of Indians that they were trying to convert in the seventeenth century, and due to the difficulties of mastering indigenous languages, missionaries often delegated the responsibility of leading group recitation, repetition, and memorization of the doctrine and spiritual songs to assistant catechists, or *temastiáns* or *madores*. These community leaders (some of whom were educated in mission schools) aided in translation, gathered the group together for instruction, and added mnemonic devices, such as melody and rhythm. The meanings of the texts of the doctrinas were explained and elaborated on in sermons and sessions led by the missionary, when he was available. However, considering that doctrine was filtered through translation—of not only words, but concepts such as morality, divinity, and sin—the meanings acquired by native converts are difficult to ascertain.[71] Setting doctrine to local melodies attached an additional layer of meaning; not only did words taken on new meanings through the translation of text, they were shaped by the meanings and emotions connected to the melodies, rhythms, or speech cadences to which they were appended. In the processes of translation, instruction, and performance, indigenous catechists and cantors exercised a great deal of power over the communication of Christian concepts and doctrine.

Music and the Construction of Christian Identity

The Indians of northern New Spain took an interest in the material culture offered by the missionaries, including tools, clothes, and cattle. But more significantly, the introduction of European diseases into the region devastated the local populations, forcing social, political, and economic reorganization.[72] Mission life offered one way of coping with the enormous changes. Music and dance flourished in the early missions of the region. As part of the education efforts of the missionaries, music and dance were successful because this method of transmit-

---

[71] Vicente L. Rafael, "Confession, Conversion, and Reciprocity in Early Tagalog Colonial Society," in Nicholas B. Dirks, ed., *Colonialism and Culture* (Ann Arbor: University of Michigan Press, 1992). For a specific discussion of doctrinas in Sonoran Jesuit missions, see Cynthia Radding, "Crosses, Caves, and *Matachinis*: Divergent Appropriations of Catholic Discourse in Northwestern New Spain," *The Americas* 55:2 (October 1988), 184-188.

[72] Daniel T. Reff, *Disease, Depopulation, and Culture Change in Northwestern New Spain, 1518–1764* (Salt Lake City: University of Utah Press, 1991).

ting information was already practiced by native groups. Furthermore, rituals (indigenous forms, those introduced by the missionaries, and the syncretic forms that developed in mission communities) provided an outlet for the relief of emotional, political, and social pressures associated with population decline and the imposition of colonial rule.[73] Community identity was constantly negotiated and re-created under these circumstances. Celebrations for special occasions elicited wide participation of soldiers, settlers, missionaries, and diverse groups of Indians. Juxtapositions of European popular religious practice, music, rites of the liturgy, and native practices characterized these fiestas and ensured their prominent mention in annual letters and reports. For example, on feast days, new converts in Sinaloa gathered together and entered towns in processions, singing the doctrina or hymns, their crosses raised and adorned with flowers.[74] At a mass baptism in San Luis de la Paz, a sung mass was followed by a public dance in the courtyard in the evening. Neophytes were allowed to dance,

> *provided that they did not dance in their former infidel fashion, but rather in a very orderly and Christian way. . . . They arranged themselves in the circle that they use in their dances, with each husband leading his wife by the hand. The dance lasted three hours and was accompanied by their drums and singing. This is how the celebration was concluded, and they all returned to their homes extremely happy.*[75]

This account taught readers of Pérez de Ribas's history that societal norms, appropriate interaction of the sexes, and ideals about Christian marriage could be introduced by presenting them within the contexts of native cultural practices. Furthermore, integrating dance into the celebration was a way to emphasize the significance of the sacrament of baptism. Still, the circular dance, accompanied by steady drumbeats and collective singing, re-created communal identity and reinforced group ties for those present.

Other accounts of indigenous religious practices in the northwest indicate that Jesuits allowed a certain degree of latitude in the integration of pre-Hispanic customs into Christian practices. Yaquis at San Ignacio Tórim constructed a large ramada, in front of which they erected and painted a huge cross. The church building was well constructed, and inside, they placed the heads of deer near the altar. Converts greeted visitors in procession, the women on one

---

[73] See Daniel T. Reff, "The Jesuit Mission Frontier in Comparative Perspective: The Reductions of the Río de la Plata and the Missions of Northwestern Mexico, 1588–1700," in Guy and Sheridan, *Contested Ground*, 17-18.
[74] Carta anua de 1599, in Zubillaga, *Monumenta Mexicana*, vol. 7, 220.
[75] Pérez de Ribas, *History of the Triumphs*, book 12, chapter 4, 702.

side, and the men in a separate line, all singing and carrying crosses.[76] Yaquis at Torim aided in the construction of the church, and exhibited decorous, Christian behavior, coming together as a group to welcome visiting clerics. Still, Torim, the largest of the Yaqui pueblos, was a site at which Christian ideas and indoctrination through the arts and Christian practices were contested. Many resisted baptism, and Father Tomas Basilio was plagued by problems of drunkenness and polygamy. A group of shamans (hechiceros) met near the pueblo to convince recent converts that the Jesuit's teachings were false. These shamans preached that after death, souls traveled underground, not to a Christian heaven, and that in the underworld, souls happily practiced "all types of vices."[77]

Three decades later, a more corporate Christian identity had emerged throughout the region, aided no doubt by the native-language doctrina written by Father Basilio, which contained Christian hymns translated into Cáhita, and Basilio's thirty years of work in the region. Corpus Christi was celebrated in 1653 when all the Yaqui pueblos came together at Torim to hear mass, take communion, eat, sing, and dance. A total of 720 Yaquis and Mayos were baptized, and 270 couples were married.[78] Specific devotions were directed toward San Ignacio (the patron saint of Torim), San Francisco Javier, and San Miguel Arcangel. Large gatherings such as this, made more attractive by the presence of abundant food, dances, games, and pageantry, were tied to Christian feast days and the observance of liturgical devotions. They also reinforced the importance of Christian baptism and marriage, establishing ties of godparentage between old Christians and new converts, and extending kin networks through marriage. By 1656, increased colonial pressures due to disease, famine, and labor demands even caused those who had fled to the mountains to escape missionization, to return to Torim and participate in the "worship of divine things."[79]

MUSIC, DANCE, AND POWER IN SEVENTEENTH-CENTURY NORTHERN NEW SPAIN

Despite the many successes reported by early missionaries to northern New Spain, some Indians of the north chose to reject their presence and intentions.

---

[76] Letter of Padre Provincial Nicolás de Anaya, 1622, cited in Francisco Zambrano, *Diccionario bio-bibliografica de la Compañia de Jesús en México*, vol. 4 (Mexico City: Editorial Jus, 1961), 95.

[77] Nicolás de Anaya, Anua del 1621, Bancroft Library (BL), M-M 227, 650-665, on microfilm, DRSW.

[78] AGN, Historia, vol. 15, exp. 30, f. 182-188.

[79] AGN, Historia, vol. 15, exp. 30, f. 196-197.

Song and dance figured in these events as well, from attacks on individual missionaries to large regional revolts. Much of the tension between seventeenth-century missionaries and those they sought to convert revolved around practices considered superstitious, immoral, or even inspired by the Devil. When missionaries attempted to prohibit or eradicate these practices, Indians resisted. Some moved their ceremonies to caves, underground kivas, or locations away from the scrutiny of the clergy. Some took individual action against the missionary by casting spells, or even attempting to kill him. Still others rallied support, prophesied the revitalization of traditions and the fall of the Spaniards, and mounted rebellions against Spanish authorities.[80]

In 1619, Jesuit Father Martín Burgensio (Martin de Bruges) evangelized the Nebome pueblos of Buena Vista, Cumuripa, Tecoripa, and Zuaque. Baptized Nebomes had left the missions to join with Aibinos, and Burgensio found them drunk, dancing a mitote while holding the severed heads of their enemies. In the confrontation that followed, a Nebome fiscal was killed, and Burgensio and others narrowly escaped with the help of faithful Indians who defended them.[81] This episode illustrates the divisions that developed within indigenous groups following missionary entrance to a region. Some chose to adopt and even defend the new customs, others viewed Christianity as something that could be taken on in pieces, coexist with native cosmology, and be cast aside as needed. Still others refused to participate in any elements of mission life. These choices drove wedges between families, kin groups, and military and trading alliances. Music was both a marker of membership in a group and an item that was selectively appropriated. It also functioned to communicate responses to Spanish presence across groups.

Because the powers of song and dance could be accessed by any group or individual, regulating them became a source of conflict in early mission communities. Church and state were often at odds over whether indigenous peoples should be able to continue to perform dances once they had been baptized into the Church. Ideas among Spaniards varied. Some believed that dancing was harmless, and even helped to create productive, happy workers. Others thought

---

[80] While it is beyond the scope of this work to provide a comparative history of seventeenth-century revolts, several monographs provide excellent coverage of first- and second-generation rebellions. See, for instance, Susan Schroeder, ed., *Native Resistance and the Pax Colonial in New Spain* (Lincoln: University of Nebraska Press, 1998); and Guy and Sheridan, *Contested Ground*. My chief concern is with the function of music and dance in the contexts of these challenges to Spanish power.

[81] Gerard Decorme, *La obra de los Jesuítas mexicanos durante la época colonial, 1572–1767* (Mexico City: Antigua Librería Robredo, de J. Porrúa e Hijos, 1941), vol. II, 347.

that some dancing might be permissible, but preferred that the dances contain European instruments, tunes, and themes. A third opinion, held most strongly by friars in mid-seventeenth-century Nuevo México, was that dances involved communication with and inspiration from the Devil, and fostered heathen behavior. One of the most contentious cases involving dance occurred during Bernardo López de Mendizábal's tenure as governor of New Mexico. Franciscan padres united in their attempts to destroy all evidence of native religious beliefs among the Puebloans. The friars thought the only way to eradicate native religion was to cut out all ceremonies and cultural elements, particularly the *catsina* dances, in which dancers with masks leaped in a circle around offerings, singing to communicate with the spirit world. Dances were performed in supplication for bountiful harvests, rain, victory, or other needs. According to the friars, neither the governor nor his mestizo lieutenant, Nicolás de Aguilar, found these dances offensive. Meanwhile, the Franciscans were embroiled in a separate conflict over authority with the governor. They were outraged when the governor suspended the father custodian's position as ecclesiastical judge, effectively removing his important power of excommunication.[82] Residents of Tesuque took advantage of the rift between church and state to complain about the Franciscans' ban on catsinas. After witnessing a performance of one dance, Mendizábal ordered the Franciscans to allow these dances to continue, provided that they were held in the open, and not in underground *estufas* (kivas).[83] Throughout the region, dancing exploded, and reports of lascivious and immoral behavior accompanied complaints of dancing by friars and settlers. In one instance, a catsina dance was even performed on the roof of the mission church at Chililí. Indigenous displays of the power of the catsinas infuriated the friars and undermined what little authority they retained. The Franciscans' unyielding attitudes toward catsinas were expressed most dogmatically in the Inquisition charges and testimony levied against Governor López de Mendizábal. Many of the governor's autos were overturned, and the new display of force, including mandatory church attendance and a ban on the catsinas, began to create an atmosphere ripe for the massive Pueblo uprising of 1680.[84]

---

[82] Andrew L. Knaut, *The Pueblo Revolt of 1680: Conquest and Resistance in Seventeenth-Century New Mexico* (Norman: University of Oklahoma Press, 1995), 110.

[83] Charles W. Hackett, trans. and ed., *Historical Documents Relating to New Mexico, Nueva Vizcaya, and Approaches Thereto, to 1773*, vol. 3, comps. Adolph F.A. Bandelier and Fanny R. Bandelier (Washington, DC: Carnegie Institute of Washington, 1937), 223-224.

[84] *Proceso contra Mendizábal*, AGN, Inquisición, 487, 593, 594, contains the lengthy suit against the governor, one of the primary charges of which was his encouragement of the catsina dances. Nicolás de Aguilar was also accused of ordering the dances. Some of the documents in this

A similar, but less vicious, controversy surfaced between the Apalachee and their new friar in 1657. Residents of Mission San Damián de Cupayca complained that they were prohibited from performing their lawful dances or playing their ball game, a celebration that included storytelling, dancing, and feasting. The governor ruled that such practices be permitted, unless they interfered with the economic obligations of the mission Indians.[85] Nearly twenty years later, Fray Juan de Paiva, father provincial of the Apalachee region, further investigated *pelota*, the ceremonies preceding it, and stories of its origins, and determined them to be antagonistic to decent Christian practices. In this instance, the caciques agreed, and the ball games, as well as festivities surrounding the competitions, ceased to be played in mission communities.

These cases reveal only selective accommodation to Christian practices, such as accepting baptism and attending doctrinal instruction, mass, and celebrations for feast days, while maintaining important pre-missionization rituals. In some cases, European stringed instruments and metal bells, as well as liturgical gestures, were incorporated into the dances and games. Disputes over these performances stemmed from the friars' desires to control the power of song, dance, and rituals—power which might easily fall under the control of the Devil, provoking barbarous behavior. In both Florida and New Mexico, dances and games were deemed un-Christian, and their performance prohibited. These mandates did not end the practices. Otermín's failed reconquest expedition to New Mexico in 1681–1682 collected testimony from Puebloans, who reported that "throughout the entire kingdom the catsina was danced, for that purpose [the Pueblos] having made many masks with the likeness of the Devil."[86]

Revolts also attempted to destroy the power of Christian ritual and those Europeans and Indians who performed it. First-generation revolts, or those that occurred within the initial period of a mission community, shared several characteristics. They were led by messianic figures, and attempted to reverse the social and political order through a revitalization of pre-colonial cultural prac-

---

case were transcribed in Hackett, *Historical Documents*, particularly 134, 157. For a discussion of missionary policy toward dance in New Mexico, see Carroll L. Riley, *The Kachina and the Cross: Indians and Spaniards in the Early Southwest* (Salt Lake City: University of Utah Press, 1999), 269-270.

[85] Amy Turner Bushnell, "That Demonic Game: The Campaign to Stop Indian Pelota Playing in Spanish Florida, 1675–1684," *Americas* 35:1 (1978), 1-19.

[86] Ralph Emerson Twitchell, ed., *The Spanish Archives of New Mexico* (Cedar Rapids, IA: Torch Press, 1914), vol. II, 57. Catsina dances are still performed today, but of course in completely different contexts.

tices. They were often a response to disastrous epidemics, which in turn led to social, political, and economic upheaval.[87]

The Tepehuan Revolt of 1616 occurred after a generation of congregation in the Jesuit missions of Santiago Papasquiaro, Santa Catalina, San Ignacio del Zape, and San Miguel de las Bocas. Tepehuan children had followed the examples of converted Tarascans brought to the missions to aid in teaching and organization. They quickly learned some Spanish and Latin, and could sing Christian songs and recite the prayers.[88] The larger communities attended the pageantry surrounding the performance of *pastorelas* at Christmas and procession of the host on Corpus Christi.[89] Still, Jesuits had to pursue the shamans, and punish them for their "vain old superstitions," and there were many who did not participate in the regimen of mission life. A shaman identified as Quatutlatas began advocating rebellion and gathering followers in the area in 1615. He called for the restoration of indigenous lands and resources, which would happen after victory against the Spaniards, including priests, and predicted that Indians killed in battle would be resurrected.[90] In the first days of the revolt in November of 1616, Father Juan Font and nine other missionaries were among the more than two hundred Spaniards killed. Those in revolt mocked and desecrated vestments, religious ornaments, and the Eucharistic host before destroying them. Following the destruction of buildings at Santiago Papasquiaro, Santa Catalina, and Zape, as well as surrounding haciendas and ranchos, the rebels drank communion wine and feasted on stores of food. Wild dances celebrated their victory.[91] Quatutlatas and his followers desired a return to life without the Spaniards, yet they selectively appropriated elements of Hispanic material culture, claiming ownership over cattle, tools, and weapons. They destroyed artifacts of mission life and mocked the processions and liturgical gestures of those who had accepted Catholicism, while celebrating their tri-

---

[87] See Susan M. Deeds, "Indigenous Rebellions on the Northern Mexican Mission Frontier: From First-Generation to Later Colonial Responses," in Guy and Sheridan, *Contested Ground*, 32-51.

[88] The 1615 carta anua stated that children at a visita of San Ignacio del Zape learned to chant the mass by memory in only one year.

[89] Cartas anuas de 1608, 1611, and 1613, in Luís González Rodríguez, ed., *Crónicas de la Sierra Tarahumara* (Mexico City: Secretaría de Educación Pública, 1987), 148, 160-165, 174-175.

[90] P. Francisco de Arista, Relación de la guerra de los Tepehuanes, December 1617, AGN, Historia, 311, and carta anua, 1616, AGN, Jesuitas, III-29, exp. 21, cited in Susan M. Deeds, "First-Generation Rebellions in Nueva Vizcaya," in Schroeder, *Native Resistance and the Pax Colonial in New Spain*, 8.

[91] Carta anua, 1616, AGN, Jesuitas, III-29, exp. 21; Deeds, "First-Generation Rebellions in Nueva Vizcaya," 9-10.

umph with dances that had been forbidden by the Jesuits. Dancing released psychological pressure and must have created a shared sense of euphoria.

Similarly, in 1632, Cobamea, a cacique of Guaspares, attacked Jesuits Giulio Pasquale and Manuel Martins and a group of eight choirboys, who were en route back to Mission Santa Inés Guairopa after performing for the dedication of a church site. Cobamea and his followers killed the entire party, including the young singers, who may have been targeted because they produced music that communicated with the Christian god. The rebels then fouled the sacred ornaments carried by the missionaries and choir, and burned the church building.[92] Messianic leaders such as Quatutlatas and Cobamea aimed to return balance to their worlds through their shamanic activity. Killing the settlers, priests, and Christian converts, and destroying churches and haciendas destroyed the world created by Spanish colonial presence, and destruction and re-creation of the universe were prominent features of native understandings of history.[93] Catholic rituals such as mass, baptism, processions, and prayers had disrupted the balance of the universe, bringing sickness and loss of autonomy to indigenous communities. Dancing after the destruction of these elements restored equilibrium and a relationship with the sacred universe.

Whereas first-generation revolts often involved attempts to reclaim control over indigenous customs prohibited under the new mission system (polygamy or dancing), revolts in the later stages of mission life did not always demonstrate these concerns. The Timucuan Revolt of 1656 targeted not the missions and their friars, but the political administration. Governor Diego de Rebolledo's failure to adhere to established procedures of gift-giving in order to reduce expenses from the Indian fund angered Timucuan leaders. The governor had ignored social practices that excused elites from performing manual labor, when he ordered caciques to carry sacks of corn to San Agustín to provision the fort in preparation for an expected English attack. Refusing to assimilate completely into the Spanish colonial hierarchy, Timucuans killed the soldiers sent to execute the governor's orders, and the rebellion spread.[94] Participants in this revolt were mission leaders, including a sacristan and *mandador*. They were not rejecting Christian life and restrictions on cultural practices, but instead attempting to "liberate themselves from the offenses and continuous injuries" of government

---

[92] AGN, Historia, vol. 15, f. 140-143.

[93] Anthony Wallace, "Revitalization Movements: Some Theoretical Considerations for Their Comparative Study," *American Anthropologist* 58:2 (April 1956), 265-267.

[94] See John E. Worth, *The Timucuan Chiefdoms of Spanish Florida, Vol. 2: Resistance and Destruction* (Gainesville: University Press of Florida, 1998), 38-65.

officials.[95] Still, in the months following the revolt, victorious Timucuans abandoned the missions and their friars, spending their time dancing and preparing for expected war.[96]

The most complex and orchestrated revolt of this period broke out in Nuevo México in August 1680. After a decade of drought, famine, and increased raiding by Apaches, indigenous shamans such as Popé led the revolt against the intolerance of Franciscans and Spanish officials, who forbade the ceremonial practices that brought order to the Puebloans' world. Queres and Tano Indians interrogated about the causes of the revolt protested the ill treatment and physical injuries they received from Spaniards. Furthermore, missionaries and officials had burned their kivas, while constantly requiring the Queres to keep the church heated, clean, and adorned. The Tano testified that these duties, as well as other labor requirements, did not allow them time to plant and take care of their own needs.[97] In essence, despite nearly a century of Spanish presence and Catholic evangelization, mounting economic and political difficulties, coupled with the Franciscans' insistence of the observance of rigidly structured days with little unregulated time, created intense pressure. Without allowing ceremonial activities like dance, which functioned as safety valves to relieve pressures and restore balance, revolt was inescapable. In the multiple initial attacks, twenty-one friars and over four hundred settlers were killed. Upon their retreat to El Paso, Governor Otermín's forces witnessed destroyed churches, shattered bells, destroyed statues, and excrement-covered vestments and altars.[98] Similar to the aftermath of other seventeenth-century revolts, widespread dancing followed the overturning of Spanish power. Kivas were uncovered and catsinas performed to seek the favor of the gods and re-create the Pueblo world.[99]

Conclusions

After the ease with which music was used as an evangelization tool in central New Spain, its use in northern frontier missions was assured. Both Franciscans

---

[95] Francisco de San Antonio, Juan de Medina, Sebastián Martínez, Jacinto Domínguez, Alonso del Moral, and Juan Caldera to the King, September 10, 1657; cited in Worth, op. cit., 63.

[96] Ibid., 68.

[97] Charles W. Hackett, ed., *Revolt of the Pueblo Indians of New Mexico and Otermín's Attempted Reconquest* (Albuquerque: University of New Mexico Press, 1942), vol. 2, 239-251. See also Gutiérrez, *When Jesus Came, the Corn Mothers Went Away*, 136.

[98] Hackett, *Revolt of the Pueblo Indians*, vol. 1, 177-178. See also Gutiérrez, *When Jesus Came, the Corn Mothers Went Away*, 134.

[99] Hackett, *Revolt*, vol. 2, 245-246.

and Jesuits could point to successes in the late sixteenth and seventeenth centuries, in the sense that they had established mission systems that were generally economically self-sufficient, with large numbers of baptisms, a chain of well-furnished mission buildings, and converts capable of reproducing European-style liturgical music. Within these mission communities, music and dance were primary conduits of information between missionaries and Indians in mission communities—from behavioral expectations to doctrine and cosmologies. Drastic demographic decline and the pressures of colonial labor and tribute systems created conditions that both encouraged the acceptance of material mission life, but also incubated first-generation revolts that rejected this life. Christian and non-Christian forms of music and dance helped to define boundaries between those who accommodated to the missions, and those who rejected the missionaries' presence. However, selective appropriation of musical practices, on the part of both Indians and missionaries, was also evident. Borrowing instruments, melodies, or gestures added layers of meanings to existing words, songs, and dances. A rich, syncretic musical culture developed in many communities, with Christian and native practices existing side by side. A closer look at the effusive compliments about the quality of music in mission communities reveals that performance of music in both central New Spain and the northern frontier regions was a way for indigenous groups to re create and assert communal identity in the face of colonial pressures.

CHAPTER 4
Music, Dance, and Community, 1680–1767

The Pueblo Revolt sent waves of concern throughout the missions of northern New Spain. Was the mission frontier too extended? How could Spain fulfill the obligations of the Patronato Real, continuing the Catholic education of thousands of incomplete converts, while protecting the financial investments and well-being of increasing numbers of soldiers and settlers? From 1680 until 1767, missionaries were eager to extend their evangelization in northern New Spain, while by the end of the period a new Bourbon state established different priorities for the empire. In the 1680s, Franciscans established new missions in east Texas among the various tribes of the Assinai confederation, and they moved into central Texas in the 1710s. Jesuits, led by Father Eusebio Francisco Kino, pushed farther north into the Pimería Alta of Sonora at the end of the seventeenth century, and began the settlement of the Californian peninsula shortly afterward. Church and state worked in tandem to reconquer New Mexico, failing once before returning permanently in 1692. The advance of the Spanish frontier was countered by indigenous rebellions, which prompted military responses, and in some cases, abandonment of the missions. The second half of the eighteenth century brought additional sociopolitical challenges, and the Society of Jesus was expelled from the empire in 1767, leaving mission communities temporarily without regular clergy. Throughout this period, indigenous communities witnessed dramatic changes due to population and labor pressures. Meanwhile, cultural change in frontier communities was enormous—relations with settlers and other tribes produced growing numbers of mestizos and children of mixed indigenous heritage. These factors caused changes in the society of the north, creating overlapping communities bound by common ties and interests, though not necessarily shared histories or cultural beliefs and practices. Throughout the 1680–1767 period, the struggles surrounding the formation of these communities, still closely tied to the missions, and resistant adaptation by indigenous groups, were mirrored in the forms and functions of music and dance. This chapter begins by looking at the ways in which the political and economic circumstances in each region of the north impacted the forms and functions of music and dance within mission communities. Within these settlements, Indians frequently dictated the terms under which music was used.[1] Then, an analysis of the careers of two prominent missionaries to the north, Father Juan María de Salvatierra and Fray Antonio Margil de Jesús, illustrates the way in which missionaries attempted to build community through the use of music and dance. Their careers also demonstrate the differences and similarities between Jesuit and Franciscan mission music and evangelization techniques. The Jesuit mission period came to an end in 1767, when all members of the Society of Jesus were ordered to report to Mexico City, and then escorted to Veracruz and across the Atlantic. Some missions were transferred into the hands of secular clergy under diocesan authority, while others were left temporarily abandoned.

COMMUNAL WORSHIP: REGIONAL SIMILARITIES AND DIFFERENCES

The two most striking forms of mission music in the northern missions from 1680 until the expulsion of the Jesuits in 1767 were the communal, repetitive, unison songs performed as part of mass or doctrinal instruction and the festive hymns, processionals, and dances performed as part of celebrations for special occasions. In both types of music, corporate identity was encouraged through the actions of missionaries, settlers, soldiers, and Indian converts from central New Spain. By example, they introduced neophytes to the appropriate intonation, postures, gestures, and responses of the mass. Participation in group worship and the introduction and repetition of popular songs created a sense of community within groups congregated in mission settlements. Meanwhile, shared liturgical practices also helped define and shape the larger frontier communities. Soldiers, settlers, and their families served as godparents at the baptisms of children at the missions, creating ties outside of the mission sphere. Indians interacted with non-Indians and mestizos in the economic sphere while working in the mines of the northwest, trading in the northeast, and encountering soldiers throughout. Baptisms, weddings, and special festivities to mark patron saint feast days brought together overlapping communities—soldiers and their families, settlers, missionaries from throughout the region, and even

---

[1] I am building on an argument made by Barr in *Peace Came in the Form of a Woman* that the terms of intercultural interaction were largely governed by indigenous patterns. While her argument applies to eighteenth-century Texas, it also bears some application with regard to music in the broader northern borderlands.

Indians who had left or never joined the mission—attracted by feasting, games, dancing, and opportunities to renew kinship ties.

Corporate worship was part of the quotidian routines of the missions of the late seventeenth and early eighteenth centuries, just as it had been in the century before. However, records indicate that by the eighteenth century, daily mass and doctrinal instruction were less elaborate, and relied more heavily on the participation of indigenous converts, than in the previous period. The expense of fabricating or transporting and maintaining and caring for instruments, the time and effort necessary to train musicians, lack of adequate missionary staff, and more tenuous post-revolt relationships between missionaries and Indians in many communities may have led to these changes. Still, mass was chanted at most missions staffed by a resident priest every Sunday and on feast days, and sometimes even more frequently. On most occasions, simple plainchant was used; the priest chanted the liturgy, with the congregation, cantors, or choir responding at the appropriate points. Missionaries trained converts and choirs to sing from memory. Some were taught to read or copy music, but choir books were not commonly listed on mission inventories, suggesting that uncomplicated rote singing was most common. Jesuit Juan Nentvig taught his choir to sing from memory, and later marveled "that these illiterate people are able to memorize chants for as many as four different types of Masses, the Psalms, and responses for pertinent burial services."[2] This is not surprising, considering that history, instructions, and cultural practices were all transmitted orally prior to Spanish contact with the Opatas at his mission of San Francisco Xavier de Guásabas. Hymns, antiphons, and devotional songs used for educational purposes, or as part of the daily routine, such as the alabado, Lord's Prayer, Salve Regina, and Ave Maria, were sung by the entire community. These songs were rarely accompanied by musicians, unless they were part of a more elaborate celebration, and the simple melodies could be easily learned by children and adults. Singing devotional songs and prayers facilitated memorization of Christian doctrine. This type of undemanding singing was far more common in the missions of the north because it was not as labor intensive and did not require the resident missionaries to have an extensive musical background. Communal singing as part of the daily routine was also much more similar to the performance practices of indigenous groups of the north, and thus was utilized due to its similarity. In some cases, individual verses or the entire text were sung separately by different groups. The cantor or missionary sang first, fol-

---

[2] Nentvig, *Rudo Ensayo*, 111.

lowed by the men, women, boys, and girls, ending with the entire community singing together.[3] Still, the economic and political circumstances in each region and the backgrounds of individual missionaries were reflected in the different types of communal music performed for daily worship and instruction, as well as song and dance performed as part of celebrations for special occasions. A survey of the northern frontier from west to east during this period reveals interesting differences and similarities among communal worship practices.[4]

The Jesuit Enterprise in Baja California

Music for communal worship in Jesuit Baja California was characterized by emphasizing music in the vernacular in doctrinal instruction and more elaborate performances on special occasions. Jesuits in this region composed songs and translated the catechism into native languages, while tying worship to meal times. Soldiers and Christianized Indian assistants played a larger role in this region than others, and liberal policies toward native dances were observed. After several evangelization attempts, which failed due to lack of indigenous cooperation, permanent Jesuit evangelization in Baja California began in 1697. Traveling from the established missions in Sinaloa, Father Juan María de Salvatierra established Nuestra Señora de Loreto Conchó in the central coast of the peninsula, bordering the Gulf of California. Loreto became the base from which the colonization of lower California continued until the Jesuit expulsion in 1767. Jesuits initially had a much greater degree of control over the military and financial prospects of Baja California than in other regions.[5] They established a model community, governed by the Jesuit missionary, and assisted by soldiers, and Indian converts, anchored by Mission Nuestra Señora de Loreto

---

[3] del Barco, *Historia natural*, 268. See also a report by Fray Manuel de San Juan Nepomuceno y Trigo, dated July 23, 1754 concerning the New Mexico missions, in Hackett, *Historical Documents*, 468.

[4] While this section cannot provide a comprehensive comparative history of the missions in these regions, political and economic conditions help to explain differences in musical forms and practices. For an overview of mission history in the north, see David J. Weber, *The Spanish Frontier in North America* (New Haven, CT: Yale University Press, 1992).

[5] Ignacio del Rio, *El regimen jesuítico de la Antigua California* (Mexico City: Universidad Nacional Autónoma de México, 2003), 12. On Baja California, see also del Río, *Conquista y aculturación en la California jesuítica, 1697–1768* (Mexico City: Universidad Nacional Autónoma de México, 1984); *Crónicas jesuíticas de la antigua California* (Mexico City: Universidad Nacional Autónoma de México, 2000); and Harry W. Crosby, *Antigua California: Mission and Colony on the Peninsular Frontier, 1697–1768* (Albuquerque: University of New Mexico Press, 1994).

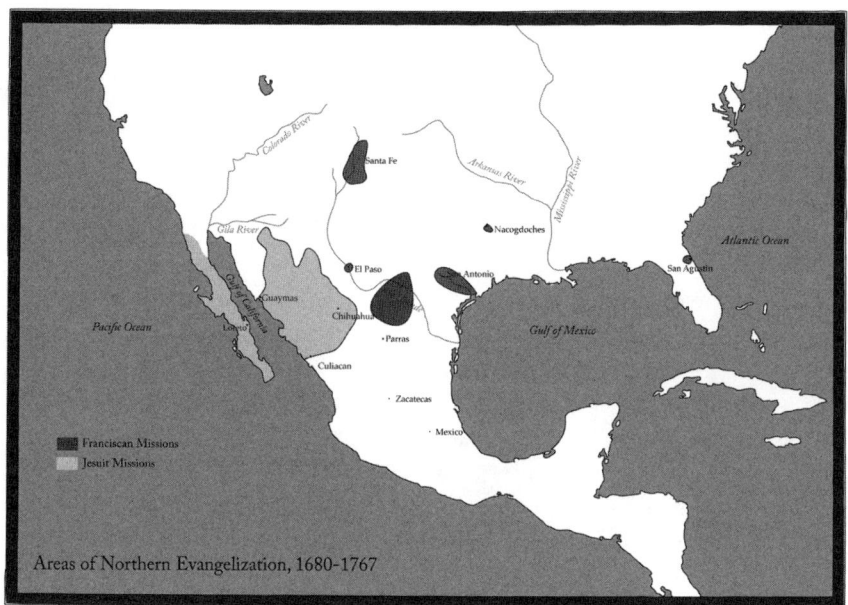

Areas of Northern Evangelization, 1680-1767

and the presidio at Loreto. Together with Christianized Yaquis, a small number of soldiers and their families served as examples of proper Christian behavior and helped to teach the litanies and responses of the liturgy. Their attendance at weekly worship, funerals, and processions and masses for holy days of obligation was required. In the early missions of Baja California, soldiers were even involved in teaching the doctrine in the Californian languages through music, a practice unique to this region.[6] Inventories from Baja California do not contain references to large numbers of instruments, although organs and stringed instruments were used on special occasions. Most often, missionary reports emphasized the repetition of doctrine, in simple songs, translated into local languages.[7] Nicolás Tamaral, who established La Purísima Concepción de Cadegomó and worked among its population between 1720 and 1730,

---

[6] Fray Manuel de la Vega, Relación del descubrimiento y conquista de las Californias, Biblioteca del Instituto Nacional de Antropología e Historia, Fondo Franciscano (hereinafter BINAH), vol. 68, f. 12-17.

[7] When missionaries entered a new territory, they were instructed to first gain proficiency in the region's language, both listening and speaking. Miguel Venegas, *Empressas apostólicas de los Pp. missioneros de la Compañía de Jesús, de la Provincia de Nueva-España*, vol. 4 of *Obras californianas del Padre Miguel Venegas, S.J.*, ed. W. Michael Mathes (La Paz: Universidad Autónoma de Baja California Sur, 1979), paragraph 1878, f. 619.

reported on the organization of time and the governance of mission communities.[8] Tamaral's correspondence included a description of daily life structured by bells, the alabado, work, doctrinal instruction and recitation, and meals. Food was closely tied to daily instruction and worship, including song, in Baja California, particularly in arid and drought-prone areas. The morning meal was served immediately after mass for those who attended, and the afternoon meal followed a period of doctrinal instruction for children and unmarried women, and work, for adults. This technique, although used elsewhere, was emphasized in Baja California due to the scarcity of food in the arid region. The imposition of such a rigid schedule of daily activities surely contributed to the demographic collapse of the natives, brought on initially by the spread of diseases such as smallpox.[9]

When compared to the Spaniards and creoles who worked in the north during the seventeenth century, as well as Franciscans in eighteenth-century New Mexico and Texas, the Jesuits who evangelized Baja California and Sonora in the mid-eighteenth century were a cosmopolitan group, including *criollos*, Italians, Germans, and Spaniards. This helps to explain why local languages, instead of Spanish, were used for instruction. It may also explain the widespread use of music for teaching doctrine. Music was part of the comprehensive education of boys in early eighteenth-century German and Italian regions, even more so than in Spain.[10] For the missions in which trained choirs or musically inclined populations were noted, in both Baja California and Sonora, a majority of the missionaries originated from central Europe or Italian provinces.[11] Father

---

[8] His 1730 letter to the padre visitador is copied in AGN, Historia, vol. 21, no. 16, f. 166-172v.

[9] See also Miguel León-Portilla, "Face and Heart of the California Missions," in Rose Marie Beebe ed., *Historical and Cultural Perspectives on the Peninsula of Baja California: Proceedings of the 19th Annual Conference of the California Mission Studies Association* (San Diego: California Mission Studies Association, 2002), 8.

[10] Joe E. Tarry, "Music in the Educational Philosophy of Martin Luther," *Journal of Research in Music Education* 21:4 (Winter 1973), 362. See also Thomas D. Culley, *Jesuits and Music: A Study of the Musicians Connected with the German College in Rome during the Seventeenth Century and of Their Activities in Northern Europe*, Sources and Studies for the History of the Jesuits, 2 (Rome: Jesuit Historical Institute, 1970).

[11] This includes Fathers Eusebio Francisco Kino and Marcus Kappus at Mission Dolores del Saric in the late seventeenth century, Father Joseph Neumann from Moravia at Santa Maria Sisoguichic and Carichic, Father Francisco Maria Piccolo at Loreto and Santa Rosalía Mulegé in the early 1700s, Venetian Pedro María Nascimbén at Santa Rosalia Mulegé from 1735 to 1754, and Bavarian Father Jacob Sedelmeyer at Mission San Pedro y San Pablo de Tubutama in the 1740s and San José de Mátape afterward. A notable exception was Father Gaspar de Trujillo, who served at Loreto in the 1740s. On the careers of some of these Europeans, see Otakar Odloz'ilík, "Czech Missionaries in New Spain," *Hispanic American Historical Review* 25:4 (November 1945),

Pedro María Nascimbén emphasized communal singing of hymns, even integrating visiting Spaniards into the community at Santa Rosalía Mulegé:

> *Every day on rising, on retiring, after the morning rosary and the evening, even at times of work, there would be sung now litanies of Our Lady, now acts of contrition, now songs in verse about Our Lord Jesus Christ and His Holy Mother, and of many saints. . . . A boatload of those who came to dive for pearls arrived at these missions and were captivated by the range of songs, most of them composed and taught by Father Pedro. Then Father Pedro arranged that these people learn some of the music and sing it.*[12]

Bohemian Jesuit Xavier Bischoff trained choirs at San Luis Gonzaga from 1746 to 1751 and at Nuestra Señora de Loreto in the 1760s. The choir at San Luis Gonzaga continued, largely under indigenous direction, when less musically talented Alsatian Jacob Baegert took over mission administration.[13] Bischoff's choir at Loreto sang so well that it was lauded by the Franciscans who arrived after expulsion.[14] In addition, these non-Hispanic Jesuits often rose to supervisory positions in their provinces and their leadership likely helped spread ideas about musical form and function more widely.

JESUITS IN THE NORTHWEST: SINALOA, SONORA, AND NUEVA VIZCAYA

In the period from 1680–1767, Jesuits continued to expand the mission frontier north and west. Reduction of populations into missions in these regions was driven by desires for economic expansion of mining, ranching, and agriculture.[15]

428-454; and on their reports to European colleges, see Ricardo García Villoslada, "Algunos documentos sobre la música en el antiguo seminario romano," *Archivum Historicum Societatis Iesu* 31 (1962), 116.

[12] Francisco Escalante to Fr. Visitador General Ignacio Lizasoáin, 1762, AGN, Jesuitas, vol. 3, part 16, exp. 2.

[13] Jacob Baegert, *Observations in Lower California*, trans. M.M. Brandenburg and Carl L. Baumann (Berkeley: University of California Press, 1952), 171.

[14] Manuel de la Vega, Relación, INAH, Fondo Franciscano, vol. 68, f. 107-107v.

[15] On the missions of Nueva Vizcaya and Sonora, see Deeds, *Defiance and Deference*; Radding, *Wandering Peoples*; Daniel T. Reff, *Disease, Depopulation, and Culture Change in Northwestern New Spain, 1518–1764* (Salt Lake City: University of Utah Press, 1991); Evelyn Hu-DeHart, *Missionaries, Miners, and Indians: Spanish Contact with the Yaqui Nation of Northwestern New Spain, 1533–1820* (Tucson: University of Arizona Press, 1981); and González Rodríguez, *Etnología y misión*.

Whereas the presence of colonists in Baja California was extremely limited, in Sinaloa, Sonora, and Nueva Vizcaya, much greater numbers of settlers were present, in all but the most remote mountainous and northernmost areas. Revolts, in which groups of indigenous peoples banded together under the leadership of marginalized leaders and shamans, rocked this region throughout the late seventeenth and eighteenth centuries. The Tarahumara revolts of the 1690s, Yaqui revolt of 1740, and Pima revolts of the 1750s left some missions in ruins, their sacred ornaments, bells, and vestments destroyed, and livestock scattered. Spanish presence increased in the mineral-rich areas to meet the threats of Indian uprisings, and zones of refuge to which Indians fleeing Spanish control could relocate became increasingly scarce into the eighteenth century. By the second half of the eighteenth century, the Diocese of Durango expanded to include the secularized missions of the Tepehuanes and Acaxees.

In the northwest, evangelized by Jesuits and a handful of Franciscans since the early colonial period, a large number of Indian and mestizo *vecinos* held positions as sacristans, catechists, fiscales, cantors, bell ringers, cooks, artisans, and laborers. They interacted with soldiers and settlers on a regular basis in the towns of the region. The most unique characteristic of mission music in Sinaloa, Sonora, and northern Nueva Vizcaya during the early eighteenth century was the prevalence of stringed instruments to accompany weekly worship, recreation, and celebrations for special occasions.[16] Stringed instruments were present in many northern missions, and community members manufactured violins and guitars by the end of the colonial period, but the most elaborate instrumental culture developed in the Jesuit missions of Sonora and northern Nueva Vizcaya, where missionaries taught Yaqui, Tarahumara, and Piman peoples to manufacture and play violins. The Jesuits may have used stringed instruments in this area due to the pre-Hispanic use of hunting bows in instrumental music among the Seri, Tarahumara, and Yaqui in this region. Increased contact with settlers in the region also likely contributed to the appearance of these stringed instruments in mission reports. Joseph Och reported that he "had Indians who made for themselves violins, harps, and even *psalterios*, and this they did with little more than an old knife and a sharp flint."[17] Stringed instruments became vital parts of the dances of Nueva Vizcaya and Sonora, and their manufacture has continued to the

---

[16] Stringed instruments were also an important part of music in the Guaraní and Chiquitos missions administered by Jesuits in South America. On the music of these missions, see Piotr Nawrot, *Indígenas y cultura musical de las reducciones jesuíticas* (Cochabamba, Bolivia: Editorial Verbo Divino, 2000); and Victor Rondón, ed., *Mujeres, negros y niños en la música y sociedad colonial iberoamericana: IV Reunión Científica* (Santa Cruz: Asociación Pro Arte y Cultura, 2002).

[17] Treutlein, *Missionary in Sonora* 122.

present day.¹⁸ Some types of aerophones were locally constructed as well, particularly flutes or recorders; reeds and strings for the locally constructed instruments were sometimes included on supply requests. Instruments could have been fabricated at missions with more extensive carpentry shops and a resident missionary or local artisan with knowledge of their production, and then sent to nearby missions for use in worship. As their presence in the region increased due to mining interests and the establishment of presidios, soldiers and settlers also participated in the construction of instruments and teaching of instrumental techniques. *Vecinos* and mission Indians were involved in the musical culture of mission communities, providing music for worship as well as entertainment for secular dances, weddings, and community celebrations. At Mission Los Santos Reyes del Cucurpe, German Jesuit Ignaz Pfefferkorn trained a choir and violin players, but other instrumentalists learned to play the harp and psalterio from Spanish settlers. The Salve Regina, Lauretanian litany, and other devotional songs were performed by this group on Saturdays, Sundays, and feast days, as well as during regularly scheduled masses.¹⁹

Playing instruments and singing were attractive occupations for mission neophytes. Practicing music required a much smaller degree of demanding physical labor than working in the fields or mines. Jesuits in Sonora may have found the Opatas and Eudeves so inclined to musical tasks because these indigenous peoples were using music-making to avoid other tasks. Ignaz Pfefferkorn exclaimed,

> *Both nations had an extraordinary inclination for music, and many individuals displayed a special musical ability. If they were shown the first principles of playing a musical instrument, they compensated for the lack of further instruction by an attentive ear and almost unceasing practices.*²⁰

Music-making empowered those who engaged in it, giving them recognition, money-making skills, and social status, along with public opportunities to blend indigenous practices with European musical practices.²¹ Some mission Indians

---

¹⁸ Constructing violins in modern Tarahumara society is a male activity of great esteem, and virtually all males can play the violin. See John G. Kennedy, *Tarahumara of the Sierra Madre: Beer, Ecology, and Social Organization* (Arlington Heights, IL: AHM Publishing Corporation, 1978), 74.

¹⁹ Ignaz Pfefferkorn, *Sonora: A Description of the Province*, trans. Theodore Treutlein (Tucson: University of Arizona Press, 1989), 246.

²⁰ Ibid., 246 (my emphasis). These sentiments were echoed by Juan Nentvig, who stated that the application and natural ability of the Opatas, Eudebes, and Pimas made them proficient in playing musical instruments. *Rudo Ensayo*, 69.

²¹ This theme will be further elaborated in Chapter 7.

gained positions of prominence within their communities, like those in central New Spain. During his 1715 visit to the missions of Nueva Vizcaya, Bishop Pedro de Tapis commented on the musical talent of Indians at Mission San Francisco Javier de Satevó, led by a Tarahumara *maestro de capilla* (chapel master) who had trained the choir to perform a sung mass and portions of the Divine Office.[22] The bishop celebrated the feast of San Ignacio at Satevó, where bajones, chirimías, a harp, violins, and an organ augmented the vocal music that was performed. The beauty and solemnity of the music inspired this important visitor, and a good number of instrumentalists and singers must have appreciated his praises. Missionaries at Satevó were encouraged to learn Nahuatl in order to communicate with a wide variety of community residents, indicating the diverse population of this northwestern frontier mission. Musicians and other indigenous officials were among the most Hispanicized residents of mission communities, serving as cultural intermediaries. Juan Nentvig commented on the proficiency of some catechists in Sonora who could read and write music, direct the choir and instrumentalists, and perform *canto llano* (plainchant) and more complex figured chant (*canto figurado*). They could also read and write, enabling them to serve as scribes. Nentvig found their proficiency as teachers to be extraordinary, because "illiterate people are able to memorize chants for as many as four different types of masses, the Psalms, and responses for pertinent burial services."[23]

Another area in which the increased interaction of overlapping communities was evident in the musical forms of the northwest was popular religious dances. In the Jesuit northwest, dancing was an area with clear blending of indigenous and Catholic cultural traditions. The First Mexican Provincial Council's mandates of 1555 had forbidden all dancing within church buildings, fearing continuance of indigenous idolatrous practices within the sacred space of the church. But the Montezuma and moros y cristianos dances, frequently held in church courtyards, quickly became important syncretic celebrations in the schools and colleges of central Mexico, including the Colegio de San Gregorio. By controlling the space and the manner in which indigenous dances were performed, and by changing some of the key characters to represent the triumph of Christianity, missionaries hoped to instill their Christian beliefs in place of indigenous religious beliefs. As seen in the early Jesuit missions, as well as the colleges of central New Spain, dances were widely practiced. The technique of bringing Christianized Indians to help start up new missions likely spread some

---

[22] Informe de Pedro Tápis, August 26, 1715, AGI, Guadalajara, 206, f. 152.
[23] Nentvig, *Rudo Ensayo*, 111.

of these syncretic dances to the northwestern frontier, where they were again combined with local native dance practices. The matachines dances still performed throughout the region for special occasions were also influenced by the overlapping communities of colonists and soldiers who interacted with mission Indians.[24] Cloth and costumes for the performance of the matachines dances were among items listed in some mission inventories.[25]

Ultimately, whether the matachines dances (or other conquest dances) performed at the missions were introduced by missionaries or Hispanic settlers is rather inconsequential. Instead, what is striking is the unique indigenous character of the dances in each region. Tarahumara matachines in both the colonial period and the present day, for example, utilize indigenous rattles as well as the Spanish-introduced (but Tarahumara-fabricated) violin.[26] Jesuit Joseph Och described a Montezuma dance in mid-eighteenth century Sonora that included dancing with red and white ribbons around a pole.[27] According to chroniclers and anthropologists, circular dances around a tall pole were characteristic of Opata, Yaqui, and Mayo dances in this region before the advent of mission life.[28] The local and indigenous characteristics of these dances, modeled after European, and possibly Mesoamerican patterns, suggest that indigenous peoples maintained a large degree of creative control over so-called religious dances, even though the times and spaces of performance may have been directed by individual missionaries.

---

[24] On matachines, see Flavia Waters Champe, *The Matachines Dance of the Upper Rio Grande: History, Music, and Choreography* (Lincoln: University of Nebraska Press, 1983); Sylvia Rodríguez, *The Matachines Dance: Ritual, Symbolism, and Interethnic Relations in the Upper Río Grande Valley* (Albuquerque: University of New Mexico Press, 1996); Brenda Rae Romero, "The Matachines Music and Dance in San Juan Pueblo and Alcalde, New Mexico: Context and Meanings" (D.M.A. diss., University of California at Los Angeles, 1993); Jesús Jáuregui and Carlo Bonfiglioli, *Las danzas de conquista* (Mexico City: Fondo de Cultura Económica, 1996); and Carlo Bonfiglioli, *Fariseos y matachines en la Sierra Tarahumara* (Mexico City: Instituto Nacional Indigenista, 1995).

[25] See, for example, the inventories in the W.B. Stephens Collection, 1744, UTNLB. The missions of Arivechi and Bacanori list costumes for the matachines among inventory items in 1738; they were also found at Saguaripa in 1751 and in the San Antonio missions in the late eighteenth century.

[26] See Dunne, *Early Jesuit Missions in Tarahumara* (Berkeley: University of California Press, 1948), 6-7; Daniel Sheehy, "Matachines," in *The Garland Handbook of Latin American Music* (New York: Garland Publishing, 2000), 353; and William Merrill, *Rarámuri Souls: Knowledge and Social Process in Northern Mexico* (Washington, DC: Smithsonian Institution Press, 1988).

[27] Treutlein, *Missionary in Sonora*, 163.

[28] See also William Curry Holden, *Studies of the Yaqui Indians of Sonora, Mexico* (Lubbock: Texas Technological College Bulletin, vol. 12, no. I, Scientific Series, no. 2, 1936); and Pfefferkorn, *Sonora*, 182-183.

Franciscans in Nuevo México, 1692–1767

While the use of instruments and hybridized forms of dance characterized mission music in the Jesuit northwest, Franciscans in Nuevo México gave up trying to purify the Puebloans of indigenous musical practices, and settled for mediocre outward displays of Christian conversion. Don Diego de Vargas and a force of soldiers, along with three Franciscans, returned to the pueblos of New Mexico in the fall of 1692. They moved quickly through the towns, announcing their return and promising that those who submitted to Spanish presence would be treated leniently for their rebellious behavior in 1680. The following year, a force of over 1,200 soldiers, Indian auxiliaries, and recruited colonists followed the banner of Nuestra Señora del Rosario, La Conquistadora, north from El Paso. Sixteen Franciscan priests and two lay brothers, largely inexperienced, were assigned to complete the spiritual reconquest of the pueblos, twenty-two fewer than Vargas had believed necessary.[29] Within a year, five of those had left the region, and it was not until September of 1694 that the remaining Franciscans petitioned to re-enter the pueblos, joined by four others the following month. When Spaniards returned to the pueblos of Pecos, Santa Ana, Jemez, and Zia, Franciscans were accompanied by the governor and a detachment of soldiers. After the exchange of gifts, and an official re-christening of the pueblos with Christian titular saints, the bells were rung, and the *Gloria* sung three times. Vargas ordered the pueblos to present their chosen leaders, (alcaldes, captains of the pueblo, captains of war, and fiscales for the mission), who were then presented with canes and rods by the governor, signifying their posts and loyalty to the government.[30] Similar ceremonies followed at each of the pueblos. The ritual repossession of these pueblos demonstrated that Franciscans in eighteenth-century New Mexico were dependent on the military and governor, and the goodwill of the Puebloans. They no longer exercised the authority to handpick community leaders, or commanded financial resources sufficient to outfit the missions with large numbers of musical instruments and ornaments. The entrada ceremonies are indicative of the substantial differences

---

[29] See John Kessell and Rick Hendricks, eds., *By Force of Arms: The Journals of Don Diego de Vargas, 1691–1693* (Albuquerque: University of New Mexico Press, 1992), 463-476; and Jim Norris, *After "The Year Eighty": The Demise of Franciscan Power in Spanish New Mexico* (Albuquerque: University of New Mexico Press, 2000), 33-34.

[30] Extracts from Governor Vargas's Journal on the Reestablishment of the Missions, September 18–October 7 and November 1–December 21, 1694, in J. Manuel Espinosa, ed., *The Pueblo Indian Revolt of 1696 and the Franciscan Missions of New Mexico* (Norman: University of Oklahoma Press, 1988), 92-99.

in the Franciscan administration of pueblos before and after 1680.[31] Ritual actions and the indoctrination of children could not ensure that Puebloans would peacefully accept Spanish presence and Catholicism. Although, in 1692, children sang alabados throughout the pueblo of Tesuque, and Father Custos Juan Álvarez stated that he heard the governor instruct his children in the doctrine, by 1695, Tewas there were singing war songs, and plotting in the house of the *hechicero*.[32] Lucas Naranjo from Cochití organized another Pueblo revolt in 1696, in which five friars were killed. Similar to the 1680 revolt, church ornaments and vestments were destroyed, but not all of the pueblos participated, and divisions ran deep between those who fought to rid the territory of Spanish presence, and those who chose not to engage in active revolt.

After the second Pueblo Revolt, Franciscan leaders had difficulty recruiting and retaining enthusiastic priests to work in communities prone to rebellion, apostasy, and idolatrous practices; the average tenure of a Franciscan friar in eighteenth-century New Mexico was two and a half years.[33] Within that timeframe, it was difficult to learn a new dialect or language, understand the social and political hierarchy of a community, and exercise authority. So, despite the instruments of hegemony employed by missionaries, including bells, repetition of doctrine, singing of Christian hymns, and appropriation of indigenous customs, Puebloans in New Mexico largely dictated the terms upon which they accepted Christianity and acculturation.[34] Those settled at Taos, for example, enjoyed a good relationship with Fray Francisco Brotóns, because he did not destroy the large number of kivas in the Pueblo.[35] In 1714, fresh from another attempt at extirpating indigenous dances and kivas, Governor Juan Ignacio Flores convened a junta of soldiers and friars to discuss several questions, including whether Puebloans should be allowed to practice body painting and enter the churches with feathers on their heads and ears.[36] The question eventually

---

[31] For differences in Franciscan administration before and after the Pueblo Revolt, see Norris, *After "The Year Eighty,"* chapters 4 to 10, and in Gutiérrez, *When Jesus Came, the Corn Mothers Went Away*, 157-162.

[32] Report of Fray Custos Juan Álvarez, in Espinosa, ed., *The Pueblo Indian Revolt of 1696*, 115-116, 175.

[33] Norris, *After "The Year Eighty,"* 3.

[34] See AGI, Mexico, 89-2-17, in CAT, manuscript 18.8b, 82.

[35] Governor Don José Chacón ordered that Indian alcaldes, supported by presidial troops, must destroy the kivas in 1708-1709, causing conflict with Bretons and other Franciscans, who feared rebellion. See John Kessell, *Kiva, Cross, and Crown: The Pecos Indians and New Mexico, 1540-1840* (Washington, DC: National Park Service, 1979), 311-312; and Norris, *After "The Year Eighty,"* 56, 60.

[36] Vélez de Escalante, Extracto, cited in Kessell, *Kiva*, 317-319.

proceeded directly to Mexico City, where authorities decided that such practices were not dangerous, but that Puebloans ought to be turned toward a more civil and Christian life without force or violence. In this, they agreed with the friar at Ácoma, Fray Antonio de Miranda, who argued that

> [a]s Catholics the Indians are obliged to detest all heathen ceremony. However, in such a critical case, one must exercise the prudence of the serpent and the simplicity of a dove. . . . One must carry the natives (weak sheep) with the patience of the gardener cultivating a recently planted garden. Little by little he removes the weeds, and through patience he comes to see the garden free of darnel. But to will that the new plant bear leaves, flowers, and fruit at once is to will not to harvest anything.[37]

After over a century of evangelization, Franciscans were making little progress in their "weeding" of the Puebloan gardens.

Franciscans depended heavily on the aid of Puebloan leaders to ensure that members of the community attended daily instruction, work, and worship; thus, they were more tolerant of practices that would have been uprooted by seventeenth-century Franciscans. They were dependent on the communities in which they served for food and protection from the growing Apache threat—and deeply fearful of the possibilities of future revolts. Furthermore, unlike the Jesuits in Sonora and Baja California, Franciscans in post-revolt New Mexico were not widely competent in indigenous languages.[38] No native-language catechisms, songs, or rhymes existed to teach doctrine, like in the Jesuit missions of the northwest. While songs for teaching purposes were sung in Spanish, and the daily communal catechism recitation (in Spanish) was led by native catechists, in most mission settlements, translators were necessary for sermons, doctrinal explanations, and confession.[39] Puebloans carefully guarded their native languages and determined the

---

[37] Miranda to Governor Flores, Ácoma, July 1714, SANM II, no. 207, translated in Kessell, *Kiva*, 319.

[38] Bishop Crespo's report from 1730, reprinted in Eleanor Adams, ed., *Bishop Tamarón's Visitation of New Mexico, 1760* (Albuquerque: University of New Mexico Press, 1954), 102-103, expressed contemptuous criticism toward Franciscans for their failure to learn native languages. Bishop Tamarón's visita report from 1760, and Fray Atanasio Domínguez's report from 1776 consistently mention the failure of Franciscans, even those who served in an area for an extensive period of time, to learn native languages.

[39] Mission communities with a larger number of Spaniards and mestizos had more familiarity with Spanish, and residents in these areas, such as Isleta, Santa Cruz de la Cañada, and Taos, confessed in Spanish and attended services without the aid of interpreters. However, most mission communities refused to learn more Spanish than that needed to engage in trade, or at least did not

terms under which they participated in mission life.⁴⁰ Franciscans in eighteenth-century New Mexico had little choice but to accept these terms. Parallel Christian and native practices existed, kivas inhabited the same spaces as mission churches, and catsina dances and alabados were performed by the same people. Even secular clergy reluctantly accepted the state of cultural accommodation in New Mexico. Bishop Pedro Tamarón y Romeral performed the sacrament of confirmation for hundreds of Puebloans during his 1760 visitation of the province, but ordered that Franciscans must demonstrate much more progress in conversions.⁴¹ The Towa at Pecos responded with a mockery of the visitation rites, juxtaposing the Christian rituals of mass and confirmation with indigenous dances and clowning. Three months following the bishop's visit, Agustín Guichí, a leader of the Pueblo, initiated a three-day re-enactment of the rituals performed by Tamarón and his entourage. Guichí and three companions dressed in garments they fashioned to resemble the clerics. They entered the Pueblo and

> *went straight to the plaza, where the Indian women were kneeling in two rows. And Agustín, the make-believe bishop, went between them distributing blessings. In this manner they proceeded to the place where they had prepared a great arbor with two seats in it. . . . Agustín . . . used the following method of confirming each one who came to him: He made a cross on his forehead with water, and when he gave him a slap, that one left and the next one came forward. . . . After the confirmations were over, the meal which had been prepared for the occasion was served. Then followed the dance with which they completed the afternoon. On the next day the diversion and festivities continued, beginning with a mass which Bishop Agustín pretended to say in the same arbor. During it he distributed pieces of tortillas made of wheat flour in imitation of communion. And the rest of the day the amusement was dancing, and the same continued on the third day which brought those disorders and entertainments to an end.⁴²*

---

let it be known that they understood the friars. In return, missionaries had difficulty learning the multiple languages and dialects, because Puebloans did not want them to learn, and because of frequent transfers. On daily liturgical activities, see Father Jacobo de Castro's visitation from 1755, Biblioteca Nacional de México (hereinafter BNM), leg. 9, no. 31, and Father Manuel de San Juan Nepomuceno y Trigo's visitation of 1750, BNM, leg. 8, no. 80.

⁴⁰ See Kessell, *Kiva*, chapter 7.
⁴¹ Adams, ed., *Bishop Tamarón's Visitation*, 48-50, 78-79.
⁴² *Relación del atentado sacrilegio, cometido por tres indios de un pueblo de la provincia del Nuevo México, y de el severo castigo, que executó la divina justicia con el fautor principal de ellos* (Mexico City, 1763), translated in Adams, ed., *Bishop Tamarón's Visitation*, 50-53.

The clergy, however, had the last laugh, when Agustín Guichí was attacked by a bear and killed (but not before repenting, confessing through an interpreter, and receiving extreme unction) on the day following the burlesque. The episode was recorded and printed in Mexico to serve as a warning to those who would doubt the power of Christian ritual.

Franciscans in Coahuila and Texas

Late seventeenth- and early eighteenth-century attempts to colonize east Texas were characterized by the ceremonial use of liturgical music to claim possession of territory, but failure of the missionary enterprise to gather converts into the missions. Alonso de Leon's 1689 entrada into eastern Texas reported promising prospects for evangelization and conversion. Caddos, Assinai, and Aís were all attracted to the majestic rites of possession practiced by the military expedition and its priests. A new missionary college in Querétaro had been founded in 1683 for the purpose of training Franciscans to convert Indians on the frontiers of New Spain, and friars were eager to begin their work. Fray Damián Mazanet led four priests and a lay brother into a Assinai village, while all sang the Litany of Our Lady, carrying crucifixes and banners on which the Virgin's image was emblazoned. The following year, friars blessed an improvised chapel, naming it Mission San Francisco de los Tejas, and chanting a mass on the feast of Corpus Christi.[43] Spaniards secured additional labor to build a more permanent site, as well as two other missions nearby, and requested and transported supplies, including large, heavy bells, into the heart of Caddo territory. In the four years that followed, they baptized children, performed marriages, and visited settlements, but were unable to convince natives to live at the mission and regularly attend doctrinal instruction or mass.[44] Caddoans were intrigued by the rituals of Catholicism, but declined to participate in the everyday routines of mission life. When Franciscans were ordered to abandon the east Texas missions in 1694, they buried the cumbersome bells and regretfully returned south.[45]

---

[43] Mazanet to Sigüenza, in Lino Gómez Canedo, *Primeras exploraciones y poblamiento de Texas* (Monterrey: Instituto Tecnológico y de Estudios Superiores de Monterrey, 1968), 25.

[44] Espinosa, *Crónica de los colegios de propaganda fide* 756. See also Barr, *Peace Came in the Form of a Woman*, chapters 1 and 2; Michael McCloskey, *The Formative Years of the Missionary College of Santa Cruz de Querétaro, 1683–1733* (Washington, DC: Academy of American Franciscan History, 1955), 104.

[45] Vito Alessio Robles, *Coahuila y Texas en la época colonial* (Mexico City: Editorial Cultura, 1938), 454.

Motivated by the French presence in the region, the Ramón expedition attempted a second settlement of eastern Texas in 1716. Franciscans were encouraged by their first encounters with the Assinai, whereupon *caddis*, or leaders, showed reverence for the image of Our Lady of Guadalupe by touching and kissing it. They later attended a solemn mass held in her honor. What the friars saw as a sign of enduring devotion to Mary and Christian worship, might easily have been an expression of indigenous efforts to recognize and honor a female presence among the Spanish expedition.[46] Furthermore, attending displays of Spanish power was a method of accumulating material goods from the colonizers, even if there was no intent to cooperate in the construction of a church. The Assinai, by showing interest in the chanting of mass, and singing of the Te Deum Laudamus, gathered many useful goods from the Franciscan missionaries who attempted to reclaim abandoned neophytes in the region. They were presented with tobacco, decorated pipes, chocolate, and hats in exchange for mimicking the gestures and postures of expedition members, but despite the ritual gestures, processions, and attentiveness of the Indians of east Texas, the missions remained empty.[47] Franciscans were ordered to abandon their conversion project in east Texas a second time in 1719 due to the Spanish war with the French, and mission bells and ornaments were once again buried, rather than left unattended, indicating the symbolic power of their sound.[48]

The Xarames, Siabanes, and Payoguanes of northern Coahuila at first cooperated more fully, initially agreeing to present their children for baptism and doctrinal instruction, even consenting to Christian marriage and attendance at communal worship. Fray Antonio de San Buenaventura y Olivares brought ornaments with him from Mexico City to adorn the church at San Francisco Solano, and Indians congregated at the mission, worked its fields, and learned the musical responses of the mass. Within eight years, however, the mission was virtually empty, which the friars attributed to the unwillingness of converts to accept the discipline of mission life.[49] The Coahuilan mission enterprise had started with great promise in 1675, but was dissolved by 1715. Converted Tlaxcalans were

---

[46] Barr, *Peace Came in the Form of a Woman*, 42.

[47] Espinosa, *Crónica apostólica*, 685. Gift giving in exchange for proper performance of Christian rituals was used elsewhere. Pimas at Pitiquín were promised gifts once they listened to Jesuit Father Adam Gilg say mass and recite the doctrine. Juan Bautista de Escalante and his soldiers showed the Pimas how to "adore the Holy Sacrament," and when the Pimas imitated the actions of the soldiers, they were given gifts. Juan Bautista de Escalante's diary, May 19, 1700, transcribed and translated, in Sheridan, *Empire of Sand*, 64.

[48] Old Spanish Missions Historic Research Collection, OSMHRC, Archivos del Colegio de Querétaro (hereinafter ACQ), reel 10, fr. 4231-4266.

[49] Espinosa report, December 11, 1708, AGI, 62-2-29, microfilm, CAT.

brought north from central Mexico to serve as fiscales, sacristans, and cantors, but even they abandoned Mission San Bernardino de la Candela when friars could not control idolatrous behavior, particularly the unbridled dances known as mitotes and the ingestion of peyote, of the Catujanos, Milijais, and Tilalajais for whom the mission had been built.[50] A rebellion in 1715 at missions San Juan Bautista and San Bernardo Coahuila temporarily halted missionary work.

By the 1720s, the situation in Coahuila and Texas began to shift due to political and demographic changes. The villa of San Antonio de Béxar was established by colonists and presidial soldiers in 1718, and missions were founded outside the town shortly afterward. The east Texas missions had been established a third time, and then relocated permanently to the San Antonio River in 1730. The pressures of epidemic disease, droughts, and incursions from Tobosos, Apaches, and Comanches forced smaller Coahuiltecan-speaking bands to seek sustenance and protection in the missions, which became temporary zones of refuge in San Antonio and Coahuila.

In the missions of central Texas and northern Coahuila, one of the largest challenges facing Franciscans was creating Christian community and cultivating religious devotion among the diverse small bands congregated in the missions. The friars attempted to do this by employing spiritual songs such as the alabado, which introduced both doctrine and the Spanish language, and by permitting altered forms of indigenous dances during well-appointed festivities on patron saint feast days. The success they enjoyed with these methods was likely because these forms of music and evangelization fit nicely with indigenous patterns. Large aggregate encampments of Coahuilteco-, Tonkawa-, and Karankawa-speaking peoples who populated the plains of Texas and Coahuila were accustomed to annual gatherings that renewed alliances, encouraged trade, and involved feasting and dancing.[51]

While Franciscans introduced the calendar of Christian festivals, gatherings at the missions were simply re-creations of indigenous practices in the region. Mass, processions, and Spanish dances were added to the fiestas so that the neophytes of the San Antonio missions "might forget their native mitotes."[52] Since music and dance were intimately connected with ritual in native tradition, missionaries believed that by changing the music, they might also change the rituals, which they perceived as much more pagan and thus threatening. However,

---

[50] Alessio Robles, *Coahuila y Téxas in la época colonial*, 272, 385.
[51] Barr, *Peace Came in the Form of a Woman*, 120.
[52] Fray Juan Agustín Morfi, *History of Texas 1673–1779*, trans. Carlos E. Castañeda (Albuquerque, NM: Quivira Society, 1935), 96.

bone flutes and rattles found in indigenous archaeological sites in south Texas were also found in mission trash heaps, indicating that mitotes and other indigenous rituals involving music survived missionization.[53] Friars at the San José Mission in San Antonio went so far as to keep the costumes worn for mitotes in a storeroom at the mission to attempt to supervise the performance of these dances.[54] By controlling the costumes, missionaries hoped to control the circumstances of their use by the Coahuiltecos, and further govern the conditions under which such dances could be performed.

BUILDING COMMUNITY THROUGH MUSICAL PERFORMANCE: JUAN MARÍA DE SALVATIERRA AND ANTONIO MARGIL DE JESÚS

The formation of Christian identity in a mission community was often dictated by the techniques used and relationships built by individual missionaries. Jesuit Father Juan María de Salvatierra and Franciscan Fray Antonio Margil de Jesús, both important early eighteenth-century evangelizers of northern New Spain, incorporated song and dance into their work.[55] The ways in which Salvatierra and Margil used music throughout their careers are numerous, but all functioned to build Christian community and solidify group identity both among new converts and between missionaries within the provinces they administered. Furthermore, Margil and Salvatierra were both revered as examples of pious and saintly men by their religious biographers. Contemporary accounts of their lives used music as an illustration of their holiness, tying Margil and Salvatierra to the larger community of saints by demonstrating their piety. An examination of the lives of these two leaders provokes a discussion about differences and similarities in Franciscan and Jesuit methods of evangelization through music.

Antonio Margil was born in 1657 in Valencia, Spain, and entered the Franciscan order in 1673. He served his novitiate at the Convento San Antonio de Denia, where he was a *corista*. After studying theology in Spain, he was ordained a priest in 1682, and he joined twenty-two other Franciscans in a journey from Cádiz to Veracruz in the following year. Their mission was to open the first colegio de propaganda fide in the Americas at Querétaro in New Spain. The

---

[53] Gilberto M. Hinojosa and Anne Fox, "Indians and Their Culture in San Fernando de Béxar," in Hinojosa and Gerald E. Poyo, eds., *Tejano Origins in Eighteenth-Century San Antonio* (Austin: Institute of Texan Cultures, 1991), 116.

[54] Ibid., 95-96.

[55] An earlier version of this section appears in "*Opus Dei*—The Work of God: Franciscan and Jesuit Music in Mexico," in Schroeder and Poole, *Religion in New Spain* (Albuquerque: University of New Mexico Press, 2007).

members of the Colegio de Santa Cruz had the dual purpose of preaching at parish missions in Spanish towns and establishing teaching missions among unconverted indigenous groups. Fray Margil worked in the southern edges of New Spain (modern-day Guatemala, El Salvador, Honduras, Nicaragua, and Costa Rica) for thirteen years, establishing missions and hospicios throughout the territory, and he served as father guardian of the Colegio de Santa Cruz from 1697 to 1700 before returning to the mission field. He helped found the Colegio de Cristo Crucificado in Guatemala in 1701, and another college at Guadalupe near Zacatecas in 1705. His final years, from 1711 to 1726, were spent establishing missions among the hostile Indians of the north. He died in the Franciscan convent of San Francisco el Grande in 1726.

Juan María de Salvatierra was born in Milan in 1658. Unlike Margil, Salvatierra is known to have had formal music training in Europe. His family was wealthy, and he learned to play the lute as a child. When the Spanish infanta Doña Margarita passed through Milan on her way to marry Emperor Leopold, young Juan was chosen to perform at the ceremonies.[56] He was educated at the Jesuit college in Parma, where he studied philosophy, music, Latin, and French. He served his two-year novitiate in Genoa. After becoming a Jesuit in Chieri, Salvatierra wrote Jesuit General Juan Paolo de Oliva asking permission to be sent to the mission field in the Americas. He listed his proficiency on the lute as among the many characteristics that made him suitable for the task of evangelization.[57] In 1675 he received his orders to travel to New Spain. He continued his studies there and taught rhetoric, serving as rector of the Guadalajara Colegio from 1693 to 1696, and as the *maestro de novicios* at Tepozotlán the following year. In 1680 he set out for the northern frontier of New Spain, where he worked among indigenous peoples of Chínipas for ten years. He was appointed *padre visitador* of the Jesuit missions in northwestern New Spain in 1690. With Father Eusebio Kino, he undertook the exploration and evangelization of Baja California in 1697. Apart from his duties as padre visitador from 1704 to 1707, he worked for the remainder of his life in the missions that he helped to found. On his way to report to the viceroy in 1717, Salvatierra died in Guadalajara.

---

[56] Miguel Venegas, *Juan Maria de Salvatierra of the Company of Jesus; Missionary in the Province of New Spain, and Apostolic Conqueror of the Californias*, trans. Marguerite Eyer Wilbur (Cleveland, OH: Arthur H. Clark Company, 1929), 66-67. Venegas says that Salvatierra had been chosen to "give an exhibition before her Majesty of the aptitude he had for dancing and playing various musical instruments." However, due to an accident, the ceremony never took place.

[57] Salvatierra to Gian Paolo Oliva, June 8, 1671, cited in Ernest Burrus, ed., *Juan Maria Salvatierra: Selected Letters about Lower California* (Los Angeles: Dawson's Book Shop, 1971), 19.

Both Margil and Salvatierra used music to promote the development of community in the mission communities they served. This was a three-stage process, in which prospective converts were first congregated into a mission and provided with examples of Christian living, that is, indigenous converts brought in from established mission communities. Salvatierra emphasized the musical training of the Indians who accompanied him. Eusebio Kino, in his diary of the exploration of Baja California, recounted that

> [a]lmost all day we were praying and chanting various prayers and praises of Our Lady in different languages—in Castilian, in Latin, in Italian, and also in the Californian language; for the six natives of California, four large and two small, whom Father Juan María had brought with him, were so well-indoctrinated and instructed in everything that they sang the prayers, since the Father Rector had already arranged them for them in pretty couplets, in this Californian language; and we said with the psalmist, Cantabiles mihi erant justificaciones tuas in coro peregrinaciones meae.[58]

Missionaries themselves also modeled piety—Margil by singing the alabado at the conclusion of masses, at mealtimes, and at night before retiring,[59] and Salvatierra by his constant singing of hymns in honor of Our Lady of Loreto.

The second phase of spreading community through music was to teach those considered most receptive to Christian doctrine, such as children and people marginalized in their own indigenous societies. Margil was known for his

---

[58] "Thy justifications were the subject of my song in the place of my pilgrimage," Psalm 118:54. Kino's diary entry (from 1701) is transcribed and translated in Herbert Bolton, *Kino's Historical Memoir of Pimería Alta; a Contemporary Account of the Beginnings of California, Sonora, and Arizona, by Father Eusebio Francisco Kino, S.J., Pioneer Missionary Explorer, Cartographer, and Ranchman, 1683–1711* (Cleveland, OH: Arthur H. Clark Company, 1919), 278. The couplet (Bolton's translation of *copla*) may refer more specifically to a short song or poem, usually with four lines.

[59] There were many different versions of the alabado used in New Spain. Margil's version was commonly sung in Texas. Espinosa, *Crónica de los Colegios de propaganda fide*, 594-595; and Espinosa, *El pelegrino septentrional atlante: delineado en la exemplarissima vida del venerable padre F. Antonio Margil de Jesús* (Mexico City: Joseph Bernardo de Hogal, 1737), 117. Some of his devotional songs were sung in California as well. See Marion A. Habig Collection, Our Lady of the Lake University, Special Collections and Archives, San Antonio, TX (hereinafter OLLUSCA). Alabados were also sung in New Mexico, and Richard B. Stark connected them to Spanish *saetas* by virtue of their elaborate, and sometimes melismatic, tunes. See Stark, "Notes on a Search for Antecedents of New Mexican Alabado Music," In Marta Weigle, ed., *Hispanic Arts and Ethnohistory in the Southwest* (Santa Fe, NM: Ancient City Press, 1983), 117-127. For twentieth-century recordings of New Mexican alabados, see the Hispano Music and Culture of the Northern Rio Grande: The Juan B. Rael Collection, a digital archive at the Library of Congress, http://memory.loc.gov/ammem/rghtml/rghome.html.

techniques involving the use of music. He taught the doctrine by setting it to music and also sang devotional songs about the Holy Family, with lyrics intended to emphasize parents' biblical duties in raising their children.[60] Similarly, Salvatierra attracted converts and taught doctrine through song. Venegas reported that Salvatierra "would sing about these mysteries, and following him, like a choir of angels, came the devout band of children who had already been baptized and who also sang the same thing in the settlements to their parents. Carried along by the same harmonious melody of this music, the parents came to learn about these same mysteries, and were moved to ask to be admitted within the portals of the Holy Church."[61]

In the third phase of doctrinal instruction through music, then, children transmitted the songs and rhymes taught by the padres and Indians from established missions to their parents and the wider community. Overlapping communities of unconverted Indians, apostates, and neophytes from other missions could then be reached by the most elaborate musical performances at fiestas for special days of the liturgical year. Margil wrote to the viceroy that his missionaries from the missionary college of Zacatecas in Texas were "always trying to find ways and means of attracting the adults."[62] On special occasions, such as Corpus Christi and Holy Week, special masses were sung in conjunction with ceremonies including feasting, dancing, and processions. Margil described the activities associated with Corpus Christi in 1695 during his time evangelizing the Lacandones in Guatemala:

> *We had four altars and arches, the usual procession, the foot soldiers on each side, discharging their guns effectively both during the Mass and the procession. . . . Some of the Lacandons carried the cross and candles, and served as sacristans and acolytes. . . . With all the reverence we could show we raised the cross and planted it in the same place, and on our knees we sang the Adoro Te, Santa Cruz. Some of the natives responded, especially the ones called Don Pedro Ytzquin and Nicolas.*[63]

This fiesta was held in conjunction with the burning of indigenous icons and the punishment of the offending individuals. The music of the mass and the melody

---

[60] One of these saetas is translated and reprinted in Benedict Leutenegger, trans., *Nothingness Itself: Selected Writings of Ven. F. Antonio Margil* (Chicago: Franciscan Herald Press, 1976), 315-316. On Spanish saetas, see "Saeta," in Stanley Sadie, ed., *New Grove Dictionary of Music and Musicians*, vol. 16 (London: Macmillan, 1980), 380-381.

[61] Venegas, *Juan Maria de Salvatierra*, 187-188.

[62] Margil to Viceroy Marqués de Valero, June 23, 1722, OSMHRC, Querétaro, reel 18.

[63] AGI, Guatemala, 153, f. 9v-14v, as transcribed in Leutenegger, trans., *Nothingness Itself*, 63.

of the hymn were linked with the show of force associated with the gunshots and the bonfire. This celebration provided an alternative to the indigenous music of the Lacandones who, painted black, were playing the cane flutes of the community as part of their spiritual rites.[64] It is interesting that both musical performances occurred at the same fiesta even though the intent was to eradicate important elements of the Lacandon culture.

Father Salvatierra seems to have also recognized the importance of dance among the indigenous peoples of Baja California. He described the dances of the Indians with great admiration, and even joined in the dance called the Nimbe, pulling Padre Pedro de Ugarte with him.[65] This earned him the admiration and affection of the Indians. On one occasion Salvatierra gave permission for the neophytes to dance as a way of distracting them from the horrors of an epidemic that was sweeping through their community. He wrote to Padre Provincial Antonio Xardón of this decision:

> *Before going to sleep, I said to Ambrosio that these people were very saddened by the deaths of their people from the epidemic of measles, and that they could have permission to dance that evening. And he told them that they could dance, and they were very happy; and then they began at midnight with a dance so sorrowful and hideous that had I not been prepared for it, I would have been fearful of treachery. And it lasted until the dawn.*[66]

Juan María de Salvatierra recognized that the Indians of Baja California used music and dancing as ways of preserving group identity in the face of social upheaval caused by the measles epidemic that decimated a native community. Despite official decrees that limited dancing to religious dances on special occasions, it was practiced by the missionaries and allowed among indigenous groups as a form of recreation and renewal. Salvatierra's actions with regard to dancing contrast greatly with those of Franciscan missionaries in New Mexico during Governor Mendizábal's tenure in the 1660s. By the mid-eighteenth century, the missionaries had become much more tolerant of local ceremonies and dances, although some were still perceived as threatening to the religious state of newly converted Indians. Franciscans in New Mexico and Texas allowed some indigenous dances to continue with few changes, as long as they were observed by a

---

[64] *Nothingness Itself*, 64.
[65] Ibid., 188-189.
[66] Salvatierra to Padre Provincial Antonio Xardón, April 3, 1710, AGN, Historia, 308, f. 398v, transcribed by Luis González Rodríguez, in "Juan María de Salvatierra y los Seris, 1709-1710," *Estudios de Historia Novohispana* 17 (1997), 254.

missionary and not perceived to be idolatrous.[67] These rituals were essential elements in drawing Indians to the missions throughout Latin America, and in forming Catholic identity that transcended racial, ethnic, and linguistic boundaries in areas where multiple ethnic groups were gathered in the same community. Salvatierra considered them the most efficient way of achieving religious identity and spiritual development, since "it was through the eyes [and ears and mouth] that devotion and charity entered the heart."[68]

Fray Antonio and Father Juan María not only used music to achieve conversion and the formation of community among indigenous converts. They also recognized that music was essential to the sustenance and spiritual health of the missionaries they supervised. Father Margil, like later Franciscans such as Junípero Serra, also sang the alabado as he walked from his college with companions through villages and towns where he was preaching missions.[69] While singing may have simply been a way to pass the time during a long walk, it also reminded missionaries of their purpose, buoyed their spirits, and informed indigenous peoples of their presence and intent. Margil, like other Franciscans, seems to have routinely ended his journeys in this manner: "We arrived at this town of Our Lady of El Viejo on the sixteenth of this month; and here we sang a Mass in honor of Our Lady with great solemnity for the success of our mission."[70] For both Franciscan and Jesuit missionaries, singing the Te Deum Laudamus or a song of praise was part of the entrada into a new area—a musical conquest of the space for God. Singing on a journey helped to sanctify the space within reach of the sound of the missionaries' voices.

Padre Salvatierra encouraged singing among the missionaries under his charge. In his role as a Jesuit administrator in Baja California, Father Juan María was concerned about the morale of the missionaries. Each year the padres were required to go to Loreto to perform the spiritual exercises of Ignatius of Loyola. While there, Salvatierra invited them to stay for chocolate, conversation, singing with the guitar, and dancing.[71] In this instance, music and dancing were used as

---

[67] For a discussion of missionary policy toward dance in New Mexico, see Carroll L. Riley, *The Kachina and the Cross: Indians and Spaniards in the Early Southwest* (Salt Lake City: University of Utah Press, 1999), 269-270.

[68] Ibid., 188.

[69] Testimonio de Fr. Simon del Hierro, in *Nothingness Itself*, as transcribed in Leutenegger, trans., 325, 328. See DaSilva, *Mission Music of California*, 20, for Fray Serra's singing of the alabado.

[70] Margil de Jesús to Fr. Tomas de San Diego Arrivillaga, February 17, 1703, Archivo de la Recolección Guatemala, no. XXIX, in *Nothingness Itself*, 93. See also descriptions of Margil's travel in Fr. Simon del Hierro's *testimonio*, reprinted in the above book, 325, 328.

[71] Miguel Venegas, *El apostól mariano representado en la vida del V.P. Juan María de Salvatierra* (Mexico City: En la imprenta de Doña Maria de Ribera, 1754), 132, 250-251.

a way to combat depression and homesickness. The exchange of folk songs and dances must have also fostered a sense of collegiality among the missionaries, who hailed from different parts of Europe and worked in Baja California in remote settings, separated by long distances. Salvatierra used music to build community within his community of Jesuit brothers, with potential converts, and in his personal relationship with God and devotion to Mary.

Song and Access to the Communion of Saints

For Antonio Margil, chanting and the liturgy were part of a daily routine connected to being a pious individual. In a letter to the Carmelite nuns in Guadalajara, he expressed his passion for Jesus Christ and revealed his desire to live a pious life:

> *Jesus and Jesus only will live in us sacramentally, and really by grace; and . . . he will be the one who prays during prayer, the one who chants in the choir, and he will be in us entirely. . . . So let us die always for Jesus, so that Jesus may always live in us and we only in Jesus and for Jesus alone.*[72]

Fray Simon del Hierro glorified Margil's piety reflected in descriptions of his daily devotions. According to Hierro's *Testimonio*, Margil never failed to say mass and hear confessions each day. He participated with fervor at communal spiritual devotions, and sang and prayed as he walked from the college at Guadalupe to his mission work. On his deathbed at the convent of San Francisco el Grande, he reportedly whispered, "My heart is steadfast, O God, my heart is steadfast; I will sing and chant praise. I shall praise you and sing in the company of the angels in glory."[73]

Biographers of other prominent missionaries also emphasized their devotion by describing their final hours. Music figured prominently in Junípero Serra's last moments. He sang *Tantum ergo sacramentum* with tears in his eyes, according to Fray Francisco Palou, immediately before passing into heaven.[74] Similarly, according to Miguel Venegas's biography, Juan María de Salvatierra died on July 18, 1717 after falling ill while en route to report to the viceroy. As he died, Venegas reported that he chanted the hymn *Ave Maria Stella* to Our Lady of Loreto, for

---

[72] Ibid., 152, from Margil to the Carmelite convent, June 9, 1710.

[73] This is a paraphrase of verses from Psalms 36 and 37, in Leutenegger, trans., *Nothingness Itself*, x.

[74] Francisco Palóu, *La Vida de Junípero Serra* (Ann Arbor, MI: University Microfilms, 1966), 287.

whom he had a special devotion.⁷⁵ Histories and menologia described other missionaries whose ascension to heaven was linked with singing. Father Miguel Nuñez de Haro, missionary at San José y San Miguel de Aguayo for over thirty years, sang the verses of a hymn in honor of Our Lady of the Good Shepherd (which he had taught to mission Indians), as he "surrendered his soul to his creator."⁷⁶ Whether singing actually occurred at the end of these missionaries' lives is not crucial. However, it is notable that music and singing were written into the dying moments of important missionaries, held up as signs of inner piety and religious devotion for those who read the biographies in the hopes of gaining inspiration for their own careers. Song provided the link that united these exemplary missionaries with the larger communion of saints at their moments of death, just as it could provide the faithful and pious a connection with the spirit world.

Differences in Franciscan and Jesuit Evangelization

The careers of these two important evangelists of northern New Spain also serve as a springboard for a discussion of the differences and similarities between Franciscan and Jesuit evangelization techniques, especially those related to the use of music. First, as demonstrated in Chapter 2, members of both orders received musical training as part of their comprehensive education in colleges and seminaries in Europe and New Spain. Jesuit colleges in Europe were renowned for their rigorous curriculum, which included music as well as languages, rhetoric, and philosophy. Many of the men who served the Church in Mexico as chapel masters, while not Jesuits themselves, were educated at Jesuit colleges in Europe.⁷⁷ Prospective missionaries were exposed to liturgical music through their own participation in worship as well as in formal classes at some seminaries. In Spain, where Margil studied, instruction in the basics of singing and playing of some musical instruments was included in seminary education. The Divine Office was chanted in choir in the morning, at noon, late in the afternoon, and again in the evening.⁷⁸ During Juan María de Salvatierra's two-year novitiate, he com-

---

⁷⁵ Venegas, *Juan Maria de Salvatierra*, 224.

⁷⁶ José Francisco Sotomayor, *Historia del Apostólico Colegio de Nuestra Señora de Guadalupe de Zacatecas: desde su fundación hasta nuestros días* (Zacatecas: Imp. y Encuadernación de La Rosa, 1889), vol. II, 161, Biblioteca Franciscana, Cholula, Mexico.

⁷⁷ For example, Ignacio de Jerusalem, *maestro de capilla* of the Mexico City cathedral from 1750 to 1769, and an illustrious composer, attended the Jesuit college in Leece, Italy. See Robert Murrell Stevenson, "Ignacio Jerusalem, 1707–1769," *Inter-American Music Review* 16:1 (Summer–Fall 1997), 59.

⁷⁸ Regina Maria Gormley, "The Liturgical Music of the California Missions, 1769–1833" (DMA diss., Catholic University of America, 1992), 27.

pleted the spiritual exercises of St. Ignatius and studied the lives of the saints. Like that of the Franciscans, the daily routine of Jesuit novitiates involved exposure to music through daily communal worship. At the Roman College, for example, seminarians participated in the choir for liturgical functions, took singing lessons, and learned liturgical melodies for an hour each day. All students had to learn both Gregorian plainchant melodies as well as *canto figurado*.[79]

Both Franciscans and Jesuits, like Margil and Salvatierra, used folk songs in their efforts to create communities among converts. Margil's use of these songs became well-known among members of the missionary colleges. In the later Alta California missions, students and future missionaries acted upon this knowledge and copied music from their home provinces for use in the mission field.[80] Thus it is possible to see the similarities between the *alabados*, or songs of praise, used in many mission communities, and the *saetas* such as those sung by confraternities in Spain.[81] Members of both orders seem to have had exposure to a wide variety of music, both instrumental and vocal, within the liturgy and in more informal devotional or spiritual songs, which they then incorporated into their evangelization efforts in local missions. Jesuits tended to sing hymns and devotional songs in Latin, or translate them into indigenous languages, while Franciscans such as Margil composed hymns in their vernacular Spanish language. Missionaries who were comfortable with their degree of musical ability and training tended to use music, as one would expect, to a greater degree than their brethren who were not musically trained.

Franciscans and Jesuits also practiced devotions to particular elements of the Christian pantheon. Juan María de Salvatierra's life reflected Jesuit devotion to Mary, which manifested itself in musical offerings at many Jesuit missions.[82] As in his later work in the missions of northwestern New Spain, Father Salvatierra found time to give special attention to the devotion of Our Lady of Loreto, who became patroness of all of lower California. In Guadalajara, while functioning as superior of the colegio, Salvatierra oversaw the founding of a holy house and chapel dedicated to Loreto. It was dedicated on November 25, 1695, in a cer-

---

[79] Ricardo García Villoslada, "Algunos documentos sobre la música en el antigua seminario romano," *Archivum Historicum Societatis Iesu* 31 (1962), 116. Canto figurado is a rhythmic version of plainchant, sometimes harmonized in a chordal manner.

[80] Owen da Silva, *Mission Music of California* (Los Angeles: Warren F. Lewis, 1941), 19.

[81] Stark, "Notes on a Search for Antecedents of New Mexican Alabado Music."

[82] This devotion has been previously noted by Pilar Gonzalbo Aizpuru, "La influencia de la Compañía de Jesús en la sociedad novohispana del siglo XVI," *Historia Mexicana* 32:2 (October–December 1982), 262-281; and Schroeder, "Jesuits, Nahuas, and the Good Death Society."

emony that involved a solemn procession and sung vespers with "excellent" music. Miguel Venegas wrote that townspeople gathered at the chapel on Saturdays to hear a choir sing the rosary and the litany to the Virgin, followed by a sermon from Salvatierra.[83] Visita reports and missionary letters mention vespers and mass on Saturdays, as well as the singing of the Litany of Our Lady of Loreto, held to honor Mary in larger Jesuit missions in both the seventeenth and eighteenth centuries.[84] Jesuits tended to sing and teach songs that were part of the liturgy, such as the Ave Maria, as well as hymns such as the Salve Regina and Vexilla Regis in Latin. Franciscans also honored Mary in this manner at their missions, but Franciscan devotion to Mary was more often expressed through the singing of spiritual songs, such as the alabado, in the vernacular.[85]

Both Franciscans and Jesuits relied on church and state officials for permission to evangelize in indigenous communities. Support of patrons and influential officials could make an enormous difference in the ornaments and supplies available to support missionary work. Music was a powerful tool that members of both orders engaged to create lasting impressions in the minds of important guests. Instrumental and vocal music had the ability to sway the minds of powerful visitors, whose reports might determine whether a mission received funding or was closed. Special musical performances were arranged for the arrival of important visitors, such as a superior of the order, a bishop, or a state or military official. These performances were not only important because they created images of pious converts, but also because they involved the coming together of the community, planning, and rehearsals. Such communal activities could have fostered ties between indigenous peoples congregated in the missions, even if they had previously been members of different ethnic groups or tribes. In one interesting case, Jesuit Pedro María Nascimbén, missionary at Mulegé, Baja California, composed a song for his neophytes to sing because he knew the father visitor was coming to punish the Indians for their lapses in Christian behavior. The song, which was to serve as an act of contri-

---

[83] Venegas, *Juan Maria de Salvatierra*, 149.

[84] See, for example, AGN, Misiones, vol. 26, exp. 27, ff. 160-163 (Anua de 1662), especially f. 160v-161, concerning Mission San Miguel de las Bocas, José Pascual to Padre Provincial 6/29/1653, AGN, Historia, vol. 19, exp. 14, f. 204-204v, concerning Mission San Felipe, as well as Pfefferkorn, *Sonora*, 269, and Crosby, *Antigua California*, 205.

[85] For example, see Father Juan Fernández to F. Provincial Tomás Altamirano, October 7, 1679, ARSI, Rome 17, f. 409r-409v, concerning San Miguel de los Ures; biography of Padre Escalera, OSMHRC, Zacatecas, 16, fr. 1431–1423, concerning Espíritu Santo de Moris Mission; and Howard Benoist and María Eva Flores, eds., *Guidelines for a Texas Mission: Instructions for the Missionary of Mission Concepción in San Antonio* (San Antonio, TX: Old Spanish Missions Historical Research Library, [1787] 1994), 5.

tion, began *"Que viva Jesús . . .* and was as tender as his kind heart could desire. And he taught his delinquent sons to sing it."[86] In this context, music not only served as a way to communicate with God (as an act of contrition), but more importantly it was a way for Nascimbén to communicate an apology to his superior and to demonstrate that the Indians under his charge could be models of piety.

At San José Mission in Texas, Governor Barrios reported that

> *[e]very Saturday, Rosary devotions are conducted with great reverence and even greater edification. There is no one who has witnessed it and has not been moved to tears by the modesty, composure, religious spirit, good voices, and instrumental music of the natives, who compose the music and sing the Rosary.*[87]

These performances of religious songs were used to communicate evidence of conversion and devout belief, even if the singers may not have understood or believed the words they sang. Missionaries and visitors were eager to demonstrate the success of their conversion efforts, and the performance of Catholic music of the liturgy was seen as proof of indoctrination. It is entirely possible, however, that indigenous performers either did not understand or did not subscribe to the words they were singing. Ironically, missionaries often complained that the same indigenous peoples, who possessed such sweet and pious voices in the churches, sounded like howling animals when performing their own songs and dances. Thus, it was not the individual, but the musical performance that communicated piety. While performances for special occasions were meant to convey piety to visitors, in practice, Franciscans confronted constant undermining of their authority by mission Indians.

Conclusions

Music was an important element of the evangelization efforts of both Franciscans and Jesuits throughout a wide geographic area during the colonial period. The evangelization techniques of the missionaries, however, changed only slightly between the late sixteenth century and the expulsion of the Jesuits in 1767. The greatest emphasis was placed on converting Indians and Hispanicizing them with as little force as possible, although violence was still

---

[86] Cited in Crosby, *Antigua California*, 205.
[87] Barrios to viceroy, May 28, 1758, Archivo San Francisco el Grande, copy in UTNLB, vol. 12, f. 62-63.

part of the conversion and acculturation processes in many places.[88] Music was used as part of evangelization in daily worship, for special occasions, and in teaching doctrine as a memorization aid. Members of both orders placed great importance on teaching children, since they were seen as "blank slates" upon which Christian and Hispanic ideals could be written.

The early Jesuit missions in the near north as well as the early Franciscan missions in New Mexico seem to have possessed more elaborate musical cultures than their seventeenth- and early eighteenth-century counterparts elsewhere in northern New Spain. At Mission Santa María de las Parras, like in other early missions, Indians sang motets and figured chant as part of the celebration of mass and the Divine Office.[89] Religious dances and a large variety of musical instruments were also used at Parras. As the resources of the orders and the Spanish Crown were spread more thinly and over a larger geographic area, the funds and efforts that could be devoted to music were more limited. The individual musical background and training of the missionaries were also very important in determining the type of music sung at the missions and the types of musical instruments constructed and played.

During the seventeenth and early eighteenth centuries, music in the missions largely consisted of chant and simple polyphony for masses and vespers as well as simpler songs, such as alabados, for teaching and ordering daily schedules. Larger missions with more resources possessed more instruments bought in central Mexico or Europe, but mission residents in many areas, particularly the Jesuit northwest, made stringed instruments. Special occasions were cause for more elaborate performances, including dance and instruments. All communal worship involving music reflecting the social, political, and economic conditions at work in the overlapping communities of New Spain's north.

Indigenous peoples were able to affect the type of music performed in their mission communities to a limited extent. Religious dance became part of the mission repertoires for special occasions such as Christmas, Corpus Christi, and Holy Week. Although the dances were not allowed inside the church, and access to costumes and instruments was sometimes controlled by the missionaries, many of the dances retained strong indigenous components. Certainly many indigenous groups continued dancing for their own special occasions (e.g., harvest or war), often at night, in a location hidden or far from missionary control.

---

[88] See Spicer, *Cycles of Conquest*, 331.

[89] Anua de 1598, in Félix Zubillaga, ed., *Monumenta Mexicana VI* (Rome: Societatis Iesu, 1961), 638.

Native peoples used music to their advantage throughout the northern frontier, quite possibly to avoid other work. Perhaps this is why Jesuits stationed at Cucurpe found the Opatas and Eudeves so eager to learn to sing and play musical instruments. Being a cantor, choir member, or instrumentalist meant avoiding or at least shortening repartimiento or other forced labor in the mines or nearby fields. Skilled musicians could also earn wages performing for secular and religious occasions in larger towns, supplementing their incomes and participating in celebrations that shared community values.

Both Franciscan and Jesuit missionaries successfully employed music as a powerful tool for teaching and attracting Indians to the missions. With the expulsion of the Jesuits and the militarization of the northern frontier in the late colonial period, Franciscans relied even more heavily on music to try to achieve the resettlement and conversion of resistant and semi-nomadic groups in the northeast and north central, while a new mission enterprise, with a much more elaborate musical culture, was founded in Alta California.

CHAPTER 5
Changing Communities, 1768–1810

The late eighteenth and early nineteenth centuries were periods of great change throughout the Spanish empire. In northwest and north central New Spain, the Bourbon reforms, and the results of a military reorganization of the northern mission–presidio frontier, called for a refocusing of financial and military resources and the consolidation of the northernmost regions into the Provincias Internas. In addition, the increasing hegemony of the Apache, Comanche, and Wichita horse cultures in the central plains posed new threats to land and resources, and created the desire for new alliances between Spaniards and Indians. Responding to threats of English and Russian presence in the region, the Spanish moved into Alta California in 1769, and a comprehensive mission system developed in that region in the following century. Farther east, the vast territory of Louisiana passed into the hands of the Spanish as a result of the Seven Years' War, and forays into this territory commenced to enhance trading relationships with the indigenous groups there.

The church also provided new dictates for religious administration as a result of the Fourth Mexican Provincial Council in 1770, the first major changes since 1585. During this period, mandates issued by civil and religious authorities throughout the Spanish empire emphasized social and religious orthodoxy, and they expressed concern about the nature of popular religious practices.[1] But in the northern frontier of New Spain, like in other rural areas of the Spanish empire, these concerns rarely translated into significant actions.[2] The music and

---

[1] During the second half of the eighteenth century, Bourbon officials exerted a greater deal of control over Church affairs, including secularizing doctrinas that had been administered by missionaries. On new rules about local festivals, see Juan Pedro Viqueira Albán, *¿Relajados o reprimidos? Diversiones públicas y vida social en la Ciudad de México durante el Siglo de las Luces* (Mexico City: Fondo de Cultura Económica, 1987); Geoffrey Baker, *Imposing Harmony: Music and Society in Colonial Cuzco* (Durham, NC: Duke University Press, 2008), 60-64.

[2] On changes in the Bourbon Church, see David A. Brading, "Tridentine Catholicism and Enlightened Despotism in Bourbon Mexico," *Journal of Latin American Studies* 15 (1983), 1-22.

dance of northern mission communities, although not always orthodox, continued to be valuable tools for encouraging acculturation and cooperation with the Spanish project of colonization. Music alone could not make loyal Christian citizens, particularly when it was used by Spaniards and their mestizo and Indian allies to reinforce Christian community, and at the same time used by Indians such as the Apache, Comanche, Seri, and Yuma, to gather energy and power with which to fight the imposition of Spanish hegemony.

This chapter examines four major topics: (1) the effects of the expulsion of the Jesuits, secularization, and the movement of settlers into Baja California and Sonora on the musical cultures of those regions; (2) music and dance in the mature Franciscan missions of Coahuila, Texas, and New Mexico; (3) the involvement of music in new explorations and missionization attempts in the Provincias Internas and the northern frontier; and (4) the establishment of an elaborate musical culture in the new Alta California missions. The sociopolitical context of late eighteenth-century northern New Spain caused missionaries to intentionally rely on the power of song to attempt to achieve conversion in many areas. Not only repetition, melody, and the addition of European instruments, but also the lyrics of mission music and the coexistence, and occasional blending of Indian and Hispanic dance practices, came to be important tools of Hispanicization. Spanish and mixed-race settlers and soldiers moved into the region in greater numbers than before, bringing with them folk religious and secular music and dance, and more opportunities for musicians to use their skills to enhance their livelihoods and standing in the larger communities. The musical cultures of late colonial Franciscan missions adapted as they reflected new political, economic, and cultural situations.

COMMUNITIES IN TRANSITION: BAJA CALIFORNIA AND SONORA

After continued conflicts with the Crown, the Society of Jesus was expelled from all Spanish territories in 1767. Forty-eight missions in Chihuahua, Sinaloa, Sonora, and Baja California were left without missionary leadership until a reduced Franciscan presence moved into the region.[3] Upheaval in the adminis-

---

On changes in personal devotional practices, see also Pamela Voekel, *Alone before God: The Religious Origins of Modernity in Mexico* (Durham, NC: Duke University Press, 2002); and Brian R. Larkin, "Liturgy, Devotion, and Religious Reform in Eighteenth-Century Mexico City," *The Americas* 60:4 (April 2004), 493-518.

[3] Francisco Morales, *Franciscan Presence in the Americas: Essays on the Activities of the Franciscan Friars in the Americas, 1492–1900* (Potomac, MD: Academy of American Franciscan

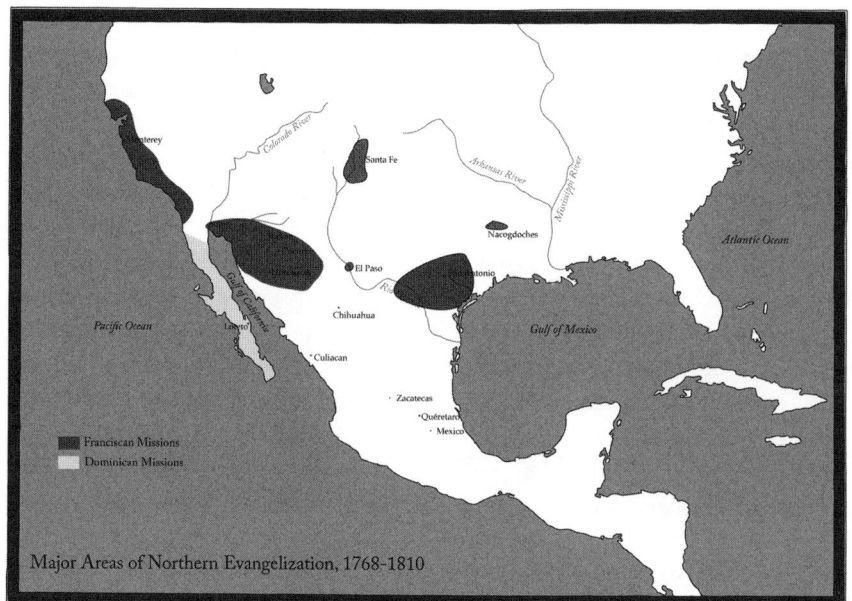

Major Areas of Northern Evangelization, 1768-1810

tration and internal cohesion of the missions undeniably affected the economic and political fabric of the regions, as did the consolidation of Spanish settlements.[4] However, indigenous residents of mission communities continued to make and play stringed instruments. Upon their arrival, this frustrated the Franciscans, who were exasperated at the Indians' lack of "industriousness" and unwillingness to fulfill missionaries' requests. Instead, "they only know how to make some musical instruments, which please them very much."[5]

The departure of the Jesuits affected the religious and cultural makeup of communities to varying degrees. Largely Hispanicized areas with more diverse populations continued to observe religious rituals, in some cases aided by secular clergy and in others by Hispanicized Indians, including reciting the doctrine, praying the rosary, ringing church bells, and burying the dead according to Catholic rites. Although many churches fell into disrepair, inventories from the first Franciscans in the most populated areas of Baja California and Sonora indicated that silver religious ornaments remained in the sacristy of the church, and

---

History, 1983), 244. On the Sonoran missions after Jesuit expulsion, see José Refugio de la Torre Curiel, "Conquering the Frontier: Contests for Religion, Survival, and Profits in Northwestern Mexico, 1768–1855" (PhD diss., University of California at Berkeley, 2005).

[4] See Deeds, *Defiance and Deference*, 131-189.
[5] Alcocer, *Bosquejo de la historia*, 157.

religious images and statues were not harmed. In northern areas without a sizeable Spanish or mestizo presence, however, the initial Franciscan reports described abandoned mission buildings, uncultivated fields, and scattered residents, who spoke little Spanish and were without religious, decorative, and ritual ornaments.[6] At San Francisco Xavier de Cumuripa, once the most important mission in the region, when the fathers rang the bells for instruction or prayers, few came.[7]

Some areas received replacement ministers more quickly than others. The sixteen Jesuits stationed in Baja California left in February 1768, and by the start of April, Franciscans arrived to replace them, planning to use established missions in Baja California to launch their new endeavor in Alta California. After several years, the Franciscans handed the Baja California missions, in a poor state after Jesuit expulsion, disease, and conflicts with civil authorities, to the Dominicans, so that they could focus on establishing new missions farther north.[8] Political concerns, particularly holding territory against foreign threats and Indian raids, often dictated settlement as much as available resources or indigenous settlement patterns. This was the case in late eighteenth-century Baja California, where Viceroy Armona ordered strategic areas settled with all possible haste in 1770.[9] Although the Dominicans had been active in conversion efforts in Oaxaca and Guatemala, their only work in the northern borderlands of the Spanish empire was in Baja California. Their methods relied heavily upon discipline and adherence to daily routines, and although a few new missions were established on the northern frontier, others saw drastic declines in their populations.[10]

Jesuits had also controlled the missions of the Pimería Alta and Pimería Baja. Several years passed before Franciscans were able to gather personnel to staff some of these mission communities, and some were abandoned or left to

---

[6] Antonio de los Reyes, *Noticia y estado*, 1772, in Fernando Ocaranza, *Los franciscanos en las provincias internas de Sonora y Ostimuri* (Mexico City: N.p., 1933), 221; and for Baja California, *Expediente sobre los Inventarios formados en la entrega de la antigua California*, AGN, Misiones, vol. 12, exp. 10.

[7] Ocaranza, *Los franciscanos*, 200-204.

[8] Francisco Palóu, *Noticias de la Nueva California* (San Francisco: N.p., 1874), 211-213.

[9] Ibid., 126-129.

[10] For example, the head mission of Loreto, which was richly decorated and had an extensive library of 466 volumes, had a population of 160 in 1772, 70 in 1782 following a smallpox epidemic, 152 in 1792, and only 37 in 1798. The presidio and surrounding area maintained a population between 450 and 600 in the last decade of the eighteenth century, but more than half of its population was Spanish or mestizo. Similarly, Mission San José de Comondú Mission, also one of the more elaborately outfitted missions, with a library of 126 books, declined in population from 216 in 1772 to 28 in 1800. See Hubert Howe Bancroft, *History of the North Mexican States and Texas*, vol. I (San Francisco: A.L. Bancroft Publishers, 1884), 738-740.

secular clergy. As they arrived in the Pimería Alta, the friars re-introduced daily patterns based on prayer, singing, and doctrinal recitation.[11] These routines, which will be discussed further in Chapter 6, not only promoted a sedentary, agriculture-based lifestyle punctuated by bells and prayers, but facilitated the learning of Spanish. The effects of the Jesuit expulsion were widespread, even as the threat to small frontier communities from the raiding bands, including Apaches and Seri, increased. Due to lack of staff and security concerns, some *visitas*, or smaller mission stations, were abandoned or their populations were encouraged to relocate to missions, such as San José de Tumacácori, which were closer to presidios and offered stable food sources and more shelter from raids. Farther south and east, some Tarahumaras in the missions administered by the Franciscan apostolic college at Zacatecas maintained houses at the *cabeceras*, or head missions, in the region. But many Indians did not live there full time, others lived in the mountains and valleys out of missionary reach, and only sometimes did they attend mass or allow their children to receive doctrinal instruction.[12] These mission communities, like those of Baja California, did not have large numbers of Hispanic settlers and remained primarily indigenous. Franciscans in these missions needed interpreters for all but the most rudimentary communication, including doctrinal instruction and preaching.[13] Although missionary control over all of Sonora decreased after 1767, some populations chose to continue living near the mission, adhering to the religious customs and daily routines introduced by the missionaries. In 1788, Father Juan Santiesteban reported a smaller population of Pimas living at his mission, but promised that they were "*gente de mucha fidelidad*," loyal to the faith, who came at the sound of the bell.[14]

By 1779, the number of missions in the north was further reduced when Pope Pius VI created the diocese of Sonora and Sinaloa, which incorporated many mission communities under the direction of the secular authorities. This administrative move recognized the changing nature of frontier communities, in which Spaniards and *vecinos* of mixed race often outnumbered Indians who chose to adopt a settled lifestyle. While some Franciscans considered the secularization

---

[11] Antonio de los Reyes to the King, September 2, 1774, AGI, Guadalajara, 586, f. 39v-40, described a daily routine similar to that used by the Jesuits. Reyes was later appointed as bishop of the Diocese of Sonora and Sinaloa, a post in which he served from 1783 to 1787.

[12] Report to the Colegio de Nuestra Señora de Guadalupe, 1778, OSMHRC, Zacatecas, reel 6, fr. 225.

[13] Pedro Corbalán, 1771, AGI, Guadalajara, 338.

[14] Fr. Juan Santiesteban to Juan María de Bohorquez, November 15, 1788, in Fernando Ocaranza, *Los franciscanos*, 164-165.

of their missions throughout the north a threat to their authority and religious duties, and an encroachment of the state into religious matters, others petitioned to be relieved of the burden of the missions newly assigned to their care.[15]

The organization and distribution of Franciscans in northern New Spain also changed during this period. A smaller percentage of friars ministered in the Chihuahua and Sonora missions than those who lived a conventual life farther south, representing a significant change over the earlier part of the century.[16] Those serving in the missions had difficulty enforcing attendance at mass, doctrinal instruction, and recitation of the prayers and rosary. In response to absences from required religious activities, friars depended on corporal punishment or aid from indigenous officials, while complaining bitterly about the lack of support from civil authorities.[17] Some of those who staffed the missions failed to observe their vows. In 1792, the provincial of Zacatecas was charged with depriving the missionaries of his apostolic college of necessary funds. As a result, some engaged in commercial activities to raise funds. Others were reprimanded for allowing women into their friaries, and leaving their missions to go to the Spanish settlements.[18] The instability and turnover in religious administration in these communities did not completely silence religious music, but even in the largest, most stable missions, reports of religious music and dance beyond simple devotional songs, such as the alabado or Salve Regina, greatly decreased during this period.

A look at the history of Mission Los Santos Reyes del Cucurpe in the Pimería Baja during both its Jesuit and Franciscan periods helps to clarify the effects of political, economic, and social changes during the colonial period on the musical culture of the community. Following a brief period of Franciscan evangelization, Jesuits formally established this mission among Eudeve and Opata settlements near the headwaters of the Río San Miguel in 1647.[19] By the

---

[15] See, for example, Fray Diego Ximenez to Viceroy Antonio María de Bucareli, December 6, 1774, Marcellino de Civezza Collection, Pontificio Ateneo Antoniana microfilm copy, University of Arizona (AZU), 305, microform reel 1, fr. 54-57

[16] Francisco Morales, "Mexican Society and the Franciscan Order in a Period of Transition 1748–1859," *The Americas* 54:3 (January 1998), 323-356.

[17] The Franciscans engaged in a running battle with Teodoro de Croix over their administration of the missions. See Juan de Prestamero to the Viceroy, August 18, 1780, AGN, Provincias Internas, vol. 258, exp. 7, f. 63-80; and Informe of Teodoro de Croix, 1781, AGN, Provincias Internas, vol. 258, exp. 8, f. 121-123.

[18] *Usurpacion de sinodos por el provincial de Zacatecas*, April 14, 1792, AGN, Provincias Internas, vol. 40, ff. 1-62.

[19] For a more detailed analysis of Cucurpe, see Thomas E. Sheridan, *Where the Dove Calls: The Political Ecology of a Peasant Corporate Community in Northwestern Mexico* (Tucson: University of Arizona Press, 1988); and Radding, *Wandering Peoples*, 38, 98-99, 172-175.

end of the seventeenth century, Cucurpe was a productive mission, and it helped to support other communities in northwestern New Spain. Jesuit fathers and the indigenous *alcaldes mayores* and catechists were successful in introducing Christianity and Hispanic lifeways to the population, as well as encouraging ranching and farming among indigenous inhabitants. The Indians at Cucurpe looked and sounded like rural peasants elsewhere in New Spain, even though their understanding of Christian concepts was surely incomplete at best. They knew how to use the Spanish colonial system to their advantage to seek protection from rival groups; residents even brought a lawsuit against a Pima Indian to protect their water and land rights.[20] Despite their outward acceptance of a Hispanic lifestyle, residents of Cucurpe and its outlying *pueblos de visita* faced unrest and violence. Like the nearby Pima and Yaqui, many resented the Spaniards' labor demands in the mines and fields. Between 1730 and the mid-1750s, revolts, disease, and Apache raids rocked Sonora, leaving Jesuits dejected over the region's lamentable state.[21]

Jesuit Juan Nentvig described the Opatas and Eudeves as more "devoted to the tilling of the land and the breeding of cattle[,] . . . more faithful to their villages, and consequently better instructed in the mysteries of Our Holy Faith," than their Pima neighbors.[22] Cucurpe's residents learned Spanish, largely complied with missionaries' requests, and after a century of evangelization were recognized as the "best Christians" and "most loyal vassals of our Lord the King" in Sonora.[23] Not surprisingly, the musical culture during the end of Cucurpe's Jesuit period was rich, with Opata and Eudeve participation as singers and instrumentalists.

Jesuits introduced liturgical music, devotional songs, and European instruments. Violins, harps, and psalterios, as well as bells of different sizes, were listed in inventories and letters.[24] Under Ignaz Pfefferkorn's leadership, the mission boasted a choir of nine or ten members, including at least four women, who sang mass, litanies, and the Salve Regina on a weekly basis. For high mass, singers alternated verses with instrumental music. On Saturday evenings, the

---

[20] Archivo de Parral, 1723B, fr. 655-688, microfilm copy, UTNLB, see excellent discussion in Radding, *Wandering Peoples*, 172-175.

[21] In 1730, Indians near Guepaca and Cucurpe revolted. Joseph Toral to Padre Provincial Joseph de Barba, 3/25/1730, W.B. Stephens Collection, UTNLB. See also Padre Juan Baptista Duquesney al Gobernador Augustin de Vildosola, San Pedro de Aconchi, April 15, 1747, Archivo Historico de Hacienda, Temporalidades, 278, no. 23, microfilm copy, DRSW.

[22] Nentuig, *Rudo Ensayo*, 56-57.

[23] Ibid.

[24] AGI, Guadalajara, 586, 1749 inventory; also Nentuig, *Rudo Ensayo*, 98, 109; and Pfefferkorn, *Sonora*, 246.

rosary, litanies, and Ave Marias were accompanied by music.[25] On principal feast days, the choir provided music for vespers on the evening preceding the feast. Processions were also common, "in order to present a visual display of the majesty of our Holy Religion to the neophytes so that they may remain impressed with its splendor and be attracted to it."[26] Visual and auditory appeals to all residents encouraged religious devotion, and music was also used for education and Hispanicization at Cucurpe. Father Juan Ortíz Zapata, Jesuit visitor to the missions in the 1670s, instructed that all who were capable should be taught to read, write, and sing for divine worship. He further ordered that the Angelus be played on mission bells in the morning, noon, and at night.[27] Cucurpe's status as a *cabecera* meant that its resident missionary and his indigenous assistants were responsible for teaching all boys and girls in the area, ages seven to seventeen, on a daily basis. Before Jesuit expulsion, children recited the catechism twice daily—once in their own language, and once in Spanish. Catechism instruction was led by native teachers (*temastianes*), some of whom could read and write music.[28]

As the largest mission in the area, Los Santos Reyes del Cucurpe served as a staging point for expeditions into the northern Pimería. Visitors, as well as nearby residents, celebrated with the mission and its rancherías on special occasions. On San Ignacio's feast day, Cucurpe reveled for three days with both religious and secular activities. Father Pfefferkorn described the festivities, including a banquet with an abundance of food, high mass with glorious music, a procession of the sacrament through the community to the mission, a bullfight, and dances. Mission residents, as well as nearby Opatas, Eudeves, and Spanish soldiers and settlers, attended this fiesta. Spanish soldiers celebrated by firing their muskets into the air, and Indians danced the Montezuma, or matachín dance.[29] A similar gathering was held for Corpus Christi. Fiestas of this type were important occasions for strengthening community identity, exchanging goods, and renewing kinship ties. After the Pima Revolt of 1751, and decades of conflict with Spaniards and other indigenous groups, celebrations were

---

[25] Pfefferkorn, *Sonora*, 264, 269; and Nentvig, *Rudo Ensayo*, 110.
[26] Nentvig, *Rudo Ensayo*, 109.
[27] Zapata, "Relación de las Misiones," 337-338.
[28] Nentvig, *Rudo Ensayo*, 109-111.
[29] Pfefferkorn, *Sonora*, 270-272. Matachines dances are described both during the colonial period and in current-day Sonora. When Campbell Pennington conducted fieldwork among the Pima Bajo in 1968 to 1971, he learned that matachines dances were then performed in Onavas (to the south and east of Cucurpe) during the Christmas season (December 16-24), on New Year's Day, and on the Sunday before Easter. *The Pima Bajo of Central Sonora, Mexico* (Salt Lake City: University of Utah Press, 1980), 249.

important "safety valves" that allowed the area's residents the ability to feast, dance, and revel.

During the second half of the eighteenth century, these gatherings became increasingly diverse. Larger numbers of soldiers and Indian auxiliaries patrolled Sonora, groups of indigenous peoples moved to seek zones of refuge, and peasants moved north from central Mexico seeking economic opportunity in the area's ranching and mining economy.[30] Interethnic marriage increased, and a mixed-race population of settlers participated in religious rites at Cucurpe and nearby mission churches. Jesuits in Sonora had difficulties extending their reach north during the troubled mid-century, and their Franciscan replacements never exercised the same degree of control in the region.[31] Still, music-making at Cucurpe continued, suggesting that religious music had become an important part of the community's culture. When Franciscan Antonio de los Reyes arrived at Cucurpe on San Antonio's feast day in 1768, he chanted mass. A choir of area residents performed at this mass "with such melodious and disciplined voices that a religious community could not do better." Perhaps due to his surprise at finding such a display of musical talent, Reyes declared that it was the happiest day he had spent in all of New Spain.[32] When Reyes reported on the mission again in 1772, he noted that the missionary was administering the sacraments and praying the Divine Office, but no musical performances or the presence of a choir were mentioned. Cucurpe and the other missions of the region experienced transitions in administrative control. The western missions of the Pimería Baja, including Cucurpe, were transferred to the friars of the apostolic college of Jalisco in 1776, the new custody of San Carlos de Sonora in 1783, and back to the Jaliscan friars in 1791. Inventories of these missions do not contain references to the violins and other stringed instruments listed earlier in the century. Presumably, instruments were taken from the church by the community members who played them.[33]

In the decades before its handover to the new diocese of Sonora at the end of the century, Los Santos Reyes del Cucurpe's population shifts reflected those of much of the northern frontier.[34] The mission was attacked by a large band of

---

[30] On population movements in eighteenth-century Sonora, and "zones of refuge," see Radding, *Wandering Peoples*, chapter 9. For the late colonial period, see de la Torre, "Conquering the Frontier," chapter 2.

[31] See Sheridan, *Where the Dove Calls*, 12.

[32] Reyes to Piñeda, Cucurpe, June 17, 1768, cited in Kieran McCarty, "Franciscan Beginnings on the Arizona-Sonora Desert" (PhD diss., Catholic University of America, 1973), 73.

[33] Some of the ornaments from the Baja California missions were also taken during the 1769–1773 period to help outfit the new missions in Alta California.

[34] Population statistics for Cucurpe and the other missions of the Opatería from 1766-1850 were compiled by de la Torre in "Conquering the Frontier," 83.

raiders in 1781, and nearly one hundred residents were either killed or captured. Others fled following the raid.[35] Military officers organized a company of Opata auxiliary troops in 1784, and together with Pima allies, they negotiated with the Apaches for peace.[36] During the late colonial period, a small number of indios, mestizos, and mulattos had moved into the region to work the land and new mines, and raise livestock, but the mission recorded few new Indian converts.[37] A 1799 census indicated that less than half of Cucurpe's population was indigenous.[38] Cucurpe's residents had also adapted to a Hispanic agrarian and ranching economy more completely than other mission communities. It was one of only three communities in which residents spoke Spanish, and Indians there understood and manipulated the Spanish legal system.[39] Music was an agent that both aided in these processes of cultural accommodation, and reflected the demographic makeup of the community. Angél Antonio Nuñez, missionary at Santa Maria Baserac to the east of Cucurpe remarked that Opata dances were seldom performed; instead, mission residents "use, practice, and know all the dances of the Spanish."[40] Processions on special occasions were accompanied by music, likely in Spanish, the language in which the resident friar preached and explained doctrine. Franciscans spent some of their meager funds on necessities, including items for the celebration of feast days.[41] On these occasions, Franciscans in the Pimería oversaw participation in games and dances considered innocent. Superstitious dances, probably those associated with sacred locations such as caves or idols, were prohibited, and missionaries attempted to discipline

---

[35] Teodoro de Croix to Juan Bautista Peru, 1782, Records of the Presidio de San Felipe y Santiago de Janos, 1706-1858, UTNLB, folder 4, section 3, 1-55.

[36] Bancroft, *History of Arizona and New Mexico*, 378.

[37] Josef Pinilla to the viceroy, November 11, 1771, AGN, Provincias Internas, vol. 152, f. 280-283; and Teodoro de Croix, Arizpe, June 30, 1781, AGI, Guadalajara, 267. This group was likely a multiethnic band, composed of those dissatisfied with the Spanish and settler presence in the region. See de la Torre, "Conquering the Frontier," 309-312. On other multiethnic raiding bands, see William Merrill, "Cultural Creativity and Raiding Bands," in William Taylor and Franklin Pease, eds., *Violence, Resistance, and Survival in the Americas: Native Americans and the Legacy of Conquest* (Washington, DC: Smithsonian Institution Press, 1994).

[38] Censo de poblacion de las misiones franciscanas de Sonora, 1799, in Ocaranza, *Los franciscanos*, 181.

[39] Ocaranza, *Los franciscanos*, 214-215. See also Radding, *Wandering Peoples*, 192-193; and de la Torre, "Conquering the Frontier," xxix.

[40] Fr. Angél Antonio Núñez, Carta edificante histórico-curiosa, escrita desde este misión de Santa Maria de Baserac, March 31, 1777, AZU, special collections, MS 193.

[41] Fr. Lorenzo Simó's report from 1788 indicated that 117 pesos and one real had been spent for the necessities and support of the people of the mission, and the fiestas of Purísima and the other saints; 186 pesos spent for the consumable goods. The church was adorned decently, but that of the visita at Tuape was in very poor condition. See Ocaranza, *Los franciscanos*, 170.

those who participated. Civil and military authorities, however, were more concerned with Seri, Apache, and Pima pacification than the dances of relatively peaceful groups, and missionaries did not receive support from military or civil officials for punishing offenders.[42]

Dancing continued to be an important form of recreation in the region around Cucurpe, in addition to its importance in re-creating history and fashioning group identity. In 1835, Ignacio Zúñiga reported that Opata cultural life included dances such as the *dagüinemaca* that re-created initial encounters between Spaniards and Indians; the *jojo*, which commemorated the arrival of Montezuma among the Aztec; and *taguaro*, a mock battle with Apache raiders accompanied by singing and rattles.[43] These dances emphasized reciprocity, created historical memory, and placed themselves in relation to others in their world.[44] Neither the Spaniards nor their ways of life were rejected; the dagüinemaca means, literally, "give to me and I shall give to you." Hispanic forms of music and dance did not completely replace indigenous forms of expression.

Mission Nuestra Señora de Loreto, the flagship of the Baja California missions, experienced changes similar to those at Cucurpe. Young boys learned the doctrine under Franciscan administration, perhaps through song, but the educational effort was not as extensive as during the Jesuit period, when both boys and girls were taught to read, write, and sing.[45] Inventories of the well-appointed mission, attended by Spanish and mestizo settlers and soldiers as well as indigenous families, listed fewer items related to music during Franciscan and Dominican administration.[46] During the Jesuit period, Loreto was known for its musicians. Reports from Jesuit visitor generals in 1729, 1744, and 1762 lavished praise on the choir and musicians, who "achieve a great harmony, and employ many chirimías."[47] Because a musical culture had flourished at Loreto, in 1773

---

[42] Ocaranza, *Los franciscanos*, 214-215. De la Torre demonstrates that the missions of this region physically deteriorated during this period, compounded by the continuing erosion of communal holdings. See "Conquering the Frontier," 188-197.

[43] Ignacio Zúñiga, *Rápida ojeada al estado de Sonora, dirigida y dedicada al Supremo Gobierno de la Nación* (Mexico City: Imprenta de Juan Ojeda, 1835), 4-7.

[44] De la Torre, "Conquering the Frontier," 271, argues that these rites "recreated historical memory, relations of reciprocity, and hope for a common future."

[45] On the Jesuit schools at Loreto, see Padre José Rotea, *Informe*, AGN, Historia, exp. 21, f. 194, and *Informe al Padre Visitador*, AGN, Historia, vol. 21, no. 15, f. 186 (1762). The Franciscans established a school for boys to teach them not only doctrine, but also how to make boats for pearling and fishing. BNAH, vol. 65, f. 230-231v, 243-246.

[46] The missions of Baja California also supplied religious ornaments to outfit the new missions in upper California. See Hackel, *Children of Coyote*, 148, and Crosby, *Antigua California*, 391.

[47] Crosby, *Antigua California*, 291 (José Echeverría, 1729); BINAH, vol. 68, f. 105 (1744); AGN, Historia, vol. 21, no. 15, f. 183v (*Informe al Padre Visitador*, 1762).

an old cupboard still contained several well-used stringed instruments—violin, harp, violón, guitar, and lyre, and the church contained a small organ and a clave.[48] Brief descriptions of liturgical books, such as missals, manuals in Castilian and Latin, as well as in the Yaqui language, bells, and a processional cross with its covering for Holy Week indicated that the church was still outfitted to publicly announce and celebrate the obligations of the liturgical year.[49] Yet in the late colonial period, it seems that Loreto lacked the organized, intentional musical culture present during the Jesuit period in Baja California and in the late colonial Alta California missions. Responsibility for music-making for recreation and religious celebrations shifted to musicians, both indigenous and non-Indian, in more informal settings.

Thus, musical activities continued in the centers with the most Hispanicized and settled populations of the northwestern frontier, even after the transition to Franciscan and Dominican administration. However, late colonial reports from the missions of northwestern New Spain do not contain vivid descriptions of musical performances or celebrations for special occasions like those in the documentary record before 1767. In smaller missions, evidence of musical activity tied to the missions is limited or completely absent. Mission Santa Rosalia Mulegé, which, under the direction of Jesuit Pedro María Nascimbén was well-known for its music, possessed only two broken bajones and three chirimías, used missals, and bells for celebrating mass in 1773.[50] As the political, social, and economic conditions of the northwestern frontier shifted during the late colonial period, the mission and its missionary often ceased to be the center of a community. Bells still pealed to guide daily activity, but perhaps, as de la Torre

---

[48] A clave is a keyboard instrument, either a clavichord, fortepiano, or a harpsichord in this context. See *New Grove Dictionary of Musical Instruments*, vol. I (London: Macmillan, 1985), 415.

[49] Padron de Yndios, Ynventario de la Iglesia, Sacristia, Utensilios de Cassa de esta Mission de Nra. Señora de Loreto, y su entrega, 1773, AGN, Misiones, vol. 12, exp. 10, f. 217-228.

[50] Of Nascimbén, Father Francisco Escalante said, "Further, touching on the point of music, I cannot do less than tell the great benefits and advantages created by Father Pedro, not only in this mission but rather in all those of this province, in that every day on rising, on retiring, after the morning rosary and the evening, even at times of work, there would be sung now litanies of Our Lady, now acts of contrition, now verses of Our Lord Jesus Christ and His Holy Mother, and of many saints, spreading light and being admired in whatever place encountered. A boat load of those who came to dive for pearls arrived at these missions and were captivated by the range of songs, most of them composed and taught by Father Pedro. Then Father Pedro arranged that these people learn some of the music and sing it." AGN, Jesuitas, vol 3, pt. 16, exp. 2. For the Franciscan inventory of 1773, see AGN, Misiones, vol. 12, exp. 10, f. 265-272. In this same expediente, inventories from Nuestra Señora de Guadalupe (f. 275), San Ignacio de Loyola Kadaacaman (f. 282), and San Josef del Cabo (f. 298v), Missions also list broken bells and instruments or harpsichords without strings.

has suggested for the Pimería Alta, native temastianes supplanted the Franciscans. They became associated with ceremonialism both within and outside the mission churches. In both areas, they functioned as ritual specialists—to instruct in Christian doctrine (inside the church) and to preserve Pima dances and ceremonialism (outside the church).[51] Musical activities might have similarly been de-centered from the missions themselves and into the wider communities. Based on the documentary evidence, similar trends in mission music and ornaments occurred in the long-established Franciscan missions farther north and east over the same period.

MUSIC AND DANCE IN LATE COLONIAL COAHUILA, TEXAS, AND NEW MEXICO

Franciscans had worked among the indigenous populations of northeast and north central New Spain from the late sixteenth century onward, but by the late colonial period, religious and civil officials expressed frustrations about the apparent lack of progress in religious conversions. The population of this region had dramatically changed from the early colonial period, with the non-indigenous population, including *gente de razón* (so-called because they were Hispanicized) and mixed-race peasants known as *"hijos de la misión."* Meanwhile, some semi-nomadic groups entered mission communities for the first time. Like in the northwest, racial categories were fluid, and referred as much to an individual's standing in a community and level of acculturation than to ethnicity.[52] The changing demographics of these areas were reflected in the music and dance of these regions in the period from 1767 to 1810. Dances and pageantry held to commemorate significant occasions contained Spanish, Mexican, and indigenous elements and participants, bringing communities together to reinforce religious and military goals. These expressions of popular religion were encouraged by the Franciscans, even when they ran counter to the desires of Bourbon reformers within church and state. In the northeastern frontier, where new converts frequently abandoned missions and refused to offer their children for doctrinal instruction, the friars could not afford to be dogmatic about ensuring orthodox religious devotions or learned routines and behavior.

[51] De la Torre, "Conquering the Frontier," 277.
[52] On racial categories in the late colonial period, see Cheryl English Martin, *Governance and Society in Colonial Mexico: Chihuahua in the Eighteenth Century* (Stanford, CA: Stanford University Press, 1996), 6-7; Laura A. Lewis, *Hall of Mirrors: Power, Witchcraft, and Caste in Colonial Mexico* (Durham, NC: Duke University Press, 2003); and Deeds, *Defiance and Deference*.

Cultural change and accommodation were prevalent in late colonial Coahuila and Texas. Instead of serving as permanent homes for large populations of Indians, late colonial missions of the northeastern frontier were meeting sites for extended family networks, only some of whom lived in nuclear families in or around the missions.[53] Migration and intermarriage between groups of Pames, Cocos, Pajalates, Xarames, and other small ethnic groups facilitated the spread of Coahuilteco as a regional language, and the friars used time-tested methods of offering food, clothing, and tools to Indians in exchange for their appearance at worship, doctrinal instruction, and confession.[54] Most of the region's indigenous population lived outside the missions, but maintained ties and occasionally reconnected with families living on mission lands. A manual written by Fray Bartholomé García facilitated the friars' work among both mission and non-mission Indians.[55]

García's manual also reflected the ongoing battle for cultural hegemony, largely fought in the arena of music and dance. While hearing confessions from Indians, friars were reminded to ask whether neophytes had eaten the flesh of others, ingested peyote, or danced mitotes.[56] Franciscans struggled with indigenous ritual practices among the new populations they sought to convert in the late colonial period. Fray Diego Jiménez observed that in area around the San Lorenzo de la Santa Cruz and Nuestra Señora de Candelaria del Cañon Missions, built on the Nueces River after entreaties by the Lipan Apaches, shamans performed rites including prophecy, sacrificial dances, healings, and blessings upon dwellings.[57] When the Marquis de Rubí toured the region in 1767, Candelaria was abandoned and San Lorenzo claimed no residents except

[53] The missions at San Antonio had the most permanent settlers of the region, particularly Mission San José y San Miguel de Aguayo. But in 1786, only two of the forty-six families at San José were descendants of the Indians for whom the mission had been built. See Fray José García, "Estado actual de las misiones de la provincia de Coahuila y Rio Grande de la misma jurisdicción," San Bernardo de Rio Grande, March 3, 1786, BL, M-M, 431:3.

[54] Of the eleven married couples listed on the register of Mission San Antonio de Valero in 1772, eight were mixed marriages. See Barr, *Peace Came in the Form of a Woman*, 156.

[55] Bartholomé García, *Manual para administrar los santos sacramentos de penitencia, eucharistia, extrema-unción y matrimonio* (Mexico City: Imprenta de los herederos de Dona Maria de Rivera, 1760).

[56] Ibid.; Barr, *Peace Came in the Form of a Woman*, 150-151.

[57] Diego Jiménez, Relación de las Misiones de la Presidencia del Río Grande del Norte, 1764, AGN, Historia, vol. 29, pt. 1, f. 182-183.

[58] Comanche attacks and the lack of interest in doctrinal instruction or residence at the mission by the Lipan Apaches prevented friars from doing much more than performing baptisms and caring for the dying. See Vito Alessio Robles, ed., *Demonstración del vastísimo obispado de la Nueva Vizcaya, 1765* (Mexico City: Editorial Porrúa, 1937); and Nicolás de Lafora, *Relación del Viaje que hizo a los Presidios Internos situados en la Frontera de la América septentrional perteneciente al Rey de España* (Mexico City: Editorial Pedro Robredo, 1939), 187.

its friars.⁵⁸ Increasing hostilities among Apaches, Comanches, and Spanish troops plagued the region and precipitated the military reorganization in the Reglamento of 1772.⁵⁹ These hostilities coincided with an increase in the mention of mitotes in the documentary records, in references to both mission and gentile Indians.⁶⁰ Even those most acculturated, the converted population of the San José Mission in San Antonio, who spoke Spanish, played the harp, violin, and guitar, and recited the rosary and other prayers, "go off to the woods to dance . . . with the pagans whenever the priests are not watching. Great care is taken to keep them from this wicked practice, and whenever they are found guilty of it, they are punished severely."⁶¹ To combat the strong attraction of these dances, Franciscans used corporal punishment. They also encouraged those who were inclined to music to learn to play stringed instruments, even drums, and promoted Spanish dances.⁶² Others only permitted mitotes and "good dances" within the mission community, "when no superstition, no question of celebrating an enemy's death, nor any sinful motive are present . . . because among the Indians it is the same as the fandango among the Spaniards."⁶³

Increasing exposure to Spanish and mestizo settlers, who rented land from the missions or acquired land as the missions were secularized, was one method of conveying outward signs of Christianity and Hispanic life: wearing appropriate dress, marching in processions, praying the rosary, singing devotional songs, dancing appropriately, and responding to the sound of the bell. Witnessing and following these outward signs of Christianity did not signify conversion to Catholicism, however. In 1778, Fray Juan Agustín Morfi found that the resident neophytes at San Juan Bautista, Coahuila, "confess, they receive the sacraments,

---

⁵⁹ These royal orders, based on Rubí's report, called for a pullback of all presidios to the Río Grande del Norte, with the exception of those that protected the Spanish settlements in New Mexico and San Antonio. For a brief summary of the Reglamento's effect, see David Weber, *The Spanish Frontier in North America* (New Haven, CT: Yale University Press, 1992), 215-222. During the late eighteenth century, the presidio, instead of the mission, became the dominant Spanish institution of the frontier.

⁶⁰ On mitotes among Coahuiltecan speakers, see William W. Newcombe, *The Indians of Texas: From Prehistoric to Modern Times* (Austin: University of Texas Press, 1972), 53-55.

⁶¹ Diario del R.P.G. Gaspar José de Solís en su visita a las Misiones de Texas, 1768, microfilm copy, OSMHRC, Archivo del Colegio de Zacatecas, reel 1, fr. 179-181.

⁶² Carlos Castañeda, *History of Texas, 1673–1779* (Albuquerque: University of New Mexico Press, 1935), Part I, 97-98; Benoist and Flores, *Guidelines*, 12.

⁶³ Ibid., 36-37. Indians at San José in San Antonio received Fray Juan Agustín Morfi with a "danza buena" on January 1, 1778, when he arrived at the mission. Fray Juan Agustín de Morfi, *Diario y Derrotero*, eds. Eugenio del Hoyo and Malcolm D. McLean (Monterrey: Instituto Tecnológico y de Estudios Superiores de Monterrey, 1967), 99.

they fast, they hear Mass, attend prayers and daily explanations of the doctrine through an interpreter; but all this is as commanded and with a grade of piety so weak as hardly to be recognizable as Christianity."[64] In addition, employing soldiers and settlers as models of Christian life to new converts was not always a desirable strategy. Gambling, drinking, and playing games were only slightly less offensive than the nighttime idolatrous dances practiced by the non-Christians. Vecinos and soldiers could engage with neophytes in appropriate recreation, which could provide a venue to release pressures of regimented life, but they had to be closely monitored.[65] Some settlers only desired "to take from the Indians all that they can, gambling with them, trading trifles for clothing and other utensils, and practicing evil."[66] Farther west, Fray Pedro Font was appalled at a fandango held at Presidio San Miguel de Horcasitas in which "a very bold widow who came with the [Anza] expedition sang some verses, which were not at all nice, applauded and cheered by all the crowd."[67] Mission Indians interacted with soldiers and settlers frequently during this period, as they traded, engaged in labor, defended territory, and worshiped. The most structured interactions occurred during principal feasts of the church year.

Indigenous converts were active participants in the demonstrations of faith hosted by the larger settlements in the region on Christmas or Holy Week and Easter. The ranchers, farmers, and soldiers who populated the small communities in Coahuila and Texas, and the more well-established towns of Nuevo México, punctuated their years with the celebrations of the church year. The friars encouraged these communal fiestas; beginning with the life of St. Francis, Franciscans showed special devotion to the images of Christ in the nativity and the passion. Dancing and *misa de gallo*, or mass in the very early hours of Christmas morning, had been a part of Nativity celebrations in New Spain from

---

[64] Descripción del Territorio del Real Presidio de San Juan Bautista del Río Grande del Norte, y su Jurisdicción, Año de 1778, AGN, Historia, vol. 29, ff. 185-204.

[65] In Nuevo México, Texas, and Coahuila, most settlers appear to have been of mixed race, although over time they sometimes "passed" in baptismal and marriage records as *españoles*. See, for instance, Oakah L. Jones, Jr., *Los Paisanos: Spanish Settlers on the Northern Frontier of New Spain* (Norman: University of Oklahoma Press, 1979); and Jesús F. de la Teja, *San Antonio de Béxar: A Community on New Spain's Northern Frontier* (Albuquerque, University of New Mexico Press, 1995).

[66] Benoist and Flores, *Guidelines*, 42-43. See also Daniel Matson and Bernard L. Fontana, *Friar Bringas Reports to the King: Methods of Indoctrination on the Frontier of New Spain, 1796–1797* (Tucson: University of Arizona Press, 1977), 122.

[67] Herbert Eugene Bolton, trans. and ed., *Font's Complete Diary: A Chronicle of the Founding of San Francisco*, Anza's California Expeditions, vol. IV (Berkeley: University of California Press, 1930), 34-35..

the time of Fray Pedro de Gante, and they were also part of Spanish folk Catholicism.[68] Celebrations for Christmas and Easter also included elements that were closely tied to indigenous practices in the regions. Coahuiltecan speakers in central Texas traditionally gathered during the winter months when food was scarce for large communal dances that served as trading fairs. Their dances lasted for days, were particularly loud at night, and involved large numbers of participants, often around a bonfire.[69] Franciscans at the San Antonio missions encouraged similar gatherings under their watchful eyes and tied to the Christian calendar. On Christmas at the San Juan Capistrano Mission, nocturnal dances were held to celebrate the Nativity. A mission inventory from 1772 included indigenous ankle rattles, *cascabeles*, and masks used specifically for these Christmas dances.[70] On Christmas Eve at Mission Purísima Concepcíon in the same area, Indians danced the matachines at the entrance of the friar's house "as long as the missionary allows it." The next day, they danced at the governor's house and the presidio.[71] The traveling dancers provided entertainment for secular and religious crowds alike, and each audience surely received a different message as they watched, just as the meaning must have been vastly different for the dancers themselves. These dances incorporated both European and indigenous meanings, dress, instruments, rhythms, and dance patterns, as they reinvented the history of cultural encounters between Europeans and Indians.[72]

Like the dances of Christmas in the central Texas missions, the mournful practices of the week preceding Easter were particularly resonant in the New Mexican pueblos. Holy Week was celebrated in New Mexico and the later Alta California missions with solemn processions. In 1776, Fray Francisco Atanasio Domínguez reported on a Via Crucis, or stations of the cross, procession. The faithful at Abiquiu, including mestizos and settlers, made stops at altars where Fray Sebastián Fernández recited prayers, on their way to a stop designated "Calvary." After the final prayers, procession participants remained after nightfall to engage in self flagellation as a form of penance, joining themselves with Christ

---

[68] See Kristin Dutcher Mann, "Christmas in the Missions of Northern New Spain," *The Americas* 66:3 (January 2010), 331-351.

[69] Diario del R.P.G. Gaspar José de Solís . . . , 1768. Solís's description of the mitotes of the Indians around Mission Rosario is particularly vivid. See microfilm copy, OSMHRC, Archivo del Colegio de Zacatecas, reel 1, fr. 164-168.

[70] 1772 inventory, San Juan Capistrano Mission, San Antonio, OSMHRC, Archivo del Colegio de Querétaro, reel 10, fr. 4271-4294.

[71] Benoist and Flores, *Guidelines*, 34-35.

[72] These themes will be considered further in Chapter 7.

by re-enacting and participating in his pain.[73] There is no evidence that Franciscans attempted to limit the practices of the *penitentes*, despite the instructions of the Fourth Mexican Provincial Council, which associated them with *castas*, drunkenness, and barbarity.[74] By the early nineteenth century, mixed-race members of the Brotherhood of Our Father Jesus of Nazareth provided spiritual leadership and visual re-creations of Christian stories in northern New Mexico.[75]

Wealthy Spanish settlers sometimes sponsored religious festivities on their own, after receiving permission from the government and assistance from the clergy. Prominent citizens petitioned the governor of New Mexico to collect alms to augment a celebration on the feast day of Nuestra Señora del Rosario. This Marian image was an important patroness in campaigns against the Comanche and their allies, and had also been a key image in the Reconquista of 1692–1693. The feast of Nuestra Señora del Rosario, described in 1776 by Fray Atanasio Domínguez, included vespers, a procession, mass, and public praying of the rosary in the streets of Santa Fe. Presidial soldiers attended and offered volleys of gunfire. Dances, including the moros y cristianos pantomime, *comedias*, and bull fighting entertained the large crowd of Indians, *genízaros*, mestizos, and Spaniards.[76] The music and dance of this communal celebration reflect and illustrate the impact of the social and political realities of life on the northern frontier of New Spain during the late colonial period. Soldiers, citizens, and Indians engaged in religious and civil activities that brought the community together to articulate themselves as followers of Our Lady, in opposition to a common enemy: the rapidly growing horse culture of the Plains that threatened the livelihood of frontier settlements. This brief description of the elaborate festivities in Nuevo México's capital contrasts starkly with the limited references to music inside the mission settlements of the colony.[77]

---

[73] Adams and Chavez, eds., *The Missions of New Mexico, 1776*, 124. Self-flagellation was one type of personal religious devotion that recalled Christ's agony and involved the mystical union of lay member and Christ. See Larkin, "Liturgy, Devotion, and Religious Reform," 496-499.

[74] *Concilio provincial mexicano IV. Celebrado en la ciudad de México el año de 1771* (Queretaro: Imprenta de la Escuela de Artes, 1898), 161. See Larkin, "Liturgy, Devotion, and Religious Reform," 510-511.

[75] Martina Will de Chaparro, *Death and Dying in New Mexico* (Albuquerque: University of New Mexico Press, 2007), 7, 27, 62, 77.

[76] Descripción del Nuevo México hecha por fray Francisco Atanasio Domínguez, 1777, BNM, leg. 10, n. 43. Copy at Center for Southwest Research, Zimmerman Library, University of New Mexico, Albuquerque, NM, f. 382-383. On the moros y cristianos dances in Spain and New Mexico, see Tomás Lozano, *Cantemos al Alba: Origins of Songs, Sounds, and Liturgical Drama of Hispanic New Mexico* (Albuquerque: University of New Mexico Press, 2007), chapter 6.

[77] Similarly, settlers in San Antonio celebrated the feast days of the Immaculate Conception and the Virgin of Guadalupe with religious services, bullfights, games, and dances, sponsored by

The late colonial missions of Coahuila, Texas, and New Mexico differed significantly from their Franciscan and Jesuit counterparts in the earlier part of the century. After the reorganization of the northern frontier, most missions were administered by a single friar, or by friars with multiple communities to administer, and Indians freely entered and left the missions at will.[78] Any troops stationed nearby were dedicated to protecting settlements from Apache and Comanche raids, and were not used to compel Indians to work and attend instruction. Missionaries relied on the cooperation of Hispanicized converts to enforce rules, teach and translate doctrine, encourage attendance at worship services, and teach music. Because he could not adequately train musicians, Fray Manuel Silva suggested that the Indian carpenter Joseph, who played the violin for mass, might be used to train converts in San Antonio to play instruments and sing in the choir.[79] Shorthanded and with little success in maintaining a regimented schedule, Fray Joseph Cárdenas, missionary at Espíritu Santo de Zúñiga in Texas, reasoned as follows:

> *It has appeared to me for now not to impose . . . the obligation of attending that [Sunday] Mass, since they are not much inclined to do it. . . . It has been necessary to proceed with much care, not obligating all of them to the continuous task of instruction outside of the assigned times, because I might push the thing that might make many of them leave. . . . Although many attend the teaching of the doctrine (but not all), some, as soon as the bell is rung, jump the wall and go away, and some stay in their houses. Even though I have tried ways to oblige them to attend, I have not been able to succeed with all of them. . . . Nor can I force them with rigor, so as not to lose all of them to flight because it can be justly feared that they are very warlike Indians, and wicked.*[80]

Cárdenas blamed the deterioration of the Texas missions on a lack of ornaments and properties, a lack of aid from the troops, and the enormous number of tasks that befell individual missionaries trying to maintain missions alone. While clearly frustrated with the political changes affecting the region in the late colonial period, he offered music as evidence of some progress in conversion.

---

the *cabildo* during the month of December. See Jesús F. de la Teja and John Wheat, "Béxar: Profile of a Tejano Community, 1820–1832," *Southwestern Historical Quarterly* 89 (July 1985), 20-21.

[78] On the decline in numbers of Franciscans ministering in late colonial New Mexico, see Will de Chaparro, *Death and Dying in New Mexico*, 5; and Jim Norris, *After "The Year Eighty": The Demise of Franciscan Power in Spanish New Mexico* (Albuquerque: University of New Mexico Press, 2000).

[79] Silva to the Governor, June 29, 1793, Béxar Archives, San Antonio, TX.

[80] Report on the conditions of Mission Espíritu Santo de Zúñiga, February 27, 1783, microfilm, OSMHRC, Archivo del Colegio de Zacatecas, reel 3, fr. 3497-3499.

On days when Fray Joseph did not say mass, some women still gathered in the church to sing the alabado before retiring to their houses.[81] Fray Juan Agustín Morfi's remarks about the Indian families at the San Bernardo and San Juan Bautista Missions in Coahuila were similar. Despite their lack of progress in conversion and acculturation to Spanish norms, women at San Juan Bautista beautifully sang the alabado and *gozos* in honor of Our Lady of Guadalupe, while the *indias* at San Bernardo divinely sang the alabado and the Salve Regina.[82] Compared to the *mexicano* cantor in San Antonio de Béxar, whose singing sounded like howling, these women certainly impressed Morfi with their outward devotion expressed through song.[83]

Music such as the alabado, and the use of guitars and violins for mass, were recorded in northeastern frontier mission reports of the late eighteenth century, but references to trained choirs, or musical performances other than dances on special occasions are limited. A few liturgical books containing music survive from the late colonial period in New Mexico, but it is unknown whether mission Indians from this period read European notation, or sang European-style polyphony or figured chant.[84] The reports of missionaries and visitors to the mature missions of New Mexico, Texas, and Coahuila do not center around music or ceremonies; they are instead concerned with the mission communities' limited resources, statistics concerning crops, herds, and populations, and concerns about Apache and Comanche raids.

On the whole, the friars in the northeastern and northwestern frontiers showed little of their former zeal in directly challenging practices they saw as incompatible with Christianity: idolatry, desertion, polygamy, and dancing. Instead they saw themselves engaged in a war with gentile Indians, and to a lesser extent, the Spanish authorities, for the souls of those who lived near the missions. They engaged in battle by using the tools that had served them well for years: repetition of religious routines, devotional songs to emphasize doctrine and moral behavior, and rations of food, clothing, and tools. They

---

[81] Ibid., fr. 3499.

[82] Fray Juan Agustín de Morfi, March 22, 1777, *Diario y Derrotero*, eds. Eugenio del Hoyo and Malcolm D. McLean (Monterrey: Instituto Tecnológico y de Estudios Superiores de Monterrey, 1967), 92.

[83] Ibid., January 1, 1778, San Antonio de Béxar y Villa de San Fernando, 99.

[84] I am grateful to John Koegel for pointing out the liturgical books in the Museum of New Mexico Collections at the Museum of International Folk Art in Santa Fe. *Missae, et orationes propriae sanctorum in Missali Romano* (Mexico City: José Jáuregui, 1772), from an unknown mission church, was used at Santa Cruz de la Cañada in the late nineteenth century, as was *Missae propriae sanctorum trium ordinum fratrum minorum* (Antwerp: Plantin, 1731), a missal for the Franciscan Third Order. See Koegel, "Spanish and French Mission Music," 18-20.

added secular and religious dances, tolerated indigenous dances deemed "appropriate," and encouraged other physical reinforcements of Christian doctrine in processions and re-creations of Christ's life. Friars such as Joseph Cárdenas were willing to overlook non-attendance at worship, or dances that previously would have been considered profane, in order to keep recent converts on their side.

New Mission Fields

Despite the troubles of staffing the existing missions of northern New Spain, a few Franciscans continued to push for expansion among previously uncongregated peoples. They received approval when the expansion aligned with the goals of the Crown—to protect areas from foreign encroachment or to establish overland supply routes. As the Marqués de Rubí's plans were implemented, Spanish officials sought alliances with former enemies, and focused on bringing about peace where possible through trade and the distribution of gifts.[85] At the same time, soldiers focused on mounting punitive expeditions against threats from those outside of the mission-town complexes who refused alliances. Franciscans such as Francisco Garcés and Francisco Antonio de Barbastro of the apostolic college at Querétaro ardently believed that religious transformation and Hispanicization could create loyal Christian subjects, even among the most resistant indigenous groups. The Querétaran and Zacatecan fathers asked permission to begin new missions in the Pimería Alta and the Gulf Coast during the late eighteenth century. These mission communities contained outward signs of progress in the form of cultivated fields and church buildings.[86] Friars attempted to impose the discipline of daily life used by the most prominent member of the colleges, Antonio Margil de Jesús, earlier in the century, and similar to the regime used by Jesuits prior to their expulsion. In all, however, they were largely unsuccessful in achieving conversion, with only one resident priest, little military protection, and insufficient material support.[87] Indians dictated the terms of

---

[85] See Max L. Moorhead, *The Presidio: Bastion of the Spanish Borderlands* (Norman: University of Oklahoma Press, 1975), 58-61.

[86] The most impressive construction project took place at San Xavier del Bac in the northern Pimería Alta, begun in the 1780s.

[87] Defining conversion is very problematic. Once baptized, converted Indians were expected to reside near the mission, confess each year, and receive communion, as well as participate regularly in mass and the festivals of the liturgical year. There is little evidence that the new Franciscan missions of the late colonial period accomplished these things with newly reduced populations. On the question of what constitutes conversion, see de la Torre, "Conquering the Frontier," xxv, as

their interactions with the missionaries, sometimes showing favor and interest in settled, Christian life. More often, however, they used the missions and their resources for food and protection, and even rejected them outright through revolt. Franciscans believed that religious routines and ornaments might keep neophytes committed to mission life, and they regularly petitioned the Crown for musical instruments. When members of the apostolic college at Zacatecas asked to found Mission Nuestra Señora del Refugio for the Carancaguases on the south Texas coast in 1794, they had to solicit alms in the Villa of Saltillo to outfit the mission with necessary ornaments, including a missal and bells.[88] By 1796, the mission's inventory also included a violin, guitar, and bandola[89] for the music of the church, as well as replacement strings for the instruments.[90] But the bands of Carancaguases and Malaguitas targeted for conversion at Refugio and nearby Nuestra Señora del Rosario refused to settle permanently in either mission, traveling back and forth between the missions and the coast, where they collected food and salvaged shipwrecks.[91]

In lieu of strong military support, and in the face of such monumental work, Franciscans turned to music as a potential pacification tool where force of arms had not been successful. For example, in the late colonial period, the clergy attempted to incorporate instruction in music as a way of enticing the Seri to accept mission life. Small numbers of Seri had first agreed to mission life in the late seventeenth century at Nuestra Señora del Pópulo. Bohemian Jesuit Adam Gilg reported that the bands who congregated around the mission were attracted to the ceremonies and routines of daily life.[92] In 1707, Miguel Almanza requested chirimías and a bajón, among other items, for use at Pópulo.[93] Almanza might have hoped that these wind instruments would reinforce the Seri association of aerophones, which made sound when blown, with

---

well as Merrill, "Conversion and Colonialism." For an excellent description of incomplete religious conversion in the Andes, see Nicholas Griffiths, *The Cross and the Serpent: Religious Repression and Resurgence in Colonial Peru* (Norman: University of Oklahoma Press, 1995).

[88] Unsigned Memoria, November 6, 1794, AGI, Guadalajara, 104, photostat (CAT), 12.4.

[89] A flat-bodied stringed instrument in the guitar family. See Malena Kuss, *Music in Latin America and the Caribbean: An Encyclopedic History* (Austin: University of Texas Press, 2004), 148.

[90] "Inventory of Mission Refugio, September 8, 1796. Microfilm, OSMHRC, ACZ, reel 1, fr. 49-50.

[91] Kathleen Gilmore, "The Indians of Mission Rosario: From the Books and from the Ground," in David Hurst Thomas, ed., *Columbian Consequences*, vol. 1 (Washington, DC: Smithsonian Institution Press, 1989), 235.

[92] DiPeso and Matson, "The Seri Indians in 1692," 33-56.

[93] Francisco Zambrano, *Diccionario bio-bibliográfica de la Compañía de Jesús en México* (Mexico City: Editorial Tradición, 1977), vol. 15, 73-74.

the breath and sound of the spirit world.

Only a small percentage of Seri groups chose to settle on mission lands and adopt Hispanic work and worship. Many others raided the missions of the San Miguel River area for food. By mid-century, the presidio at Pitic, originally established to keep peace among the Seri, was moved to Pópulo, and its lands, which had been farmed by Seri converts, were distributed among Hispanic and mestizo settlers. Spanish military officials answered Seri protests with the capture and deportation of women. Enraged, many Seri bands joined with disaffected Pima, and attacked Spaniards from their strongholds in the Cerro Prieto and Tiburón Island for the next quarter-century.[94] Pressures of famine and war brought about the piecemeal surrender of extended family groups, and by 1772, Franciscans again attempted to congregate the Seri at Carrizal near the coast. The mission was destroyed and Fray Crisostomo Gil de Bernabé killed in less than a year. During the next twenty-five years, Franciscans lamented the poor state of the missions in the lower Pimería, where only one broken bell aided in bringing the faithful to worship.[95] In the last decades of the eighteenth century, officials again tried to settle groups of Seri near Pitic, with the aid of the military. Although some moved to San José de Pimas and Pitic, a smallpox epidemic decimated the population in the early 1780s.[96] Frustrated at the lack of success among this population, Bishop of Sonora José Joaquín Granados wrote to the viceroy requesting musical instruments for the settlement at Pitic in 1791. Unusual about this series of letters was the reasons given by Granados for this request, emphatically repeated over a period of eight months, until the viceroy supplied the instruments. The bishop reasoned that musical instruments would "quiet the discontent" of the unruly Seris and forge a "perpetual peace and incorruptible society" in the Hispanic-style mission communities to which the Seris were to be reduced.[97] Granados recognized the impact of the introduction of musical instruments among the Tarahumara, Yaqui, and Pimas, and he hoped that, once introduced in Seri territory, violins, harps, chirimías, and bajones might entice the resistant Seri to adopt a Hispanic, Christian lifestyle. In the previous century, bands of Seris who settled at Pópulo had reportedly embraced the rituals introduced by Jesuit fathers.

---

[94] Spicer, *Cycles of Conquest*, 105-112.
[95] Fray Miguel Josef Arenibar to viceroy, October 1773, AGN, Provincias Internas, vol. 232, f. 69-70.
[96] Comandante Felipe de Neve to the King, 1781, AGI, Guadalajara, 267.
[97] Granados to viceroy Jacobo Ugarte y Loyola, March 31, 1791, AGN, Provincias Internas, vol. 235; Ugarte y Loyola to Granados, November 17, 1791, AGN, Provincias Internas, vol. 235, microfilm copy, DRSW.

Once again, however, Seris would only accept missionization on their own terms. In the early 1790s, they came to Pitic when they needed food and protection from Apache raiders, completely abandoning the complex several times. Eventually, more began to appear at Pitic and Banamichi for mass. Fathers Roque de Medina and Ignacio Zavalos instructed boys and girls under fourteen, and the missionaries requested additional ornaments and livestock. By 1798, Father Juan Felipe Martínez enthusiastically reported that they could recite the rudiments of the faith, and the older boys assisted at mass, having forgotten their depraved customs.[98] In 1799 there were over two hundred Indians residing in the community.[99] Ultimately the mission enterprise failed and many Seris found more benefit in raiding Spanish ranches and settlements. While the use of music, religious ornaments, tools, and livestock to attract semi-nomadic groups to relocate to permanent mission communities was sometimes successful, these strategies had most impact in a climate rocked by instability and devastated by ecological change and disease, and among children. The Seris selectively incorporated small elements of Hispanic life, including musical instruments, but these alone could not forge the perpetual peace and incorruptible society sought by Granados and the Franciscans.[100]

The cultivation of these new mission fields sometimes produced disastrous results for the missionaries. In 1781, four priests, including Father Francisco Garcés, were killed at the Colorado River, along with colonists recruited from Sonora, while trying to compel the Yumas to accept Christianity and a sedentary agricultural life. Fray Francisco entered the Colegio de Santa Cruz de Querétaro in 1763, and was particularly diligent in his service in the choir. In 1768, he was assigned to San Xavier del Bac, and over the next twelve years he traveled, sometimes alone, into territory populated by the Yumas.[101] Viceroy Antonio de Bucareli made arrangements for the founding of mission-presidio-town complexes on the Gila and Colorado Rivers that could be protected by

---

[98] Fr. Juan Felipe Martinez to Virrey Conde de Revillagigedo, February 15, 1798, AGN, Provincias Internas, vol. 235, f. 237-238.

[99] Censo de población de las misiones franciscanas de Sonora, 1799, in Ocaranza, *Los franciscanos*, 181.

[100] Early twentieth-century ethnographies of the Seri include descriptions of a unique violin that "sings" the songs, instead of providing a distinct instrumental accompaniment. There is some question about whether the Seri violin is descended from the Spanish violin, or whether it is entirely indigenous. See Diane D. Dittemore, "A Comparison of Seri and Western Apache One-Stringed Fiddles" (Master's thesis, University of Denver, 1978); and Thomas Vennum, Jr., "Locating the Seri on the Musical Map of Indian North America," *Journal of the Southwest* 34:2 (Autumn 2000).

[101] Juan Domingo Arricivita, *Crónica seráfica y apostolica del Colegio de Propaganda Fide de la Santa Cruz de Querétaro* (Mexico City: N.p., 1792).

presidios at Buena Vista and Horcasitas. Soldiers and their families colonized the new settlements and helped to acculturate the Indians gathered there, participating in doctrinal instruction and the songs, gestures, and routines of the liturgy. Garcés was performing mass at Concepción on July 17, 1781, when Yumans attacked the church and houses. Another group assaulted the settlement at Bicuñer immediately preceding mass. All of the men were killed, and women and children were enslaved. The next day Garcés and Barraneche were beaten to death even though some of the new converts pled for their lives to be spared. In this case, Yumans understood the daily routine that Franciscans attempted to impose as they resettled potential converts. Ultimately, instead of embracing the restructuring of their lives, they ruptured the liturgical routine by attacking during mass.

While Spaniards attempted to missionize the remaining nomadic peoples of the northwestern frontier and the Gulf Coast, they undertook different efforts in the vast interior of the North American continent. The territory of Louisiana passed into Spanish administration in 1763. Documents from this region indicate that colonial officials in the new northeastern frontier were chiefly concerned with defending the territory against foreign threats, regulating the lucrative fur trade, and establishing diplomatic relations with indigenous groups. Jesuits had worked to convert and educate Indians in this area, particularly in their mission at Kaskaskia, but they did not undertake a large-scale missionary presence like that of northern New Spain during the same period.[102] Once under Spanish rule, extending Christianity in the form of the Franciscan missions to this region was not a priority, nor a practical possibility. Even the expeditions mounted to explore territory and secure Indian alliances made provisions for liturgical obligations, but lacked the elaborate religious and musical components of seventeenth- and early eighteenth-century entradas in east Texas.[103] Instead, military and diplomatic forays, often undertaken by

---

[102] See Christopher Bilodeau, "They Honor Our Lord among Themselves in Their Own Way": Colonial Christianity and the Illinois Indians, *American Indian Quarterly* 25:3 (Summer 2001), 352-377; Koegel, "Rural Musical Life in the French Villages in Upper Louisiana," 13-25; and Mary Borgia Palm, *Jesuit Missions in the Illinois Country, 1673–1763* (Cleveland, OH: Sisters of Notre Dame, 1933). French Capuchins had also evangelized the area around Natchitoches and the Red River in the first half of the eighteenth century.

[103] Antonio de Ulloa's instructions to Captain Francisco Rui for an expedition to the mouth of the Missouri River called for a chaplain to accompany the group. On Sundays and feast days, members of the expedition were to participate in mass and the chanting of the Salve Regina, for the purpose of "trying so far as Christian customs are concerned to preserve all those of Spain." Antonio de Ulloa, March 14, 1767, in Louis Houck, ed. and trans., *The Spanish Régime in Missouri*, vol. I (Chicago: R.R. Donnelley & Sons, 1909), 3.

Frenchmen who had pledged loyalty to the Spanish Crown, were not accompanied by regular clergymen.[104] Armed with gifts of medals, flags, and staffs, which recognized an indigenous leader's authority, they negotiated truces, facilitated trade, and reported to Spanish officials about the large Indian populations of the Plains.[105] Official instructions for holding councils with the Indians designated the protocols for gift-giving, but these rituals did not involve music or dance.[106]

The Power of Music in the Alta California Missions

In contrast to the waning religious activities farther east in the last part of the eighteenth century, the Alta California chain of missions was supported by the interests of the Bourbon state, which resulted in a robust military presence, two resident Franciscans per mission, and sufficient material goods.[107] The Franciscan missionary project in Alta California focused on control over the indigenous populations through punitive expeditions, cultural hegemony, and a combination of force and persuasion. While they still had to be flexible in their imposition of rules, Franciscans did not hesitate to mete out corporal punishment or refer offenders to the presidios for discipline when they felt it was warranted, even when physical punishment was on the decline in other areas of New Spain.[108] In their final mission chain, Franciscans relied on the lessons they had

---

[104] Athanase de Mézieres and Vial were two of the most important Frenchmen who traveled extensively in upper and lower Louisiana. Mézieres later became governor of the region, while Pedro Vial traveled extensively among Santa Fe, San Antonio, and Missouri.

[105] John C. Ewers, "Symbols of Chiefly Authority in Spanish Louisiana," in John Francis McDermott, ed., *The Spanish in the Mississippi Valley, 1762–1804* (Urbana: University of Illinois Press, 1974), 272-284. Small metal bells were among the items used as presents for meetings with indigenous groups. See, for example, Francisco Cruzat, "Effects Delivered to Don Manuel Perez, 1787," in Louis Houck, ed. and trans., *The Spanish Régime in Missouri*, vol. I (Chicago: R.R. Donnelley & Sons, 1909), 269.

[106] Francisco Rui, "Instructions for Holding Council with the Indians, March 6, 1769," in Houck, *The Spanish Régime in Missouri*, vol. I, 46-48.

[107] Excepting the first few years during which the initial missions were founded, all missions except for San Diego were self-supporting and contributed food and livestock to the presidios and small settlements of *gente de razón*. See Hackel, *Children of Coyote*, chapter 3.

[108] On the flexibility of Franciscan labor demands and indigenous desires to leave the missions, see Hackel, *Children of Coyote*, 287. On corporal punishment in California, see Hackel, 332-338. Manuals for the administration of Indian communities, and in particular Alonso de la Peña Montenegro's *Itinerario para Párrocos de indios,* recommended corporal punishment of Indians and compared priests to fathers punishing their children. See William B. Taylor, *Magistrates of the Sacred: Priests and Parishioners in Eighteenth-Century Mexico* (Stanford, CA: Stanford University Press, 1996), 215-221.

learned in the preceding centuries of evangelization among the native peoples of the Americas. Like in other areas, they were aided by disease and ecological change, which vastly changed the context in which Indians chose whether to seek life within the mission communities.[109]

Franciscans exercised greater political authority in Alta California, as Jesuits had earlier in the century in Baja California. The Crown depended on the mission chain to claim territory, seal the northern frontier and its silver mines, and provide for settlers and presidios in the province. In contrast, other contemporaries engaged in a larger number of disputes with military and civil authorities in New Mexico, Texas, Sonora, and Chihuahua. The mostly Spanish-born friars, members of the College of San Fernando, used music to impart doctrine, facilitate cultural and linguistic change, and structure daily life.[110] Officials endorsed the use of music in the new missions of Alta California and the Philippines in an 1808 instruction manual written by Fray Mariano Lopez Pimentel, as "one of the most effective methods for congregating the Indians, taming them, civilizing them, and catechizing them, without the expense of troops, nor arms, and without danger to the lives of Hispanic youth, and with utility to the church, and the Crown."[111]

From the start, religious song and gestures were an integral part of establishing these communities. José de Galvez spearheaded the planning for the entrada, or formal entrance, into Nueva California from the south. By the summer of 1769, the bedraggled land and sea expeditions, reduced by nearly one-quarter due to disease and hunger, congregated to officially claim the territory for the King. On the dual feast day of the Holy Cross and Nuestra Señora de Carmel, Fray Junípero Serra sang a high mass under a shelter that served as

---

[109] The Alta California missions have received more scholarly attention than most regions, due to the availability of ample documentation stretching well into the nineteenth century. See Hackel, *Children of Coyote*; Sandos, *Converting California*; Albert L. Hurtado, *Intimate Frontiers: Sex, Gender, and Culture in Old California* (Albuquerque: University of New Mexico Press, 1999); Lisabeth Haas, *Conquests and Historical Identities in California, 1736–1936* (Berkeley: University of California Press, 1995); and Robert Jackson and Edward Castillo, *Indians, Franciscans, and Spanish Colonization: The Impact of the Mission System on California Indians* (Albuquerque: University of New Mexico Press, 1995).

[110] On the background of the Alta California Franciscans, see Hackel, *Children of Coyote*, 53. Music in the Alta California missions has been well-documented by musicologists and historians. See, in particular, Sandos, *Converting California*, chapter 9, and the many works of musicologist William Summers, as well as Craig Russell, *From Serra to Sancho: Music and Pageantry in the California Missions* (London: Oxford University Press, 2009).

[111] *Reglamento de enseñanza civil, política, y cristiana, para los hijos de los infieles de la Asia y América: en su colegio de misiones, de estas lenguas de los infieles asisaticos y americanos*, section entitled "De la música y artes liberales," AGI, México, 2735, exp. 2.

a temporary church.[112] Serra followed a similar routine, involving soldiers and converted Baja Californianos, in each mission he founded. Music not only sanctified the space claimed by entradas, it also likely provided familiarity and comfort to expedition members. Fray Pedro Font, chaplain of Juan Bautista de Anza's expedition to the San Francisco Bay, was an accomplished musician and copied plainchant choirbooks.[113] When Spaniards entered northern California, like in rituals farther south, the music of the Te Deum Laudamus and the chanting of mass accompanied the ceremonies, which were occasionally witnessed by local indigenous groups.[114] The natives of California also used music in their initial encounters with the newcomers. In late September 1769, a group of Chalon Indians in the Monterey region did not trade with the Spaniards, but instead threw handfuls of earth into the air and played on a pipe.[115]

Just as in other mission fields, Franciscans incorporated the music of the mass and the Divine Office as soon as possible, for it attracted neophytes to worship and demonstrated the solemnity and majesty that they hoped to convey. Devotional songs were used to help teach doctrine and encourage attendance at instruction, as well as in processions. By the early nineteenth century, a strong musical culture flourished in the new Alta California missions, beginning with the work of Padre Junípero Serra, who taught Indians at Mission San Carlos to sing the alabado and devotional songs up until his death in 1784. Missions Santa Barbara, Santa Clara de Asís, San José, and San Antonio de Padua boasted European-style choirs, orchestras, and large music books, some of which remain extant.[116] Indians were taught to produce copies of musical manuscripts at a

---

[112] Serra to Francisco Palóu, July 8, 1769, San Diego, in Antoine Tibesar, ed. and trans., *Writings of Junípero Serra I* (Washington, DC: Academy of American Franciscan History, 1966), 141-142.

[113] Catalan Friar Pedro Font (1738–1781) was a member of the apostolic college in Querétaro, a missionary in Sonora, and possibly choirmaster for the college in the 1760s. See Koegel, "Spanish and French Mission Music," 26.

[114] This topic will be more thoroughly discussed in Chapter 7. Fray Pedro Font described the rituals associated with claiming possession in his diary of the expedition. See Bolton, *Font's Complete Diary*.

[115] Fray Juan Crespí, September 29, 1769, in Alan K. Brown, ed. and trans., *A Description of Distant Roads* (San Diego, CA: San Diego State University Press, 2001), 533-535.

[116] Summers, "New and Little Known Sources of Hispanic Music from California," 17-18, lists music books in the archives of Santa Clara University and the Archdiocese of Los Angeles, while his article "Music of the California Missions: An Inventory and Discussion of Selected Printed Music Books Used in Hispanic California, 1769–1836," *Soundings: Collections of the University Library* IX (June 1977), 23-24, lists music books in the collections of the Santa Barbara Mission Archive, the University of California, Santa Barbara Library, Bancroft Library, and Stanford Museum. A complete listing of California mission music sources appears in Russell, *From Serra to Sancho*.

scriptorium founded by Padre Narciso Durán at Mission San José.[117] These large books contain music intended for use by a choir, with plainsong, as well as more than two hundred polyphonic works for the ordinary of the mass, Divine Office, and devotional songs for use in processions, prayers, or teaching. A mass for orchestra and double choir by noted composer Ignacio Jerusalem was found in mission archives and might have been performed in the region.[118] Surviving music from the Alta California missions includes a wide variety of compositional styles, from the plainchant of missals, to two-voice polyphony in parallel thirds, to settings of the mass for double choir and orchestra. The musical repertoire indicates that the Franciscans who served in this region were intentional in their use of music, having copied scores and reproduced manuscripts for use in more than one mission.[119]

Song was part of the daily routine and weekly worship services. Raymundo Carillo informed his superiors that neophytes at Missions Santa Barbara, San Gabriel, San Luis Obispo, San Antonio, and San Carlos attended catechism instruction in Spanish in the mornings. The Franciscans celebrated high mass each Sunday, and on other days, those gathered prayed the rosary and sang the Salve Regina or an alabado.[120] At Mission San Juan Bautista, friars

> *induced the children to sing the prayers as they learnt them. The Our Father was accordingly sung in one loud tone without variation until the end of a sentence, when a stop or inflexion was made. Sometimes this prayer would be sung after one of the psalm tones. Thus in a few days boys and girls would be able to sing the prayer aloud and together.... The Hail Mary was acquired in the same way, with the difference that it was sung after a Spanish melody, and then became the most popu-*

---

[117] Summers, "New and Little-Known Sources of Hispanic Music from California," 16.

[118] William Summers, "Spanish Music in California: A Reassessment," in *Report of the Twelfth Congress of the International Musicological Society, Berkeley, 1977* (Kassel: American Musicological Society, 1981), 371-379. Summers concludes that Mission Santa Barbara was the only church that was known to have possessed both the personnel and the pipe organ; the mass might also have been performed at Missions San José or Santa Clara without an organ. Jerusalem died in Mexico City in 1769. See also George Harshbarger, "The Mass in G by Ignacio Jerusalem and Its Place in the California Mission Music Repertory" (DMA diss., University of Washington, 1985).

[119] See William J. Summers, "The *Misa Viscaina:* An Eighteenth-Century Musical Odyssey," in David Crawford, ed., *Encomium Musicae: Essays in Memory of Robert Snow* (Hillsdale, NY: Pendragon Press, 2002), 131, and "Recently Recovered Manuscript Sources of Sacred Polyphonic Music from Spanish California," *Ars Musica Denver* (1) 1994: 13-30.

[120] Raymundo Carrillo to P.P. José Joaquín de Arrillaga, Santa Barbara, October 13, 1802, AGN, Provincias Internas, 216, exp. 1, f. 107-107v.

lar hymn. It could be heard at the homes, at work, at the play of the children, on the march, and above all in the church and in the popular processions. . . . Singing formed part of the morning and evening devotions, and during the Sunday Masses and afternoon exercises.[121]

At San Juan Bautista, one of the most extensive programs of music education was put in place. Melody was used as a mnemonic device and in the liturgical services, and song was part of the daily routine of the neophytes. The mission also included a school for musicians to augment worship elsewhere in the region. Dance and instrumental melodies enlivened daily life and celebrations of Christian and Indian fiestas, even when the padres tried to prevent them, or meted out punishment for dances in which men and women, and gentiles and Christians freely mixed.[122]

In Alta California, music was used to rejoice at the birth of a new church building, the baptism of a new convert, or the matrimonial union of two Christians. In San Diego, a band from Mission San Luis Rey provided dancing music to celebrate the wedding of Mariano Guadalupe Vallejo.[123] The close presence of soldiers and settlers brought secular music into the mission communities, including marches, fandangos, and waltzes.[124] Couples near the presidios sang and stomped their feet rhythmically as they danced the *barrego*, accompanied by soldiers on violin and guitar.[125] Fray Estevan Tápis stated that "it was the custom of the young Indians at Mission Santa Barbara to gather in the kitchen-court or the main mission patio and dance, sing, or play games to the accompaniment of music."[126] Multiple examples of music for the Office of

---

[121] Zephyrin Englehardt, *Mission San Juan Bautista: A School of Church Music* (Santa Barbara, CA: Mission Santa Barbara, 1931), 21-22.

[122] Raymundo Carillo to José Joaquín Arrillaga, October 13, 1802, Santa Barbara, AGN, Provincias Internas, 216, exp. 1, f. 111-111v.

[123] Mariano Guadalupe Vallejo, "Historical and Personal Memoirs Relating to Alta California," trans. Earl R. Hewitt (Berkley: University of California Bancroft Library, 1875), 191. I have not found reference to music and dance in earlier mission weddings, but there is some evidence that indigenous cultures used dance to celebrate heterosexual unions. Jesuit Juan Nentvig described an Opata "marriage" ceremony in the mid-eighteenth century that involved singing and dancing.

[124] The presence of secular music is particularly well-documented during the later colonial period in Franciscan missions in Alta California. See, for example, Maynard Geiger and Clement Meighan,eds. and trans., *As the Padres Saw Them: California Indian Life and Customs as Reported by the Franciscan Missionaries, 1813–1815* (Santa Barbara, CA: Santa Barbara Mission Library, 1976), 36-37.

[125] Georg Heinrich von Langsdorff, *Remarks and Observations on a Voyage around the World from 1803 to 1807*, ed. Richard Pierce and trans. Victoria Moessner, vol. 2 (Kingston, Ontario: Limestone Press, 1993), 107.

[126] Cited in Ray and Engbeck, *Gloria Dei*, 16.

the Dead also lamented the incomprehensible number of deaths in the region.¹²⁷

The music of the California missions aided in the acculturation of those who sang and heard it, even when the meanings of Christian concepts may have been less than clear.¹²⁸ Doctrinal instruction occurred in Spanish, but also in native languages, because of the immense number of indigenous languages and dialects friars had to master. Songs, particularly those in Spanish, and images reinforced the concepts recited as part of the simplified catechism. Common themes of these songs and devotional paintings reflected some of the most persistent struggles of the missionaries. Emphasis on the devotion of Mary and Joseph to each other and God, and to the Christ Child belied the friars' difficulty in enforcing monogamous marriage and Hispanic gender roles.¹²⁹ One version of the alabado, a religious song of praise sung widely in California and Texas, began with a verse dedicated to the divine sacrament, and continued as follows:

> *Y la limpia Concepción*
> *De la Reina de los cielos,*
> *Que, quedando Vírgen pura,*
> *Es madre del Verbo eterno.*
>
> *Y el glorioso San José*
> *Electo por dios inmenso*
> *Para padre estimativo*
> *De su hijo, Divino Verbo.*¹³⁰

---

¹²⁷ See Grayson Wagstaff, "Franciscan Mission Music in California, c. 1770–1830: Chant, Liturgical, and Polyphonic Traditions," *Journal of the Royal Musical Association* 126:1 (2001), 54-82, esp. 61-66.

¹²⁸ Mariano Guadalupe Vallejo, for example, recounted a visit with neophytes after doctrinal instruction through song. Although Vallejo said that the Indians did not understand the meaning of the words, they sang it nonetheless. Alvarado, "History of California, 1769–1847," vol. I, BL, 41. On music and acculturation, see Sandos, *Converting California*, chapter 9.

¹²⁹ On marriage and gender in the California missions, see Albert L. Hurtado, *Intimate Frontiers: Sex, Gender and Culture in Old California* (Albuquerque: University of New Mexico Press, 1999); Antonia Castañeda, "Engendering the History of Alta California, 1769–1848: Gender, Sexuality, and the Family," in Ramón A. Gutiérrez and Richard J. Orsi, eds., *Contested Eden: California before the Gold Rush* (Berkeley: University of California Press, 1998), 230-259; Hackel, *Children of Coyote*, 182-227.

¹³⁰ Angel de los Dolores Tiscareño, *El colegio de Guadalupe: lo ideal* (Zacatecas, México: Lejeune, Flores, and Company, 1905), 113, at UTNLB, attributes this version of the alabado to Fr. Antonio Margil de Jesús. Fr. Owen da Silva, in *Mission Music of California* (Los Angeles: Dawson's Book Shop, 1941), 112-113, translates this stanza as follows: "Honor Joseph, spouse of Mary/ The chosen of God in heaven/ To his paternal arms so tender/ The Incarnate Son was

Mary and Joseph as parents, specially chosen by God to bear and raise Jesus, figure prominently in these stanzas. By singing this song daily, Indians were reminded not only of Christian doctrine, but also of their duty to follow the example of the Virgin Mary and San José. The texts of other devotional songs, written by the padres for singing outside of formal worship services, transmit similar messages. In a section of the choirbook compiled by Estevan Tápis, missionary at San Juan Bautista, entitled "Letras al Patriarca San José," a song in four-part polyphony characterizes Joseph as the "dulce esposo de María, y de Jesús fiel tutor."[131] Song and the twice-daily recitation of doctrine reinforced the concepts presented to new converts through paintings and devotional prints, specially ordered by Junípero Serra and subsequent missionaries to aid in their explanations of Catholicism.[132] The amount of money spent on artwork, vestments, religious ornaments, and musical instruments was astounding, but these items were surely essential to try to convey Christian concepts and impress upon new converts the majesty of the Church.[133] We have no way of knowing how Indians understood the songs and artwork, but the colors, rhythms, melodies, and symbols of these cultural items were impressive enough that supply requests from the missionaries consistently included them.[134]

---

given." The first three stanzas of Margil's alabado are the same as the lyrics given in da Silva's collection of religious songs from Alta California. Alabados will be discussed further in Chapter 6.

[131] The translated lyrics are as follows: "Sweet husband of Mary, and faithful teacher of Jesus." *Dulce esposo de María* is found in the Tápis choirbook, Mission San Juan Bautista.

[132] For Serra's requests for religious art, see Serra to Verger, June 20, 1771, Monterrey; and Serra to Pangua, August 22, 1775, Monterrey, in Tibesar, ed. and trans., *Writings of Junípero Serra*, vol. I, 221, and vol. II, 319. On religious art in the California missions, see Hackel, *Children of Coyote*, 161-170. For religious art throughout New Spain, see Robert H. Jackson, "Visual Representations of Religious Conversion in Spanish American Missions," *Boletín* 25:2 (2008), 5-30; and Susan Anderson Kerry, "Preliminary Observations on Angels in Religious Art in New Spain," *Boletín* 25:2 (2008), 31-48.

[133] Hackel, "Beyond Words: Liturgical Art and Music in the California Missions" (paper presented at *Encuentros*/Encounters 2009: Music of the California Missions, University of California at Riverside, January 30, 2009), 9-13. Between 1809 and 1811, 380 pesos were spent on musical instruments, a sizeable investment in guitars, flutes, horns, and strings for violins, guitars, and bass instruments; but an even larger investment, over 6,000 pesos, was invested in paintings of saints and those depicting the Via Crucis, or stations of the cross.

[134] See Hackel, *Children of Coyote*, 148-152, for an overview of devotional art and its use in the Alta California missions. On religious artwork in New Spain, see Clara Bargellini, "Stars in the Sea of the Church: The Indian in Eighteenth-Century New Spanish Painting," in Joseph J. Rishel and Suzanne Stratton, eds., *The Arts in Latin America, 1492-1820* (New Haven, CT: Yale University Press, 2006); and Gauvin Bailey, *Art on the Jesuit Missions in Asia and Latin America, 1542-1773* (Toronto: University of Toronto Press, 1999).

Marian devotion was particularly encouraged in statuary, paintings, and small devotional prints, as well as hymns and songs, perhaps because a female deity resonated with indigenous spiritual beliefs. Gabrielinos revered a virginal woman named Chukit, who was impregnated by the son of God via lightning. At Mission San Carlos, specific Indian women were revered, and given gifts, because they controlled rain and the growth of plants.[135] For the Franciscans, Mary was an important role model of selflessness and unquestioning devotion to God, as well as chaste and pure behavior that missionaries wanted to cultivate in their churches. Missionaries' annual reports and responses to circular letters indicated that singing the Salve Regina and praying the Hail Mary was part of the daily routine of mission life throughout Alta California. Some young women learned to sing the Salve Regina not only in Spanish or Latin, but also in their own language.[136] Mary was lauded as "toda hermosa/ tan linda y tan bella que al sol a ventajas," a refuge and a queen for the heavens and the earth.[137] The words of the simple devotions and antiphons like the Salve Regina were repetitive, set to easily memorized tunes, sometimes with four-part harmony, and were sung by men and women alike.

Devotional songs such as the alabado, *cántico de alba* (morning hymn), and *gozos* (praise songs) also facilitated linguistic acculturation. Their verses, set to memorable tunes with rhythmic structures suitable for walking in procession, combined to involve physical and auditory engagement with doctrine, Spanish grammar, and common words, and the tasks and sights of the indigenous world. A song praising Mary's Immaculate Conception, a concept foreign to indigenous beliefs, likely resonated more with the Costanoans at San José in its references to the sun, dawn, and nocturnal animals, than in its explanation of Mary's conception without sin.[138] The sky and moon, and the pain and sorrow of death

---

[135] Hackel, *Children of Coyote*, 165; and Edward D. Castillo, "Gender Status Decline, Resistance, and Accommodation among Female Neophytes in Missions of California: A San Gabriel Case Study," *American Indian Culture and Research Journal* 18 (1994), 70.

[136] Fray Vicente de Santa María and Fray José Señán to Governor Don Diego de Borica, October 21, 1800, San Buenaventura, AGN, Provincias Internas, vol. 216, exp. 1, f. 93v.

[137] "Eres toda hermosa," Durán choirbook, Mission San José, 1813, BL, MSS C-C 59.

[138] The third verse of this gozo is "Como la culpa traydora a el sol no pudo mirar/ tampoco pudo aguardar que amaneciese la aurora/ pues huye de vos Señora este nocturno animal/ Sois concebida Maria sin pecado original." Craig H. Russell's translation is as follows: "As the traitorous temptor couldn't look upon the sun/ neither could it endure the coming of dawn, so this nocturnal animal flees from you, Lady/ You were conceived, Mary, without original sin." The next verse compares Mary to the wheat for sacramental bread, another analogy that would have resonated with daily life at the missions, where women ground the wheat, mixed the dough, and baked the bread that would become the host. The song is located in the Durán choirbooks from Mission San José.

are also themes expressed in songs composed by friars for use in teaching and devotion, ones that reinforced Spanish vocabulary used in the mission communities, but also related Christian concepts to the physical and emotional aspects of indigenous life.[139] Tying Christian concepts the natural world opened the door for indigenous acceptance of doctrine on their own terms, and made Christian beliefs not only more accessible, but also more appealing.

Thus, the musical landscape of Alta California reflected the complicated, sometimes dual, identities of many of its residents. Mission residents could match the tone, inflection, melodies, and rhythms of European-style plainchant and polyphony, often even learning the music by ear. Conforming to European performance and musical standards, however, did not mean that native Californians abandoned their native musical practices. Like in other areas of the Spanish empire, archaeological and documentary evidence points to an abundance of native dances and the use of some indigenous instruments within mission communities, often by the same native peoples who beautifully performed Catholic religious music.[140] Dance was an important expression of identity in pre-Hispanic California, performed during communal celebrations and as part of the rituals of the Spanish Church and Crown. Most friars in Alta California permitted indigenous dances to continue during the day within the mission complex. Perhaps friars felt conflicted about punishments for and prohibitions on dancing after the whipping of several baptized Indians at Mission San Diego for participating in a dance contributed to a massive revolt that killed a friar and destroyed church buildings in 1775.[141] Governor Pedro Fages prohibited baptized Indians from organizing and performing dances in 1782. Not all friars enforced this edict, and those who did were once again reminded of the importance of ritual life to Indians when Gabrielinos revolted in 1785 in response to prohibitions on ceremonial dances and activities.[142]

Vivid descriptions of indigenous dances by early nineteenth-century visitors to California provide a glimpse of native cultural practices. Fray Pedro asked Indians at Mission San José to adorn themselves and dance for visitors from a Russian expedition in 1806. Georg Heinrich von Langsdorff, the expedition's doctor, observed that "jumping rhythmically and making all kinds of body

---

[139] See, for example, the lyrics to "Eres toda hermosa" in the Durán choirbook, BL, MSS C-C 59.

[140] Larry Warkentin, "The Rise and Fall of Indian Music in the California Missions," *Latin American Music Review* 2:1 (Spring–Summer 1981), 49.

[141] Maynard Geiger, *The Life and Times of Fray Junípero Serra* (Washington, DC: Academy of American Franciscan History, 1959), vol. II, 60.

[142] Hackel, *Children of Coyote*, 263-264.

movements and grimaces, they portray scenes from war and domestic life with the help of bows and arrows and with feathers held in their hands and on their heads. Their music consists of singing and clicking produced by a little stick split on one end."[143] Men and women danced separately, but near each other, and the dances continued throughout the day. At Mission San Carlos, Raymundo Carillo reported that the native population adorned themselves with body paint and regalia and danced for Spanish visitors.[144] The constant movement of new groups into the missions from the countryside, and the frequent interactions of missionized and gentile populations, meant that indigenous cultural practices and goods moved into the settlements and rancherías surrounding the missions. This fluidity allowed for the constant re-creation of culture. Indigenous dances might be altered to fit new contexts, and rattles or drums added to European instruments that accompanied a religious procession. The Esselen at Mission San Carlos Borromeo used the appointment of Pablo Vicente Solá as governor of California in Monterey as an occasion to dance.

> *They arranged themselves across the front of the plaza, and at the sound of the chirimías, the leaders began first to leap about, wearing on their heads their great feather headdresses, and drawing their legs up together. . . . Finally they stopped in front of the governor and made as if to discharge arrows at him. . . . When they had surrendered their weapons, the musicians of all the tribes, . . . played Indian dances and all the Indian men and women took part in the dancing which concluded the native celebration.*[145]

In this instance, the Esselen people likely seized the opportunity to engage in native cultural traditions by tying them to a Spanish civil ceremony, although their interpretation of the meaning of the dance might have been entirely different from Spanish perceptions. Even the dedication of a church building contained elements of both Christian and autochthonous sacred music. When workers placed the last tile on the roof of Mission San Buenaventura, Chumash men reportedly danced the Blackbird Dance following a mass of thanksgiving in the church.[146]

---

[143] von Langsdorff, *Remarks and Observations on a Voyage around the World*, 114-117. See also Hackel, *Children of Coyote*, 80-81.

[144] Raymundo Carillo, October 13, 1802, AGN, Provincias Internas, 216, exp. 1, ff. 104v-111, cited in Hackel, *Children of Coyote*, 80.

[145] Juan Alvarado, "History of California, 1769–1847," vol. I, 54, BL.

[146] Fernando Librado, John Peabody Harrington, and Travis Hudson, *The Eye of the Flute: Chumash Traditional History and Ritual* (Santa Barbara, CA: Santa Barbara Museum of Natural History, 1977), 84-85.

Evidence of the tension between Christianized and native identities is also evident in the actions of musicians in the California missions. Jayme, a leader of the choir at Mission Santa Barbara, was one of the first to participate in the Chumash Revolt in 1824, but also one of the first to seek pardon and return to mission life.[147] Choir members often came from the groups of young boys baptized and raised in the mission, and some, such as Hortulano at Mission Santa Clara, served as godparents at multiple baptisms of mission recruits.[148] They were among the most acculturated mission residents, with the most exposure to Spanish and Latin, and frequent contact with the missionaries, as well as participation in the daily rituals of the church.[149] Still, some choir members, likely those who came to the mission as adults, were ritual specialists in their indigenous communities as well, and in the space outside mission walls, they donned costumes and body paint and danced in elaborate performances that communicated indigenous history and group identity.[150]

The complex, textured musical culture of Alta California harkened back to the complexity of the mission music of the sixteenth- and early seventeenth-century Jesuit missions in the north, and the Franciscan missions in New Mexico, where missionaries commanded greater resources and exercised more complete control over neophytes.[151] In comparison with other regions of the Spanish empire, California mission music most closely resembled the type of music performed in the cathedrals of frontier dioceses, such as Durango and Guadalajara. Far from being isolated, rural outposts insulated from European and creole

---

[147] Daniel Krieger, "Music and the Psychology of Colonization in the California Missions" (paper presented at *Encuentros*/Encounters, 2009, University of California-Riverside, January 30, 2009).

[148] James Sandos, "Professionalization of Music: Choristers at Mission Santa Clara, 1800-1845, and the Mystery of Mission San Antonio" *Diagonal* 2009, http://cilam.ucr.edu/diagonal/issues/2009.html, data from Early California Population Project database, Huntington Library, San Marino, CA.

[149] For more on this theme, see Sandos, *Converting California*, chapter 9. The social standing of musicians will also be discussed further in Chapter 7.

[150] Hackel, *Children of Coyote*, 81, 138. Coexistence of indigenous and Hispanicized practices can also be seen in the arrangements by which Indians at many of the California missions were granted *paseos* to leave the mission and collect foods such as sardines, birds, and other native subsistence foods, even when mission harvests were bountiful. See Hackel, *Children of Coyote*, 84-88.

[151] Theodore Göllner and William Summers have argued that the music and notation of the California mission manuscripts are an extension of sixteenth-century musical practices that persisted in rural areas of Spain until the late eighteenth century, then were brought to Alta California by the Spanish Franciscans during the late eighteenth and early nineteenth centuries. See Göllner, "Two Polyphonic Passions from California's Mission Period," *Anuario: Yearbook for the Institute for Inter-American Musical Research* 6 (1970), 67-76; and Summers, "Music of the California Missions," 19-20.

trends in religious music, the musicians and chapelmasters in frontier areas, like several of the friars in California, were well acquainted with trends in religious music.[152] In the cathedral of the Diocese of Durango, for example, in 1761 the *maestro de capilla* had fifty-seven choirbooks from which to select music to augment worship. Some were illuminated, and the books contained processional and devotional songs, as well as music for the Divine Office and settings of the mass for different times of the church year. They contained parts for different voices, and some contained music for the use of the cathedral's instrumentalists—among them organists, violinists, and horn players.[153] An inventory of the choral library in 1788 listed music books printed in Spain, Venice, and Rome, and the liturgy of the Divine Office, particularly matins and lauds, was sung.[154] The musical culture of the Durango cathedral shifted in the period after 1784, when the performance of elaborate Italianate-style compositions declined and the musical chapel was disbanded. In this period, Durango cathedral music was similar to that of California missions such as San José, Santa Clara, San Antonio, Santa Barbara, and Santa Inés, with instrumentalists, singers, and hand-copied scores of music for the mass and office, and even propers for the feast days of the church year.[155]

What accounts for the differences between the religious music of the Alta California missions and that of late colonial missions elsewhere in northern New Spain? A primary reason for the expansive music performed in Alta California was the talent and interest of the inhabitants of the region. Without exception, the friars reported that neophytes were eager to learn, and achieved proficiency quickly, in European-style music. Neophytes at Mission San Juan Bautista learned to play instruments easily, and even adapted indigenous melodies to the new instruments.[156] Father José Señán remarked that the Chumash at Mission San Buenaventura were "very much inclined to sing and to play any kind of string or wind instruments."[157] California Indians, like others throughout the northern frontier, possessed a strong tradition of using song, instruments, and

---

[152] See Drew M. Davies, "The Italianized Frontier: Music at Durango Cathedral, Español Culture, and the Aesthetics of Devotion in Eighteenth-Century New Spain" (PhD diss., University of Chicago, 2006).

[153] AGI, Guadalajara, 556, f. 15.

[154] AGI, Guadalajara, 550, f. 201-206, 89.

[155] On Durango cathedral music and musicians during the eighteenth and early nineteenth centuries, see Davies, "The Italianized Frontier," chapter 2. For a complete listing of extant musical books and manuscripts in Alta California, see Russell, *From Serra to Sancho*.

[156] Felipe Arroyo de Cuesta, *Preguntas y Respuestas*, May 1, 1814, in Geiger and Meighan, *As the Padres Saw Them*, 135-136.

[157] Ibid., 134.

dance to re-create their history, invoke the blessings and protection of the spiritual world, and communicate values and beliefs. Visitors immediately observed the importance of ritual song and dance to *californio* culture. Georg Heinrich von Langsdorff wrote that "among all their pastimes they prefer dancing," and described the skill with which Indians near Mission San Francisco made costumes. While at Mission San José, he noted that coastal and interior groups, who rarely interacted socially, performed dances that conveyed their histories and reenacted a battle.[158] In 1824, French visitor Duhaut-Chilly described a dance-drama in which "the harmony was plaintive and wild, moving the nerves, rather than the soul. While the actors rested, a horn was blown to drive away evil spirits."[159]

Another explanation of Alta California's rich musical culture lies in the resources, both human and material, available to the Fernandino friars. The California missions were prosperous enough to sustain two friars per mission, which meant that one of the resident friars might devote more attention to music instead of being consumed with other matters of daily administration. Although the guidelines of apostolic colleges stated that at least two friars should work in each mission community, the Tarahumara missions, those in Sonora, and the New Mexican Franciscan missions were generally staffed by only one resident friar in the late eighteenth and early nineteenth centuries, and some friars were even responsible for several communities simultaneously.[160] With two resident friars in Alta California, missions received two annual allowances of 350 to 400 pesos, which could be spent to procure goods in Mexico City. Missionaries augmented their annual allowance by selling surplus crops and material goods manufactured in mission communities to presidios and settlers, as well as through the fur trade.[161] These resources, human and material, allowed missionaries to purchase musical instruments, strings, books, and even uniforms.

The missionaries themselves also differed from those elsewhere in the northern frontier. The friars of the Colegio de San Fernando, located in Mexico City, administered the province of Alta California. In contrast to those who served in

---

[158] von Langsdorff, *Remarks and Observations on a Voyage around the World*, vol. 2, 96-97, 116.

[159] Nellie van der Grift Sanchez, *Spanish Arcadia* (San Francisco: Powell Publishing Company, 1929), 310, cited in Larry Warkentin, "The Rise and Fall of Indian Music in the California Missions," *Latin American Music Review* 2(1) (Spring–Summer 1981), 48.

[160] On the declining numbers of Franciscans in the late colonial period, see Morales, "Mexican Society and the Franciscan Order in a Period of Transition, 1748–1859," 331-335.

[161] Hackel, *Children of Coyote*, 274-276, 278.

the other missions of northern New Spain, missionaries to Alta California were mostly Spanish-born. Most lived in Mexico City, the capital of the viceroyalty and site of a rich musical culture, for a period of time before making the journey north. Prominent among the Fernandinos serving in Alta California was Juan Bautista Sancho, who had directed choirs in Spain before coming to the Americas. Between 1795 and 1796, Sancho copied music from the Convento de San Francisco in Palma, Mallorca, for his use in the new mission field.[162] Another musician and former choirmaster in Zaragoza, Florencio Ibáñez, demonstrated great skill in his notation and illumination of five large choir books from Mission San Antonio de Padua.[163] Ibáñez was also credited with introducing a *pastorela*, performed at Christmas throughout the Alta California missions.[164] Popular in rural Spain, pastorelas involved the community in a re-creation of the shepherds' visit to the Holy Family following the birth of Christ. The pastorela included both solo and choral passages, and in other areas of New Spain these dramas drew large crowds to the church on Christmas Eve.[165]

Another composer and musician, Fray Narciso Durán, was most remarkable for a system of musical notation that he employed to more easily teach Costanoans at Mission San José. He produced a large choirbook for use with orchestras and singers that compiled music used elsewhere in California and New Spain.[166] Durán firmly believed that music was a key component of religious conversion, and he was diligent in the training of neophytes. All musicians under

---

[162] J.B. Sancho was one of fifteen natives of Mallorca who ministered in Alta California between 1769 and 1850. On Sancho, see William J. Summers, "Sancho: Alta California's Preeminent Musician," in *Juan Bautista Sancho, Pioneer Composer of California* (Palma, Mallorca: Universitat de les Illes Balears, 2007), and "Music of the California Missions: An Inventory and Discussion of Selected Printed Music Books Used in Hispanic California, 1769–1836," 16.

[163] Maynard Geiger, *Franciscan Missionaries in Hispanic California* (San Marino, CA: Huntington Library, 1969), 124-125.

[164] Summers, "Sancho: Alta California's Preeminent Musician," 69, 76-77.

[165] Documents also mention the performance of pastorelas in the Jesuit Tepehuan missions of Nueva Vizcaya in the early seventeenth century. See cartas anuas of 1608, 1611, and 1613, in González Rodríguez, *Crónicas de la Sierra Tarahumara*, 148, 160-165, 174-175. On medieval extraliturgical music associated with Christmas, see Richard H. Hoppin, *Medieval Music* (London: W.W. Norton, 1978), 52-53, 172; and Gustave Reese, *Music in the Renaissance*, rev. ed. (New York: W.W. Norton and Company, 1959), 491. On the pastorela in California, see Margaret Cayward, "The Pastorela, a Christmas Play of Mission-Era California" (paper given at *Encuentros*/Encounters, University of California at Riverside, January 30, 2009); and Mann, "Christmas in the Missions of Northern New Spain," 331-351.

[166] Selections of Durán's choirbook were published by da Silva as *Mission Music of California*. Durán appears to have copied the *Misa Viscaina*, likely the work of Basque Friar Martin de Crucelaegui, of the San Fernando college to Alta California, transliterating it into the simplified notation style of his choirbook. See "The *Misa Viscaina*," 131, 134-137.

Durán's tutelage were required to learn instrumental and vocal music, and he recommended the use of a single chant melody for each proper of the mass for use on Sundays. All music for high mass was to be accompanied by an orchestra.[167] Alfred Robinson described a feast day in which Durán's choir performed:

> *The music was well executed for it had been practiced daily for more than two months under the particular supervision of Father Narciso Durán. The number of musicians was about thirty; the instruments performed upon were violins, flutes, trumpets and drums; and so acute was the ear of the priest that he would detect a wrong note on the part of either instantly, and chide the erring performer.*[168]

Fray Narciso's musical talents, combined with his belief in the power of song to convey doctrine and enforce Christian values and beliefs, cultivated a rich musical culture at Mission San José, made possible by his simplification of musical notation and by numerous rehearsals.

One of the last Franciscans to minister in Alta California was also an ethnographer. Missionary at San Juan Bautista from 1808 to 1833, and afterward at the northern mission of San Miguel Arcángel, Felipe Arroyo de la Cuesta preserved both indigenous language and music. He transcribed melodies sung by the Mutsun into musical notation.[169] Following a tradition of employing familiar tunes to teach doctrine, Fray Felipe wrote his own music for use in evangelization. These settings of simple hymn tunes contained texts in Spanish, as well as in the Mutsun dialect. Fray Felipe reused a small book unfinished by a scribe to write out plainsong and two-part masses and songs for use by the choir at San Miguel after Mexican Independence.[170]

Not every Alta California mission boasted trained choirs and expert instrumentalists, because not all Franciscans in the region had extensive musical training. Fernando Martín and José Sánchez commented that the Ipai and Tipai at Mission San Diego had been supplied with instruments, and "they would become proficient if they had someone to teach them."[171] Indigenous talent was not enough to drive a mission's musical program; a friar dedicated and able to

---

[167] The prologue to Durán's choirbook is translated in da Silva, *Mission Music of California*, 29-33.

[168] Alfred Robinson, *Life in California* (New York: Da Capo Press, [1846] 1969), 124.

[169] Victoria Lindsey Levine, ed., *Writing American Indian Music: Historic Transcriptions, Notations, and Arrangements* (Middleton, WI: Published for the American Musicological Society by A-R Editions, 2002); and Robert Stevenson, "Written Sources for Indian Music until 1882," *Ethnomusicology* 17 (1973), 6-14.

[170] Summers, "New and Little-Known Sources of Hispanic Music from California," 23.

[171] Preguntas y Respuestas, December 23, 1814, in Geiger and Meighan, *As the Padres Saw Them*, 133.

teach music, including performance technique and instrumental accompaniment, was also necessary.

Other accomplished singers and instrumentalists, such as Fray Antonio Margil de Jesús and Jesuit fathers Juan María de Salvatierra and Pedro Nascimbén, had evangelized elsewhere in the northern frontier using music. But nowhere else in northern New Spain had there been such a systematic and cooperative effort, led by a cluster of expert musicians, to teach music, train choirs and orchestras, and even produce musical manuscripts for performance elsewhere. With the resources and talent, Franciscans in California left fragments of an incredibly rich musical repertoire, performed by indigenous peoples who had long made music part of their daily lives.

Song, Dance, and the End of the Colonial Mission Era

In the nineteenth century, only a few new missions were established near Indian population centers in remote areas. The Dominicans founded two more missions in Baja California, and Franciscans attempted to congregate and missionize remaining nomadic peoples in Texas, the Pimería Alta, and Nuevo Santander. Existing missions during the late colonial period were gradually secularized, their ornaments and communicants transferred to the care of diocesan clergy, and the land distributed among settlers. From 1810–1821, the Spanish Crown was in turmoil and paid scant attention to the missions. Revolutionary activity in the north led to a halt in supplies, such as musical instruments, shipped from Mexico City. Those in the most impoverished areas continued as missions into the Mexican national period, as more colonists moved into the regions. The patriarchal system of mission hierarchy did not match new republican ideals, and strict control of mission communities declined everywhere except in Alta California. Mission lands were sold to colonists or parceled out to mission inhabitants, and the remaining mission churches decreed to transfer to diocesan control in 1833.[172] Secularization must have affected the musical cultures of mission communities to a degree, but evidence suggests that music-making for both Catholic and native ceremonies continued after the friars departed. Newspaper accounts in Alta California reported on performances of ensembles with mission ties well into the 1900s, and many manuscripts from these missions are still extant in library collections.[173] The work of folklorists and

---

[172] Peveril Meigs, *The Dominican Mission Frontier of Lower California* (Berkeley: University of California Press, 1935), 155-156.

[173] Russell, *From Serra to Sancho*, 399-415.

ethnomusicologists in the early twentieth century recorded strong traditions of devotional songs with mission roots in the American Southwest, and stringed instruments such as violins and guitars have been in continuous use in northern Mexico and the U.S. Southwest since their introduction during the late sixteenth and early seventeenth centuries.[174]

Conclusions

It is impossible to overlook the many differences in the music performed in mission communities across this vast geographic region and over a span of more than 250 years. However, the musical culture of all but a few regions and time periods differed substantially from cathedral music in central Mexico. It was simpler, performed by Indian singers and instrumentalists with informal training, and intended to edify the Church. The song and pageantry of mission communities instilled Catholic values and taught indigenous inhabitants not only Catholic doctrine, but also how to become productive vassals of the King. Even so, northern frontier missions were not so disconnected and isolated from Mexico City as might be imagined.[175] Musical instruments, including difficult-to-transport organs, and items such as cloth, strings for violins and guitars, liturgical books, and massive bells were transported north to supply missionaries with goods for attracting and retaining Indians in the missions.

The early Jesuit missions in the near north as well as the early Franciscan missions in New Mexico seem to have possessed more elaborate musical cultures than their seventeenth- and eighteenth-century counterparts elsewhere in northern New Spain, except in the late colonial Alta California missions. At Mission Santa María de las Parras, like in other early missions, Indians sang motets and figured chant as part of the celebration of mass and the Divine Office.[176] Religious dances and a large variety of musical instruments were also used at Parras. As the resources of the orders and the Spanish Crown began to be spread more thinly and over a larger geographic area, the funds and efforts that could be devoted to music were more limited. As evidenced in the cases of Mission Los Santos Reyes del Cucurpe

---

[174] For example, see the Juan B. Rael Collection of New Mexican folk songs at the Library of Congress, as well as the work of anthropologists such as Frances Densmore.

[175] For a similar discussion of the importation of paintings, sculpture, and artisans to frontier missions in Nueva Vizcaya, see Clara Bargellini, "At the Center on the Frontier: The Jesuit Tarahumara Missions of New Spain," in Thomas DaCosta and Elizabeth Pilliod, eds., *Time and Place: The Geohistory of Art* (Aldershot: Ashgate Publishing, 2005), 113-128.

[176] Anua de 1598, in Félix Zubillaga, ed., *Monumenta Mexicana VI* (Rome: Societatis Iesu, 1961), 638.

and the Alta California mission chain, the individual musical backgrounds and training of the missionaries were crucial in determining the type of music sung at the missions and the types of musical instruments constructed and played.

Evidence suggests that in the seventeenth and eighteenth centuries, missionaries, cantors, and mission choirs largely performed mass in plainchant or simple polyphony. Vespers services followed the same pattern, and both services contained Latin texts. Daily song also included devotional songs in Castilian, such as alabados, for teaching and encouraging popular religiosity. Larger missions with more resources possessed more instruments purchased in central Mexico or Europe, but mission residents in many areas, particularly the Jesuit northwest, manufactured stringed instruments. Special occasions were cause for the most elaborate performances, which featured dance, feasting, games, decorations, and multiple types of musical instruments. Communal worship involving music reflected the social, political, and economic conditions at work in the overlapping communities of New Spain's north, in which Indians increasingly maintained contacts with Spaniards and mixed-race peasants.

In the late eighteenth and early nineteenth centuries, more military force was used to try and contain and pacify the Indians of the north, particularly in the Pimería Alta, Alta California, and Texas. This resulted in a renewed interest in using music as a hegemonic device. The musical culture of the Alta California missions, established in the late eighteenth century, and not secularized until after the colonial period, was distinct from that of other northern mission areas in the late colonial period. In the Alta California missions, Indians were required to maintain residence at the mission pueblos; in some cases this was enforced by physically locking young members of the community in their quarters in the evenings. More consistent and controlled populations, as well as greater numbers of dedicated friars, in these missions resulted in a great deal of musical training, including very large choirs and orchestras. Franciscans in Alta California also had the benefit of knowledge of evangelization techniques that had proven successful in other parts of Spanish America. Policies for the use of music in worship were more restrictive during the late colonial period; instruments were not commonly used in mass except for on special occasions, and plainsong was again the preferred form for liturgical music. However, indigenous influence was still present in the wide variety of native dances and songs that were performed mostly outside of the missions.

Over time, then, the musical culture of the northern missions experienced little substantial change when compared to the changes in Catholic music in Europe and Latin American cathedrals. Musical form and content, as well as instrumentation, of the mission music was simple. It included forms such as plainsong chant, simple organum, and instruments such as the organ, strings, and woodwinds—all common in late-Renaissance liturgical music in Europe. The earliest and latest missions seem to have had more resources and musical performances most similar to those of the same period in central Mexico and the cathedrals of the northern frontier. In the late sixteenth century, motets were sung in the colleges and cathedrals of central New Spain, as well as in the missions of Nueva Vizcaya and New Mexico. In the early nineteenth century, Ignacio de Jerusalem's masses were performed in the cathedrals of the Spanish empire and found in the library of Mission Santa Barbara.

Finally, indigenous peoples shaped the music performed in their mission communities. Their fingerprints were on the stringed instruments built in some communities, the costumes assembled for dramas and dances, and the drums and rattles used in processions and dances. The timbre, volume, and inflection of the words they sang were influenced by their understanding of the music. Religious dance became part of the mission repertoires for special occasions such as Christmas, Corpus Christi, and Holy Week. Although the dances were not allowed inside the church, and access to costumes and instruments was sometimes controlled by the missionaries, many of the dances retained strong indigenous components. Certainly many indigenous groups began, continued, or intensified dancing for their own special occasions (e.g., harvest or war), often at night, in locations hidden or far from missionary control.

Indigenous peoples used music to their advantage throughout the northern frontier, quite possibly to avoid other work. Perhaps this is why Jesuits stationed at Cucurpe found the Opatas and Eudeves so eager to learn to sing and play musical instruments. Those who practiced and performed music avoided much harsh physical labor, and could also supplement their income by performing for secular or religious celebrations outside the missions.

Jesuit and Franciscan missionaries successfully utilized instrumental and vocal music to attract Indians to the missions, to evangelize and teach them, and to celebrate important events. But it is also clear that indigenous peoples were able to engage with these uses of music, in some cases to their advantage. Beyond music's function as a teaching tool, however, it was also important in the restructuring of daily and ritual concepts of time and space. The next two chapters will consider these topics.

Part III
Song, Time, and Space

Mission San Juan Capistrano, San Antonio, Texas. Photograph by David R. Mann.

CHAPTER 6
Music and the Restructuring of Time

In a hyberbolized account of the immense power of bells, Jesuit historian Peter Masten Dunne wrote of the encounter of the natives of the island of San José with the bells of the mission at La Paz, Baja California:

> *When the peal of the bell of the Angelus rang out at noon, the natives were at first pleased and knelt with the fathers to pray, and even asked that the ringing continue. But the faster strokes upon the bell at the end of the Angelus threw them into a turmoil of fright. The chief fainted and fell into Ugarte's lap, and the bell ringer was stopped lest others collapse. The chief was wrapped in a warm blanket and revived with a little wine.*[1]

The contrast between the heroic Jesuit fathers and the naïve indigenous peoples, overwhelmed by the pealing bells, serves to highlight the dramatic power ascribed to sound in the missions of northern New Spain. The musical landscape of northern New Spain was dramatically altered by Spanish-introduced bells and liturgical music. The restructuring of the auditory landscape in this territory through performed sound was one tentacle of Spanish efforts to impose hegemony. Whether music and bells caused fainting due to their massive, unexpected sound, or whether they reorganized the daily schedules of indigenous peoples of the north, they were important agents in the colonization process.

This chapter examines the role of music, particularly musically structured daily routines, songs, and bells, in the restructuring of daily time in the mission communities in northern New Spain. Music was an agent of colonization with tremendous hegemonic potential to impact the conversion and Hispanicization processes. An analysis of the prescribed and reported daily schedules of north-

---

[1] Dunne, *Black Robes in Lower California*, 184-185.

ern New Spain demonstrates how music was involved in demarcating time. The functions and significance of bells and alabados as communicative devices and markers of routines are evident in northern missions throughout the colonial period. Not only daily, but also yearly cycles of ritual time were restructured through the missionaries' imposition of a new, Christian ceremonial calendar. This chapter emphasizes the importance of music and bells in the cultural processes of Hispanicization that were crucial to the Spanish project of colonization undertaken by missionaries.

The Hegemonic Power of Music

Music is a cultural system that defines, orders, and maintains the structure of societies.[2] Indigenous authors recognize that culture (including music and dance), a collective way of manifesting identity, is the "soul of native civilization," in the past, present, and future.[3] By attempting to restructure culture, Spaniards aimed to change the souls of the civilizations they encountered, and the Indians of the borderlands region responded in various ways. Music was integrally involved in the definition and ordering of the lives of indigenous peoples who lived in or near mission communities. Music has intrinsic connections with time: meter, rhythm, repetition, and resolution are all elements of musical composition and performance. Spaniards and missionaries rationalized the ordering of time through music for both religious and economic purposes. Hearing bells and singing the alabado or Salve Regina came to be taken for granted as part of the natural order of daily activities—an indicator of music's involvement in the hegemonic processes of Spanish colonialism.

Music's power was pervasive. One did not have to be a musician to take part in some capacity in a musical performance. Not only musicians, but also listeners, those involved in rehearsal or practice, those who provided material or space for performance, and those who danced, participated in making music.[4] The entire mission community, then, would share in the process of music. Those who were singers, instrumentalists, catechists, or bell ringers had active roles. Still, everyone living within the range of mission bells was at least passively con-

---

[2] Dorothy Sara Lee, "Toward an Understanding of Music and Identity in the Social World," in Caroline Card, ed., *Discourse in Ethnomusicology II: A Tribute to Alan P. Merriam* (Bloomington, IN: Ethnomusicology Publications Group, 1981), 1.

[3] Theodore S. Jojola, "Introduction: Technology and Native American Culture," *Wicazo Sa Review* 13:2 (Autumn 1998), 6.

[4] Christopher Small, *Musicking: The Meanings of Performing and Listening* (Hanover, NH: University Press of New England, 1998), 9.

nected with musical performance. Physiological research shows that exposure to music affects humans in two distinct ways: directly, as the effect of sound upon the cells and involvement in organs; and indirectly, by affecting the emotions, which in turn influence bodily functions.[5] With this degree of influence over human daily functions and emotions, it is easy to see how music could become such an important element in the colonization arsenal.

In colonial situations, those with power often fear the "other" and try to control them through the reshaping of space and time. In the case of missionaries evangelizing foreign territory and resistant indigenous groups, reshaping daily schedules was one of the ways to eliminate perceived chaos and disorder and establish control over the population. One of the goals of the colonizers was to obtain power at the lowest possible cost through the creation of loyal colonial subjects.[6] Disciplining indigenous peoples subtly through reliance on a musically structured daily schedule was an effective means of achieving this goal. Through daily music and the ringing of bells, even those who did not participate in the activities of mission life were impacted by the new daily schedules.[7]

Another method used to gain control in colonial situations was to colonize time through the frequent repetition of new tasks and ideas. Repetition was an important component of missionary teaching techniques and essential for establishing hegemony, particularly in areas where indigenous peoples vastly outnumbered their colonizers. Prayers, songs, and the physical gestures and routines of the liturgy were introduced quickly after missionaries entered an area. Prayers such as the Our Father, and other parts of the doctrine, such as the Ave Maria and the Credo, were often translated and recited or sung several times a day.[8] Mass was said, at the minimum, on Sundays; often it was performed daily. All of these elements became components of the daily and weekly routines of the mission. Repetition was a key component in daily music, the liturgy (including responses, litanies, and refrains), and the routines of which they were a part. The multiple layers of repetition served to discipline time and bodies, just as

---

[5] David Tame, *The Secret Power of Music: The Transformation of Self and Society through Musical Energy* (Rochester, VT: Destiny Books, 1984), 137.

[6] Foucault, *Discipline and Punish*, 218.

[7] For music as part of the disciplining regimen of the Jesuit missions of Paraguay, see Guillermo Wilde, "Toward a Political Anthropology of Mission Sound: Paraguay in the seventeenth and eighteenth centuries," Eric Ederer, trans., *Music and Politics* 1:2 (Summer 2007): 1-36.

[8] Spicer, *Cycles of Conquest*, 296, summarizes this element of repetition. I have many examples of the repetition of prayers, doctrine, and hymns in my database, particularly in the daily schedules cited in n. 26.

[9] Jeremy S. Begbie, *Theology, Music, and Time* (Cambridge: Cambridge University Press, 2000), 173.

repetitive strategies in musical compositions function to create a sense of direction and goal orientation.[9] When repetition was coupled with a melody, it acquired even more power. As Frederick Nietzsche observed,

> *This is what happens to us in music. First one has to learn to hear a figure and melody at all, to detect and distinguish it, to isolate it and delimit it as a separate life. Then it requires some exertion and good will to tolerate it in spite of its strangeness. . . . Finally there comes a moment when we are used to it, when we wait for it, when we sense that we should miss it if it were missing; and now it continues to compel and enchant us relentlessly until we have become its humble and enraptured lovers who desire nothing better from the world than it and only it.*[10]

Through repetition of the liturgy, outward acts of Catholicism, such as attending mass, performing the gestures and assuming appropriate postures for worship, and following the imposed daily schedule became so routine as to almost not be noticed.[11] Successful indoctrination in Catholicism and guaranteed economic productivity did not necessarily follow from the colonizing of time, but rigid daily schedules combining music and repetition certainly helped establish the atmosphere for conversion and Hispanicization.

Daily Routines at the Missions

Michel Foucault wrote, "For centuries the religious orders had been masters of discipline: they were the specialists of time, the great technicians of rhythm and regular activities."[12] Time discipline began with the training of novices, and guidelines for the delegation of their hours date to the thirteenth-century *Speculum disciplinae*.[13]

Although the political and economic organization of the numerous indigenous groups of the north differed greatly, these groups did not follow Hispanic patterns of daily work, meals, and rest time. Indians' daily lives were filled with activities such as hunting, gathering food and water, trading, visiting kin, rear-

---

[10] Frederick Nietzsche, *The Gay Science: With a Prelude in Rhymes and an Appendix of Songs*, trans. W. Kaufmann (New York: Random House, 1974), 262.

[11] Anthropologists John and Jean Comaroff discuss this as an important indicator of hegemonic power. See *Ethnography and the Historical Imagination*, 29.

[12] *Discipline and Punish*, 150.

[13] This work, which provides a structure for daily practice of the novices, was originallly attributed to St. Bonaventure, but more recently thought to be the work of his secretary, Bernard of Besse. See Regis J. Armstrong, Wayne J. Hellman, and William Short, eds. and trans., *The Founder: Francis of Assisi: Early Documents* (New York: New City Press, 2000), 29-30.

ing children, preparing food, and attending dances, competitions, and games. Those who lived in villages or rancherías built homes, planted and tended crops, ground corn, and fashioned baskets, pots, and tools.

Missionaries introduced daily schedules in mission communities, to ensure that indigenous time was spent on tasks deemed productive and civilized by the missionaries. The ultimate goal of the Crown was to create productive workers in the form of loyal, Christian citizens, and so the imposition of strict daily schedules in the mission was crucial to both religious conversion and economic profitability. Schedules relied heavily on the repetition of liturgical and musical elements, such as the ringing of church bells, the oral recitation of prayers, and the singing of hymns. The installation of these routines was encouraged through the use of material and sociopolitical benefits offered by the missionaries: food, clothing, relative stability, and protection from rival groups.[14] In the initial stages of mission establishment, the introduction of a daily routine was essential, but not easily implemented. Indigenous peoples, particularly those with differing settlement patterns (such as ranchería or seminomadic groups), were not easily convinced to commit to living in permanent villages, which often combined members of different ethnic and even linguistic groups. The transition from non-Western concepts of time, where life was ordered by engaging in specific tasks, to a rigid monastic schedule, where hours for prayer, worship, and work were all appointed, was often incomplete.[15] Where missionaries were successful in reducing at least a small population of individuals to mission life, a daily routine was crucial to the success of their endeavors. It helped to establish an orderly pattern of life, develop interest in mission activities, increase productivity in labor, and instill self-discipline and religious devotion.[16]

Ideally, daily activities in mission communities began with the ringing of the bell(s) at dawn to call the population to worship. After morning worship, which consisted of the recitation of prayers, or canonical hours of Prime or Lauds, or a daily mass, the morning meal was eaten. Adults went off to work while children received doctrinal instruction. A midday meal and siesta were followed by worship, instruction, and then the evening meal. The day typically ended with a

---

[14] See Spicer, *Cycles of Conquest*, 372-373.

[15] On Western time discipline, see E.P. Thompson's classic article, "Time, Work-Discipline, and Industrial Capitalism," *Past and Present* 38 (1967), 56-97. For an example of colonizing everyday routines during the nineteenth-century British evangelization of southern Africa, see John and Jean Comaroff, "The Civilization of Consciousness," in *Ethnography and the Historical Imagination*, 258-259.

[16] For a general overview on daily schedules at Jesuit missions in New Spain, see Richard Schmutz, "Jesuit Missionary Methods in Northwestern Mexico," *Journal of the West* 8:1 (1969), 83.

procession (including singing) from the mission church to individual residences. Variations in the type of worship, specifics of doctrinal instruction, food served, and daily tasks performed were common, but the prescribed blueprint seems to have remained consistent throughout the mission period and over a large geographic area.[17]

This daily routine was most closely based on the patterns of daily life followed by the regular clergy in colleges, convents, and hospices in Europe and New Spain.[18] The earliest missionaries to New Spain, such as Franciscan Fray Pedro de Gante, instructed indigenous youths in central Mexico to discipline their lives through the structure of the liturgy, including major emphasis on music. Fray Pedro reported to the King that his students at the Convento de San Francisco awoke and sang the Office to Our Lady, followed by attendance at daily conventual mass. After mass, they were instructed in reading, writing, and singing, learning the Catholic doctrine, articles of faith, and commandments at the church by singing them so that they could teach others in the pueblos. After the canonical hour of None, they ate a meal and rested. In the afternoon they sang the Office of the Dead, a penitential psalm, or the Canticum Gradum. Students then had time for individual reading and reflection before vespers. Between the hours of Vespers and Compline in the evening, they ate supper, practiced reading and writing Spanish, and received instruction in preaching. Three times a week they said matins before retiring.[19] This highly regimented daily schedule emphasized the duties of the religious to worship God through the praying of the Divine Office and daily mass.

Franciscans and Jesuits in the missions of northern New Spain adapted routines such as Fray Pedro's to the indigenous populations among whom they worked, stressing communal meals where food was scarce, and employing music, dance, and drama to teach doctrine among groups with rich traditions of

---

[17] Schedules vary from those written by individual missionaries, to directives or circular letters sent from superiors about how to structure days at the mission. They were largely written by individuals whose motives were to justify their presence in the area, secure funding, and emphasize their accomplishments; thus it is difficult to determine whether they were consistently implemented. Daily schedules appear to have been similar in the Guaraní and Chiquitos missions administered by the Jesuits. See José Cardiel, *Misiones del Paraguay—Declaración de la verdad* (Buenos Aires: Imprenta de Juan A. Alcina, 1900), 247-252.

[18] On musical practice in Spain, see Lourdes Turrent, *La conquista musical de México* (Mexico City: Fondo de Cultura Económica, 1996), 40. For New Spain, see Espinosa, *Crónica de los colegios de propaganda fide*, 173-174; and Francisco de Florencia, *Historia de la Provincia de la Compañía de Jesús de Nueva España* (México City: Editorial Academia Literaria, 1955 [1694]), 6, 88.

[19] Pedro de Gante to the King, 6/23/1558, photostat copy, Lota Mae and Jefferson Spell Collection, UTNLB, box 139, folder 1, 230-231.

music and dance. Missionary accounts of repetitive, musically structured daily routines reveal fascinating details about daily life at the missions. From details in the letters and reports that document these schedules, it is clear that the ideal structure was difficult to achieve.

One of the most detailed descriptions of daily routine in northern mission communities was documented at Mission San Diego de los Jemez, administered by Fray Joaquín de Jesús Ruíz, in a report from 1776. The report was written at the request of the bishop to provide advice for his successor, and to serve as a model for the administration of other missions in Nuevo México. An examination of this report helps elucidate the role that music played in the restructuring of time in mission communities. A comparison of this schedule with other data about the missions, as well as with schedules of other missions operating during the same time period, reveals more about the roles of music and the liturgy in the acculturation and evangelization processes.

The Hemish migrated to the Cañon de San Diego from the northwest in the late thirteenth century.[20] European contact was first made in 1541; at this time the Hemish were one of the largest and most powerful civilizations in the region. They were a classic example of the village people described by Edward Spicer, with an agricultural and hunting-based society, participation in extensive trade networks, and a social structure including warriors, craftsmen, and religious leaders. The territory of Nuevo México was colonized by Juan de Oñate and his band of colonists in 1598, but Franciscans did not enter Hemish territory until 1618, when two missions were established. There were sporadic uprisings by Jemez Pueblo residents against the Franciscans until the general Pueblo Revolt of 1680, in which one of the Franciscans ministering at San Juan de los Jemez was killed. The pueblos were destroyed by Don Diego de Vargas in 1694, and the population was forced to congregate into a single village, Mission San Diego de los Jemez. In 1696 they again revolted, killed the Franciscan priest, and moved west, where many joined the Navajo. In the eighteenth century, some of the Hemish returned to the pueblo, called Walatowa, and participated in aspects of mission life.

Mission San Agustín de la Isleta was originally founded as San Antonio de la Isleta in 1613 by Fray Juan de Salas. Isleta Pueblo, similar to the settlements of the Hemish, was occupied by village peoples largely focused on agriculture and hunting. It was also destroyed in the Pueblo Revolt of 1680 (although some Isletans did not participate in the revolt), but was rebuilt and reoccupied by the

---

[20] For a native history of Jemez Pueblo, see Joe Sando, *Nee Hemish: A History of Jemez Pueblo* (Albuquerque: University of New Mexico Press, 1982).

Franciscans when Spaniards returned to New Mexico in 1692. A growing number of Spaniards, mestizos, and *genízaros* (non-Puebloan indigenous peoples) settled in the region during the eighteenth century. Troubles with Fray Juan Junco caused Bishop Domínguez to transfer Fray Joaquín from Jemez to the less-disciplined Isleta in 1776, ordering him to impose the same regime there as at his old post. The mission continued to be administered by Franciscans until its secularization in the early nineteenth century, and it is still an operating parish today.

In the 1770s, both missions were located in compact settlements. This type of social and economic arrangement aided the evangelization efforts of the Franciscans, who could utilize the proximity of the residents to the mission church. Fray Joaquín's description of the liturgical routine, which is quite detailed in its provisions, is as follows:

> *The bell is rung at sunrise in summer, and in winter a little later; when the catechumens gather in the churchyard each has his own place assigned to him, the fiscal endeavoring to see that they do not change their places, so that the father teacher may easily see if any are missing, and not delay the roll call. The method for prayer is to put all the little ones, boys as well as girls, in front, separated from one another by a distance of half a vara, so that they cannot talk or amuse themselves with gestures that distract their attention. In the same way the larger girls are placed behind the children, with their faces uncovered, not being permitted to cover them with their shawls, for then they occupy themselves in chewing exquite, or in some other nasty habit that they practice. After them come the young men, in the same order as those first named. Two young cantors stand up with the catechism in their hands and begin the recitation in a loud voice, and all respond. They recite first from the "Todo Fiel Christiano" as far as the "Credo," then from the "Salve" as far as the "Sacramentos," and then the explanation of the principal mysteries, closing each recitation with the angelical salutation and the alabado of the Holy Trinity. At the last the responsory is sung, accompanied by the tolling of the bell.*
>
> *The cantor for the week repeats the prayer together with the sacristans, and the little serving girls with the fiscal for the week, in the same order as the catechism. At the ringing of the Ave Marías these last repair to their cells and recite the Angelus. When there is work to be done in the way of sweeping, white-washing, or any other task in the convent, they [the men and women] are not permitted to work together, for they do not behave as they ought, and from this come intrigues...*
>
> *The chimes are rung twice after sunrise, so that mass begins at eight. The married people assemble in the following manner: Each married man brings his wife and kneels with her at his side, in their assigned place, according to the directions of the register, in such a way that two men are in the center with their wives at each side, the women not being permitted to be together because mass cannot be heard for*

> *their conversations, nor do they pay any attention to the prayers. . . . Two young cantors stand up facing the people, and intone the prayer, as in the daily catechism. If any married woman is missing, her husband brings her, he being compelled to do this. If it is a man who is missing, the* fiscal mayor, *or his assistant, goes to bring him.*
>
> *Prayers being finished, the mass begins, the musicians play until the elevation of the host, and the cantors intone the* alabado. *After mass is over, the married people [go out] in the best order possible. The best way of explaining the mysteries to them is on Saturday following the catechism, as soon as they finish the rosary, for then they are alone and do not divert themselves with the citizens, to whom the explanation is given on Sundays.*[21]

Fray Joaquín de Jesús Ruíz's description belies a concern with physical control over the Hemish congregated at Mission San Diego. The Franciscans maintained this control through structured daily schedules as well as by allying with some members of the native population and employing them as agents in the acculturation process. A 1773 report by Pedro Fermín de Mendinueta, governor of New Mexico, indicated that quite a few Indians were involved in the local governance of mission communities.[22] The *alcalde* and his assistants, the *tenientes*, served as the political and military leadership of the congregated pueblos. Spiritual governance in mission communities was aided by the appointment of sacristans, *fiscales*, and cantors. Sacristans were responsible for maintenance of the mission, while fiscales and cantors aided in the gathering of the community and religious instruction. In other missions, catechists, bell-ringers, and choir members also participated in spiritual governance. In the case of the missions of Jemez and Isleta, the fiscal mayor was responsible for calling together the neophytes every day for the recitation of prayers and doctrine, taking roll call, and retrieving those who were missing from liturgical functions such as the mass. Cantors filled a different role than the fiscales. They led the recitation of the prayers, the ten commandments, and the articles of faith, all of which were recited or chanted in unison. Cantors were also responsible for intoning the prayers during mass and leading the singing of the hymns. These jobs would have required a loud, clear voice and singing ability. Perhaps quite a few community members were capable of being cantors; Ruíz mentioned that the job changed hands weekly. Mendinueta confirmed this assumption by stating that even though the people follow the cantor's voice during the recitation of

---

[21] AGN, Historia, vol. 25, in Hackett, *Historical Documents*, 502-503.
[22] Pedro Fermín de Mendinueta to Viceroy Bucareli, published in Mark Simmons, ed. and trans., *Indian and Mission Affairs in New Mexico, 1773* (Santa Fe, NM: Stagecoach Press, 1965), 16-17.

prayers, "all seem to know what they are saying by memory."[23] Despite the level of doctrinal memorization attained by the catechumens, comprehension of the prayers was apparently elementary at best, a common problem in missionary endeavors everywhere.[24] The final occupation listed in the Ruíz passage is that of musician. Distinction of this role from that of the cantor indicates that musicians were responsible for instrumental music. Musical training at these missions, then, must have included both instrumental and vocal instruction, or perhaps by the eighteenth century, Hispanic-style music and instruments were already incorporated into the community's culture.

The description of the daily liturgical schedule testifies to the complex efforts taken by the friar to prevent disorder. He emphasized the need to arrange the seating of his students during instruction to prevent off-task behavior such as spitting and writing on the convent walls. In addition, he prohibited girls from covering their faces with shawls to hide misconduct, separated women during mass to prevent talking, and segregated men and women during work periods. While flight and open rebellion were tactics of resistance practiced by indigenous populations during the early phases of mission life, by the later generations of missionization, a more subtle undermining of the padre's power was prevalent, particularly among the women. A 1754 report by Fray Manuel de San Juan Nepomuceno y Trigo concerning the northern New Mexico missions noted that the Indians of San Agustín de la Isleta "give the father plenty of opposition with their witchcraft and idolatry."[25] By emphasizing the structure of a daily routine, Ruíz may have hoped to further acculturate these Indians and combat idolatry by placing importance on proper behavior. Both these reports, however, attest to the persistence of indigenous culture and an undercurrent of resistance, despite missionary presence in the area for over a century.

Ruíz's description highlighted most prominently the daily activities of the doctrineros, whom Mendinueta defined as young, unmarried members of the community.[26] Married men and women were responsible for the labor at the missions, which occurred after the morning prayers and mass, and before the evening call to prayer. At Isleta, mission labor consisted of grinding corn (women), tending the mission's vegetable garden, and planting and caring for

---

[23] *Indian and Mission Affairs in New Mexico, 1773*, 18.

[24] See, for example, Vicente L. Rafael, "Confession, Conversion, and Reciprocity in Early Tagalog Colonial Society," in Nicholas B. Dirks, ed., *Colonialism and Culture* (Ann Arbor: University of Michigan Press, 1992), 65-88.

[25] Fray Manuel de San Juan Nepomuceno y Trigo, description of the missions of New Mexico, July 23, 1754, translated and transcribed in Hackett, *Historical Documents*, 462.

[26] *Indian and Mission Affairs in New Mexico, 1773*, 17.

fields of corn and wheat. At Jemez, the work differed only slightly; cotton production and weaving were important there as well.[27] The day was punctuated by the ringing of the Ave Marias on the bells, a signal to halt work and pray.

A comparison of the 1773 description of mission governance with data from Alonso de Benavides's *Memorial*, written in 1630, highlights differences in missionary techniques and indigenous actions in the early and late phases of mission life. Reports from both phases document the importance of bells in gathering the people for daily prayers and mass in the morning, and dismissal in the evening. A census of the village was taken to make sure that no one was unaccounted for. Singing and recitation of the prayers were also parts of the prescribed daily routine during both centuries, although the songs were different. Alabados and the Salve Regina were sung in unison when the community gathered with Ruíz in the eighteenth century. Initially, much like other early mission communities, Franciscan missions in New Mexico boasted choirs, which could perform the mass and canonical hours in parts, often accompanied by string or reed instruments or an organ. Descriptions of daily schedules show greater participation and study of music during the early phases of missionization, likely by boys who had been entrusted to the missionaries for religious education. However, in the mature missions, participation by the entire community in music, although not as difficult or large a repertoire, indicates that liturgical music may have been one area in which conversion efforts made an impact.

Differences in the descriptions of daily life over time are more revealing. Ruíz's late eighteenth-century report placed a much greater emphasis on social control and heading off misconduct. In contrast, Benavides remarked that in the early seventeenth century, "When we ring the bell for mass, they all come as well scrubbed and neat as can be. They enter the church to pray as though they had been Christians forever. And the young boys and girls, who morning and afternoon always come to catechism, apply themselves without exception and with the greatest of care."[28] The daily routine of the early New Mexico missions was much more structured by the obligations of the liturgy. The mission communities, according to Benavides, gathered for daily celebration of the canonical hours of prime and vespers, as well as for mass. All of these services included singing by a choir.[29] In the mature missions of New Mexico and throughout the north, economic activities increased in importance and liturgical routines

---

[27] This information comes from the Nepomuceno y Trigo report, 462, 464 (cf. n. 25).
[28] Baker Morrow, trans., "How Well They Take to Christian Practices," in Morrow, *A Harvest of Reluctant Souls*, 42.
[29] Ibid.

became less complex to allow more time for agriculture, ranching, mining, and interaction with the local economies.

When Fray Juan de Jesús Ruíz's schedule is compared with the daily routines of other mature missions in northern New Spain, several similarities emerge. First, as the most obvious audible signals of the mission, bells held a position of importance in structuring time. They called the community together in the morning and signaled times for work, meals, and prayers. Even Indians who did not participate in these events were constantly reminded of them. Mass, prayers, and the singing of the alabado contributed to the rhythm of the mission. Meals were eaten in common, particularly during the early phases of evangelization or in areas like Baja California, where the pre-Contact indigenous population had largely subsisted on foraging and hunting. As many historians have observed, food was an important incentive used by missionaries to encourage attendance at communal worship, held immediately before meals were served.[30]

The challenges of daily life, including how to best instruct and prevent undesired behaviors, are evident throughout the reports of daily schedules in both regions. Christian ideas about prudent sexual behavior, monogamous marriage, and modesty were frequently counter to indigenous practices. Daily schedules penned by both Franciscans and Jesuits demonstrate a preoccupation with appropriate interaction of the sexes. Males and females were routinely separated for doctrinal instruction and mass. In Missions Loreto and La Purísima in Baja California, men and women even sang verses of the alabado and responses of the prayers separately.[31]

Perceived "backsliding" and resistance to Christian teachings, particularly among the adults, was another challenge facing missionaries throughout the Spanish empire. This problem was even more pronounced in the later stages of missionization, although missionaries were hesitant to jeopardize their positions by punishing it too harshly. In the missions of New Mexico, Baja California, and throughout the north, Franciscans and Jesuits tried to combat this by removing children from the influence of their parents and by rewarding the behavior of loyal Indians through leadership positions. Parents were separated from their children in nearly all of the samples of mission schedules. Conversion and Hispanicization were best achieved by installing children in convent schools, teaching them Spanish and doctrine, and modeling appropriate behavior. In the

---

[30] See Spicer, *Cycles of Conquest*; and Radding, *Wandering Peoples*.
[31] Salvatierra, description of Mission Loreto in Bayle, *Misión de la Baja California*, 216; and Nicolas Tamaral, 1730 report, reproduced in Manuel de la Vega, Relación, BINAH, vol. 68, f. 99v-100.

New Mexican missions, this process was started during the early mission period, but largely abandoned because it required cooperation on the part of parents after the reconquest. In Baja California, the Jesuits appear to have had sporadic success with these methods, perhaps due to the number of children orphaned or abandoned by their parents. Still, it is doubtful that a consistent, organized schooling effort was present throughout the eighteenth century—four separate reports about Loreto (dating from 1698, 1717, 1760, and 1769) mention the formation of a school for children.[32] The operation of a mission school was a strategy that depended on a number of factors, including the number of indigenous people at the mission, the ability of the missionary to attract and retain students, and the aid of Christianized Indians.

In addition to their focus on the education of children, missionaries tried to change inward spiritual behavior by first focusing on the outward signs of civilization, such as appropriate dress, cleanliness, and popular devotional practices. Jesuits, Franciscans, and the Dominicans who took over the Baja California missions in 1776 all emphasized the importance of neatly dressed and freshly bathed neophytes. Father Miguel Hidalgo admonished the Dominicans to "gather the boys and girls in the church to recite the doctrine, and afterward they will leave in a procession singing it, and go to the well, or spring, to wash their hands and face, since it is necessary to get them accustomed to keeping themselves clean."[33] While serving at Nuestra Señora de Loreto Conchó, Father Xavier Bischoff practiced the custom of *visita del Santissima Sacramento*, in which the Host was processed throughout the plaza and homes near the mission. In the evenings, the procession from the mission back to the homes of the married couples ended when the neophytes used holy water to make the sign of the cross before entering their homes. "How great was his zeal and dedication!" exclaimed Fray Manuel de la Vega.[34] The actions involved in these processions reinforced doctrinal concepts, such as the importance of the sacraments, through outward actions, such as walking behind the cross, singing or chanting the prayers, and making the sign of the cross. Late eighteenth century *doctrinas* under the care of friars from the missionary college at Querétaro ended their days with the ringing of the bells at sunset. Recitation of the prayers and catechism, in Spanish, was led

---

[32] Salvatierra letter, 1698, transcribed in Manuel de la Vega, Relacion, BINAH, vol. 68, f.13; Informe of Padre José Rotea, 1717, AGN, Historia, vol. 21, f. 194; Fr. Bischoff report, 1760, transcribed in Manuel de la Vega, Relación, BINAH, vol. 68, ff. 107-107v.; Palou report, 1769, vol. 65, f. 230-231v.

[33] Hidalgo, circular letter to Dominicans in Baja California, 1784, AGI, Audiencia de Guadalajara, 586, f. 332v.

[34] *Relación*, BINAH, Fondo Franciscano, vol. 68, f. 107-108 (several folios not numbered).

by the priest. After praying the rosary, the community sang the alabado or the Salve Regina before returning to their homes.[35] When these actions were coupled with the morning mass, the days of the neophytes were bounded at the rising and setting of the sun by the obligations of the liturgy.

Finally, when considering the daily schedules penned by missionaries and prescribed routines advocated by superiors, we must question the veracity of the descriptions of daily life. Despite the ideal descriptions of bells calling the population of the community to the mission, mass being sung daily, and doctrine being taught every afternoon or evening, it is unclear how many Indians really attended these activities. Jacob Baegert, Jesuit missionary to Baja California, lamented that his ideal picture of a mission, including a well-defined daily schedule, adherence to liturgical conventions, and residence in Hispanic-style communities, was sadly inaccurate:

> *One imagines if one comes to a mission, one would meet there well-dressed people living together in huts, living on agriculture the way people do in Europe. And so you can say mass in a nice way, can hear a lot of confessions on Sundays and holidays and give communion, can sing vespers and the Salve, and could have a lot of enjoyment with them. . . . However, with these ideas one is again cruelly cheated.*[36]

Baegert was unable to convince indigenous people to congregate at his mission, cultivate fields, and adhere to the daily routine of mission life. His comments are a far cry from Father Nicolas Tamaral's lengthy description of daily life less than twenty years earlier, which involved the ringing of bells, daily mass, gender-segregated recitation of doctrine in the morning, noon, and night, singing of the alabado, and praying the Ave Maria and the rosary in call-and-response format. This tightly packed schedule of liturgical obligations, work, and meals, depended on the participation of catechists, cantors, corn-grinders, cooks, firewood-gatherers, and fiscales—a large segment of the community.[37] Missionaries and visitors general had motives to exaggerate the efficacy of their evangelization efforts, particularly when asking for more supplies and greater funding. Superiors within the orders might also generalize the success of an individual

---

[35] Noticia y estado actual de los misiones que en la provincia de Sonora administran los P.P. del Colegio de Propaganda Fide de Querétaro, 1784, AGI, Guadalajara, 586, f. 39v-40.

[36] Jacob Baegert, letter of September 11, 1752, translated and transcribed in Elsbeth Schulz-Bischof, trans., *The Letters of Jacob Baegert, 1739–1761: Jesuit Missionary in Baja California*, ed. Doyce B. Nunis, Jr., Baja California Travel Series, 45 (Los Angeles: Dawson's Book Shop, 1982), 157.

[37] Padre Nicolas Tamaral to Padre Visitador General, 1730, AGN, Historia, v. 21, no. 16, f. 166-172v.

missionary in a particular area to the success of the entire area under his charge. In the late eighteenth and early nineteenth centuries, particularly in Alta California, where larger populations were living in the missions and adhering to the daily routines, corporal punishment and confinement in mission barracks had much to do with the successful restructuring of time and acculturation. In 1781, Teodoro de Croix, comandante general of the Provincias Internas, criticized Franciscans for their use of punishment. Indians who did not attend instruction sessions in the rosary and doctrine, as well as mass, were subject to whipping. Neophytes were required to obtain permission from the friars before leaving or if they did not feel well enough to work.[38] Disciplining daily lives took on added meanings in this context.

While musically structured daily routines endorsed and reinforced the social conditions and power relations under which they were created, musical activities within daily time could also extend, question, and even reject these social conditions.[39] Some indigenous peoples chose to extend the social conditions and power structure of the mission routine by tying themselves to the structure. They learned Spanish, prayers and doctrine, performed music, and adopted Hispanic dress, food, musical instruments, and customs. Converted Indians became leaders in the community: catechists, fiscales, and musicians. They had access to the Christian god in communication through song. Widespread illness and death, as well as dislocation and chaos due to the introduction of European diseases may have convinced many to take this path. Others questioned the liturgical routines by mocking them, or by adding them to a host of musical activities in which they already participated. If the Christian mission day was marked by bells at sunrise and sunset, then musical activities that reproduced native power structures were held after nightfall.[40] Some were aware of the demands represented in the bells' peals, but disregarded them. Bishop Domínguez reported in 1776 that

> *the Indians of Picuris and Taos outdo all the rest in all the general customs. . . . Perhaps the little ones may be playing in the street, now in the pueblo, now a little*

---

[38] AGN, Provincias Internas, vol. 258, f. 118-120.

[39] On the need to recognize that social conditions and power relations embedded in music were not totalizing, see Jeremy Begbie, *Theology, Music, and Time* (Cambridge: Cambridge University Press, 2000), 14, n. 18.

[40] For example, Indians at Mission Rosario in Texas were called together by Father Solís to recite the rosary and the mysteries of the faith and sing the alabado. They recited the doctrina before mass and after doctrinal explanation. But the same report laments that these Indians were fond of mitotes and danced around bonfires at night. Father Solís, report to the Father Guardian, 1767, OSMHRC, Archivo del Colegio de Zacatecas, reel 1, fr. 149-216.

way off, but within sight, and as soon as the bell rings they forget their game and run to take refuge in their nest. Therefore it is necessary for the fiscales to order them to come to Mass or catechism by the town crier's voice. And if there is no such summons, the bell may break [with ringing for all the attention they pay to it]. ... The little boys and girls, are absolutely in puribus until they are twelve to fourteen years old. In this regard Father Claramonte forced them to half cover themselves by whipping them, and as a reward for this good work, he was accused of imprudence with minors.[41]

Rejection of the daily routines of mission life, as evidenced in the subtle acts of defiance above, as well as the revolts discussed in Chapter 3, were also carried out through musical activities, particularly post-revolt dancing. In addition, knowledge of the routines of missionaries could be used to reject the missionaries' presence. Indians and mestizos at Mission Santiago de las Coras in Baja California knew that Jesuit Lorenzo Carranco was accustomed to saying mass between six and seven each morning, then retiring to his house to pray and recite the Divine Office. Indians and mestizos, after attending morning mass and reciting the doctrine, found the Jesuit in his house, where they killed him. Afterward, they entered the church, gathered and burned the crosses, images, statues, chalice, missal, and other sacred ornaments.[42]

Bells and the Musical Landscape

As the heralds of daily routines in mission communities, bells were a key part of establishing and maintaining daily discipline and the restructuring of time. The largest and most cumbersome supplies to transport to the northern frontier, bells must have been important to justify the expense and trouble. Large bells took on human qualities: they were named, christened and blessed, sheltered in the imposing towers and arches built to house them, and even buried when a mission was abandoned.[43] A prayer for blessing mission bells, from a 1762 manual, gives an indication of the power ascribed to their ringing:

Bless this bell with our prayers, and through the power of the holy cross pour into it ... a heavenly blessing, so that with the hearing of its sound the inhabitants of this

---

[41] Eleanor Adams and Fray Angélico Chávez, eds., *The Missions of New Mexico in 1776* (Albuquerque: University of New Mexico Press, 1956), 258-259.

[42] José Gutiérrez Casillas, *Diccionario bio-bibliográfica de la Compañia de Jesús en México*, vol. XV (Mexico City: Editorial Jus, 1974), 421-422.

[43] Tomás Lozano, *Cantemos al Alba: Origins of Songs, Sounds, and Liturgical Drama of Hispanic New Mexico* (Albuquerque: University of New Mexico Press, 2007), 635-636.

place may gather with eager spirit into the church to the praise and honor of your name. May it receive such power, that in whatever place it will sound the prince of darkness may flee and tremble with fear, and flee terrified with all his servants, never more may he dare to disturb the clouds, nor may he dare to injure our crops, or to trouble those serving you, omnipotent God, you who live and reign forever.[44]

Where conquered Indians were not forced to live within the mission walls, they were at least required to live *bajo campana*, or beneath the bell—no more than a half-league from a church's bell tower.[45] Setting these boundaries ensured Spanish hegemony over the auditory landscape of the area. The sound of bells could then intrude into the daily lives of all people in the area, subjecting them to an auditory daily routine and aiding in acculturation. Bells defined territory for individuals living within range of their sound.[46] The intensity of the bells' ringing must have been a powerful sound in the north, where the only other sounds were human voices, animals, and the noises of everyday work and recreation. Perhaps the sounds of thunder and Spanish weapons (both sounds associated with power) were the only noises that could compare with the immense sound made by the tolling of large metal bells. Because it was impossible to escape the intensity of their sound, bells served to center and define the restructured spaces of mission communities as well as mark the time of these spaces.

Bells were not a uniquely European introduction in New Spain. Clay crotales, idiophones with conical form and a circular rim, were present in southern and central Mesoamerica. By 1000, clay crotales were found as far north as present-day Arizona and New Mexico.[47] Small crotales could be worn as jewelry (on a necklace or ankle bracelet) and used as percussion instruments during dances. The Codex Mendoza depicted forty large crotales as part of the yearly tribute owed Montezuma.[48] Crotales in Mesoamerica and the north were used primarily in ceremonial contexts and became valuable trade commodities. Metal bells, however, were relatively uncommon before the arrival of the Europeans, and their value was great due to the durability of metal and its importance as a trade good.

---

[44] Diego Osorio, *Manual para administrar los santos sacramentos, arreglado al ritual romano, con el orden de bendiciones, Exequias, Procesiones y otras cosas necesaria...* (Calatayud: Imprenta de Juan Aguirre, 1762), in Biblioteca Franciscana, Cholula, Mexico.

[45] See Bushnell, *Situado and Sabana*, 96. See also Melchor de Bartiromo, S.J., account of the Juan Bautista de Escalante expedition, April 20, 1700, translated in Sheridan, *Empire of Sand*, 57.

[46] See Alain Corbin, *Village Bells: Sound and Meaning in the Nineteenth-Century French Countryside*, trans. Martin Thom (New York: Columbia University Press, 1998), 95.

[47] Percival Price, *Bells and Man* (Oxford: Oxford University Press, 1983), 71-73.

[48] Codex Mendoza, f. 40r, cited in ibid., 73.

Spaniards brought portable metal bells with them to be used in worship during the initial phases of conquest. Bells had been an important part of structuring time, signaling communities to gather, and warding off evil in Counter-Reformation Europe, and thus they were essential elements in colonizing the peoples of the Americas. In 1585 the Third Mexican Provincial Council decreed that all churches and monasteries should follow the lead of the Cathedral of Mexico in ringing bells daily for the Ave Marias, mass, and vespers.[49] The Ave Maria, or Angelus bells, were sounded three times daily, at sunrise, noon, and sunset. At their sound, a uniform signal of three strokes sounded three times each, followed by nine strokes, the faithful were to pray the Ave Maria three times.[50] In addition, church bells were to be struck three times each afternoon as a remembrance of Christ's death.[51] The sounds of bells marked the passage of daily time, dictated prayer life, and structured the day's activities, but also served as a reminder of Christian teachings.[52]

In the north, bells were an essential part of the start-up items requested by Franciscans and Jesuits establishing new frontier missions. A *memoria* from Franciscan Pedro Romero de Terreros not only requested ten large bells, varying in size, for the bell tower of a new mission that was to be established on the San Xavier River, but also three smaller hand bells for use during mass.[53] Other than the sacred vessels and vestments needed for the celebration of the sacrament, and a yearly ration of maize, Fray Pedro requested only bells and other items necessary for the maintenance of mission life.[54] Because bells were viewed as necessary for the resettlement, instruction, and teaching of non-Christians, even poorer missions were furnished with at least one bell.[55] Before bell towers could be constructed, bells were mounted on large poles or boards. In the Yaqui pueblos, men carried bells from supply caravans on logs stretched across their shoulders. These were hung on trees next to the chapel before being mounted in more permanent structures.[56]

---

[49] *Concilio III*, 317.

[50] Price, *Bells and Man*, 121.

[51] This instruction was included in the provisions of both the Third and Fourth Provincial Councils. See Larkin, "Liturgy, Devotion, and Religious Reform," 504.

[52] The Angelus bells are still rung daily in some regions, from rural Mexico to Ireland and the Philippines.

[53] AGI, México, 1933A, f. 12, 1758.

[54] Pedro Pérez de Mezquia to Pedro Romero de Terreros, September 17, 1758, Genaro García Collection 191, f. 8, UTNLB.

[55] Fray Joseph Francisco Mariano Garza, Memoria for Mission Refugio, November 16, 1794, AGI, Guadalajara, 104-1-1 in CAT, 12.4.

THE FUNCTIONS OF BELLS

Mission bells served many different functions in the lives of frontier communities.[56] They were markers of time, bearers of news, and signals of the completion of rites of passage. First, and most prominently, bells served as signals for the entire community to gather in front of the church for mass, a parish census, meals, work, or doctrinal instruction. A neophyte was placed in charge of sounding the appropriate signal on the bell, usually by pulling a rope attached to the clapper. Skill and reliability were required to fulfill this job, and the bell ringer had to know the appropriate sequence and rhythm of bell tones needed to convey the message for the occasion. Catechumens were taught to respond to the sound of the bells by congregating in the church patio, sometimes in two lines, one of men, and one of women.[58] At other times during the day, particular bell signals could convey different information. The Angelus bells were an indication for individual prayer, while other specific patterns of bell-ringing began and ended communal meal time, doctrinal instruction, and recreation time.[59] Individual missions had different daily routines with regard to bell signals. At Loreto in Baja California the nine mission bells were rung three times daily. The Angelus bells sounded at sunrise. The bells were then rung at three in the afternoon to honor the hour of Christ's death, and in the evening after sundown to signal neophytes to pray the *De Profundis*, a psalm for the deceased.[60]

Compliance with the sound of the bell was an important outward sign of Hispanicization. Once the actions of a community had been regulated by the pealing of bells, missionaries reported the news as a sign of their success. Alonso de Benavides, for example, boasted that in such a short period of time, the missions and pueblos of Nuevo México were filled "with churches, with wayside crosses, and . . . inhabitants greeting one another with their voices praising the Holy Sacrament of the Altar, and the Holy Name of Jesus Christ, and at the sounding of the bell for the Ave Marias, they get down on their

---

[56] Polzer, *Rules and Precepts*, 42.

[57] Bells were also important in the daily lives of urban communities. See Geoffrey Baker, *Imposing Harmony: Music and Society in Colonial Cuzco* (Durham, NC: Duke University Press, 2008), 32-35.

[58] AGN, Misiones, vol. 26, exp. 27, f. 160, Jesuit Anua de 1662 concerning the Tarahumaran pueblos.

[59] On bells as a signal for the distribution of food, see Georg Heinrich von Langsdorff, *Remarks and Observations on a Voyage around the World from 1803 to 1807*, ed. Richard Pierce and trans. Victoria Moessner, vol. 2 (Kingston, Ontario: Limestone Press, 1993), 93.

[60] From a report by Jacob Baegert cited in Dunne, *Black Robes*, 150.

knees, wherever the tone reaches them."[61] Pérez de Ribas was attesting to the Christian devotion of the Yaquis when he wrote that "at the first sound of the bell both young and old came running from their little houses, both throughout the week and on feast days."[62] Responding to the sound of the bells was an important step in the Hispanicization and indoctrination of the indigenous peoples of the north. Don José Gallardo issued instructions in 1750 intended to reform the labor system and discipline the "vagabond" and unproductive Indians of the Provincias Internas. Second among the six regulations was that "all work, acts, and offices of each town must be carried out at the precise pealing of the bell."[63] When Franciscans in Nuevo Santander were having difficulty in keeping potential converts from fleeing the mission and in enforcing attendance at mass on feast days, they took comfort in the fact that at least Indians routinely came from their homes when called by the bells.[64] Bells could also signal disorder and produce a response very different than acculturation over the musical landscape. On two separate occasions, the apparent ringing of bells by themselves was viewed by Jesuits as an omen of coming unrest among the Tarahumara population.[65]

At Mission Purísima Concepción in San Antonio, an area populated not only by Indians, but also Spaniards, separate strokes of the bells signaled first- and second-class feast days. In this community, bell-ringing signified power relationships based on racial and ethnic categories. On first-class feasts, both Spaniards and Indians were required to attend worship, and the bells pealed at noon, in the evening, and before mass. On second-class feasts, which only Indians were required to observe, the bells were rung only in the evening and before mass. Every Saturday was marked by a single pealing of the bells before mass.[66] In this mission, the sound of the bells not only gathered the faithful, but also reinforced ethnic differences. Canary Islanders, Spaniards, and mestizos knew which bell tones applied to them, and Indians were instructed to answer

---

[61] *Memorial of 1630*, section entitled, "Lo que deve aquel Reino a vuestra Magestad," in Morrow, *A Harvest of Reluctant Souls*, 46.

[62] Pérez de Ribas, *History of the Triumphs of Our Holy Faith*, book 5, chapter 17, 366.

[63] Report and instructions of Visitador José Rodríguez Gallardo, AGN, Provincias Internas, vol. 176, exp. 6.

[64] Report on the missions of Nuevo León and Nuevo Santander to Fr. Juan Ballesteros, 1797–1798, W.B. Stephens Collection, 1394, 52, UTNLB. See also Fr. Juan de Santiesteban to Juan María de Bohorquez, November 15, 1788, in Ocaranza, *Los franciscanos* 165.

[65] Bernabe Francisco de Gutiérrez to Padre Provincial Francisco Ximenez, April 28, 1676, AGN, Misiones, vol. 26, f. 220v; and Joseph Neumann to the governor, Sisoguichi, December 25, 1696, and December 30, 1696, cited in Deeds, *Defiance and Deference*, 97.

[66] Benoist and Flores, *Guidelines*, 3.

to a different sound. All the settlement heard the bells and knew to which ethnic group their ringing was directed.

The sound of the bell conveyed information both to the mission community as well as to anyone within reach of its sound. For this reason, it could also be used as information for those wishing to attack the missions at a time when they could capture or kill congregated groups. Juan María de Salvatierra was cautious about ringing the mission bell at Loreto when he sensed a rebellion was imminent: "I very much wanted to celebrate mass with all possible solemnity; but the concern and the numerous signs of an impending attack did not give us a chance to ring the bell, for fear that they might start the assault during mass."[67]

Bells also rang out to welcome visitors, or warn of approaching danger in the form of invaders, fire, or flood. The Jesuit annual letter of 1649 described the reception given visitors to the pueblos of Nueva Vizcaya. Indian leaders and musicians with chirimías and trumpets greeted missionaries and officials, and the patio of the church was decorated with flowers and arches. The community then processed to the church while singing the prayers. When the party arrived at the church, the bells were pealed in honor of the visitors.[68] Ringing of mission bells announced the transfer of the Baja California missions from Franciscan to Dominican administration in 1772.[69] When they announced baptisms or marriages, bells informed the community of the culmination of Christian rites of passage. In these situations, bells reinforced appropriate behavior on the part of new converts and further inculcated inclusion into the Christian community. Bell-ringing could reflect divisions and hierarchies present in a community between converted and unconverted or in ethnic and social groups, but at the same time it was heard by all, and thus guaranteed a measure of symbolic equality among individuals by giving a rhythm to their lives and marking the completion of rites.[70]

As markers of ceremonial or ritual time, bells were involved in the formal possession of mission territories and the celebration of major Christian festivals. They were also indicators of rites of passage, such as baptisms, marriages, and deaths. Upon reoccupation of the pueblos of New Mexico in 1694, Governor Don Diego de Vargas ordered the ringing of mission bells as a sign of reposses-

---

[67] Salvatierra to Ugarte, November 27, 1697, in Ernest J. Burrus, ed., *Juan Maria de Salvatierra, S.J.: Selected Letters about Lower California* (Los Angeles: Dawson's Book Shop, 1971), 120.

[68] AGN, Misiones, vol. 26, exp. 5, f. 86-99v.

[69] Francisco Palou, *Historical Memoirs of New California*, vol. 1 (New York: Russell and Russell, 1966), 255-256.

[70] Corbin, *Village Bells*, 79.

sion of the land and its peoples.[71] The first Corpus Christi celebrated at Mission San Carlos de Monterey in Alta California was cause for the ringing of celebratory bells. In 1770, Junípero Serra marked the feast by chanting mass and holding a procession "accompanied by peals of bells and repeated volleys from the cannon on the packet and from the muskets and guns of the soldiers."[72] Although Palóu's primary intent was likely to mark the Christian feast day with appropriate solemnity and pomp, this demonstration certainly had the additional effect of illustrating (very loudly) Spanish power. It also signaled the restructuring of ritual time, in which the Catholic liturgical calendar was layered upon indigenous seasonal cycles. Ceremonial bells were not only supposed to announce specific occasions, they also were intended to sanctify the space over which they sounded and drive away demons in the air, who were thought to be horrified by their sound.[73]

Bells announcing the death of a neophyte were all too common in frontier missions. The enormous toll of European diseases on the native populations must have made this type of bell-ringing a somber reminder of the effects of Spanish presence in the area. Not only were bells tolled to announce a death, they were sometimes rung as part of the weekly routine to remind the faithful to pray for the souls of the dead. Andrés Pérez de Ribas described the reaction of Sinaloan converts to these bells:

> *When the bell is rung at the appointed time of the evening for the souls of the dead, . . . all the Sinaloans immediately kneel and begin praying aloud two decades of the rosary, regardless of where they are or what they are doing. In this way each week they complete their devotion and prayers for their dead.*[74]

These bells served as a constant reminder of the tremendous losses of human life that occurred following Spanish contact with indigenous populations. Together with life-sized statues of the crucified or entombed Christ, and paintings of martyrs, heaven, and hell, they must have kept death at the forefront of neophytes' minds. Missionaries capitalized on these sounds and sights to remind new Christians to strive for the "good death," illustrated in art, religious manuals, and devotional books.[75]

---

[71] AGI, Guadalajara, 140, exp. 5.
[72] Francisco Palou, *Historical Memoirs of New California,* vol. II, ed. Herbert Bolton (New York: Russell and Russell, 1966), 295-296.
[73] See Corbin, *Village Bells,* 101-102.
[74] Pérez de Ribas, *History of the Triumph of Our Holy Faith,* book 3, chapter 26, 258.
[75] Dying well included writing a will, receiving the last rites, and saying the prayers prescribed by the manual. On the "good death," and artwork associated with death and dying, see Martina

Bells rung at death likely aided in the development of a counterideology to Catholicism present in the missions of the lower Tarahumara in the early seventeenth century. The Jesuits were viewed not as holy priests, but instead as sorcerers of the Spaniards. Conversion to Christianity was thought to make the land sterile, baptism was seen as causing illness or signaling death, and the pealing of church bells was thought to attract diseases.[76] Perhaps it is for these reasons that bells were often desecrated during indigenous rebellions, not only among the Tarahumara, but throughout the northern frontier.

Control over bell-ringing was an important marker of political and social power, and this power was sometimes contested. A 1689 dispute in San Augustine, Florida, centered around Father Alonso de Leturiondo's practice of ordering the church bells rung whenever he traveled through the streets to a residence to perform the sacrament of extreme unction. Governor Diego de Quiroga y Losada complained to the King that this noisy practice, particularly when it occurred at night, interfered with proper defense of the coastal city. Padre Alonso argued that the bells caused the faithful to accompany priests with their prayers and presence. The Crown's solution, not handed down until four years after the incident that prompted the dispute, was to permit the ringing of the bell once to signal the departure of the viaticum, and to encourage priests to ring a handbell as they traveled to a deathbed.[77] Occasionally, indigenous peoples contested the power of the bells, or appropriated it for their own use as a tool of resistance. Bells were broken or destroyed in rebellions, and church bells were even rung to gather participants in the Yaqui rebellion of 1740.[78]

Alabados

Bells were the primary markers of time in mission communities, but some liturgical forms were also used to restructure time and establish Spanish-style routines. Alabados, alabanzas, and older Latin hymns were important symbols in the musical structuring of mission life. Alabados were hymns, a form of Christian poetry, designed for communal singing with the purpose of praising

---

Will de Chaparro, *Death and Dying in New Mexico* (Albuquerque: University of New Mexico Press, 2007), 12-27.

[76] Merrill, "Conversion and Colonialism in Northern Mexico," 138. See also Deeds, "Indigenous Rebellions," 38.

[77] The entire dispute is described and documented in Amy Turner Bushnell, *Situado and Sabana*, 182-184.

[78] Spicer, *The Yaquis*, 44.

God.[79] These hymns punctuated the days of those in the mission community with auditory declarations of Christian belief. They were important tools in the acculturation process and involved the entire community. Missionaries viewed the singing of alabados by neophytes outside of prescribed contexts (in the course of daily worship and teaching) as an important indicator of Christian devotion and piety.

There is evidence of alabados being sung in the missions of northern New Spain as early as the late seventeenth century. They were simple devotional songs with chorus and verses, perhaps sung to familiar chant-like melodies.[80] The lyrics were in Spanish, unlike the Latin liturgical texts, which made up almost the entire corpus of music sung in the early northern missions. Although the texts of alabados during the colonial period could vary between different regions, within the individual mission, the text was consistent and sung to a particular tune in a way that gained mnemonic power.[81] Simple melodies and the repetition of verses throughout a day ensured that the songs were quickly retained. Extant alabado texts range from three to over ten stanzas in length, and often begin with the words, "*alabado sea*" or "praised be." The lyrics most often praised the Eucharist, but also referenced Mary, Jesus, or a particular saint. Although their form was similar to the eight-syllable quatrain common in Spanish poetry, it is unclear whether alabados originated in Spain or New Spain.[82]

---

[79] This particular section is concerned with alabados mentioned in the colonial record. Alabados are still sung today in many parts of the greater Southwest, but their form and purpose seem to differ somewhat from those found in mission communities during the colonial period.

[80] Written music for the alabados is virtually nonexistent until the nineteenth century. Reports like the Ruíz daily schedule earlier in this chapter, however, speak of the "intonation" of the alabado, perhaps suggesting that the melodies were similar to those of liturgical chant. Early recordings of alabados from California and New Mexico are sung without instrumental accompaniment. It is difficult to determine performance context for the colonial period, but elaborate instrumentation seems unlikely given that they are often mentioned in missions without large inventories of instruments.

[81] For texts and their relation to tunes as mnemonic devices, see Robert Jourdain, *Music, the Brain, and Ecstasy: How Music Captures Our Imagination* (New York: Aron Books, 1997), 256.

[82] See Thomas Steele, S.J., *The Alabados of New Mexico* (Albuquerque: University of New Mexico Press, 2005); Juan B. Rael, *The New Mexican Alabado* (Stanford, CA: Stanford University Press, 1951), 18-19; John D. Robb, *Hispanic Folk Music of New Mexico and the Southwest: A Self-Portrait of a People* (Norman: University of Oklahoma Press, 1980), 612; and Richard B. Stark, "Notes on a Search for Antecedents of New Mexican Alabado Music," in Marta Weigle, ed., *Hispanic Arts and Ethnohistory in the Southwest* (Santa Fe, NM: Ancient City Press, 1983), 117-125, for speculation on the origin of alabados in New Mexico. Franciscan Father Owen da Silva describes the California alabado in his 1941 description of music in the California missions (*Mission Music of California*, 120). He implies that there was only one alabado with twenty-four verses. This does not seem to be the case throughout the entire north, although it is probable that one form was sung in Alta California. See also Russell, *From Serra to Sancho*, 137-143.

Both Franciscans and Jesuits utilized alabados in their missionary endeavors in the north, but they were more commonly sung in Franciscan missions.[83] The only other references to the singing of alabados in Jesuit missions are in the Pimería Alta and Baja California missions. Alabados were common, on the other hand, in the Franciscan missions of Sonora, Alta California, Texas, and New Mexico. This is consistent with my earlier observations that Jesuits were more likely to use hymns or prayers set to music in Latin or vernacular languages in their evangelization efforts, whereas Franciscans encouraged singing in vernacular Castilian. Jesuit emphasis on the Latin texts of the liturgy may have derived from the Counter-Reformation spirit and Tridentine legislation, which deemed Latin a more appropriate language for praising God. In addition, Jesuits tended to emphasize teaching in the native language, and were more likely to use it and Latin for prayers and songs. Spicer theorized that Franciscans, on the other hand, by the early 1700s focused on turning neophytes away from native languages as quickly as possible in favor of Spanish. They believed that in order to understand Christianity, it was necessary to understand the Spanish language.[84] Although some Franciscans did learn indigenous languages and use them in preaching, singing was more likely to be in Spanish than Latin or an Indian language. Alabados, then, written in Spanish were frequently used as teaching tools, useful for learning both doctrine and language, by the friars, while Jesuits used other songs, including Latin prayers set to music.

Perhaps the most widely known alabado, and one of the few for which we have lyrics from the colonial period, is one written by Fray Antonio Margil de Jesús and circulated through the *colegios de propaganda fide* at Zacatecas and Querétaro.[85] Margil's biographer, Eduardo Enrique Ríos, stated that this alabado, with a few minor changes, was translated into Nahuatl and published in Mexico by Franciscan Fray Juan de Cabrera.[86] The lyrics of this song of praise emphasized purity and stressed the importance of leading a life free of sin. The singing of this alabado in Alta California supports James Sandos's argument that the friars there focused on sin in their teachings in an attempt to

---

[83] Alabados were also sung in New Mexico following the reconquest of the territory in the 1690s and may well have been sung there in the first half of the seventeenth century. See AGI, Guadalajara, 140, exp. 5.

[84] See Spicer, *Cycles of Conquest*, 327-328, for a discussion of the differences in Jesuit and Franciscan attitudes toward the use of Spanish in evangelization.

[85] Espinosa, *Crónica de los colegios de propaganda fide*, 594-595.

[86] *The Life of Fray Antonio Margil* (Washington, DC: Academy of American Franciscan History, 1959), 23, n. 16.

instill a sense of Christian guilt in converts and compel them to more decorous behavior.[87]

In Margil's alabado, praise was sung not only of the Divine Sacraments, but also the Immaculate Conception, Mary, and St. Joseph. While praise of Mary is common in many Catholic hymns, Joseph appears less frequently. Margil may have included San José as a way of emphasizing the Christian family unit, with married parents and their child. A focus on the family of Mary, Joseph, and Jesus may have stemmed from a need to reinforce the model Christian family, with a mother/nurturer and a father/provider, among the indigenous peoples with whom he worked. Margil's alabado was sung as part of the home mission's evangelization work in areas near the college, by the Franciscans living at the missionary college in Zacatecas in the eighteenth century:

> *It is common practice for missionaries to travel through haciendas, ranchos, and along the road gathering inhabitants in the evening to recite part of the Rosary, for the missionary to give them a short teaching on the virgin, and sing with them the alabado.*[88]

Father Marion Habig concluded that Franciscans at Zacatecas and Querétaro learned Margil's alabado, as well as other hymns he composed to honor Mary, and spread them throughout the territory to which they were sent as missionaries.[89] There is evidence to suggest that this was the case; Pedro Font's diary of the Anza expedition describes the first line of the alabado sung at San Gabriel in Alta California as "*alabado y ensalzado sea el divino sacramento,*" the same as the first line of Margil's alabado.[90] Junípero Serra, president of the Alta California missions, may have been responsible for the propagation of this version of the alabado. Father Sánchez at Mission San Gabriel stated that "the alabado . . . is sung in all the missions and in the same key. Indeed, the fathers sing it even though they may not have good voices, since uniformity is the best."[91] The alabado was generally sung following mass or doctrinal instruction in the missions of California and Texas. In other areas, alabados were sung in the morn-

---

[87] James Sandos, "Social Control in Spain's North American Frontiers: Choice, Persuasion, and Coercion in Alta California, 1769–1821" (paper presented at Social Control on Spain's North American Frontiers: Choice, Persuasion and Coercion Conference, Meadows Museum of Art, Southern Methodist University, Dallas, TX, April 6, 2002), 22.

[88] Undated [late eighteenth century] training manual for missionaries at Zacatecas, OSMHRC, Zacatecas, reel 13, fr. 1003.

[89] Marion A. Habig Collection, OLLUSCA, box 9.

[90] Bolton, *Font's Complete Diary*, 179-180.

[91] Ibid.

ing and at sunset, in processions, and as part of special occasions, such as celebration of the harvest, the installation of indigenous officials, and the honoring of special visitors to the mission.[92]

Regardless of the times of day at which it was sung, an alabado was repeated often within the weekly routine of a mission. Repetition was an important element in imprinting the alabado tune and text firmly in the minds of the Indians. For example, the daily routine recorded for the Baja California missions in 1730 contains a description of the restructuring of time through not only the ringing of the bells, but also the singing of the liturgy. An ordinary day was as follows: the Ave Marias were played on the bells, and then the families came to the church, prayed and saluted the Holy Virgin, singing the alabado, first the men, then the women, followed by both men and women together. After breakfast they went about separate chores, some to work, some to tend the sick and elderly. Those who had no other occupation helped with the mass, which was celebrated daily, and afterward said prayers and sang the alabado as described before. The men worked in the fields or building the church; the women spun cotton and wool. A temastián instructed the ranchería peoples in the basics of the faith so that they could confess. At 10:00 the bell was rung and the children came to the church to recite the doctrine and sing the alabado. At midday the bell was rung, and on their knees, all saluted the Holy Virgin and sang the alabado again. After they ate posole, they rested until 2:00 and then continued with their work. At 5:00 the bell was rung and the boys and girls were called to the church to recite all the prayers and the doctrine, singing the alabado in chorus at the end. In the evening the Ave Marias were played and all knelt to salute the Holy Virgin. After they ate dinner, they went to the church and recited with the padre (in chorus) the rosary, litanies, and the alabado. Then they left, the men with their temastián and the women with their temastiana, and the married people to their homes.[93] In this daily schedule, the alabado was sung a total of six times. In addition, the song itself was repetitive, with chorus-and-verse form, and the first stanza repeated at the end.

Just as bells signaled the beginning and ending of the days in many mission communities, the singing of the alabado bounded the day at Mission San

---

[92] See, for example, a report on Mission Espíritu Santo, Texas, 1787, OSMHRC, Zacatecas, reel 7, fr. 5058-5059; Fray Antonio Reyes, "Noticia y estado," September 30, 1772, cited in John Kessell, *Friars, Soldiers, and Reformers: Hispanic Arizona and the Sonora Mission Frontier, 1767–1856* (Tucson: University of Arizona Press, 1976), 69-70; Bayle, *Misión de la Baja California*, 218; Benoist and Flores, *Guidelines*, 11, 35; and Fray Solís to Padre Guardian, 1767, OSMHRC, Zacatecas, reel 16, fr. 1452.

[93] AGN, Historia, vol. 21, f. 171.

Gabriel Árcangel de los Temblores in Alta California. The Franciscan padre stationed at San Gabriel assembled the neophytes for mass at sunrise, followed by the singing of the alabado. At sunset, they again recited doctrine in unison and then ended the day's instruction by singing the alabado.[94] The Salve Regina was sung both at the beginning and end of missionaries' interactions with neophytes in other missions. This hymn, a Marian antiphon with Latin text, was used by both Franciscans and Jesuits as part of the daily routine in areas where the alabado was not as popular.[95] It was frequently part of the daily routine in missions established prior to the end of the seventeenth century. The Salve and the alabado were sung either in unison by the entire congregated group, or by groups (divided by age and/or gender) singing alternate verses.

Like the singing in their religious background at conventos and colleges in Europe and New Spain, the missionaries advocated communal singing of hymns and doctrine. Singing in unison has been shown to inspire laborers to work at an optimum level.[96] It is no surprise, then, that missionaries encouraged group singing of an alabado, the Salve Regina, litany, or another prayer before community members went off to the fields, mission workshops, or their homes for work or sleep. Teaching these Christian songs and repeating them daily had the additional goal of instilling the hymns as those to be sung by workers as they went about their daily tasks. This not only further reinforced conversion efforts through repetition of Christian concepts, but also furthered the process of Hispanicization through the singing of songs in the Spanish language. Confirmation of the success of teaching alabados as an evangelization and acculturation tool was evidenced by reports of Indians singing the hymn as they traveled, worked, or in their homes. Fray Isidro Félix de Espinosa was pleased with his instruction efforts at San Diego de Tesuque, New Mexico, when he wrote, "It is a pleasure to hear the children singing alabados throughout the pueblo, and

---

[94] Bolton, *Font's Complete Diary*, 179-180.

[95] The Salve Regina in its original Latin form was sung in Jesuit and Franciscan missions in Nueva Vizcaya, Sonora, Baja California, and Texas. In addition, a hymn in Spanish also called "Salve," with the opening line "Dios te salve, Maria," was sung in Alta California and Texas. See Antonio de los Reyes to the King, September 2, 1774, AGI, Guadalajara, 586, f. 39v-40; a biography of Padre Vicente Escalera, OSMHRC, Zacatecas, reel 16, fr. 1431-1423; Benoist and Flores, *Guidelines*, 7; Theodore Treutlein, "The Relation of Philipp Segesser: The Pimas and Other Indians [1737]," *Mid-America* 27 (1945), 160-164; Father Juan Fernandez to F. Provincial Tomas Altamirano, October 7, 1679, ARSI, Rome, 17, f. 409r-409v, in Sheridan, *Empire of Sand*, 32; Pfefferkorn, *Sonora*, 269; and Auto de inventario y embargo de bienes de Pedro Correa, vecino de Parral, June 1667, AGN, Inquisición, vol. 602, exp. 6.

[96] Tame, *Secret Power of Music*, 145. This bears comparison to the songs sung by prison workers or spirituals sung by slaves while working.

the governor instructs his children in Christian doctrine in the evenings, for I have heard him do so from my house."[97] In this example, Indians reportedly sang a Christian song outside the required context of the mission. This indicates at least a degree of acculturation, and although it is likely that the singers may not have grasped or endorsed the concepts about which they were singing (at least initially), they were still memorizing and repeating teachings of the Church. Fray Margil's alabado ends with the phrase, "Rather than sin, death." The repeated singing of such ideas must have had some effect on the indigenous peoples who learned the alabado by heart. Teaching alabados, then, not only aided in the restructuring of time, but also in the "colonization of consciousness"—a reconstruction of the daily worlds of the conquered through theological messages such as Christian domesticity, purity, and the holiness of the sacraments.[98]

Restructuring of Ritual Time

The performed sound of alabados and mission bells restructured time on a daily and weekly basis for those within their auditory range. Music in the missions of northern New Spain was further heard, repeated, structured, positioned, and presented as an exterior marker of piety. It heralded the installation of a new encompassing social order based on spectacle and performance.[99] Music was regimented and repeated in the context of daily routines, but it also became part of the restructuring of yearly celebrations and ceremonial time. The layering of indigenous rituals with Christian ceremonies, a major component of Hispanicizing the Indians, was a common goal of the regular clergy. Andrés Pérez de Ribas frequently wrote about *casos de edificación*, that is, instances where missionaries, aided by divine grace, substituted Christian rituals for native rites and beliefs.[100]

The Catholic ceremonial year was structured by a series of liturgical seasons (Advent, Christmas, Epiphany, Lent, Easter, and Pentecost), and punctuated by the celebration of specific feast days within these seasons. Christian feast days honored specific events in the life of Jesus Christ or the Church, and commemorated contributions of the saints. The imposition of religious festivals in colonial situations was an effective means of weakening indigenous religious bonds.

---

[97] Espinosa, *Crónica de los colegios de propaganda fide*, 115-116.
[98] Comaroff and Comaroff, *Ethnography and the Historical Imagination*, 258.
[99] Jacques Attali, *Noise: The Political Economy of Music*, trans. Brian Massumi (Minneapolis: University of Minnesota Press, 1985), 23.
[100] Daniel Reff, preface to Pérez de Ribas, *History of the Triumphs of Our Holy Faith*, 4.

The aim of this type of restructuring of ceremonial time was to make converts act according to new markers of time, set by the Church, and to dissolve loyalty to old autochthonous markers of time. The cycle of Catholic festivals regulated many aspects of public life as well as social and individual life in mission communities. Food was stored for feasting at celebrations, musicians rehearsed and sometimes traveled to partake in festivities, and gifts were distributed. Pérez de Ribas described the importance of the celebration of Christian festivals when he wrote about the dedication of a new church building at Zuaque, to which neighboring Indian nations were invited:

> *They could see that with Christ's law they were not being stripped of festivals and honorable and holy celebrations, which replaced their former profane and atrocious ones. Care was taken to solemnize this celebration through all possible means of joyful and pleasing spectacle; . . . therefore, nothing was spared in terms of music, dances, and fires that could be had in such a poor land. . . . The dances and drums that once called the Zuaque to war against the Christians, which they triumphantly celebrated with severed heads, were now celebrating festivals for Christ and His Most Holy Mother.*[101]

Music was interwoven into the reorganization of ceremonial time in mission communities. Specific liturgical and devotional songs were performed for different feast days. Members of the community processed from their homes to the church patio to the beat of indigenous percussion instruments and the sound of Christian devotions.

Like the processions, many of the celebrations of the newly restructured ritual calendar contained a combination of Catholic and indigenous elements. Instead of merely imposing the new Christian cycle of feasts, missionaries chose to integrate these feast days with existing indigenous practices and ceremonies. Franciscans in New Mexico scheduled the celebration of Christ's birth so that it coincided with the preparatory days the Puebloans observed before celebrating the winter solstice. Specific dances performed by clans and societies were part of the indigenous celebration of the solstice; friars attempted to integrate them into European dance-dramas such as matachines and moros y cristianos dances.[102] In Baja California, a mass baptism of forty infants at San Francisco Xavier Biaundo was timed to coincide with the ripening of the first fruits of the *pitahaya*, or prickly pear cactus. The baptism was preceded by a ceremony in which *californios* presented Father Piccolo with their corn and crops, and it

---

[101] Pérez de Ribas, *History of the Triumphs of Our Holy Faith*, book 3, chapter 12, 225.
[102] See Gutiérrez, *When Jesus Came, the Corn Mothers Went Away*, 84.

concluded with hours of dances and feasting.[103] Although rituals surrounding harvest differed by group, they generally included feasting, singing, dancing, relaxation of marital ties, games, pantomimes, and mimicry.[104] Jesuit missionaries permitted, even encouraged, these activities, so long as they were directed toward Christian devotion for All Souls' Day or saints' feast days in the Christian calendar at nearly the same time.[105] For example, Opatas and Eudeves at Cucurpe in Sonora sang the Office for the Dead and attended mass in addition to their customary singing, dancing, and feasting. In addition, on a mat woven from palm leaves, Indians placed "offerings for the consolation of the souls in Purgatory, as was the custom. One brought a handful of beans, peas, or maize; another some pinole or posole. Still others gave tortillas. . . . These offerings were afterward distributed by the missionary."[106] In seventeenth-century Nueva Vizcaya, Jesuits attempted to insert lavish ceremonies for Catholic feast days into the ritual time of Acaxees and Xiximes to compete with indigenous ceremonies. These ceremonies included elaborate processions and food, which was in short supply following uprisings in the area, to attract the attendance of the Indians.[107]

The colonization of ceremonial time did allow some space for indigenous actors to reshape their own cultures. It is important to consider that ritual festivals held by the Church could also open the door for indigenous cultural practices, which were incompatible with efforts to impose ideological and behavioral standards. Missionary-sponsored festivals had dimensions that escaped missionary control.[108] The practice of trying to colonize ritual time through the establishment of new ritual calendars could open a space for indigenous peoples to engage in some of their own cultural practices in public and with a wider audience. More specific instances of indigenous ethnogenesis connected with celebrations for special occasions will be discussed in the next chapter.

---

[103] Manuel de la Vega, Relación, BINAH, vol. 68, f. 56v.
[104] See del Barco, *Historia natural*, 192; and John Augustin Donohue, *After Kino: Jesuit Missions in Northwestern New Spain* (Rome: Jesuit Historical Institute, 1969), 141.
[105] See Crosby, *Antigua California*, 215-216; and Radding, *Wandering Peoples*, 69.
[106] Pfefferkorn, *Sonora*, 270-271.
[107] Deeds, "Defiance and Deference," 28.
[108] Malte Rolf, "Constructing a Soviet Time: Bolshevik Festivals and Their Rivals during the First Five-Year Plan: A Study of the Central Black Earth Region," *Kritika: Explorations in Russian and Eurasian History* 1:3 (2000), 470-471.

Conclusions

The regulation of time—both daily and ceremonial—was of great importance to the missionaries, who were concerned both with religious conversion and acculturation. Aligning one's day with the sound of the bell was an indication of civilization and order for Franciscans in Alta California. They were asked to respond to an early nineteenth-century circular letter that asked, "How do they [the neophytes] know and distinguish the seasons of the year? Do they have their own calendars or are they the same they had in their pagan state? How do they regulate the hours of the day for the distribution of sleep, meals, and labor?"[109] The friar at Mission San Juan Bautista replied to this letter by stating, "They have no calendar neither of months nor of the year. . . . In their pagan state . . . they did not reckon with hours for their rest, meals, or labors. Each one lived according to his pleasure. Our neophytes' lives are guided in all these things by the mission bell."[110] The Franciscans considered that their reorganization of time at San Juan Bautista was successful when Indians were convinced, forcefully or otherwise, to abandon their former cycles of time and subscribe to the mission's routine. Both ceremonial and daily schedules of time became regimented as most indigenous groups were Hispanicized and incorporated into the empire throughout the northern frontier of New Spain.

It is important to note, however, that the reshaping of indigenous concepts of time was not total. Despite the optimism of the Franciscans at San Juan Bautista about the neophytes' adherence to the dictates of the bells, in other areas foot dragging and work slowdowns, often perceived by the missionaries as laziness, were common. Padre Joseph Roldán, Jesuit missionary in Sonora, lamented, "the people never go to work, only a few; . . . the few who do go to labor in the fields go more to eat and visit than to work."[111] Indigenous peoples could also outwardly conform to the dictates of Hispanicization while not internalizing culture and Christianity. For example, Father Joseph Neumann, missionary and later visitor in the missions of the Jesuit Tarahumara province, summed up his experience with the Indians among whom he worked:

---

[109] Preguntas y Respuestas (question 16), 1813, published in Geiger and Meighan, *As the Padres Saw Them*, 81.

[110] Ibid., 83.

[111] Padre Joseph Roldán, "Luz con que se deben mirar las sementeras que los Jesuitas hacen en sus misiones," BNM, Fondo Franciscano, 32/662, cited in Radding, *Wandering Peoples*, 69.

> *These Indians are by nature and disposition a sly and crafty folk, from whom sincerity is not to be expected.... They say one thing to their people when in the presence of the missionaries and later in secret they say another directly contrary.... Superficially the governors conformed to the wishes of the fathers, and their lives had the appearance of probity, but all the while they were secretly seeking the favor of their people by tolerating and cloaking their offenses.*[112]

These examples illustrate the difficulty in ascertaining the degree of acculturation to daily schedules or Christian ceremonial calendars obtained in individual missions.

Was the musical restructuring of time, both daily and ritual, in mission communities successful? In the short term, missionaries met a great deal of resistance. In some cases, indigenous peoples simply removed themselves from the auditory boundaries established by the bells and singing of Christian hymns. Over the course of the colonial era, however, this musical restructuring, when coupled with the overwhelming pressures of disease, dislocation, and economic and political conditions, helped lead to the acculturation of a large number of indigenous peoples in northern New Spain. As an initial step in the processes of conversion and acculturation, the musical colonization of time was an effective means of establishing hegemony without expending a great amount of military power.[113] It is clear that the hegemonic effects of music on daily and yearly schedules were not complete. Indigenous peoples' lives may have, in the long run, been disciplined through the colonizing of time, but there was still room for indigenous agency, some in the form of "weapons of the weak" such as slander, work slowdowns, and foot dragging. In addition, the restructuring of ceremonial time through the imposition of a Christian calendar of feasts left much space for indigenous ethnogenesis and cultural accommodation in musical performances for special occasions. It is to a more complete examination of the performances for special occasions, and their role in the restructuring of sacred space, that I now turn.

---

[112] Father Joseph Neumann, cited in Spicer, *Cycles of Conquest*, 311.
[113] Spicer, *Cycles of Conquest*, 324-325.

CHAPTER 7
Music and the Restructuring of Physical and Social Space

Fray Pedro Font, traveling with the expedition of Juan Bautista de Anza, near San Francisco, California, in 1776, reported a curious event:

> At sunrise the ten Indians came, one behind another, singing and dancing. One carried the air, making music with a little stick, rather long and split in the middle, which he struck against his hand and which sounded something like a castanet. They reached the camp and continued singing and dancing for a little while. Then they stopped dancing, all making a step in unison, shaking the body and saying dryly in one voice, "Ha, ha, ha!" Next they sat down on the ground and signaled to us that we must sit down also. . . . They invited us to go to their village . . . [and] followed us with their singing and dancing, which I interrupted by chanting the alabado, as we did every day on beginning the journey, but as soon as I finished they continued their singing and shouting with greater vigor and in a higher key, as if they wished to respond to our chant. After going a short distance we came to the village, . . . the Indians welcoming us with an indescribable hullabaloo. . . . They led us to the middle of the village where there was a level spot like a plaza, and then began to dance with other Indians of the place with much clatter and yelling.[1]

Contests over the possession of the environment in northern New Spain occurred throughout the colonial period. From Fray Pedro's description, it is clear that both missionaries and indigenous peoples claimed and structured sacred space by performing rituals related to music and dance. This amazing encounter between Spaniards singing hymns and Indians singing and dancing foretold struggles over the control of sacred space, defined through music-making, rituals, and reshaping the land.

This chapter discusses the restructuring of space, both physical and social, through performances of music and dance. Missionaries aimed to restructure

---

[1] Bolton, *Font's Complete Diary*, 366-368.

physical space through construction projects and ritual actions. Ceremonies for territorial possession and processions attempted to sanctify land and dedicate it to God. Structures were erected to accommodate the missionaries' religious goals and liturgical needs. Defense of indigenous lands was crucial to group identity in northern mission communities, and Indians guarded caves, hilltops, and sacred territories where they could practice dances and ceremonies.[2] Indigenous groups concentrated on the restructuring of social space by carving out niches in which they could inhabit the colonial world while recreating their own cultural beliefs and practices. They remade social structure as they accepted roles in mission governance, or competed for power with the new order. Women in northern New Spain restructured gendered space by using music. Celebrations on special days during the liturgical year opened up possibilities and spaces for indigenous groups to re-create culture. Through the processes of ethnogenesis and cultural adaptation, Catholic special celebrations were made indigenous, and traditions were reinvented, so that by the nineteenth century, popular religiosity exhibited a great deal of syncretism.

Possession, Repossession, and Procession

The Anza expedition was the start of the last major *entrada* into northern New Spain, the incorporation of Alta California into the Bourbon Spanish empire. Similar to the rites of possession practiced in the early colonial period, those of the late eighteenth century involved large doses of ceremony and performance. Mission San José was formally established in 1797 in the presence of soldiers, colonists, Indian converts, and auxiliary troops, as reported by Fermín Francisco de Lasuén:

> *On this day, Sunday, feast of the Most Holy Trinity, I blessed water, the grounds, and a large cross, which we venerated and erected, in a beautiful place called* oroyjon *by the natives. . . . Immediately afterwards we sang the Litany of All Saints and celebrated the holy sacrifice of the mass in an* enramada *which we set up the preceding evening and decorated it from floor to roof with many different flowers. I preached a sermon to the troops and to the Christian Indians who had gathered there, and brought my portion of the solemn function to an end by solemnly singing the Te Deum Laudamus. In this manner, possession was taken of this region, and*

---

[2] In *Wandering Peoples*, Cynthia Radding elaborates on the ties between land and identity, in a concept she terms "ethnic space." She also discusses the importance of indigenous religious sites in "Crosses, Caves, and *Matachinis*."

so was begun the mission dedicated to our glorious patriarch San José, in accordance with the superior orders of His Excellency the viceroy of New Spain.[3]

First, Franciscans chose a suitable spot and a feast day on which to dedicate the mission; this was often the name given to it. Then, an *enramada* with a small altar was built so that mass could be said in a covered, although rudimentary, shelter. A blessing was said, the Litany of the Saints was intoned by those who knew it, mass was chanted, and then the officiant preached a sermon for the gathered assembly of soldiers and curious onlookers. The ritual always concluded with the singing of the Te Deum Laudamus, a hymn of thanksgiving. In these ceremonies, music was an integral part of claiming the space for God and King. It purified the ground and communicated feelings of thanksgiving to God. When Indians were present for the ceremonies, according to missionary accounts, the religious songs piqued their curiosity and encouraged them to investigate the new visitors.[4] As a result, the formal entradas and dedication ceremonies in late eighteenth-century New Spain were deliberately stylized with outward symbols of Catholicism: vestments, banners, music, altars, and arches decorated with flowers and foliage. Missionaries and government officials hoped that the pomp with which their arrival was celebrated would demonstrate the immense power of church and state. In addition, if outward symbols of Catholicism and material gifts could pacify the indigenous peoples and attract them to the mission communities voluntarily, precious military resources could be spared from aiding in forced relocation and conquest.

Repossession ceremonies occurred throughout the colonial period and were more lavish and military in character than initial entradas. They were meant to reestablish Spanish and Catholic control over a specific place, and thus they emphasized the material and military might of the Spanish entrada force. For example, the Aguayo expedition to reestablish missions in eastern Texas aimed to impress the indigenous peoples with the chanting of a mass by Father Margil, the ringing of large, unearthed church bells, playing of clarins and drums, firing of salvos, a great banquet, and the distribution of gifts of clothing.[5] Soldiers

---

[3] Lasuén to Don Diego de Borica, June 11, 1797, in *Writings*, Finbar Kenneally, ed. and trans. (Washington, DC: Academy of American Franciscan History, 1965), vol. 2, 30-31. Similar ceremonies took place at San Juan Bautista and San Carlos de Monterey. See AGI, Guadalajara, 104-6-17, 1776, CAT, 7-8, pp. 6, 37.

[4] See, for example, a description of the Aguayo expedition into eastern Texas, 1721-1722, AGN, Historia, vol. 28, photocopy in CAT, 26.2, pp. 79, 88, as well as Dunne, *Black Robes in Lower California*, 161, which contains a description of Padre Guillén's singing of the Litanies and the alabado, which allegedly attracted nearby Indians in 1719.

[5] AGN, Historia, vol. 28, photocopy in CAT, 26.2, pp. 79, 1721-1722.

were prominently featured in the processions, and their weapons were on display. Even though the occasion was cast as a celebration of the people's re-embracing of Catholicism and the missions, it was clearly a demonstration of military prowess. Even the music was more military than religious in character, particularly the clarins and drums.

In another interesting case of repossession, Andrés Pérez de Ribas described a procession from Guancevi to Zape to reinstall a statue of Mary that had been damaged in the Tepehuán Revolt of 1616. Triumphal arches decorated with flowers and leaves were set up along the procession route. A memorial was erected at the location where two Jesuits were slain during the uprising. Spaniards and Christianized Indians made up the procession. Once at Zape, the statue was replaced while hymns were sung. Solemn vespers was chanted in the evening, lit by torches, and Spanish soldiers fired a salute at the conclusion of the service. The next morning, a high mass was sung.[6] Zape held importance as a pre-Hispanic religious site, and Catholic icons were installed at an indigenous holy site in an attempt to take over the sacred space. It is unclear whether this specific site was further contested, but complaints about Tepehuan dancing continued well into the seventeenth century.[7]

Similar to entradas and repossession ceremonies were religious processions mounted for specific liturgical occasions, common in the missions of the north. Both civic and religious processions were common in late medieval and Renaissance Europe.[8] Civic processions welcomed visitors to town, celebrated peace treaties, and displayed the power of nobles. Religious processions paraded Marian images, statues of the saints, and the Eucharistic host through city streets.[9] Processions in the northern frontier of New Spain were much less elaborate, but conveyed the importance ascribed to religious artifacts and symbolically demarcated sacred space. Father Diego Osorio's 1762 *Manual para administrar los santos sacramentos*, frequently listed in late eighteenth-century mission inventories from Texas, Coahuila, Sonora, and New Mexico, included instructions and prayers for processions for many purposes: major and minor feast days, purification, to bring rain, to bring serenity, in time of war, in time of

---

[6] Pérez de Ribas (taken from the anua of 1623), cited in Peter Dunne, *Pioneer Jesuits in Northern Mexico*, 171.

[7] Kieran McCarty and Dan S. Matson, "Franciscan Report on the Indians of Nayarit, 1673," *Ethnohistory* 22:3 (Summer 1975), 214-215.

[8] See Barbara A. Hanawalt and Kathryn L. Reyerson, eds., *City and Spectacle in Medieval Europe* (Minneapolis: University of Minnesota Press, 1994).

[9] Pope John XXII ordered that Corpus Christi be celebrated with Eucharistic processions in 1318.

sickness, hunger, or any tribulation, and for Corpus Christi.[10] Osorio instructed clergy to ensure that the community followed behind the cross in an orderly fashion. Individual psalms were listed for each type of procession, and processions (except on Corpus Christi) were to end at the door of the church, followed by the celebration of a solemn mass.[11]

Descriptions of processions indicate that Osorio's *Manual* was followed. José Antonio Alcocer, chronicler of the friars of the Zacatecas college, described processions of Nuestra Señora de Refugio in the missions of New Mexico and Texas administered by his college. During the procession and mass that followed, the image of Refugio, part of the procession, entered the church, "robbing the hearts of the inhabitants."[12] Alcocer continued, "the commotion of the places with only this entrance of the Holy Virgin is remarkable. From that moment the sins in very many stop and they already begin to treat seriously the important business of salvation."

Upon entering the church, those at the head of the procession sang the following:

> *Venid, pecadores,*
> *Venid y cantemos*
> *Tiernas alabanzas*
> *Al Refugio nuestro*
>
> *Come, sinners,*
> *Come and let's sing*
> *Tender songs of praise*
> *To our Refuge*

A song of invitation to the mission echoed the same themes:

> *Dios toca en esta misión*
> *Las puertas de tu conciencia,*
> *Penitencia, penitencia,*
> *Si quieres tu salvación.*
>
> *God touch in this mission*
> *The doors of your conscience*
> *Penitence, penitence*
> *If you want your salvation.*

---

[10] Osorio, *Manual para administrar los santos sacramentos.*
[11] Ibid., 210-234.
[12] Alcocer, *Bosquejo de la historia*, 188.

After singing about sin and salvation, the missionary proceeded to explain the doctrine of the Church to those gathered.[13] The feast of Refugio launched renewed evangelization and conversion efforts among the Indians. This special occasion, however, was more than a gathering of individuals for a procession and performance of liturgy. The procession through the town marked the physical space as sacred ground. The image of Refugio blessed the space she occupied, and had the additional power, when coupled with entreaties expressed in song, of turning the hearts of sinners to God.

Constructing Sacred Space

Rituals of possession, the procession of holy images, and the ringing of church bells (thought to ward off agents of the Devil), all helped to create sacred space in the midst of chaotic colonial communities. Human ritual actions involving song, instruments, and the repetition of the Catholic liturgy separated holy ground from profane space, and purified the area of demonic influences. Fray Junípero Serra wrote to Francisco Palóu that a Corpus Christi procession and mass would surely "drive out any little devils that might lurk in the land."[14] Indigenous ideas about what constituted sacred space differed significantly from those of the missionaries. Land was much more than territory to be conquered—it was synonymous with the people themselves. Loss of land, in which the sacred universe resided, meant a destruction of the people.[15]

Whereas space in which Catholic holy rites were celebrated had to be covered (either in an outdoor structure or inside the church itself), many indigenous groups exercised their religious ceremonies outdoors in natural places thought to have divine significance, including groves of trees, springs, or caves. For example, Edward Spicer detailed the Yaqui concept of *huya aniya*, which he theorized could be traced to pre-Conquest society.[16] Huya aniya, or the "tree-world," was distinct from the human-built world exemplified by the Spanish-style pueblo surrounding a central courtyard and church building. In the natural world, great beings lived and exercised their powers. Under Spanish rule, huya aniya could be transformed into sacred town land through human action

---

[13] The *Aljaba Apostólico-Guadalupana* (Mexico City: Imprenta de Andrade y Escalante, 1860), includes texts of songs and saetas used by members of the Apostolic College at Zacatecas. I have consulted a later copy in the Biblioteca Franciscana in Cholula, Mexico. On the music sung for this particular occasion, see Alcocer, *Bosquejo de la historia*, 188, n. 10.

[14] Serra to Palóu, June 13, 1770, in Tibesar, ed., *Writings of Junípero Serra*, vol. I, 176-179.

[15] Sando, *Nee Hemish*, 8.

[16] Spicer, *The Yaquis*, 63-70.

undertaken by ritual specialists such as singers and dancers. Still, important religious rites and significant performances for special occasions, such as the Pascua dances, even among the converted Yaquis, were held outside of the church buildings in the open air of the courtyard.

For the missionaries, restructuring space involved not only ceremonial possession ceremonies, processions, and songs, but also building physical structures. Before constructing a permanent church building, open-air chapels or covered ramadas were used for religious rites by both Franciscan and Jesuit missionaries. These temporary spaces made sacred by their cover, altars, and the rituals performed inside them often remained in use for many years. Architectural historians have argued that open-air structures helped in the conversion process, since indigenous peoples were accustomed to celebrating religious ceremonies outdoors.[17]

Attempting to restructure physical space by building a new structure on top of an existing indigenous holy place was a common practice of Spanish colonialism. In both Mesoamerica and South America, new churches and cathedrals were erected on the foundations of Mexica, Maya, and Inca temples. In New Mexico, Franciscans directed the construction of mission churches on top of kivas, places where sacred Puebloan rites took place.[18] Jesuits at Torim ordered the construction of a shrine to the Queen of Angels (Mary) on a hill overlooking the river in a place considered holy to the Yaqui. According to Andrés Pérez de Ribas, "they did this so that the piety and worship of the Christian religion would prevail where malice and superstition had abounded."[19] The ceremony held for the dedication of the shrine was elaborate, involving music, dances, and feasting.

Missionaries were also concerned that acts they considered profane, such as drunkenness, gambling, and some native dances, not take place within the sacred space surrounding the missions. Jesuit José Pascual reported that he believed the Tarahumaras he was evangelizing had been controlled, because their drinking no longer occurred within the village, but in an out-of-the-way

---

[17] On the history of churches in Mexico, see George Kubler, *Mexican Architecture of the Sixteenth Century* (New Haven, CT: Yale University Press, 1948); John McAndrew, *The Open-Air Churches of Sixteenth-Century Mexico: Atrios, Posas, Open Chapels, and Other Studies* (Cambridge, MA: Harvard University Press, 1965); and Robert J. Mullen, *Architecture and Its Sculpture in Viceregal Mexico* (Austin: University of Texas Press, 1997); and Jaime Lara, *City, Temple, Stage: Eschatological Architecture and Liturgical Theatrics in New Spain* (Notre Dame, IN: University of Notre Dame Press, 2004).

[18] Gutiérrez, *When Jesus Came*, 82.

[19] Pérez de Ribas, *History of the Triumphs of Our Holy Faith*, book 5, chapter 19, 371.

spot.[20] Indians realized the importance that missionaries attached to the sacred space of the churches and sometimes used this knowledge to resist attempts to eradicate indigenous customs. In the Santo Domingo Pueblo, dancers responded to Franciscan attempts to limit their native dances by "very noisily" performing catsina dances on the roof of the mission church.[21]

Architecturally speaking, the scale of a building and the attention paid to its appearance conveyed the social importance and status attached to the events that occurred inside it.[22] In the case of northern frontier missions, this was very apparent. The church was the largest structure in the area, certainly larger than any previous indigenous building, and could be seen easily from long distances.[23] The structure and interior of the church dictated the sacred actions and relationships inside the building. Benches or open space in the nave were for the neophytes, who were to sit and listen to the priest and choir. The choir and acolytes were seated in raised areas of the sanctuary, behind the altar and an imposing cross, or in an elevated loft overlooking the assembly. Catechumens who were learning the doctrine remained behind the baptismal font in the vestibule. Even the physical spaces of the church reflected the social order of a Christian community. Spanish attempts to colonize physical space and time were met with indigenous responses, which together had the effect of reshaping the social landscape of mission communities.

RESTRUCTURING SOCIAL SPACE

By assigning ritual importance to specific individuals, music had the capacity to restructure social relations in the northern missions. The installation of a new indigenous leadership in mission communities, loyal to the missionary, was crucial to the success of the mission endeavor. When they were able to decipher them, missionaries and civil officials capitalized on native power rivalries and kin networks in their appointment of governors, tenientes, fiscales, and catechists. Missionaries recruited indigenous leaders, who accepted for a wide vari-

---

[20] José Pascual report on the Tarahumara, June 29, 1652, in *Documentos para la historia de México*, 4th ser., vol. 3, 179-207, as cited in Thomas E. Sheridan and Thomas H. Naylor, eds., *Raramuri, a Tarahumara Colonial Chronicle, 1607–1791* (Flagstaff, AZ: Northland Press, 1979), 29.

[21] Declaration of Fray Fernando de Velasco, June 14, 1662, Santo Domingo, transcribed in Hackett, *Historical Documents*, 132.

[22] Christopher Small, *Musicking*, 20.

[23] Despite being the largest structure in the area, the mission church would not have been the first structure erected by Spaniards. Most often, physical space was first colonized with acequias and milpas.

ety of reasons. To keep these positions, leaders participated in acculturation and evangelization efforts directed toward their kin. In 1694, Indian leaders at Mission La Purísima Concepción de Nuestra Señora de Caborca welcomed a new band to the mission, convincing them to present their children to Father Eusebio Kino for baptism. In what appears to be as much a business deal as a religious sacrament, parents were given meat, pinole, and gifts of clothing in return for having their children sprinkled with water and assigned Christian names.[24] Joining the Christian community, and bringing others into the mission fold, had its advantages.

Even in small communities, a significant number of the population—young and old, men and women—served the missionary as governors, *madores* (notaries), fiscales, sacristans, altar boys, members of the choir or orchestra, bell ringers, temastianes (catechists), cantors, cooks, and servants. Each of these positions came with special duties and privileges. Notaries, catechists, and choir masters were among the few Indians likely to be literate in the Spanish language.[25] Choir members and instrumentalists were allowed to sit in specially constructed areas during mass, often in a raised stall. In Mexico, as well as in Protestant churches of the colonial United States, seating in church buildings was a pronouncement of social order and a manifestation of social ranking.[26] Some mission churches were constructed with outdoor balconies. Architectural historians have theorized that these balconies, entered through the choir loft, may have accommodated musicians during outdoor celebrations and processions, placing them in clear view of the entire community.[27] Bell-ringers may have held the most important positions. They were entrusted with the most powerful communicative devices in the area, and they also had access to bell towers, which, where present, were the most commanding vantage points and strategic defense locations in a town.[28]

---

[24] Manuel de la Vega, Relación, BINAH, vol. 68, f. 114-114v.

[25] Juan Nentvig, *Descripción Geográfica . . . de Sonora*, Germán Viveros, ed. (Mexico City: Archivo General de la Nación, 1971), 164-165; Cynthia Radding, "Sonora-Arizona: The Común, Local Governance, and Defiance in Colonial Sonora," in Jesús F. de la Teja and Ross Frank, eds., *Choice, Persuasion, and Coercion: Social Control on Spain's North American Frontiers* (Albuquerque: University of New Mexico Press, 2005), 187-189; Sandos, Converting California, 145-146.

[26] Rhys Isaac, *The Transformation of Virginia, 1740–1790* (Chapel Hill: University of North Carolina Press, 1982), 323-357, cited in Beezley, Martin, and French, *Rituals of Rule, Rituals of Resistance*, xv.

[27] Thomas A. Drain, *A Sense of Place: Historic Churches of the Southwest* (San Francisco: Chronicle Books, 1994), 67.

[28] A cacique in the Florida province of Apalachee used the bell tower of the church of Ivitachuco as part of his defenses. See Bushnell, *Situado and Sabana*, 158.

Indians who showed proficiency in singing or playing instruments were given positions as musicians by the resident missionaries. Training at the mission could lead to paid positions within larger communities, and provide skills that would increase economic prospects.[29] Instrumentalists, singers, and cantors performed at weddings, civil celebrations, and masses for the dead. Antonio José Ortiz's estate, for example, spent 600 pesos on his funeral expenses, including 54 pesos for a sung novena of masses with response, and 19 pesos, and 4 reales for a cantor.[30] Musicians were also excused from other duties, including seasonal labor drafts for agricultural work. In 1763, in the pueblo of Satevó, over thirty Tarahumara men were able to avoid repartimiento labor by aiding in the organization of liturgical events.[31] Indigenous peoples who became musicians, teachers, or other officials gained the trust of the missionaries and Spanish administrators, entitling them to more privileges and access to material goods. Although cooperating with the resident missionary or accepting a position in pueblo governance translated into higher prestige within overlapping communities, it also increased their connection to the colonial apparatus. Fray José Viader's musicians at Mission Santa Clara de Asís in Alta California were even issued blue uniforms with brightly colored caps to uplift morale and forge group unity.[32] But by accepting positions as musicians or community leaders, Indians could increase their dependence on the Spanish colonial system for their welfare and social position.

Massive restructuring of physical and social space also created internal strife and power struggles between missionaries and Indians, and within indigenous communities. Relationships could tear a kin network, clan, or family apart when some chose to accommodate and operate within the new power structures, while others called for revolt and rejection of the mission.[33]

One of the most common conflicts in mission societies, brought about by the restructuring of physical and social space, occurred between clergy and

---

[29] James Saeger also found evidence of this in the Guaycuruan missions of South America. *The Chaco Mission Frontier: The Guaycuruan Experience* (Tucson: University of Arizona Press, 2000).

[30] Ortiz family papers, New Mexico State Records Center and Archives, box 1, folder f2, documents 9-13, cited in Martina Will de Chaparro, *Death and Dying in New Mexico* (Albuquerque: University of New Mexico Press, 2007), 91.

[31] Cheryl English Martin, "Indigenous Peoples," in Louisa Schell Hoberman and Susan Migden Socolow, eds., *The Countryside in Colonial Latin America* (Albuquerque: University of New Mexico Press, 1996), 193.

[32] Ray and Engbeck, *Gloria Dei*, 18.

[33] John Kessell argued that Pecos Pueblo was nearly destroyed by conflicts over whether to participate in the 1696 Pueblo Revolt.

hechiceros. These shamans, both men and women, competed with missionaries for the allegiance of adults in congregated mission communities. Like missionaries, shamans performed medicine and functioned as intermediaries with the spiritual universe. Furthermore, their ritual actions, including chanting, involved much repetition. Franciscans in Florida, as elsewhere, both needed and fought against the power of shamans in indigenous societies.[34] Shamans and *herbolarios* maintained connections with the larger natural world due to their specialized, ritual knowledge. They were important leaders in Timucuan society, and their significance intensified with the introduction of native diseases to the peninsula. Epidemics in the early part of the seventeenth century led Fray Francisco Pareja to write that "half of the Indians have died from the cause of the great plagues and contagious diseases they have suffered."[35] The presence of native healers provided some mitigation against the rapid spread of disease, which only heightened with the congregation of communities into larger settlements at missions like San Juan del Puerto. Furthermore, shamans helped to lead rituals performed in conjunction with death and burial. Actions connected with healing practices were largely permitted by Franciscans in Florida, particularly the preparation and application of herbs and medicines.[36] However, the friars attempted to censor such practices, prohibiting consumption of hallucinogens and drink. They introduced similar strategies, including ritual speech, gestures, and songs to demonstrate their abilities to communicate with the spiritual world and bring about healing and psychological comfort. This created rivalries for power and influence within the community, and Fray Francisco's confessional manual, which contained numerous questions regarding healing practices, indicates that competing shamanic influence was a matter of great concern in the region.[37]

Attempts to curtail shamanic influence over cultural practices led to revolts, conflict, and murder attempts in northern missions. In 1736, German Jesuit Francisco Wagner narrowly escaped an ambush led by a shaman and his

---

[34] Tamara Spike, "To Make Graver This Sin: Conceptions of Purity and Pollution among the Timucua of Spanish Florida" (PhD diss., Florida State University, 2006), retrieved August 18, 2007, from ProQuest Digital Dissertations database.

[35] Francisco Pareja to the King, January 17, 1617, Woodbury Lowery Collection, Library of Congress, Washington, DC.

[36] Herbs given to induce "bad birth" or cause abortion were specifically included in questions of the confessional manual. *Confesionario,* f. 146-147. See Spike, "To Make Graver This Sin," 41-42, for a discussion of the types of herbs likely used.

[37] Jerald Milanich and William Sturtevant, trans. and eds., *Francisco Pareja's 1613 Confessionario: A Documentary Source for Timucuan Ethnography* (Tallahassee: Florida Division of Archives, History, and Records Management, 1973).

followers at Mission San José de Comondú.[38] Most of the mission community remained loyal to Wagner, but some left to join the shamans. A 1785 conspiracy at Mission San Gabriel de los Temblores was led by Nicolás José, a baptized Gabrielino, with ties to the mission administration, and Toypurina, a young unbaptized woman with "superstitious" practices, both tied to important families in the region. They encouraged neophytes to join in rebellion against the priests and soldiers, who had forbidden ceremonial dances. In her testimony before officials after her arrest, Toypurina expressed anger at the padres, soldiers, and others who had moved to Mission San Gabriel, because "they had come to live and establish themselves in her land."[39] Power struggles such as this one, directed not only at Spaniards, but also other Indians, revealed deep divides over the restructuring of physical and social space in mission communities.

Restructuring Gendered Space

Just as music and ritual performance were agents in the reshaping of social hierarchy in mission communities, they also acted as catalysts in the reshaping of women's roles and social space in the north. Women were intimately involved with music and dance in northern indigenous communities prior to the arrival of the Spaniards. Unlike their counterparts in central Mesoamerica, women in the north participated in key ceremonial songs and dances, particularly those for mourning, preparation for war, and celebration of successful hunts or battles. Although some songs were specifically designated as those performed solely by males or females, communal dances often involved participation of both sexes together. This would later considerably disturb the Franciscan and Jesuit missionaries to the area, who spent ample time trying to instill Christian mores of modesty and decency in their indigenous converts.[40]

Also unlike the important role played by women singers and dancers of northern New Spain, European women's participation in Catholic devotional music was very limited. In 1563, the Council of Trent decreed that women could participate in the mass and Divine Office only by singing the responses and appropriate prayers in chant. Women were not allowed to chant scripture, including psalms and lessons, and females were prohibited from singing figured

---

[38] Crosby, *Antigua California*, 234.
[39] Steven W. Hackel, "Sources of Rebellion: Indian Testimony and the Mission San Gabriel Uprising of 1785," *Ethnohistory* 50:4 (Fall 2003), 656.
[40] See, for example, Pérez de Ribas, *History of the Triumphs of Our Holy Faith*, 210.

chant or polyphony.[41] The Third Mexican Provincial Council extended restrictions to New Spain. Women's music-making was limited to congregational chanting during mass, and no woman was allowed to enter the choir stall (and thus participate as a member of a choir) under the penalty of excommunication.[42] In processions, such as those for Corpus Christi and other feast days, men were to march separately from women "in order to avoid many disadvantages which are born of this practice."[43] This practice was also noted by Jesuit Jacob Baegert during his time in Cádiz, Spain, before traveling to Mexico. In his description of a neighborhood procession honoring the Virgin, he remarked that "men and women are never found together in a procession, either the men are alone or the women."[44] Separation of the sexes during opportunities for social interaction, including special celebrations, attendance at church, and education, was considered proper behavior and was enforced whenever possible.[45]

The Bourbon period in New Spain brought further legislation regarding females and the liturgy. Preoccupation with morality led the Fourth Mexican Provincial Council, held in 1771, to remind the clergy that women could not serve as choir members. The religious were particularly to guard against the excesses of women singing any type of lyrical (or secular-style) music in the church.[46] Even boys and girls were to be separated when being taught the catechism and doctrine, a practice that was common in frontier areas as well. When girls and boys were educated apart from each other, the missionary could emphasize "proper" gender roles while teaching doctrine. It also reduced the chance that inappropriate physical contact between unmarried youths could occur. Decency and morality were of great concern in both central Mexico and the north. Pedro Tamarón y Romeral, bishop of Nueva Vizcaya, reminded clergy under his jurisdiction that women's heads must be covered upon entrance to the church. They were not permitted to gather inside the church unless accompanied by their husbands, and women's dances were never to be permitted.[47]

Challenges to restricted gendered spaces within New Spain's Catholic Church were present in both central Mexico and frontier areas. Although

---

[41] Robert Hayburn, *Digest of Regulations*, 29.
[42] *Concilio III*, 310.
[43] Ibid., 320.
[44] Baegert's letter of January 12, 1750, in Schulz-Bischof, *The Letters of Jacob Baegert*, 81.
[45] See Asunción Lavrin, "Women in Colonial Mexico," in Michael C. Meyer and William H. Beezley, eds., *The Oxford History of Mexico* (Oxford: Oxford University Press, 2000), 258-259.
[46] *Concilio IV*, 157.
[47] *Demostracion del vastísimo obispado de la Nueva Vizcaya, 1765: Durango, Sinaloa, Sonora, Arizona, Nuevo México, Chihuahua y porciones de Texas, Coahuila y Zacatecas* (Mexico City: Antigua Librería Robredo, de José Porrúa e Hijos, 1937), 397.

women did not participate in choirs or as teachers of music in Mexico City, some were able to participate in religious music to a limited degree. Sor Juana Inés de la Cruz, one of the most learned women of the Mexican seventeenth century, taught herself to play music, studied music theory, and even began writing a treatise on musical theory at the suggestion of the viceroy's wife. Among her writings were many villancicos, forms of Christian poetry, that were set to music by male composers.[48] At the College of San Gregorio, eighteenth-century Nahua women participated in confraternities and helped to organize college celebrations for Holy Week.[49] Despite the very limited space in which women could participate in devotional activities involving music, then, some were able to exercise agency even in the metropolis of the colony.[50]

In northern mission communities, however, women were able to carve out larger roles in liturgical music and restructure gendered space through their participation in song and dance. In one of the earliest examples of a female holding an important position in a mission community, Andrés Pérez de Ribas described a sixteenth-century Christian Indian woman who had previously been a slave in Culiacán. Jesuit missionaries promoted this woman to the position of temastiana, or catechism teacher, in their work among the Guasave people.

> *Her fervor for teaching the catechism was so great that she made her people come to church twice a day to repeat this exercise. Now even at night, a time that they used to set aside for their superstitious dances, they assembled of their own free will to chant the catechism.*[51]

Women also served as temastianas and cantoras (singing leaders) in both Franciscan and Jesuit missions in Sonora, Nueva Vizcaya, Baja California, Texas, and New Mexico. Some missionaries chose women to instruct women and girls

---

[48] Pulido Silva, "Mexican Women in Music," 121.

[49] Schroeder, "Jesuits, Nahuas, and the Good Death Society," 72-73.

[50] The music of nuns in colonial Latin America has been examined by Josefina Muriel, "La música en las instituciones femeninas existente en el Archivo Histórico del Colegio de San Ignacio de Loyola, Vizcaínas," in *Una mujer, un legado, una historia: homenaje a Josefina Muriel* (Mexico City: Universidad Nacional Autónoma de México, 2000), 221-226; and "Las mujeres en la música del virreinato," in *De la historia: Homenaje a Jorge Gurría Lacroix* (Mexico City: Universidad Nacional Autónoma de México, 1985), 201-206. I am grateful to John Koegel for introducing this work to me. For music in the convents of Peru, see Geoffrey Baker, *Imposing Harmony: Music and Society in Colonial Cuzco* (Durham, NC: Duke University Press, 2008), esp. 111-127; and Kathryn Burns, *Colonial Habits: Convents and the Spiritual Economy of Cuzco, Peru* (Durham, NC: Duke University Press, 1999), 103-106.

[51] Pérez de Ribas, *History of the Triumphs of Our Holy Faith*, book 2, chapter 11, 134.

in doctrinal matters, while male temastianes were responsible for the supervision of the males' learning.[52]

At Mission San José Comondú in Baja California, two neophyte women, Inés and Chepa, were selected as the cantors for the entire mission community. They were chosen for their strong voices and musical talent, and they led the daily devotions, including singing.[53] Women in important positions such as temastiana or cantora could gain material benefits from their leadership roles. They might receive gifts of clothing or food and be taken away from imposed domestic tasks such as spinning, weaving, or cooking. These women learned to speak and read Spanish and had important roles in organizing festivities for special occasions.

More frequently, women appear in the colonial documentation as members of mission choirs. This is particularly apparent in the Jesuit missions of the Pimería Alta in the eighteenth century. The purity of their voices, their dedication, and their ability to memorize the devotional songs prompted missionaries to utilize their talents. Women singers were noted by chroniclers, perhaps because their presence was so different from the usual practice in Europe and central New Spain, and the beauty of their voices was often emphasized. Cristóbal de Cañas, for example, wrote that the devotion of women singing the Ave Maria and litany moved the bishop to tears during his visita of Sonora.[54] Ignaz Pfefforkorn boasted that two women among the singers he trained

> were especially conspicuous for the purity and sweetness of their voices and for their vocal technique. When in the year 1767 the Marquis de Rubí, commander in chief of the royal troops in the Kingdom of Mexico, remained with me a couple of days on his journey through Sonora, he was surprised by a Salve Regina which these two women sang together. Their singing so astonished him that he leaped up in church and told me that he had never heard such glorious voices even in Madrid.[55]

Membership and successful performance in mission choirs was a recognition of talent and placed these women near the top of the social hierarchy in the mission pueblos. Jesuit Joseph Och even acknowledged that there was competition among the Pima girls at his post for the coveted position of choir member.[56] Like cantoras and temastianas, choir members could expect material benefits

---

[52] See, for example, a report on the status of Mission Espíritu Santo de la Bahía, 1778, OSMHRC, Zacatecas, reel 3, fr. 3465-3472.
[53] Crosby, *Antigua California*, 238, from reports about the mission ca. 1740.
[54] Relación sonorense, 1730, paragraph 40, in González R., *Etnología*, 298.
[55] Pfefferkorn, *Sonora*, 246-247.
[56] Treutlein, *Missionary in Sonora*, 136.

from their participation in the colonial apparatus. In addition, singing in the mission choir often entailed travel throughout the region for featured participation in celebrations for special occasions.

In the two examples cited above, Cristóbal de Cañas and Ignaz Pfefferkorn mentioned women singers performing songs directed to the Virgin Mary—the Ave Maria and Salve Regina. Missionaries likely encouraged female devotion to Mary as a way of instilling Hispanic Christian ideas of domesticity into indigenous converts. Mary was depicted as the perfect mother, nurturer, and wife to San José (who also appeared prominently in alabados). In Alta California, as in other areas of the Spanish empire, Marian devotion might have been connected with pre-Contact beliefs. Gabrielinos believed in a virgin, Chukit, who was impregnated by lightning and bore the son of god. At Mission San Carlos, neophytes gave gifts to old women who claimed to have the power to make seeds and fruit grow.[57]

Christian domesticity and ideas about decorousness and modesty saturated the structuring of daily life at the missions. In many missions, both Jesuit and Franciscan, women and men and boys and girls were separated for doctrinal instruction, singing, work, and even eating.[58] Even missionary discourse regarding singers was gendered, with women being described as pure, sweet, devoted, and virtuous. Male singers, on the other hand, were more often characterized as proficient, talented, or in possession of strong and clear voices.

Even though women were ideally separated from men to avoid interaction of the sexes during the daily routine, special occasions provided opportunities for greater mixing. Women, according to the mandates of the Church, were not allowed to participate in dances on these occasions. However, in the north, this rule was frequently overlooked. In most northern missions, dancing by women was permitted as long as the women did not make direct physical contact with men during the dance. Pérez de Ribas elaborated on the precautions he took to ensure decent behavior during a dance of the Ahome:

> *They understood that there could be no drunkenness, which was ruled out by their acceptance of the catechism. I told them that I would agree to their request so long as the men and women did not dance together. The wise Ahome understood my misgivings, which was noteworthy in a nation so new to the faith. They answered me, "Our father . . . you will see how modestly the maidens and young men dance and*

---

[57] Hackel, *Children of Coyote*, 164-165.
[58] See Crosby, *Antigua California*, 238; "Relación sonorense," paragraph 38, in González R., *Etnología*, 297; Hackett, *Historical Documents*, 502-503; Report on the status of Mission Espíritu Santo de la Bahía, 1778, OSMHRC, Zacatecas, reel 3, fr. 3469.

how the maidens dance separately with particular dignity." . . . *Although the young women danced in sight of the young men of the pueblo, they did not raise their eyes to look at them, nor did they touch the clothing or mantas with which they danced.*[59]

Indigenous rules of gendered space were altered by Christian mores regarding the proper behavior of women in this instance. However, the Hispanic Christian concept of appropriate gender roles did not include dancing at all. Thus indigenous women of the Río Zuaque as well as in other northern missions were able to restructure Catholic gendered space through adapting their dances so that they were allowed as part of Christian celebrations. In some dance-dramas, such as the matachines and moros y cristianos performances, women and men participated in the same dance. Differing degrees of contact were allowed in different areas. Father Och ensured that women and men were on different sides of the dance area,[60] while matachines dancers at Cucurpe were separated into two rows.[61] In San Antonio, however, indigenous mitotes were allowed in the mission courtyards, and participation of men and women was permitted as long as "no superstition, no question of celebrating an enemy's death, nor any sinful motive are present . . . because among the Indians it is the same as the fandango among the Spaniards."[62]

Generally, in northern New Spain, women had more latitude to participate in the liturgy than their indigenous, mestizo, and Spanish counterparts in both New Spain and Europe. In some areas they were able to obtain prestigious leadership positions, while in others they were choir members, dancers for special occasions, or participants in communal worship. The notable exception to this conclusion was in the Franciscan missions of Alta California. With few exceptions, women in Alta California did not participate in mission choirs or orchestras.[63] Dictates about women singing in parts were also followed; where polyphonic music was sung, as in Europe and in the cathedrals of Spain's American colonies, the higher voice parts were sung by boys. Perhaps this had to do with a more rigorous enforcement of rules and a more stringent focus on neophyte discipline advocated by Father Junípero Serra, founder and president of the Alta California missions. Because Serra possessed a sense of religious determination reinforced by

---

[59] Pérez de Ribas, *History of the Triumph of Our Holy Faith*, 210.
[60] Treutlein, *Missionary in Sonora*, 165.
[61] Pfefferkorn, *Sonora*, 182-183.
[62] Benoist and Flores, *Guidelines*, 37.
[63] James Sandos, "Professionalization of Music: Choristers at Mission Santa Clara, 1800-1845, and the Mystery of Mission San Antonio" *Diagonal* 2009, http://cilam.ucr.edu/diagonal/issues/2009.html, data from Early California Population Project database, Huntington Library, San Marino, CA.

a personal piety that led him to asceticism,[64] this may have impacted his views toward women's roles in the missions. Comments by Fermín Francisco de Lasuén, president of the Alta California missions at the turn of the nineteenth century, prompt another possible explanation. He observed gender roles among the indigenous peoples who inhabited the missions:

> *We must not fail to note here how different women are. . . . In their native state they are slaves to the men, obliged to maintain them with the sweat of their brow. They are ill-treated, trampled on by them even to the point of death if, on returning to their huts after spending the entire night in raids or in dancing, the entire morning in play, and the entire evening in sleeping they find that the women have made no provision for food for them.*[65]

The pre-Contact gender roles of these mission residents also affected the degree to which women sought to challenge proscribed gendered behavior in the Alta California missions. In other areas of the north, where women had actively participated in rites involving music and dance, they were also more likely to continue that participation in religious rites at the missions.

Why were there significant differences between the limited gendered space prescribed by the Council of Trent and the Mexican Provincial Councils and the broader musical roles assumed by women in the north? Women were able to gain some prestige through their involvement in music due to pre-existing gender roles in their indigenous communities. In the missions, women played critical roles in the success or failure of an evangelizing endeavor. They were often the main targets of missionaries, who tried to ensure conversion of their family by focusing on their personal conversion.[66] Many women used this to their advantage, and used this cultural contact (as well as sexual contact, in other situations) to help themselves and their children.[67] Frontier conditions were also likely responsible for some of the relaxation of rules. In the north, gender

---

[64] Ibid., 2.

[65] Lasuén to Fray Miguel Lull, June 19, 1801, in Finbar Kenneally, trans. and ed., *Writings of Fermín Francisco de Lasuén* (Washington, DC: Academy of American Franciscan History, 1965), vol. 2, 204-205.

[66] This occurred despite the frustration of missionaries with many women's resistance to attending annual confession, where they were supposed to discuss their improper behavior, including sexual sins.

[67] Much has been written about how women responded to colonial rule in general, and specifically to missionization. See, for example, Guy and Sheridan, *Contested Ground*, 13-15; Susan Schroeder, Stephanie Wood, and Robert Haskett, eds., *Indian Women of Early Mexico* (Norman: University of Oklahoma Press, 1997); and Susan Socolow, *The Women of Colonial Latin America* (New York: Cambridge University Press, 2000).

boundaries, as well as those of race and class, were blurred due to the lack of strong state control over much of the territory. In addition, a shortage of laborers due to European-introduced diseases and refusal of some Indians to relocate to mission villages meant that men were needed for agricultural, ranching, and mining labor and could not be spared for religious duties in choir or teaching.

How does the position of women in the musical culture of the missions of the north compare with other data regarding women's gendered space in northern New Spain? Cheryl Martin, in her study of colonial Chihuahua, concluded that

> *for women, correct behavior won them a certain amount of deference and respect, and more benign treatment within the existing set of rules that allocated privilege and responsibility according to gender, but not the freedom to alter them in any meaningful way.... In other words, patriarchy furnished a relatively stable, non-negotiable set of governing principles even when all other rules came into question.*[68]

In Martin's study, boundaries that limited mobility due to race, class, and gender were at times blurred in the north, but patriarchy was still dominant and prevented women from challenging prescribed gender roles. The evidence of women participating in music in the north supports Martin's assertion that correct behavior led to deference, respect, and better treatment within the mission system. However, women musicians who rose to the positions of cantora, temastiana, and choir member challenged the all-male hierarchy of the Catholic Church in the frontier missions. They successfully circumvented patriarchal provisions from central Mexico and European Catholic authorities to carve out space for participation and leadership roles in the performance of the liturgy.

Other scholars of the north have also noted the ability of women to challenge patriarchy in the far north through other means. Susan Deeds recognized women's violation of norms of domesticity and assumption of more material roles through sexual power and magic.[69] Cynthia Radding found that indigenous women in Sonora were able to gain a degree of control over their situations in regard to reproduction and labor in the reconstituted societies of mis-

---

[68] Cheryl English Martin, *Governance and Society in Colonial Mexico: Chihuahua in the Eighteenth Century* (Stanford, CA: Stanford University Press, 1996), 183.

[69] See "Double Jeopardy: Indian Women in Jesuit Missions of Nueva Vizcaya," in Schroeder, Wood, and Haskett, *Indian Women of Early Mexico*, 255-272, and "Magic, Fantasy, Gender, and Power in Nueva Vizcaya" (paper presented at Social Control on Spain's North American Frontiers: Choice, Persuasion and Coercion Conference, Meadows Museum of Art, Dallas, TX, April 6, 2002).

sion communities.[70] James Sandos argued that women were able to exercise agency by using the colonial system to their advantage, accommodating to patriarchal mores when it suited their interests.[71] Of course, it is impossible to know whether women were accommodating by choice or because they were forced into patriarchal relations. Challenges to the male-dominated sphere of religion were possible through the use of music in northern missions, although there were still areas in which women did not participate, such as in the playing of musical instruments. Thus, gendered space was reconstituted in many missions in northern New Spain through a combination of pre-existing indigenous customs and frontier conditions that necessitated male labor in other areas and included a propensity to disregard rules that were seen as impractical.

PERFORMANCES FOR SPECIAL OCCASIONS

From the sixteenth century on, Indians were required to commemorate the Christian holy days of Christmas, Circumcision, Epiphany, Easter, Ascension, Pentecost, Corpus Christi, the Nativity, Purification, Annunciation, and Assumption of Mary, and the feast days of Saints Peter and Paul. Other festivals could be celebrated at the discretion of local secular or regular clergy, and on these days Indians were not to work, but instead to attend worship. Fiestas celebrated for Christian holy days, important visitors, or other occasions in the life of the pueblo had five central purposes. First, they were important agents in acculturation. As discussed in Chapter 6, the imposition of these holidays helped to uproot or at least redirect native religious celebrations and adapt them to the Christian liturgical calendar. Attendance at the festivals was dictated by the ringing of specific celebratory peals on the church bells. Indians were to come to the celebrations freshly bathed and dressed in their Spanish-style peasant clothing. Festivities, including European-style processions, were held in the center of the constructed pueblos in the church and its courtyard.

Second, the observance of Catholic rituals was important in evangelization and religious instruction in mission communities. As commemorations of crucial events in the lives of Jesus Christ, Mary, key saints, and the history of the church, these festivals helped teach basic tenets of the Catholic faith in a lively and entertaining manner. They also attracted the unconverted, who often participated in the festivities for material benefit and revelry. At times, mass bap-

---

[70] *Wandering Peoples*, 137-141, and "Sonora-Arizona: The Común, Local Governance, and Defiance in Colonial Sonora," 3.
[71] "Choice, Persuasion, and Coercion," 28-29.

tisms or wedding ceremonies were held in conjunction with the fiestas. Jesuits particularly held these ceremonies on the feast day of St. Ignatius, the founder of the order. On St. Ignatius Day in 1687 at Mission Dolores in the Pimería Alta, Father Eusebio Kino baptized "the governor of our town, his wife, and more than forty other adults and infants. Several Spaniards from Bacanuchi came to this solemn baptism, as did also Father José de Aguilar and his choir from Cucurpe." In Kino's optimistic view, this celebration made other unconverted Indians in the area "so content and enthusiastic that they are pleading for missionaries and holy baptism for themselves and their people."[72]

For the celebration of St. Ignatius's feast day at Dolores, like other large festivities, the entire mission community, as well as people from surrounding pueblos, came together to perform acts that bound them together. The gathering of indigenous peoples from an entire area to jointly observe feast days was particularly important for establishing community identity in northern New Spain, where disease and relocation had reconstituted many indigenous communities. Indigenous neophytes from central Mesoamerica had also relocated to the north to serve as model converts in some areas. The result was the fracturing of many indigenous communities and the building of new communities, surrounding the missions, comprised of members of different ethnic groups and cultural backgrounds. Through joint participation in musical performances at celebrations for special occasions, group identity could begin to be forged. A 1787 letter to the friars at Mission Purísima Concepción in San Antonio instructed that other missionaries in the area were to attend the celebration in honor of La Purísima, and that the musicians from Missions San Antonio and San Juan should be requested to join.[73] The participation of musicians from an entire region was common in the north, particularly since individual mission choirs were small. In some instances, instrumentalists and singers from a mission and those nearby worked closely for months practicing music for a particular religious service.[74] This daily rehearsal surely bound the musicians together as a group for the occasion, and perhaps it forged longer-lasting ties.

---

[72] Kino to Father Mansilla, Dolores, August 6, 1687, in Ernest Burrus, trans. and ed., *Kino's Plan for the Development of Pimería Alta, Arizona, and Upper California: A Report to the Mexican Viceroy* (Tucson: Arizona Pioneers' Historical Society, 1961), 211.

[73] Benoist and Flores, *Guidelines*, 7.

[74] For example, Alfred Robinson, a New England merchant, described the elaborate music performed for San José's feast day at Mission San José in Alta California in 1831: "The music was well executed . . . for it had been practiced daily for more than 2 months. . . . [T]he instruments performed upon were violins, flutes, trumpets, and drums." See Ray and Engbeck, *Gloria Dei*, 14.

Special occasions, though religiously based, were largely forms of entertainment. Along with processions, mass, and vespers, were fireworks, dances, decoration of the church and surrounding area with flowers and greenery, feasting, mimicry and pantomime, games, bullfights, military parades, costuming, gift exchanges, and even the pomp of "flying banners and blowing whistles."[75] They involved no small degree of preparation: Indians gathered resources from mission food stores, butchered livestock, prepared enormous quantities of food, rehearsed performances, and housed visitors. At the Jesuit mission of Loreto in Baja California, the community came together to celebrate the feast days of major saints, Christmas, Corpus Christi, Easter, and some of the holy days of the Virgin. On these days, the missionaries killed bulls and gave the meat to the Indians. There was an abundance of fruits as well, including watermelons, and the priests handed out clothes or tobacco as gifts to those in attendance.[76] These forms of entertainment also functioned as safety valves in which indigenous peoples could participate in revelry without uprooting the fragile Spanish hold on frontier territory. Cristóbal de Cañas's 1730 report on conditions in Sonora detailed the celebration of Santa Rosalía's feast day at the mission of Arispe, held in a manner so that the Indians there would be able to let out energy through entertainment, while not "damaging their honesty."[77] By controlling the types of entertainment and the material goods present at a fiesta, resident missionaries could hope to ensure that pagan dances, gambling, drunkenness, and the ingestion of hallucinogens would not occur.

The elaborateness of a celebration was often indication of the degree of importance attached to the event. While Corpus Christi in New Mexico was occasion for feasting, dances, processions, and elaborate liturgical services, the arrival of Governor Bernardo López de Mendizábal to Socorro in 1659 was heralded only with the pealing of bells, playing of trumpets, and Fray Benito de la Natividad sprinkling holy water on the governor and his caravan. Mendizábal, who was not favored by the Franciscans, was disappointed with the lack of pomp displayed by the mission and its friars. In a testimony about the event, he complained, "[T]hey should receive me like the Most Holy Sacrament on the Feast of Corpus Christi."[78]

---

[75] Joseph Och, transcribed in Treutlein, *Missionary in Sonora*, 164.
[76] del Barco, *Historia natural*, 398.
[77] Cristóbal de Cañas, "Relación sonorense," 1730, paragraph 40, transcribed in González Rodríguez, *Etnología y misión*, 299.
[78] Cited in Joseph P. Sánchez, *The Rio Abajo Frontier, 1540–1692: A History of Early Colonial New Mexico* (Albuquerque, NM: The Albuquerque Museum, 1987), 111.

Finally, celebrations for special occasions were important symbols and re-creations of Spanish and Catholic hegemony and social hierarchy in borderlands society. As Clifford Geertz noted, all political authority needs a "cultural frame" to define itself and put forth its claim to legitimacy.[79] Cultural phenomena help to root the symbolic power of the governing elite, justifying their existence through establishing their connection with "transcendent things." Celebrations for special occasions, whether liturgical feasts or state holidays, served as a cultural frame in New Spain. They connected church and state with the seemingly transcendent, although invented, traditions of celebrating everything from the birth of an heir to the throne to the death and resurrection of Christ. Music and dance were agents in the constant re-creation of legitimacy. Jesuit Juan Nentvig realized this when he reported that processions were performed on special occasions with appropriate dignity "in order to present a visual display of the majesty of our holy religion to the neophytes so that they may remain impressed with its splendor and be attracted to it. Their disposition *piae affectionis* [impressionable nature] is to believe through their eyes rather than their ears."[80]

Corpus Christi in the North and Central Mexico[81]

An analysis of the feast of Corpus Christi, a Catholic feast honoring the Holy Eucharist and the transubstantiation of Christ, provides interesting insight into the restructuring of physical and social space through music and ritual. Pope Urban IV first recognized Corpus Christi, celebrated on the Thursday after Trinity Sunday, as a feast in 1264, and devotion expanded throughout the fourteenth century, spreading to Castile and Aragon. The Council of Trent called the celebration of the festival a "triumph over heresy."[82] By the seventeenth cen-

---

[79] Clifford Geertz, "Centers, Kings, and Charisma: Reflections on the Symbolics of Power," in R. Sean Wilentz, ed., *Rites of Power: Symbolism, Ritual, and Politics Since the Middle Ages* (Philadelphia: University of Pennsylvania Press, 1985), 15-16, 30. See also Armando Guevara-Gil and Frank Saloman, "A 'Personal Visit': Colonial Political Ritual and the Making of Indians in the Andes," *Colonial Latin American Review* 3:1-2 (1994), 3-36, for a description of how visitas reinforced colonial order.

[80] AGN, Historia, vol. 393, published as *Rudo Ensayo: A Description of Sonora and Arizona in 1764* (Tucson: University of Arizona Press, 1980), 109.

[81] I chose to discuss the feast of Corpus Christi instead of Easter and Holy Week due to the availability of more comparative material for central Mexico and other areas of Latin America. I wanted to be able to contextualize celebrations for special occasions in northern New Spain and provide comparison with those in core areas.

[82] Carolyn Dean, *Inka Bodies and the Body of Christ: Corpus Christi in Colonial Cuzco, Peru* (Durham, NC: Duke University Press, 1999), 1.

tury, the celebration of Corpus Christi had become quite elaborate, making it one of the most important days in the liturgical year. Religious dramas and the moros y cristianos dances, embodying the theme of the triumph of Christianity, marked celebrations of this feast in Spain. Enormous processions and masses involving elaborate music were two main characteristics of Corpus Christi celebrations in both Europe and colonial territories.

In northern New Spain, the feast day honoring the Blessed Sacrament was observed according to the dictates of the First Mexican Provincial Council. Indians were exempt from manual labor on this day, and the baptized, including presidial soldiers, and settlers, were instructed to attend a special high mass in honor of the occasion. Corpus Christi fiestas attracted large crowds from throughout the region. Several missions in an area might combine to hold one celebration, or the revelry might continue for a week, with separate festivities at individual missions. The five Franciscan missions in San Antonio, Texas, for example, sometimes held their own Corpus Christi services, each on a different day, all of which attracted Indians and settlers from the region. The goal of the resident missionaries was to establish their mission's celebration on the feast day itself, a feat that demonstrated the mission's important status.[83]

In a nod to the forms of indigenous spiritual ceremonies, observance of Corpus Christi in the larger mission communities of northern New Spain involved processions and nighttime revelry with feasting and dancing. Mass at the Jesuit mission of Loreto in Baja California was held outside in a small covered ramada. Neophytes processed to the outdoor altar. Some carried lighted candles or torches, while others held statues of the saints from the chapel. Soldiers from the nearby presidio also marched in the procession, carrying their guns and firing a salvo at the elevation of the host.[84]

A mission's Corpus Christi procession was occasion for the display of the mission's wealth and material effects. During Father Kino's tenure at Mission Dolores, the mission obtained a monstrance made of gilded silver that was paraded through the settlement. The Jesuit mission at Mátape also featured an elaborate *custodia*, which housed the sacraments during the procession.[85] A surprising number of missions in this frontier territory list custodias among church ornaments in their inventories. Some, such as the reliquary at Dolores,

---

[83] See Benoist and Flores, *Guidelines*, 35.
[84] Dunne, *Black Rober in Lower California*, 151.
[85] Herbert Bolton, *Kino's Historical Memoir of Pimería Alta* (Cleveland: Arthur H. Clark Company, 1919), 137-138.

were gifts from wealthy benefactors. The existence of such ornaments is proof that frontier missions were not as economically isolated from central Mexico as might be supposed.[86]

Corpus Christi in northern missions was occasion for the explanation of doctrine through religious dramas, and the performance of Christian rites for the many people assembled. In 1653, all fifteen pueblos in the Ostimuri province of Sinaloa gathered for a large celebration at Torim. Food, music, festivities, communion, preaching, devotions to San Ignacio, San Francisco Javier, and San Miguel Arcangel were performed. An enormous outdoor service, where 720 were baptized and 270 couples were married, highlighted the fiesta.[87] The Jesuit missionary at Nuestra Señora de la Concepción de Caborca used the 1706 feast day to instruct catechumens in the doctrine and to baptize those who had professed their faith.[88]

While there are scattered data on Corpus Christi celebrations in northern New Spain during the colonial era, more data are available about commemorations in the centers of Spain's American colonies.[89] In Mexico City and Cuzco, festivities for Corpus Christi were highly elaborate pageants involving most of the city in a giant procession complete with dancing, costumes, fireworks, and theatrical performances. Musical and dance elements of the celebrations in the large cities included hymns sung during the procession, dances within or following the procession, religious dramas (sometimes held in the cemetery of the cathedral), mass, and the volley of bells, in which all of the city's church bells pealed at once. Indigenous musicians and dancers traveled from far away to participate.

In Mexico's capital, Corpus Christi was the largest and most important annual festival. It was only occasionally superceded by the ceremonies held for the entrance of a new viceroy or the oath of allegiance to a new king. By 1618, the cost of hosting the event totaled 21 percent of the city government's disposable income.[90] In the north, while Corpus Christi was an important feast day celebrated in Jesuit and Franciscan missions, as well as towns under the care of secular clergy, it was not the most important festival of the liturgical calendar.

---

[86] Bargellini notes that some reliquaries in the north even came from Italy. Many silver pieces were produced in Mexico. See "At the Center of the Frontier," 113-134.

[87] AGN, Historia, vol. 15, exp. 30, f. 182-188.

[88] Bolton, *Kino's Historical Memoir of Pimería Alta*, 175.

[89] See Curcio, "Saints, Sovereignty and Spectacle"; Curcio-Nagy, "Giants and Gypsies: Corpus Christi in Colonial Mexico City"; Dean, *Inka Bodies*, and "Ethnic Conflict and Corpus Christi in Colonial Cuzco," *Colonial Latin American Review* 2:1-2 (1993), 93-120; Baker, *Imposing Harmony*, 35-55; and David P. Cahill, "Popular Religion and Appropriation: The Example of Corpus Christi in Eighteenth-Century Cuzco," *Latin American Research Review* 31:2 (1996), 67-110.

[90] Curcio-Nagy, "Giants and Gypsies," 3.

Instead, missionaries devoted more attention to celebrations for the feast day of the mission's patron saint, and particularly to the many activities of Holy Week, culminating in the observance of Easter. Although, like Mexico City's celebrations, Corpus Christi in northern missions was well attended by a mix of Indians, clergy, soldiers, and settlers, Holy Week, celebrated in the spring, involved more complex liturgical events than the summer feast of Corpus Christi. In Baja California and the Pimería Alta, Easter was the one occasion on which Indians from surrounding rancherías were required to come to the mission to confess and receive doctrinal instruction.[91] Processions involving self-flagellation or neophytes carrying crosses and wearing thorn crowns in imitation of Christ were another prominent feature of Holy Week celebrations in the north that separated them from processions on other occasions.[92] Religious dramas depicting the Passion of Christ were also featured during Holy Week in some northern missions.[93] The *Miserere* was commonly sung by the choir and congregation for services on Good Friday or Holy Saturday. In duration and complexity, then, Holy Week and Easter were more important celebrations than the feast of Corpus Christi in the north throughout the colonial period. Corpus Christi was more important in core cities than on the frontier due to its function as a state, as well as religious, holiday. Perhaps Easter also resonated more in the north due to its symbolization of the cycle of death and rebirth, a common theme in indigenous cosmology. Holy Week also fell during the spring, instead of early summer, at a time that may have coincided more with the planting season in the agricultural cycle of some indigenous groups.[94]

---

[91] del Barco, *Historia natural*, 398; and Cristóbal de Cañas, "Relación sonorense," 1730, paragraph 43, in González Rodríguez, *Etnología y misión*, 301.

[92] These processions were common throughout the north in both Franciscan and Jesuit missions. See the report of José Pascual, June 29, 1653, on Mission San Felipe, AGN, Historia, 19, exp. 144, f. 204-204v; Dunne, *Lower California*, 151-152; Jesuit carta anua of 1599 concerning Sinaloa, Zubillaga, *Monumenta Mexicana*, vol. VII, 220-221; Pérez de Ribas, *History of the Triumphs of Our Holy Faith*, book 6, chapter 19, 422; Molina, *Estado de la provincia de Sonora*, 1730, 14; Benoist and Flores, *Guidelines*, 3.

[93] Merrill, *Rarámuri*, 178-180, discusses the liturgical drama introduced for Easter by Jesuits among the Tarahumara. Spicer, *The Yaquis*, 114-115, discusses the origins of the Yaqui passion play, or Waehma. Some services in Alta California for Tenebrae, on Good Friday, involved elements of liturgical drama as well. See Joseph Halpin, "Musical Activities and Ceremonies at Mission Santa Clara de Asis," *California Historical Quarterly* 50:1 (March 1971), 39-40. Processions at Mission Concepción in San Antonio also involved a reenactment of the passion of Christ. See Benoist and Flores, *Guidelines*, 3.

[94] Anthropologist William Merrill explains that the modern-day Rarámuri (Tarahumara) celebration of Holy Week reflects an association between the end of a yearly agricultural cycle and the disruption of their universe, embodied in a conflict between Our Father and the Devil that occurs

In large cities, the Corpus Christi fiesta was a mirror of society, expressing ethnic divisions and reinforcing the colonial status quo. Location in the large procession that wound through Mexico City was indicative of social standing and reinforced group and ethnic identity. Guilds, cofradías, regular and secular clergy, inquisitors, parish members, Indians, and government officials, including the viceroy and audiencia members, all had specific places within the procession. Each of these groups followed an initial parade of costumed individuals and dancers, including *gigantes, cabezudos, diablillos*,[95] and sometimes a large dragon (*tarasca*) symbolizing sin conquered by the Holy Spirit. The marchers were ethnically and socially divided according to the class hierarchy in the colonial capital.

On the other hand, the celebration itself was also an event that brought disparate elements of society together in a common demonstration of faith. This encouraged social integration and identification with the larger community of the entire city. Those who were not involved in the procession participated in the event as spectators, and this crowd was largely heterogeneous. While the joint participation of diverse elements in society in such an event did not ensure social harmony, it may have at least temporarily suspended social barriers and caused individuals to identify as members of the larger society of Mexico City.[96]

Corpus Christi in northern New Spain also involved the participation of various groups in society. Neophytes, unconverted indigenous peoples, and clergy attended mass and formed processions in mission communities. Where present, soldiers, government officials, and Spanish and mestizo settlers also shared in the festivities, interacting with the mission Indians who were a part of their larger community. Celebrations in the northern missions generally involved processions, but they were, of course, much less elaborate due to the smaller population and more limited resources. For example, in the mid-eighteenth century at the Jesuit mission of Cucurpe,

> *The village magistrate carried the canopy in the Corpus Christi procession. The canopy was flanked by twelve well-dressed Indians carrying as many lanterns with*

---

during Holy Week. See "Rarámuri Easter," in Rosamond B. Spicer and N. Ross Crumrine, eds., *Performing the Renewal of Community: Indigenous Easter Rituals in North Mexico and Southwest United States* (Lanham, MD: University Press of America, 1997), 380.

[95] Gigantes were huge people made of wood and dressed in finery. Cabezudos were individuals who dressed in costumes and wore big heads made of wood and paper. Diablillos, or little devils, wore masks and sometimes accompanied the giants and cabezudos. See Curcio-Nagy, "Giants and Gypsies," 5-6.

[96] Ibid.

> *burning candles. A double column of Spaniards, tapers in hand, preceded and followed the Blessed Sacrament, and an escort of 30 or 40 Spaniards marched on both sides of it. Walking directly in front of the Blessed Sacrament the singers and musicians rendered devout songs. The populace preceded and followed the procession in the most orderly fashion and prayed the rosary. After benediction at the altars, which were erected according to custom, the Spaniards fired their muskets. Twelve mortars were also fired.*[97]

This procession did not include giants, dragons, nor costumed dancers, but it did involve the entire community circling the mission in the process of venerating the Eucharistic host. Order in this procession, like those in Mexico City, reinforced social hierarchy and ethnic division. The magistrate, assisted by other officials, had the important task of carrying the canopy. Indians who had important roles in the community were selected to carry lanterns and they dressed in their finery for the occasion. Spaniards, not indigenous neophytes, escorted the sacrament itself, indicating their social prestige. Those marching closest to the host were the singers and instrumentalists. These individuals played an important role in the solemnity of the occasion, and they were rewarded with an enviable place in the procession. The procession was a re-creation of the hegemony of the Spanish state; soldiers fired ammunition to celebrate the festivities, but this action also symbolically repossessed the territory. Although the entire community participated as a whole unit in the celebration, integrating peoples of different ethnic backgrounds, the boundaries between race and class were still present.

A similar symbolic possession of territory tied to Corpus Christi demonstrated social hierarchies to Indians in East Texas. In May 1689, Alonso de León's expedition to the far northeast patched together a Corpus Christi celebration shortly after encountering the Assinai. Fray Damián Mazanet chanted mass, and the governor of the Assinai, with all his caciques and members of his community attended. After mass, there was a procession with the host, which was elevated. Although they were invited to process with the expedition members, León afterward handed the cross to the Assinai *caddí* and told him, through an interpreter, that his people would have to subject themselves to the priests, learn the doctrine, and become Christians. When the caddí nodded his approval, salvos were fired. The ceremony concluded with gift-giving, including three Indians given to León to take to the viceroy. While the Spaniards surely understood this ceremony as one in which they took possession of the land and its inhabitants

---

[97] Pfefferkorn, *Sonora*, 270.

through the Corpus Christi procession, the Assinai more likely understood it as a ritual gift exchange between two parties. Beads, ribbons, the cross, and Franciscans were exchanged for a peace pipe and three indigenous men.[98]

Corpus Christi in Mexico City was as much a civil as religious celebration, a tribute to Mexico City and its inhabitants, celebrating the representative portions of the city's population. Much responsibility was given to different groups to prepare songs, dances, costumes, and altars. The municipal council paid for much of the festival, including fireworks, bullfights, and banquets, and on occasion commissioning plays and dances. In return, civil officials expected a prominent marching location in the procession, preferably following the Eucharistic host. In the north, Corpus Christi was still primarily a religious feast. While Spanish colonial officials and soldiers participated in areas such as Santa Fe where they were present, much of the northern frontier was not completely incorporated by the state.[99] The focus of the day was the procession and the mass that followed. Where evening festivities also included dancing and feasting, however, these secular activities were probably of greater interest to a majority of the area's population and visitors who came specifically to participate in the revelry.[100]

While Corpus Christi celebrations in northern missions did not have the same degree of civil focus as those in Mexico City and Cuzco, they may have been as much civil as religious in nature for the indigenous peoples of the community, particularly in the late colonial period. In comparison, contemporary Rarámuri Holy Week festivities, which have their roots in dramas introduced by missionaries during the colonial period, developed not syncretic religious, but secular meanings.[101] These meanings are connected to the political organization of the pueblos introduced by the missionaries. Over time, the authority of indigenous officials, which originally rested in the positions granted to them by missionaries, became associated with service to the community. Celebrations for special occasions in the Rarámuri pueblos became a way of legitimating the

---

[98] Espinosa, *Crónica de los colegios de propaganda fide*, 673-674. For a more in-depth look at diplomatic ceremonies between Spaniards and Indians in east Texas, see Barr, *Peace Came in the Form of a Woman*, chapter 1.

[99] Bishop Tamarón presided over a Pontifical Mass and Corpus Christi procession in Santa Fe during his visit in 1760. The street through which it passed was decorated with branches and altars, soldiers fired salvos, and a large crowd was present. See Eleanor Adams, ed., *Bishop Tamarón's Visitation of New Mexico, 1760* (Albuquerque: Historical Society of New Mexico, 1954), 54.

[100] Some Spaniards, for example, built homes near the Tepehuan mission of Santiago Papasquiaro specifically for residence during fiestas. See Susan Deeds, *Defiance and Deference*, 167-168.

[101] "Rarámuri Easter," 412-413.

authority of pueblo officials and emphasizing the communities' political organization. This interpretation of the civil importance of modern Holy Week festivities at Basíhuare resonates with the significance of Corpus Christi celebrations in re-creating state authority and reaffirming civic identity.

In Mexico City, the pageantry of Corpus Christi was greatest during Hapsburg rule over New Spain. By the second half of the eighteenth century, the Bourbon focus on order and social morality limited some of the elements of the celebration that were deemed profane, such as the giants.[102] In effect, these restrictions dramatically cut the central role of Indians in the festivities as paid dancers, giants, and other costumed characters. Similarly, the Fourth Mexican Provincial Council, held in 1771, also reflected the Bourbon preoccupation with social order. Under Archbishop Antonio Lorenzana, the Council tried to curtail public acts of self-flagellation by decreeing that processions involving penitentes were not to be held for Holy Week. The Fourth Provincial Council furthermore admonished those who attended Corpus Christi processions to practice decency, modesty, and decorum.[103]

It is difficult to ascertain whether these Bourbon mandates were followed in the north. As a frontier area, it was largely outside of direct state control, as evidenced by the lack of adherence to other mandates from Spain and Mexico City. Because Indians were responsible for organizing and performing the labor for most of the festivities for Corpus Christi, as well as other feast days, it is likely that indigenous participation remained strong. Descriptions of Corpus Christi processions throughout the colonial period and across the entire northern frontier are relatively similar. With respect to Holy Week, the presence of self-flagellation in processions was not curtailed either, although reports of the same were more common in the seventeenth and early eighteenth centuries.[104] Corpus Christi may have declined in importance in the north, as in Mexico City, during the reign of the Bourbons, but energies devoted to organizing this fiesta may have simply been transferred to preparations for Holy Week and Easter, which seem to become more elaborate over the same time period. At Mission

---

[102] Curcio-Nagy, "Giants and Gypsies," 20-21; and Brian R. Larkin, "Liturgy, Devotion, and Religious Reform in Eighteenth-Century Mexico City," *Americas* 60:4 (April 2004), 493-518.

[103] *Concilio Provincial Mexicano IV, celebrado en la ciudad de México en el año de 1771* (Querétaro: Imprenta de la Escuela de Artes, 1898), 161, 164-165.

[104] See, for example, José Pascual's report on Mission San Felipe, June 29, 1653, AGN, Historia, vol. 19, exp. 144, f. 204-204v; Dunne, *Lower California*, 151-152; Sheridan and Naylor, *Rarámuri*, 29; Jesuit carta ánua, 1599, in Zubillaga, *Monumenta Mexicana*, vol. VII, 220-221; Pérez de Ribas, *History of the Triumphs of Our Holy Faith*, book 6, chapter 19, 422; and Molina, *Estado de la provincia de Sonora, 1730*, 14. Penitential practices appeared in New Mexico throughout the nineteenth century, despite the orders of bishops prohibiting them.

Concepción in San Antonio, the missionary was given the option of holding other festivities to supplement the obligatory mass on Corpus Christi. Matachines dances, presumably deemed to be more religiously appropriate, were to be substituted for the presence of gigantes if a procession was held.[105] The missionary was directed, however, to hold at least three separate processions during Holy Week, including songs and a liturgical drama re-enacting the passion of Christ.[106]

Thus the celebration of Corpus Christi in the North differed only slightly from festivities in Mexico City. It was not the most important feast of the year, but still held an important place in the imposed cycle of Christian holy days. Corpus Christi processions in both the capital and the frontier north were a mirror of society and reflected hierarchical divisions at the same time that they brought the entire community together in a common celebration. As in many religious festivals, the state (in the north, represented by the military) also figured in the celebration. A general decline in the elaborateness of the ceremonies for Corpus Christi took place in Mexico City following Bourbon acquisition of the Spanish throne, and this may also have been the case in the north, although data are limited. Special occasions, such as Corpus Christi, were involved in social control of frontier areas through their re-creations of hegemony. However, they could also be used by Indians as a way to gain material benefits. At the Jesuit missions of Zape and Tizonazo in Nueva Vizcaya, for example, fiestas prompted many Indians, who had left their homes to seek employment or were forced out due to labor requirements, to return to seek food and participate in the festivities.[107]

INDIGENOUS RESPONSES TO THE USE OF MUSIC IN THE MISSIONS

No matter how spectacular the pageantry designed by Catholicism, evidence suggests that the indigenous peoples in mission communities often rejected the messages conveyed in these rituals even when they did not display their defiance in open rebellion.[108] While open rebellion was certainly present in northern missions, responses to colonialism in musical form were generally more subtle. The most common response to the missionaries' agenda, prompted by only partial understanding of Christianity, was an incomplete conversion characterized by

---

[105] Benoist and Flores, *Guidelines*, 35.
[106] Ibid., 3.
[107] Deeds, *Defiance and Deference*, 170.
[108] *Rituals of Rule, Rituals of Resistance*, xxix.

participation in both indigenous and Catholic religious systems.[109] Other responses ranged from outright rebellion to apparent conversion to Catholicism and adoption of an Hispanic lifestyle. In the north, where colonization was a long and tenuous process, outward conversion to Christianity and Hispanicization could take several generations to take root in a community. Some groups of the north, such as the Hopi, rejected Christianity and adoption of a Hispanic lifestyle completely.

Ethnogenesis, or the continual re-creation of culture under colonial rule, was a common reaction to the creation of new communities in missions from disparate groups gathered together under colonial rule. This continuous cultural process was at the same time reproductive and transformative; it allowed for the persistence of parts of indigenous cultures while not limiting their capacity for change and accommodation over time.[110] Musical performances for special occasions played an integral part in indigenous ethnogenesis. Mission Indians were able to reshape their culture in an ongoing process that allowed them to fuse their diverse traditions of music and dance with those of the Catholic liturgy. Sometimes they engaged in reciprocal transculturation with missionaries, who appropriated native forms and practices, while introducing Christian themes into dances and harvest celebrations.[111] For example, Jesuit Francisco de Arista wrote from the mission at Parras in 1607, "[I]f they want to dance, they say that the music will concern God. . . . On some of the principal feast days we form processions in which all the new Christians carry crosses made from flowers. They attend the divine rites with such reverence and attention, that, with each passing day, they show more and more of their good nature and understanding of the church's holy matters and ceremonies."[112] Because the missionaries were unaware of indigenous meanings behind the dances performed by the Parras mission Indians and eager to see some signs of conversion, the Indians

---

[109] Klor de Alva, "Spiritual Conflict and Accommodation in New Spain: Toward a Typology of Aztec Responses to Christianity," in George Collier, et al., eds., *The Inca and Aztec States: 1400–1800* (New York: Academic Press, 1982), 351-352, cited in Peterson, *Paradise Garden Murals of Malinalco*, 14.

[110] See Karen Powers, *Andean Journeys*, 9. Although Powers uses ethnogenesis to refer to cultural re-creation in specific ethnic groups, I have chosen to apply this concept to late-colonial-period reconstituted ethnic groups (in some cases, fictitious kin groups) found in most northern missions.

[111] Barbara Ganson uses the term "transculturation" to describe cultural regeneration and the reciprocal relationships between Guaraní peoples and Jesuits in their South American missions. *The Guaraní under Spanish Rule in the Río de la Plata* (Stanford, CA: Stanford University Press, 2003), 12.

[112] Francisco de Arista, quoted in Pérez de Ribas, *History of the Triumphs of Our Holy Faith*, book 11, chapter 6.

were able to maintain some of their cultural identity by convincing the missionaries that the dances related somehow to God. Through the process of ethnogenesis, the dances may have been altered to fit the Christian imperatives and their context changed, but indigenous peoples still maintained a degree of control regarding their content.

People on the margins of society often refashion and reinvent rituals to keep their identities alive, and these involve music and dance.[113] Thus, the performance of dances originally intended for various indigenous occasions was transferred to the celebration of Christmas by the ethnic groups inhabiting the mission of Loreto in Baja California:

> *Hundreds of neophytes came to the festivities and more than a hundred of these new Christians performed native dances. . . . These Indians have more than 30 dances, all different. They are performed in costume, and they are designed to give instruction in various pursuits and occupations, such as making war, fishing, traveling, carrying babies, packing loads, and other things of this sort. The boy of three or four prides himself on properly playing his part in the dances.*[114]

In this case, indigenous peoples were able to continue passing on their traditions of dance, even to young children, through reshaping their culture to meet the demands of the colonial situation. Instead of having to perform their dances in secret, they simply integrated them into the festivities surrounding the mission's celebration of the birth of Christ. This fiesta opened up a space for indigenous expression of ethnogenesis and allowed a more public and widespread display of indigenous culture.

Indigenous musical traditions, such as the use of percussion and the connection of dance with ritual, were combined with European traditions associated with the mass and Divine Office, and reincorporated into the devotional practices of both Indians and missionaries. The persistence of indigenous dances in the pueblos of New Mexico as well as among surviving indigenous communities in the greater Southwest is evidence of the resistant adaptation of indigenous cultures. Music and dance, as incorporated into popular religious practices, were crucial agents of ethnogenesis. The elaborate Catholic ceremonies that mission Indians organized and performed in their new communities served the purpose of substantiating their status as new Christians in the eyes of the Spaniards. This allowed communities some protection against exploitation and land encroach-

---

[113] Small, *Musicking*, 97-98.
[114] Juan María Salvatierra to Pedro Ugarte, April 1, 1699, as transcribed in Bayle, *Misión de la Baja California*, 100-101.

ment while also symbolizing the existence of a new community brought about by ethnogenesis.[115]

The so-called "weapons of the weak"[116] identified by James Scott—gossip, slander, foot dragging, sabotage, backsliding, and work slowdowns—were also part of the spectrum of indigenous responses to the imposition of Catholic music in the missions. Padre Narciso Durán complained of indigenous musicians in Alta California:

> *Since the Indians are so short on memory that out of 10 or 12 hardly two remember the following day what they learned the day before, it follows that if these two or three, whom we may say excel, fall sick or their voices change, or they are missing for any other reason, the others, who sing only by being towed and following the rest, are stranded, and one must teach them again.... The ecclesiastical chant was so faulty that the one song the boys knew, the Asperges, had neither feet nor head, and seemed a howl rather than a song. And let us not speak of the masses, for in telling you, scarcely without exaggeration, that they did not know how to answer Amen, you can judge the rest for yourself.*[117]

Durán's remarks are notable because most reports of indigenous musicians in Alta California and throughout the north continually praise the dedication and quality of indigenous musicians. In this case, however, it appears that the musicians could have been deliberately sabotaging the religious music.

Music was involved in revolts against the imposition of colonial rule as well. Performances for special occasions were sometimes opportunities for Indians to rise up against the power structure of the mission and military. Popular revolts sometimes coincided with a Catholic feast because group celebrations provided a convenient means for expressing discontent with and even destroying elements of Spanish control in the area.[118] Elements of celebrations for special occasions were internalized enough by indigenous peoples to become targets of resistance or symbols of empowerment. In the first-generation Tepehuan rebellion, rebels celebrated their victories over the Spaniards with mock processions, including Indian women dressed as the Virgin Mary, crosses, and other religious ornaments. Ritual feasting and dancing continued at night, and sacred objects and vestments were desecrated.[119] Mocking of the missionaries and the liturgy also took place after the Yuma revolt in 1781. Every night after the massacre at San

---

[115] Merrill, "Conversion and Colonialism," 151.
[116] Scott, *Weapons of the Weak*.
[117] Quoted in Ray and Engbeck, *Gloria Dei*, 10.
[118] See *Rituals of Rule, Rituals of Resistance*, xxii.
[119] Deeds, *Defiance and Deference*, 33.

Pedro y San Pablo, Indians processed around the area where the mission had stood, singing songs in hymn form with unintelligible words, and carrying candles in their hands.[120]

SYNCRETISM AND POPULAR RELIGIOSITY[121]

A particularly unique musical ethnicity developed in the mission communities of northern New Spain during the colonial era. This musical ethnicity was constantly changing and dialogic, neither wholly European nor indigenous. Missionaries introduced new Christian practices that were negotiated within the pueblos, and the music that resulted was mixed, containing both European and indigenous influences and meanings.[122] New percussive instruments, dances, and rhythms became part of the devotional music on the northern frontier. Native music was appropriated and placed in new religious contexts, given European form, and sometimes accompanied by woodwinds and stringed instruments.

Syncretism, or a combination of European and indigenous elements, is the most prominent feature of popular religion in the colonial borderlands. Art historian Jeanette Peterson identified three types of syncretism in her study of colonial murals in Malinalco, Mexico.[123] First, syncretism was manifested in a "double mistaken identity,"[124] where each culture brings a different set of associations to the same object. The use of unison *a capella* chants in praising god(s), discussed in the first two chapters, was common to both indigenous and European cultures and is an example of this type of syncretism. Even though this type of music might have sounded at first hearing wholly Catholic, each party

---

[120] Zephyrin Englehardt, *The Franciscans in Arizona* (Harbor Springs, MI: Holy Childhood Indian School, 1899), 148.

[121] Parts of this section have been published in Kristin Dutcher Mann, "Music and Popular Religiosity in Northern New Spain," *Catholic Southwest* 12 (2001), 7-27.

[122] The concept of syncretism has been criticized by some as being too binary to describe the changes that occurred in indigenous culture and religion following the Conquest. See Thomas Abercrombie, *Pathways of Memory and Power: Ethnography and History among an Andean People* (Madison: University of Wisconsin Press, 1998). I use the term as a way of discussing the specific processes that affected religious music. I find Peterson's categories of syncretism useful for comparison with similar processes in music and dance. The musical ethnicity that developed in the borderlands region is the result of the processes of cultural enmeshment that brought together indigenous and European musical elements.

[123] *The Paradise Garden Murals of Malinoco*, 8-9.

[124] See James Lockhart, "Some Nahua Concepts in Postconquest Guise," *History of European Ideas* 6 (1985), 477, who identifies this concept. Louise Burkhart, *The Slippery Earth: Nahua-Christian Dialogue in Sixteenth-Century Mexico* (Tucson: University of Arizona Press, 1989) develops Lockhart's ideas further.

most likely retained the interpretation from its own culture. Indians were singing new words and tunes, but in a form that was traditionally intended to praise and supplicate their own gods or provide healing. The missionaries could change the words and melody of such chants, but changing the context would be far more difficult.

A second form of syncretism involved the merger of native and European Christian images to form a new, hybridized icon. This type of syncretism also appeared in the music and dance of the northern missions. The tunes of indigenous music merged with the words of the Catholic liturgy to create blended musical forms of prayers such as the Rosary, Salve Regina, and Our Father. At a Christmas celebration at the Parras mission, Indians gathered to sing and dance, and this type of hybridized syncretism was present:

> *They were adorned with feathers of various colors from guacamayas and other birds. They held arrows in their hands, as was their custom, and sang words that were no longer barbarian but rather Christian. . . . The songs of our Indians, translated from their language, in which they sang, went as follows: "God our Lord is worthy of praise; the feast of Our Lady makes us happy; let men praise Our Lady and mother; let us worship the place where Our Lady is found, she who is the Mother of God and Our Lord." These motets were repeated and sung in the tone and rhythm that they use.*[125]

In this example, indigenous dances and traditional dress were combined with Hispanic Christian themes and words as well as Jesuit emphasis on the Virgin Mary. The content of the songs was Christianized, but the language and rhythm retained Indian characteristics. Padre Felipe Arroyo de la Cuesta, musician and missionary at San Juan Bautista in Alta California, facilitated this type of syncretism when he set indigenous texts in the indigenous language to the tunes of familiar devotional songs used in the mission.[126]

The third type of syncretism occurred when unique indigenous forms were used to convey Christian themes. These events indicate very little sincerity in Christian conversion; indigenous forms very likely retained much of their older meanings. Franciscans and Jesuits pointed to the pious celebrations of their communities on Catholic feasts. These indigenous gatherings, however, which featured dancing and feasting, were often simply pre-Contact celebrations, such as that for the harvest of the pitahaya fruit, that were moved to appropriate feast days in the Catholic calendar, such as All Souls Day.

---

[125] Pérez de Ribas, *History of the Triumphs of Our Holy Faith*, book 11, chapter 10, 669-670.
[126] See "Oro Molido," 1819, Bancroft Library, MS 60, cited in da Silva, *Mission Music*, 127.

Jesuit Father Eusebio Kino attempted to use an indigenous form to induce Christian devotion. He implemented a syncretic nighttime mass for the celebration of Christmas at Mission San Bruno, and supplemented the mass with feasting, music, lights, and dancing in the church.[127] Baja Californian Indians were accustomed to observing important rituals at night with feasting and dancing, and Kino seems to have been striving to place the Christian feast into a pre-existing indigenous form in order to increase participation.

Instead of tacitly accepting the instruction of the missionaries, indigenous groups throughout the borderlands maintained and adapted their cultural traditions in order to survive in the new political and religious situation. Syncretism and ethnogenesis occurred because they were the best way to hold on to some pre-existing practices and traditions. By modifying dances, for example, to reference the Virgin Mary and the Devil, they were allowed to continue under the watchful eyes of the missionaries. By aligning festivals with Christian saints' days or religious feast days, the dancing, music, revelry, and feasting could continue under a different name. Mission pueblos and churches furnished convenient meeting places for community ceremonial gatherings and political activities, particularly among groups who refused to fully relocate into compact villages.[128] The missionaries, as well, benefited from the blending of cultural elements and encouraged native practices as a way of easing their charges into Catholicism. After all, a pueblo full of potential converts congregated around the mission was much preferable to an empty mission, regardless of the piety of the neophytes.[129] They recognized that hybridized traditions involving dance were opportunities for converts to release pressure, frustration, and emotion—much more desirable than the eruption of tension in revolts.

Cultural accommodation and adaptation, then, characterized the popular religiosity of the colonial borderlands. This can best be seen outside of the official liturgy of the church in newly composed music as well as in the development of syncretic religious dance-dramas from indigenous forms. Alabados and other simple songs composed for teaching doctrine were likely influenced by local indigenous tunes and rhythmic patterns. The choirbooks of Fray Narciso Durán, a Franciscan who worked in the nineteenth-century Alta California missions, include formal masses and settings for the offices as well as more informal alabados and hymns. These songbooks were influenced by the indigenous musicians

---

[127] Dunne, *Black Robes*, 33.
[128] Merrill, "Conversion to Christianity," 141.
[129] For a typology of Tarahumara responses to Jesuit conversion efforts, ranging from outright rejection to acceptance of Catholicism and its ceremonies, see ibid., 149-151.

of the area and have been called the missionaries' attempt to capture and express the qualities of indigenous California music.[130]

Accommodation and adaptation was also evident in the importance of dance in mission communities of northern New Spain. Although dance was not a part of official liturgy practiced by missionaries, it was a key component of sacred indigenous music. Both Franciscans and Jesuits attempted to incorporate some of the elements of indigenous ritual into the Catholic rites they promoted. This resulted both in the introduction of European-style dances as well as the redirecting of pre-existing dance and music. The missionaries attempted to sanitize the music and dances of the Indians in order to disassociate autochthonous rituals from music. They wanted to capture indigenous music and incorporate it into the hegemonic European culture of New Spain. In New Mexico, Franciscans emphasized the celebration of rituals that paralleled native dances and cultural practices. For example, the catsina cult was compared with the Christian cults surrounding saints and Marian images. Corn dances were allowed to continue in conjunction with devotions to saints associated with agriculture.[131] Some dances, including matachines, moros y cristianos, and Pascua dances, have persisted in popular religious culture into the current day. Celebrations in the borderlands today include processions and singing with both indigenous and European components. Edward Spicer described one such procession to a Yaqui Catholic church on Sunday morning. A group of men and women sang hymns to the Virgin Mary in the style of plainchant. Accompanying them, however, was a man bare to the waist wearing a mask and headdress of a deer and dancing with a gourd rattle.[132] This juxtaposition of ritual activities indicates the degree to which indigenous practices merged with Catholic beliefs to form hybridized religious devotions.

Other than musical forms, many indigenous groups continue to make European-style instruments introduced by the missionaries. Most notable among these instruments are the Tarahumara-made violins. A modern ethnographer of the Tarahumaras asserted that "the Tarahumaras are literally a society of violinists. A violin can be found somewhere in the possession of most families, and virtually all men play . . . these wooden stringed instruments, entirely hand-carved and constructed."[133] Similarly, the harp introduced by Spaniards

---

[130] Ray and Engbeck, *Gloria Dei*, 3.
[131] Gutiérrez, *When Jesus Came*, 82.
[132] Spicer, *The Yaquis*, 59.
[133] John G. Kennedy, *Tarahumara of the Sierra Madre: Beer, Ecology, and Social Organization* (Arlington Heights, IL: AHM Publishing Corporation, 1978), 74.

among the Seri Indians of Sonora has also become a central part of modern Seri music and dance.[134]

The use of music in the missions, as well as the imposition of a Christian cycle of feasts involving ritual celebrations, opened up a space in which indigenous peoples could respond to the colonial power structure. It is clear that many indigenous practices involving music and dance, particularly nocturnal dances, persisted in the north. Others were refashioned as part of the ongoing cultural processes of ethnogenesis and cultural adaptation. Even missionaries may have adopted some indigenous practices in order to try and relate Christianity to those they were attempting to convert. Jesuits at Temeichic, for example, adopted the Tarahumara practice of using music in healing rituals when they chanted mass during an exorcism against malignant spirits attacking a convert.[135] Other friars welcomed the assistance of native remedies and herbs in their healing efforts.

Physical and social space was restructured by the use of music in the missions. Songs and processions, as well as the ringing of bells, could make holy ground out of the desert. They could also create conflict within groups and reveal new indigenous leaders, including women, who participated in the performances as a way of improving their status. Religious holidays such as Corpus Christi and Holy Week were celebrated differently in the north than in central Mexico, but they were important occasions for establishing group identity and reflecting a community's social hierarchy. Finally, the blend of indigenous and Catholic religious traditions that developed into the popular religion of the borderlands region was reflected in the religious music and dance of the area. Neither wholly indigenous nor entirely European in origin, this music's power was in its ability to achieve religious accommodation and the restructuring of space and time in reconstituted mission communities. Music and dance, particularly in the context of performances for special occasions, could be effectively employed by indigenous peoples in their attempts to respond to the pressures of colonialism. Song was not merely a tool of domination or a method for educating the unconverted; its power could also be harnessed to serve the interests of indigenous actors.

---

[134] On Seri music, see Thomas Bowen and Edward Moser, "Material and Functional Aspects of Seri Instrumental Music," *The Kiva* 35:4 (1970), 178-200.

[135] Carta anua de 1676, Tarahumara pueblos, AGN, Misiones, vol. 26, f. 216v.

Conclusions

> *For do but note a wild and wanton herd*
> *Or race of youthful and unhandled colts*
> *Fetching mad bounds, bellowing and neighing loud,*
> *Which is the hot condition of their blood;*
> *If they but hear perchance a trumpet sound,*
> *Or any air of music touch their ears,*
> *You shall perceive them make a mutual stand,*
> *Their savage eyes turned to a modest gaze*
> *By the sweet power of music.*
>
> —William Shakespeare, *The Merchant of Venice*, Act V, Scene I

Shakespeare's description of the power of music displays early modern European ideas about music's supernatural ability to affect nature and human behavior. It bears comparison to Fray Mariano López Pimentel's previously cited discussion of the power of music as a conversion tool over two hundred years later in his instruction manual for Franciscans of the Province of San Diego:

> *This is an effective medium for taking in the gentiles, bringing them together and congregating them daily, and after playing it a while exhorting them, and instructing them, civilizing them, taming them, catechizing them, and converting them. Oh, with what pleasure would they attend to hear the divine word through hearing music? Oh, with what pleasure would they sing the hymns of praise that they would learn for this purpose!*[1]

In Pimentel's view, indigenous peoples were wild beings who required taming, and music was the sweet elixir designed for this purpose in the missions he oversaw. Clerics throughout Spain's colonial mission system recognized music's ability to form group identity, affect behavior, and communicate doctrine and cul-

---

[1] Reglamento de enseñanza civil, politica y cristiana, para los hijos de los infieles de la Asia y América: en su colegio de misiones, de estas lenguas de los infieles asiáticos y americanos, AGI, México, 2735, exp. 2, 1808.

ture. The indigenous peoples of northern New Spain also understood the power of song and dance to open communication with the sacred, restore order to the universe, and transmit history, culture, and tradition.

This study has analyzed the varied forms of music present in the mission communities of northern New Spain from the late sixteenth century until the end of the colonial period. Three major factors contributed to the forms of music present in mission communities over this period: the background and training of missionaries, the musical practices of native groups of the region, and the sociopolitical context of larger overlapping communities with which the mission was involved. The juxtaposition of these factors created unique musical landscapes in the various regions of northern New Spain.

Missionary training included daily exposure to ecclesiastical chant, and missionaries were also shaped by the cultures and popular religious practices of the regions from which they came. Missionaries like Antonio Margil de Jesús and Juan María de Salvatierra frequently used music in their work, and both had a great deal of experience with song, and in the case of Salvatierra, dance and instrumental music, in their education and early careers. In missions staffed by those who could command the power of music, it became a powerful method of indoctrination and inculcation of religious identity. However, other missionaries, like Jesuit Jacob Baegert, who had no formal musical training, were likely much less confident in their ability to harness the power of music effectively. When Baegert wrote to his brother, he requested that he be sent books of songs or hymns, perhaps as a way of bolstering his ability and confidence in using music to work with Indians who had exhibited interest in European-style liturgical music.[2] More elaborate music was found in missions where missionaries, or indigenous converts, could teach instrumental music and even manufacture violins, flutes, or chirimías. Still, even those missionaries without specific talents, could teach doctrine using simple folk songs and hymns.

Forms of music in mission communities were also shaped by the people who inhabited these communities. Groups who ascribed a great deal of importance to music, such as the Seri, were targeted for evangelization and pacification through musical instruction.[3] Those peoples who quickly responded to

---

[2] Baegert to Father George Baegert, October 12, 1750, in *The Letters of Jacob Baegert*, 110.

[3] Recall the example from Chapter 5 in which repeated requests for musical instruments for Seri missions were eventually granted. Granados to viceroy, March 31, 1791, AGN, Provincias Internas, vol. 235; Ugarte y Loyola to Granados, November 17, 1791, AGN, Provincias Internas, vol. 235, microfilm copy in DRSW. The Seris, however, were never effectively reduced into mission pueblos despite the use of music.

European-style songs and instruments, such as the Opatas and Eudeves, received more musical training; thus, musical performances tended to be more elaborate in the mission communities they populated. Descriptions of liturgical dances in the colonial missions of northern New Spain reveal many local characteristics—dancing around a pole, the use of masks or specific costumes, particular rhythms or harmonization patterns, and storylines that emphasized the triumph of good over evil. In many areas, the music of the Catholic liturgy, including the singing of the alabado, was added to an existing repertoire of ceremonial and quotidian songs, which continued to be used (albeit with alterations such as the incorporation of European instruments), outside of liturgical worship. That missionaries were at least partially successful in using music as a teaching tool is evident in the cultural transfer that took place when hymns such as the alabado or the Salve Regina were sung outside of the context and space of the church, in private homes, fields, or recreational spaces not controlled by the missionaries.[4] Over several generations, these Christian songs acquired religious significance and became, along with liturgical ceremonies, an integral part of the popular religiosity of the borderlands.

Third, the sociopolitical contexts of New Spain's northern frontier region affected the forms of music performed in mission communities. Regional differences, due to the control exercised by missionaries, the presence of soldiers and settlers, or earlier histories of revolts and church–state conflicts, all impacted the nuances of musical forms and performance within individual communities. Over time, mission music in general changed, with the most elaborate musical cultures exhibited in the earliest missions of the near north and New Mexico, and the latest Alta California missions. These periods of more intense musical performances and repertoire bookended the vast majority of the mission period, in which hymns and daily liturgical chant, along with occasional performances for special feast days were the most common forms of mission music.

How did the end of the mission era impact the forms of music that became part of popular religiosity in the north? Although this question is beyond the scope of my study, it is possible to offer a few generalizations. The handover of missions to secular clergy, and, to a lesser degree, the 1767 expulsion of the Jesuits, did not greatly change the function of music in mission communities. After the initial years of congregation and widespread doctrinal instruction in

---

[4] Beth Aracena argues that Jesuit introduction of European music among the Araucanian people of South America had lasting power because of their use of indigenous language. Performances outside of established ceremonial contexts in the church are evidence of this transfer. See "Singing Salvation," 20-21.

individual missions, music was less of an evangelization tool and an expression of changing identity. Although still largely European in form, music gained a place in the popular religiosity of both Indian communities and increasingly diverse parishes in areas to which Spanish and multiethnic settlers migrated and established homes. Many missions were the places of worship for settlers, seasonal laborers, and soldiers long before they were secularized, and intermarriage between these colonists and converted Indians increased the racial mixture of these congregations, blurring ethnic boundaries. Still, even under secular control, the fiestas for holy days of obligation continued, and the increasing number of *cofradías* and religious societies in the nineteenth century involved even more of the population in the planning and execution of such events. Musical performances for special occasions continued to include indigenous dances, processions, the singing of hymns and devotional songs, and the rituals of the liturgy. In some areas, mission choirs continued under the direction of indigenous or mestizo leaders, instead of the resident missionary, while in others they were disbanded. Musical instruments rarely appear on the inventories of missions upon secularization, and then, they are described as in poor condition or broken. This suggests that instruments, costumes, and processional accoutrements passed into possession of the community and individual performers as the celebrations to which they were tied increasingly became individual and collective expressions of identity. Instruments also likely passed into the hands of musicians in the interim between Jesuit expulsion and Franciscan takeover of the missions in northwestern New Spain.[5] Secularization and changes in religious leadership may have had short-term effects on the music in a particular church, but in the long run, the music introduced by the missionaries and refashioned through dialogic processes involving the wider community, constituted a crucial element of culture, and continued to change, reflecting the dynamic identity of the community.

Altogether, however, the purpose of this study has been to analyze not only the forms, but the functions of music and dance in New Spain's northern mission communities. What was the primary function of song in the missions? Far beyond its use as a tool of evangelization and teaching, music was also an instrument of social control used by the missionaries, with the ability to reconstruct time and space. Furthermore, it communicated cultural understandings between and within groups. Music was at the core of identity formation. It was an instrument of adaptation, cultural accommodation, resistance, and an agent in ethno-

---

[5] See, for example, inventories of the Baja California missions from 1768 and then again in 1772, in Kennealy, *The Writings of Fermín Francisco de Lasuén*, vol. I, 5-34, which contain no instruments other than bells for these missions in 1768, but include some instruments in 1772. Jesuit inventories from the 1760s contain musical instruments as well.

genesis employed by indigenous peoples within the webs of power, and constraints of disease, dislocation, and depopulation that characterized their lives.

Music's use as a tool of evangelization stretches back to Franciscan beginnings in the Middle Ages. The lauda, or spiritual songs, were used by the friars to incorporate folk songs with the teaching of Catholic doctrine. When Franciscans and the newly established Society of Jesus arrived in New Spain to convert the indigenous population, it is not surprising that music was one of the first and most effective tools used to attract Indians to doctrinal instruction and participation in the rites of the Church. Its use was endorsed by official Catholic bodies, such as the Council of Trent and the Mexican Provincial Councils. As missionaries traveled northward, establishing missions and preaching doctrine, music again proved an invaluable aid in captivating the curiosity of indigenous peoples and teaching Catholic concepts. But music might not have proven such an effective tool if not for the importance of song and dance in indigenous groups of the north. Despite the wide variety of ethnic groups in northern frontier areas, music and dance were crucial elements of both daily life and ritual ceremonies. Music structured communication with the wider universe, provided access to power, and shaped corporate identity. Songs, instruments, and dances functioned as communication conduits within ethnic groups, between different groups, and with supernatural beings. It was not unfamiliar, then, when missionaries suggested that their God could be addressed through songs and the ceremonies of the mass. Nor was the practice of dancing to recreate history and impart cultural values alien to missionaries, who had witnessed moros y cristianos dances and liturgical drama in Europe and Central New Spain.

As part of the colonization weapons arsenal, song was intimately involved in the exercise of colonial power, and it functioned as a means of achieving social control in the unincorporated frontier areas of northern New Spain. Because of the mnemonic power of song, particularly when used as part of a daily routine, missionaries were able, in ideal situations, to reorder the lives of those who congregated in mission communities in an attempt to promote Hispanic goals of economic production and cultural accommodation. Every mission possessed at least one bell, and bells became part of the musical landscape of the north, establishing Hispanic schedules for work, sleep, meals, instruction, and worship. Music was then integrally involved in the attempt to establish cultural hegemony over Indians in northern missions. The degree to which music was effective as an instrument of acculturation is questionable. Certainly bells became an inescapable sound in northern pueblos, reminding all, not just converts, of the power of Church and State. But reports such as the following, penned by Father Echeverría in 1729, were likely exaggerated:

> *All those who live in the pueblo go to mass, which is celebrated every day. The men sit on the right side of the church; the women, by themselves, on the left. When the mass is finished, they praise the Lord in song; the men sing first, and the women follow. The boys remain for instruction in Christian doctrine, and likewise, in a separate section, the girls. In the afternoon they gather for the Rosary, which they repeat in chorus. This whole place has become a heaven. . . . The men come to church in their trousers and shirts of sack-cloth; the women wear their flannel petticoats and cotton chemises. . . . [Loreto is] a new, happy, miniature Christian kingdom.*[6]

This report and other official missionary correspondence (sources upon which my research is largely based) often present pictures of ideal mission life. It is difficult to assess the veracity of these reports; Echeverría could have been referring to the activities of only a small number of Indians who chose to congregate in the mission. He could also have been presenting a rosy picture of mission life in order to obtain necessary funds or impress officials with the success of evangelization and acculturation efforts. What we do not have, unfortunately, is an indigenous account of daily life at Loreto, nor at other northern missions, to provide an alternative perspective.

However, it is possible to speculate on the role that music played in the lives of indigenous peoples responding to the imposition of colonial rule in northern New Spain. Song and dance, as integral elements in indigenous culture, provided a means of maintaining and reshaping community identity. Music's role in the process of ethnogenesis allowed ethnic groups, whether true or constructed, to refashion their cultures through the integration and appropriation of songs and musical instruments such as the violin. In some modern indigenous communities, as Merrill and other cultural anthropologists have shown, musical culture remains an essential part of community identity. Although missionaries saw the internalization of European musical forms as a marker of indigenous piety, Indians may have selectively accommodated to this element of mission life as a way of gaining the missionary's favor and access to material benefits, such as reduced work, additional food, positions in mission government, or gifts. Over time these musical forms took on additional religious significance as Catholicism became rooted in mixed communities.

Performances for special occasions, whether civil or religious, opened up spaces for Indians to reinvent rituals in order to maintain a degree of control over their culture. Indigenous dances were combined with Christian themes and incorporated into celebrations for saints' feast days. Mission courtyards provided

---

[6] Echeverría to Marqués de Villapuente, October 28, 1729, BNM, Archivo Franciscano, caja 4/55.1.

venues for congregation for such dances and they moved from being prohibited (or moved to locations far away from the missionaries' control) to being featured as part of the festivities for a Christian feast, and even complemented with feasting, fireworks, and rest from physical labor.

Music also provided opportunities for the restructuring of social space by individual Indians. Membership in a choir or orchestra entitled the musician to exemption from (or at least a reduction in) other forms of labor. It involved extra travel and increased participation in celebrations throughout the region. Indians who held musical offices, such as cantor, music teacher, or choir member held offices important in the structure of the community. In some cases they assisted in their villages' governance. Being a musician, cantor, catechist, or instrumentalist meant achieving a degree of social prestige. For women, music provided a way of renegotiating gendered space in northern missions. Although mandates restricting the participation of women in the liturgy were handed down by Church bodies in both Europe and New Spain, these dictates were ignored in many northern missions, allowing women to advance to honorable positions such as cantor or choir member. Gendered space was reconstructed in northern New Spain through a combination of pre-existing indigenous customs and frontier conditions, which necessitated male labor in other areas and included a tendency to disregard rules that were seen as impractical.

Responses to the liturgical music of the missions, then, took on a range of forms, from acceptance to accommodation to gain material benefits. In some cases, music and dance were incorporated into indigenous resistance to colonial rules, either through passive means or outright rebellion. Dance and the mockery of liturgical songs and rituals were components of indigenous resistance to colonial rule in some revolts. In these cases, Indians internalized the rites of the Church enough to effect reversals of ritual roles when they had achieved victory over the colonizers. This is evidence of the power of music and its availability to be harnessed by both colonizers and colonized in the struggle for cultural dominance. Indigenous dances persisted throughout the frontier, although they incorporated some European elements, such as instruments or musical form.

Thus, while music may have started out merely as an evangelization tool and part of the attempt to impose cultural hegemony in the northern missions, as the colonial period progressed, Indians were able to strategize ways to use it to their advantage. The function of song and dance in the missions became inextricably tied to the construction of identity, both individual and group. It helped to plant the seeds for multiple identities—as Catholics, members of reconstituted mission communities, and as members of ethnic groups. Community identity in many areas of the borderlands today owes much to the syncretic forms of dance and liturgical ceremony, such as the matachines and the alabado, that had their roots in the colonial missions. One has only to consider the words of Hemish historian Joe Sando to begin to understand the long view of the results of the meeting of musical cultures in New Spain's north:

> *Having Indian blood or claiming Indian ancestry does not make one an Indian, according to Pueblo values; one has to be an active participant in Indian life. . . . The pueblo is known throughout Indian country for its many feast days. . . . During the entire Christmas season the figure of the Christ Child remains at the host family's home in a specially decorated area, usually in the living room—it represents the stable in Bethlehem. An animal dance is generally held to coincide with the birth of Christ, and all game animals known and beneficial to the people are represented. During my childhood, the Jemez people used to roast corn in the fireplace, and while that was going on, other members of the family would draw pictures of wild game animals and birds, as well as farm crops, on the wall next to the fireplace. All this was in hopes that the birth of Christ would also result in the birth of the animals and plants being drawn on the wall. . . .*
>
> *Of course, alongside the Christian calendar, there remain the traditional Indian ceremonial dates, which are not open to the general public. . . . The non-Indian has learned belatedly that Indian ceremonials are not blatant orgies, but well-organized, sacred dramas, dedicated to the Creator in thanksgiving, or pleading for more blessings.*[7]

In this description, celebrations for Christian feast days are considered markers of traditional Indian life for the Jemez. Waiting for the birth of Christ paralleled waiting for important resources, and the Catholic ritual calendar commingled with Indian ceremonial dance-dramas. The strategic reinvention of traditions and the reformulation of cultural practices that have taken place over centuries of the interaction of musical influences speaks to new social and political contexts in modern-day northwestern New Mexico—whether it is defending traditional practices, passing along shared history, or claiming land rights.

In conclusion, the music and dance of the missions of northern New Spain are a lens through which the effects of sustained contact between the European colonizers, in the form of missionaries, and indigenous ethnic groups can be studied on a small scale. Often overlooked or relegated to the margins of cultural history, this music is significant because it allows us a glimpse of indigenous actions and responses to colonialism in a region where the colonial record is dominated almost exclusively by Spanish voices. The power of song and dance lay in music's ability to reshape colonial cultural encounters, restructure time and space, and forge new religious identities.

[7] Sando, *Nee Hemish*, 217-222.

Bibliography

Manuscript Collections

Archivo de las Indias, Seville (AGI)
Archivo General de la Nación, Mexico City (AGN)
Archivum Romanum Societatis Iesu, Rome, microfilm copy in Vatican Film Library, St. Louis University, St. Louis, Missouri (ARSI)
Bancroft Library, University of California, Berkeley (BL)
Béxar Archives, San Antonio, Texas
Biblioteca del Instituto Nacional de Antropología e Historia, Fondo Franciscano, Mexico City (BINAH FF)
Biblioteca Nacional de México, Mexico City (BNM)
Catholic Archives of Texas, Austin, Texas (CAT)
Documentary Relations of the Southwest, Office of Ethnohistorical Research, University of Arizona, Arizona State Museum, Tucson, Arizona (DRSW)
Juan B. Rael and Charles Lummis recordings, Archive of Folk Culture, American Folklife Center, Library of Congress, Washington, DC (LOC)
Mission Santa Barbara Archive Library, Santa Barbara, California (MSBA)
Old Spanish Missions Historical Research Collection, Our Lady of the Lake University, San Antonio, Texas (OSMHRC) microfilm collections from the Archivo del Colegio de Querétaro and Archivo del Colegio de Zacatecas
Our Lady of the Lake University Special Collections and Archives, San Antonio, Texas (OLLUSCA)
University of Arizona Main Library Special Collections, Tucson, Arizona (AZU)
University of Texas, Nettie Lee Benson Latin American Library, Austin, Texas (UTNLB)

Printed Primary Sources and Ethnographies

Adams, Eleanor B., ed. *Bishop Tamaron's Visitation of New Mexico, 1760*. Historical Society of New Mexico Publications in History, XV. Albuquerque: Historical Society of New Mexico, 1954.

Adams, Eleanor B., and Angélico Chávez, eds. *The Missions of New Mexico in 1776.* Albuquerque: University of New Mexico Press, 1956.

Alcocer, José Antonio. *Bosquejo de la historia del colegio de Nuestra Señora de Guadalupe y sus misiones, año de 1788.* Edited by Rafael Cervantes. Mexico City: Editorial Porrúa, [1788] 1958.

Alessio Robles, Vito, ed. *Coahuila y Texas en la época colonial* (Mexico City: Editorial Cultura, 1938.

———, ed. *Demonstración del vastísimo obispado de la Nueva Vizcaya, 1765.* Mexico City: Editorial Porrúa, 1937.

Aljaba Apostólico-Guadalupana. Mexico: Imprenta de Andrade y Escalante, 1860.

Anderson, Arthur, J.O., ed. and trans. *Psalmodia Christiana.* Salt Lake City: University of Utah Press, 1972.

Armstrong, Regis J., Wayne J. Hellman, and William Short, eds. and trans. *The Founder, Francis of Assisi: Early Documents.* New York: New City Press, 2000.

Arricivita, Juan Domingo. *Crónica seráfica y apostolica del Colegio de Propaganda Fide de la Santa Cruz de Querétaro.* Mexico City: N.p., 1792.

Ayer, Mrs. Edward E., trans. *The Memorial of Fray Alonso De Benavides, 1630.* Chicago: R.R. Donnelly and Sons, 1916.

Baegert, Jacob. *Observations in Lower California.* Translated by M.M. Brandenburg and Carl L. Baumann. Berkeley: University of California Press, 1952.

Bahr, Donald, ed. *O'odham Creation and Related Events, As Told to Ruth Benedict in 1927 in Prose, Oratory, and Song.* Tucson: University of Arizona Press, 2001.

———. *The Short, Swift Time of Gods on Earth: The Hohokam Chronicles.* Berkeley: University of California Press, 1994.

Bancroft, Hubert Howe. *History of the North Mexican States and Texas,* vol. 1. San Francisco: A.L. Bancroft Publishers, 1884.

Benavides, Alonso de. *Revised Memorial of 1630.* Albuquerque: Gran Quivira Society, 1945.

Benoist, Howard, and María Eva Flores, eds. *Guidelines for a Texas Mission: Instructions for the Missionary of Mission Concepción in San Antonio.* Translated by Benedict Leutenegger. Documents Relating to the Old Spanish Missions of Texas, I. San Antonio: Old Spanish Missions Historical Research Library, 1994.

Bolton, Herbert Eugene, trans. and ed. *Font's Complete Diary of the Second Anza Expedition.* Anza's California Expeditions, vol. IV. Berkeley: University of California Press, 1930.

Bonaventure, Saint, Cardinal. *The Life of St. Francis.* Translated by Emma Gurney Salter. N.p.: J.M. Dent, 1904.

Brown, Alan K., ed. and trans. *A Description of Distant Roads.* San Diego: San Diego State University Press, 2001.

Burrus, Ernest J., ed. *Juan María Salvatierra: Selected Letters about Lower California.* Los Angeles: Dawson's Book Shop, 1971.

———. *Kino escribe a la duquesa.* Rome: Jesuit Historical Institute, 1965.

———. *Kino's Biography of Francisco Javier Saeta, S.J.* Translated by Charles Polzer. Rome: Jesuit Historical Institute, 1971.

Burrus, Ernest J., trans. and ed. *Kino's Plan for the Development of Pimería Alta, Arizona, and Upper California: A Report to the Mexican Viceroy.* Tucson: Arizona Pioneers' Historical Society, 1961.

Cartas de Indias. Madrid: Imprenta de M. G. Hernández, 1877.

Castañeda Delgado, Paulino. *Los memoriales del Padre Silva sobre predicación, pacífica, y repartimientos.* Madrid: Instituto Gonzalo Fernández de Oviedo, 1983.

Celano, St. Thomas of. *St. Francis of Assisi: First and Second Life of St. Francis, with Selections from Treatise on the Miracles of Blessed Francis.* Edited and translated by Placid Hermann. Chicago: Franciscan Herald Press, 1963.

Chávez, Angélico, O.F.M., trans. and ed. *"The Oroz Codex." Relation of the Description of the Holy Gospel Province in New Spain and the Lives of the Founders and Other Noteworthy Men of Said Province.* Washington, DC: Academy of American Franciscan History, 1972.

Concilio provincial mexicano IV. Celebrado en la ciudad de México el año de 1771. Querétaro: Imprenta de la Escuela de Artes, 1898.

Constituciones de el Arzobispado, y provincia de la muy ynsigne, y muy leal Ciudad de Tenuxtitlan, México de la Nueva España. Concilio I. Mexico City: Juan Pablos, 1555. Nettie Lee Benson Latin American Library, University of Texas, Austin.

da Silva, Owen F. *Mission Music of California.* Los Angeles: Warren F. Lewis, 1941.

del Barco, Miguel. *Historia natural y crónica de la antigua California.* Edited by Miguel León-Portilla. Mexico City: Universidad Nacional Autónoma de México, 1988.

de León, Alonso. *Historia de Nuevo León, con noticias sobre Coahuila, Tejas y Nuevo México.* Mexico City: N.p., [1649] 1909.

de Mora, Vicente. *Los informes de Fray Vicente de Mora sobre Baja California en 1777.* Edited by Salvador Bernabéu Albert. Mexico City: Embajada de España, 1992.

Decorme, Gerald. *La obra de los Jesuitas mexicanos durante la época colonial, 1572–1767.* Mexico City: Antigua Librería Robredo, de José Porrúa e Hijos, 1941.

Demostracion del vastísimo obispado de la Nueva Vizcaya, 1765: Durango, Sinaloa, Sonora, Arizona, Nuevo México, Chihuahua y porciones de Texas, Coahuila y Zacatecas. Mexico City: Antigua Librería Robredo, de José Porrúa e Hijos, 1937.

Densmore, Frances. *Music of Acoma, Isleta, Cochiti and Zuñi Pueblos.* Washington, DC: Bureau of American Ethnology, Smithsonian Institution, 1957.

———. *Papago Music*. Washington, DC: U.S. Government Printing Office, 1929.

———. *Yuman and Yaqui Music*. Washington, DC: Bureau of American Ethnology, Smithsonian Institution, 1932.

Díaz del Castillo, Bernal. *The Conquest of New Spain*. Translated by J.M. Cohen. London: Penguin Books, 1963.

DiPeso, Charles, and Daniel Matson. "The Seri Indians in 1692 as Described by Adamo Gilg, S.J." *Arizona and the West* 1, no. 7 (1961): 33-56.

Dunne, Peter Masten, trans. and ed. *Jacobo Sedelmayr: Missionary Frontiersman Explorer in Arizona and Sonora, Four Original Manuscript Narratives, 1744–1751*. Tucson: Arizona Pioneers' Historical Society, 1955.

———, ed. "Juan Antonio Balthasar, Padre Visitador to the Sonora Frontier, 1744–45: Two Original Reports. Tucson: Arizona Pioneers Historical Society, 1957.

Dunne, Peter Masten, and Ernest J. Burrus, eds. "Four Unpublished Letters of Anton Maria Benz, Eighteenth Century Missionary to Mexico." *Archivum Historicum Societatis Iesu* 24 (1955): 3-45.

Espinosa, Fray Isidro Félix de. *Crónica de los Colegios de Propaganda Fide de la Nueva España*. Edited by Lino Gómez Canedo. Franciscan Historical Classics, 2. Washington, DC: Academy of American Franciscan History, 1964.

———. *El peregrino septentrional atlante: delineado en la exemplarissima vida del venerable Padre F. Antonio Margil de Jesús*. Mexico City: Joseph Bernardo de Hogal, 1737.

Flint, Richard, and Shirley Cushing Flint, eds. and trans. *Documents of the Coronado Expedition, 1539–1542: "They Were Not Familiar with His Majesty, Nor Did They Wish to Be His Subjects."* Dallas, TX: Southern Methodist University Press, 2005.

Florencia, Francisco de. *Historia de la Provincia de la Compañía de Jesús de Nueva España*. Mexico City: Editorial Academia Literaria, [1694] 1955.

Foster, E. A., trans. and ed. *Motolinía's History of the Indians of New Spain*, Berkeley, CA: Cortés Society, 1950.

García, Bartholomé. *Manual para administrar los santos sacramentos de penitencia, eucharistia, extrema-unción y matrimonio*. Mexico City: Imprenta de los herederos de Dona Maria de Rivera, 1760.

García Villoslada, Ricardo. "Algunos documentos sobre la música en el antigua seminario romano." *Archivum Historicum Societatis Iesu* 31 (1962): 107-138.

Geiger, Maynard, and Clement W. Meighan, eds. and trans. *As the Padres Saw Them: California Indian Life and Customs as Reported by the Franciscan Missionaries, 1813–1815*. Santa Barbara, CA: Santa Barbara Mission Archive Library, 1976.

González Rodríguez, Luis, ed. *Crónicas de la Sierra Tarahumara*. Mexico City: Secretaría de Educación Pública, 1984.

---. *Etnología y misión en la Pimería Alta, 1715–1740*. Mexico City: Universidad Nacional Autónoma de México, 1977.
Hackett, Charles Wilson, trans. and ed. *Historical Documents Relating to New Mexico, Nueva Vizcaya, and Approaches Thereto, to 1773*. Compiled by Adolph F.A. Bandelier, and Fanny R. Bandelier. Vol. 3. Washington, DC: Carnegie Institute of Washington, 1923.
---, ed. *Revolt of the Pueblo Indians of New Mexico and Otermín's Attempted Reconquest*. 2 vols. Albuquerque: University of New Mexico Press, 1942.
Hammond, George Peter, trans. and ed. *Narratives of the Coronado Expedition*. Albuquerque: University of New Mexico Press, 1940.
Houck, Louis, ed. and trans. *The Spanish Régime in Missouri*, vol. 1. Chicago: R.R. Donnelley & Sons, 1909.
Ignatius of Loyola. *The Constitutions of the Society of Jesus*. Translated by George E. Ganss. St. Louis: Institute of Jesuit Sources, 1970.
Kenneally, Finbar, trans. and ed. *Writings of Fermín Francisco de Lasuén*. Washington, DC: Academy of American Franciscan History, 1965.
Kessell, John, and Rick Hendricks, eds. *By Force of Arms: The Journals of Don Diego de Vargas, 1691–1693*. Albuquerque: University of New Mexico Press, 1992.
Lafora, Nicolás de. *Relación del Viaje que hizo a los Presidios Internos situados en la Frontera de la América septentrional perteneciente al Rey de España*. Mexico City: Editorial Pedro Robredo, 1939.
Langsdorff, Georg Heinrich von. *Remarks and Observations on a Voyage around the World from 1803 to 1807*. Edited by Richard Pierce. Translated by Victoria Moessner. Vol. 2. Kingston, Ontario: Limestone Press, 1993.
Leutenegger, Benedict, trans. *Management of the Missions in Texas: Fr. Jose Rafael Oliva's Views Concerning the Problem of the Temporalities in 1788*. Edited by Marion A. Habig. Old Spanish Missions Historical Research Library's Documentary Series, 2. San Antonio, TX: Old Spanish Missions Historical Research Library, 1977.
---. *Nothingness Itself: Selected Writings of Ven. Fr. Antonio Margil*. Chicago: Franciscan Herald Press, 1976.
Leutenegger, Benedict, and Marion A. Habig, eds. *The Zacatecas Missionaries in Texas (1716–1834): Excerpts from the "Libros de los Decretos" of the College of Zacatecas (1707–1722)*. Austin, TX: Historical Survey Committee, 1973.
Leutenegger, Benedict, trans., and Marion Habig, ed. *The Texas Missions of the College of Zacatecas in 1749–1750*. San Antonio, TX: Old Spanish Missions Historical Research Library, 1979.
Lumholtz, Karl. *Unknown Mexico: A Record of Five Years Exploration among the Tribes of the Western Sierra Madre; in the Tierra Caliente of Tepec and Jalisco; and among the Tarascos of Michoacán*. London: Macmillan, 1903.
Mathes, W. Michael, ed. *Obras californianas del Padre Miguel Venegas, S.J.* 4 vols. La Paz: Universidad Autónoma de Baja California Sur, 1979.

Matson, Daniel S., trans. "Letters of Friar Pedro Font, 1776–1777." *Ethnohistory* 22, no. 3 (1975): 263-293.

Matson, Daniel S., and Bernard L. Fontana, trans. and eds. *Friar Bringas Reports to the King: Methods of Indoctrination on the Frontier of New Spain, 1796–1797.* Tucson: University of Arizona Press, 1977.

Menideta, Fray Gerónimo de. *Historia eclesiastica indiana.* Mexico City: Editorial Porrúa, [1598] 1971.

Milanich, Jerald, and William Sturtevant, trans. and eds. *Francisco Pareja's 1613 Confessionario: A Documentary Source for Timucuan Ethnography.* Tallahassee: Florida Division of Archives, History, and Records Management, 1973.

Missae, et orationes propriae sanctorum in Missali Romano. Mexico City: José Jáuregui, 1772.

Missae propriae sanctorum trium ordinum fratrum minorum. Antwerp: Plantin, 1731.

Morfí, Fray Juan Agustín de. *History of Texas 1673–1779.* Translated by Carlos Castañeda. Albuquerque, NM: Quivira Society, 1935.

———. *Diario y Derrotero.* Edited by Eugenio del Hoyo and Malcolm D. McLean. Monterrey: Instituto Tecnológico y de Estudios Superiores de Monterrey, 1967.

Morrow, Baker, trans. and ed. *A Harvest of Reluctant Souls: The Memorial of Fray Alonso de Benavides 1630.* Niwot, CO: University of Colorado Press, 1996.

Motolinía, Toribio de. *Historia de los indios de la Nueva España.* 2 vols. Edited by Salvador Chávez. Mexico City: Hayhoe, 1941.

Nentvig, Juan. *Rudo Ensayo: A Description of Sonora and Arizona in 1764.* Translated and edited by Alberto Francisco Pradeau and Robert R. Rasmussen. Tucson: University of Arizona Press, 1980.

Neumann, Joseph. *Historia de las sublevaciones que contra los misioneros de la Compañía de Jesús y sus auxiliares promovieron las naciones indias ante todo la tarahumara.* Edited by Josef Opatrny. Prague: Ibero-Americana Pragensia Supplementum VI, 1994.

Ocaranza, Fernando. *Los franciscanos en las provincias internas de Sonora y Ostimuri.* Mexico City: N.p., 1933.

Osorio, Diego. *Manual para administrar los santos sacramentos, arreglado al ritual romano, con el orden de bendiciones, Exequias, Procesiones y otras cosas necesarias. Dispusolo el r.p. Fr. Diego Osorio, Ex-Lector de Teología Moral, Predicador General, Calificador del Santo Oficio, Notario Apostolico, Chronista General de todas las Provincias de Nueva España, cura Ministro por sy Magestad de la primitiva Parroquia de Naturales de este Reyno, y Vicario de la Capilla del Señor San Joseph en el Convento de N.P. San Francisco de Mexico.* Calatayud: Imprenta de Juan Aguirre, 1762.

Palóu, Francisco. *Historical Memoirs of California.* Edited by Herbert Eugene Bolton. New York: Russell and Russell, 1966.

———. *Noticias de la Nueva California.* San Francisco: N.p., 1874.

Pennington, Campbell W., ed. and trans. *The Pima Bajo of Central Sonora, Mexico.* Vol. 2. Salt Lake City: University of Utah Press, 1980.

———. *Vocabulario en la lengua nevome: The Pima Bajo of Central Sonora, Mexico.* Vol. 2. Salt Lake City: University of Utah Press, 1979.

Pérez de Ribas, Andrés. *History of the Triumphs of Our Holy Faith among the Most Barbarous and Fierce Peoples of the New World.* Translated and edited by Daniel T. Reff, Maureen Ahren, and Richard K. Danford. Tucson: University of Arizona Press, 1999.

Pérez de Villagrá, Gaspar. *Historia de la Nueva México, 1610.* Critical and annotated Spanish/English edition, translated and edited by Miguel Encinas, Alfred Rodríguez, and Joseph P. Sánchez. Albuquerque: University of New Mexico Press, 1992.

Pfefferkorn, Ignaz. *Sonora: A Description of the Province.* Translated by Theodore Treutlein. Tucson: University of Arizona Press, 1989.

Polzer, Charles, trans. *Kino's Biography of Francisco Javier Saeta, S.J.* Edited by Ernest J. Burrus. Sources and Studies for the History of the Americas, IX. Rome: Jesuit Historical Institute, 1971.

Polzer, Charles. *Rules and Precepts of the Jesuit Missions of Northwestern New Spain.* Tucson: University of Arizona Press, 1976.

Porrúa Turanzas, José, ed. *Documentos para la historia eclesiastica y civil de la provincia de Texas o Nuevas Philipinas, 1720–1779.* Madrid: Ediciones José Porrúa Turanzas, 1961.

Priestly, Herbert Ingram, trans. *A Historical, Political, and Natural Description of California by Pedro Fages, Written for the Viceroy in 1775.* Ramona, CA: Ballena Press, 1972.

Recopilación de leyes de los reynos de las Indias. Madrid: Julian de Paredes, 1681. Reprint. Madrid: Consejo de la Hispanidad, 1943.

Robinson, Alfred. *Life in California.* New York: Da Capo Press, [1846] 1969.

Salvatierra, Juan María. *Juan María de Salvatierra, S.J.: Selected Letters about Lower California.* Translated by Ernest J. Burrus. Edited by Edwin Carpenter and Glen Dawson. Baja California Travel Series, 25. Los Angeles: Dawson's Book Shop, 1971.

Sánchez García, José Hermengildo. *Crónica del Nuevo Santander.* Mexico City: Colegio Regiones, 1990.

Santa María, Fray Vicente de. *Relación histórica de la colonia del Nuevo Santander.* Edited by Ernesto de la Torre Villa. Mexico City: Universidad Nacional Autónoma de México, 1973.

Schroeder, H.J. *Canons and Decrees of the Council of Trent.* St. Louis: B. Herder Book Company, 1950.

Schulz-Bischof, Elsbeth, trans. *The Letters of Jacob Baegert, 1749–1761: Jesuit Missionary in Baja California.* Edited by Doyce B. Nunis, Jr. Baja California Travel Series, 45. Los Angeles: Dawson's Book Shop, 1982.

Tamarón y Romeral, Pedro. *Demonstración del vastísimo obispado de la Nueva Vizcaya, 1765: Durango, Sinaloa, Sonora, Arizona, Nuevo México, Chihuahua y porciones de Texas, Coahuila y Zacatecas.* Mexico City: Antigua Librería Robredo, de José Porrúa e Hijos, [1765] 1937.

Tibesar, Antonine, ed. and trans. *Writings of Junípero Serra.* Vol. 1. Washington, DC: Academy of American Franciscan History, 1966.

Treutlein, Theodore, trans. and ed. *Missionary in Sonora: The Travel Reports of Joseph Och, S.J., 1755–1767.* San Francisco: California Historical Society, 1965.

———. "The Relation of Philipp Segesser: The Pimas and Other Indians [1737]." *Mid-America* 27 (1945): 139-187, 257-260.

Venegas, Miguel. *El apostól mariano representado en la vida del V.P. Juan María de Salvatierra.* Mexico City: Imprenta de Doña Maria de Ribera, 1754.

———. *Juan María de Salvatierra of the Company of Jesus; Missionary in the Province of New Spain, and Apostolic Conqueror of the Californias.* Translated by Marguerite Eyer Wilbur. Cleveland, OH: The Arthur H. Clark Company, 1929.

Vetancurt, Agustín de. *Menologio franciscano de los varones más senalados, que con sus vidas exemplares, perfección religiosa, ciencia, predicación evangelica en su vida, y muerte, illustraron la Provincia de el Santo Evangelio de México.* Mexico City: N.p., 1697.

———. *Teatro mexicano: descripción breve de los sucessos exemplares, historicas, politicos, militares, y religiosos del nuevo mundo occidental de las Indias.* Mexico City: María de Benavides, 1698.

Zapata, Juan Ortíz. "Relación de las misiones, 1678." *Documentos para la historia de México.* 4th Series. Vol. 3. Mexico City: N.p., 1853–1857, 301-419.

Zubillaga, Félix, ed. *Monumenta Mexicana.* Vol. 6. Rome: Societatis Iesu, 1956.

———. *Monumenta Mexicana.* Vol. 7. Rome: Societatis Iesu, 1961.

Zúñiga, Ignacio. *Rápida ojeada al estado de Sonora, Dirigida y dedicada al Supremo Gobierno de la Nación.* Mexico City: Imprenta de Juan Ojeda, 1835.

Secondary Sources

Abercrombie, Thomas. *Pathways of Memory and Power: Ethnography and History among an Andean People.* Madison: University of Wisconsin Press, 1998.

Alegre, Francisco Javier. *Historia de la Compañía de Jesús.* 3 vols. Mexico City: N.p., 1841.

Alcocer, José Antonio. *Bosquejo de la historia del colegio de Nuestra Señora de Guadalupe.* Mexico City: Editorial Porrúa, 1958.

Almaráz, Félix. *Crossroad of Empire: The Church and State on the Río Grande Frontier of Coahuila and Texas, 1700–1821.* San Antonio: Center for Archaeological Research, University of Texas at San Antonio, 1979.

American Folklife Center. *The Federal Cylinder Project: A Guide to Field Cylinder Collections in Federal Agencies*. Studies in American Folklife, no. 3. Washington, DC: American Folklife Center, Library of Congress, 1984.

Aracena, Beth K. "Singing Salvation: Jesuit Musics in Colonial Chile, 1600-1767." PhD diss., University of Chicago, 1999.

———. "Viewing the Ethnomusicological Past: Jesuit Influences on Araucanian Music in Colonial Chile." *Latin American Music Review* 18, no. 1 (1997): 1-29.

Arenas Frutos, Isabel. "Al norte de la Nueva España: diversidad de experiencias evangelizadoras." In *Franciscanos en América*, edited by Francisco Morales, O.F.M. Mexico City: Curia Provincial Franciscana, 1993.

———. *La iglesia en Florida en el siglo XVII*. Seville: N.p., 1981.

Arróniz, Othón. *Teatro de evangelización en Nueva España*. Mexico City: Universidad Nacional Autónoma de México, 1979.

Attali, Jacques. *Noise: The Political Economy of Music*. Translated by Brian Massumi. Minneapolis: University of Minnesota Press, 1985.

Bahr, Donald. "Native American Dream Songs, Myth, Memory, and Improvisation." *Journal de la Société des Americanistes* 80 (1994): 73-93.

Bailey, Gauvin. *Art on the Jesuit Missions in Asia and Latin America, 1542–1773*. Toronto: University of Toronto Press, 1999.

Baker, Geoffrey. *Imposing Harmony: Music and Society in Colonial Cuzco*. Durham, NC: Duke University Press, 2008.

Bangert, William V. *A History of the Society of Jesus*. St. Louis: The Institute of Jesuit Sources, 1972.

Bargellini, Clara. "At the Center on the Frontier: The Jesuit Tarahumara Missions of New Spain." In *Time and Place: The Geohistory of Art*, edited by Thomas DaCosta and Elizabeth Pilliod, 113-128. Aldershot: Ashgate Publishing, 2005.

———. *Misiones y presidios de Chihuahua*. Chihuahua: Gobierno del Estado de Chihuahua, 1997.

———. "Objetos artisticos, viajeros : cuales, como y porque llegaron al Nuevo México?" In *El camino real de tierra adentro, historia y cultura*. Chihuahua: Instituto Nacional de Antropología e Historia, 1997.

———. "Stars in the Sea of the Church: The Indian in Eighteenth-Century New Spanish Painting." In *The Arts in Latin America, 1492–1820*, edited by Joseph J. Rishel and Suzanne Stratton. New Haven, CT: Yale University Press, 2006.

Bargellini, Clara, Salvador Alvarez, and Chantal Cramaussel. *Misiones para Chihuahua*. Mexico City: D.R. Grupo Cementos, 1994.

Barr, Juliana. *Peace Came in the Form of a Woman: Indians and Spaniards in the Texas Borderlands*. Chapel Hill: University of North Carolina Press, 2007.

Barth, Pius J., O.F.M. *Franciscan Education and the Social Order in Spanish North America, 1502–1821*. Chicago: N.p., 1945.

Bayle, Constantino. *Historia de los descubrimientos y colonización de los padres de la Compañía de Jesús en la Baja California*. Madrid: Librería General de Victoriano Suárez, 1933.

———. *Misión de la Baja California*. Madrid: La Editorial Católica, 1946.

Begbie, Jeremy. *Theology, Music, and Time*. Cambridge: Cambridge University Press, 2000.

Berry, Mary. "Franciscan Friars." In *New Grove Dictionary of Music and Musicians*. Vol. 6. Edited by Stanley Sadie, 776-777. London: Macmillan, 1980.

Bermudez, Egberto. *La música en el arte colonial de Colombia*. Bogotá: Fundación de Música, 1994.

Bilodeau, Christopher. "'They Honor Our Lord Among Themselves in Their Own Way': Colonial Christianity and the Illinois Indians." *American Indian Quarterly* 25, no. 3 (Summer 2001): 352-377.

Bolton, Herbert Eugene. *The Hasinais: Southern Caddoans as Seen by the Earliest Europeans*. Norman: University of Oklahoma Press, 1987.

———. *Kino's Historical Memoir of the Pimería Alta: A Contemporary Account of the Beginnings of California, Sonora, and Arizona*. Cleveland, OH: Arthur H. Clark Company, 1919.

———. *The Mission as a Frontier Institution in the Spanish-American Colonies*. El Paso: Texas Western College Press for Academic Reprints, 1960.

———. *Rim of Christendom: A Biography of Eusebio Francisco Kino, Pacific Coast Pioneer*. New York: Russell and Russell, 1960.

———. *The Spanish Borderlands: A Chronicle of Old Florida and the Southwest*. New Haven, CT: Yale University Press, 1921.

Bonfiglioli, Carlo. *Fariseos y matachines en la Sierra Tarahumara*. Mexico City: Instituto Nacional Indigenista, 1995.

Borges, Pedro. *Métodos misionales en la cristianización de América, siglo XVI*. Madrid: Consejo Superior de Investigaciones Científicas, Departamento de Misionología Española, 1960.

Bossy, John. "The Mass as a Social Institution, 1200–1700." *Past and Present*, no. 100 (August 1983): 29-61.

Bowen, Thomas, and Edward Moser. "Material and Functional Aspects of Seri Instrumental Music." *The Kiva* 35, no. 4 (1970): 178-200.

Brading, David A. "Tridentine Catholicism and Enlightened Despotism in Bourbon Mexico." *Journal of Latin American Studies* 15 (1983): 1-22.

Brown, Steven, and Ulrik Volgsten, eds. *Music and Manipulation: On the Social Uses and Social Control of Music*. New York: Berghahn Books, 2006.

Bruning, Walter M. "Zur Vorgeschichte Der Masse 'Pro Propagatione Fidei' Eine Bittschrift Aus Der Sonoramission in Jahre 1707." *Archivum Historicum Societatis Iesu* 8 (1939): 319-327.

Burke, Peter. "Bakhtin for Historians." *Social History* 13, no. 1 (1988): 85–90.

Burkhart, Louise. "A Doctrine for Dancing: The Prologue to the *Psalmodia Christiana*." *Latin American Indian Literatures Journal* 11, no. 1 (1995): 21-33.

———. *Holy Wednesday: A Nahua Drama from Early Colonial Mexico*. Philadelphia: University of Pennsylvania Press, 1996.

———. "Pious Performances: Christian Pageantry and Native Identity in Early Colonial Mexico." In *Native Traditions in the Postconquest World*, edited by Elizabeth Hill Boone and Tom Cummins, 361-381. Washington, DC: Dumbarton Oaks Research Library and Collection, 1992.

———. *The Slippery Earth: Nahua–Christian Dialogue in Sixteenth-Century Mexico*. Tucson: University of Arizona Press, 1989.

Burns, Kathryn. *Colonial Habits: Convents and the Spiritual Economy of Cuzco, Peru*. Durham, NC: Duke University Press, 1999.

Burrus, Ernest J. "Two Lost Mexican Books of the Sixteenth Century." *Hispanic American Historical Review* 37 (1957): 310-320.

Bushnell, Amy Turner. *Situado and Sabana: Spain's Support System for the Presidio and Mission Provinces of Florida*. Anthropological Papers of the American Museum of Natural History, no. 74. New York: American Museum of National History, 1994.

———. "That Demonic Game: The Campaign to Stop Indian Pelota Playing in Spanish Florida, 1675–1684." *Americas* 35, no. 1 (1978): 1-19.

Cahill, David P. "Popular Religion and Appropriation: The Example of Corpus Christi in Eighteenth-Century Cuzco." *Latin American Research Review* 31, no. 2 (1996): 67-110.

Caldwell, John. "Lauda." In *New Grove Dictionary of Music and Musicians*, vol. 14, edited by Stanley Sadie, 367. London: Macmillan, 2001.

Campbell, T.N. *Ethnohistoric Notes on Indian Groups Associated with Three Spanish Missions at Guerrero, Coahuila*. Archaeology and History of the San Juan Bautista Mission Area, Coahuila and Texas, Report no. 3. San Antonio: Center for Archaeological Research, University of Texas at San Antonio, 1979.

Cardiel, José. *Misiones del Paraguay—Declaración de la verdad*. Buenos Aires: Imprenta de Juan A. Alcina, 1900.

Castañeda, Antonia. "Engendering the History of Alta California, 1769–1848: Gender, Sexuality, and the Family." In *Contested Eden: California before the Gold Rush*, edited by Ramón A. Gutiérrez and Richard J. Orsi, 230-259. Berkeley, CA: University of California Press, 1998.

Castañeda, Carlos. *History of Texas, 1673–1779*. Albuquerque: University of New Mexico Press, 1935.

Cayward, Margaret. *Musical Life at Mission Santa Clara de Asís, 1777–1836*. Santa Clara, CA: Santa Clara University, 2006.

———. "The Pastorela, a Christmas Play of Mission-Era California." Paper presented at *Encuentros*/Encounters 2009, University of California at Riverside, January 31, 2009.

Ceballos Ramirez, Manuel. *De historia e historiografía de la frontera norte.* Nuevo Laredo: Universidad Autónoma de Tamaulipas, 1996.
Cervantes, Fernando. "The Devils of Querétaro: Scepticism and Credulity in Late Seventeenth-Century Mexico." *Past and Present* 130 (February 1991): 51-69.
Champe, Flavia Waters. *The Matachines Dance of the Upper Rio Grande: History, Music, and Choreography.* Lincoln: University of Nebraska Press, 1983.
Chase, Gilbert. *A Guide to the Music of Latin America.* Washington, DC: Pan American Union/Library of Congress, 1962.
Christelow, Allan. "Father Joseph Neumann: Jesuit Missionary to the Tarahumaras." *Hispanic American Historical Review* 19, no. 4 (1939): 423-442.
Colley, Charles. "The Missionization of the Coast Miwok Indians of California." *California Historical Society Quarterly* 49 (1970): 143-162.
Comaroff, John, and Jean Comaroff. *Ethnography and the Historical Imagination.* Boulder, CO: Westview Press, 1994.
Contreras Arias, Juan Guillermo. *Atlas cultural de México, Música.* Vol. 10. Mexico City: Secretaría de Educación Pública, 1987.
Coolidge, Dane, and Mary Roberts Coolidge. *The Last of the Seris.* New York: E.P. Dutton and Company, 1939.
Corbin, Alain. *Village Bells: Sound and Meaning in the Nineteenth-Century French Countryside.* Translated by Martin Thom. New York: Columbia University Press, 1998.
Crosby, Harry W. *Antigua California: Mission and Colony on the Peninsular Frontier, 1697–1768.* Albuquerque: University of New Mexico Press, 1994.
Culley, Thomas D. "A Documentary History of the Liturgical Music at the German College in Rome: 1573–1674." PhD diss., Harvard University, 1965.
———. *Jesuits and Music: A Study of the Musicians Connected with the German College in Rome during the Seventeenth Century and of Their Activities in Northern Europe.* Sources and Studies for the History of the Jesuits, 2. Rome: Jesuit Historical Institute, 1970.
———. "Musical Activity in Some Sixteenth-Century Jesuit Colleges." *Analecta Musicologica* 19 (1980): 1-29.
Culley, Thomas D., and Clement J. McNaspy "The Place of Art in the Old Society." *Archivum Historicum Societatis Iesu* 40 (1971): 213-245.
Curcio, Linda A. "Saints, Sovereignty and Spectacle in Colonial Mexico." PhD diss., Tulane University, 1993.
Curcio-Nagy, Linda. "Giants and Gypsies: Corpus Christi in Colonial Mexico City." In *Rituals of Rule, Rituals of Resistance,* edited by William Beezley, Cheryl English Martin, and William French, 1-26. Wilmington, NC: SR Books, 1994.
Davies, Drew M. "The Italianized Frontier: Music at Durango Cathedral, Español Culture, and the Aesthetics of Devotion in Eighteenth-Century New Spain." PhD diss., University of Chicago, 2006.

Dean, Carolyn. "Ethnic Conflict and Corpus Christi in Colonial Cuzco." *Colonial Latin American Review* 2, nos. 1-2 (1993): 93-120.

———. *Inka Bodies and the Body of Christ: Corpus Christi in Colonial Cuzco, Peru.* Durham, NC: Duke University Press, 1999.

Dean, Carolyn, and Dana Leibsohn. "Hybridity and Its Discontents: Considering Visual Culture in Colonial Spanish America." *Colonial Latin American Review* 12:1 (2003): 5-35.

Deeds, Susan M. *Defiance and Deference in Mexico's Colonial North: Indians under Spanish Rule in Nueva Vizcaya.* Austin: University of Texas Press, 2003.

———. "Double Jeopardy: Indian Women in Jesuit Missions of Nueva Vizcaya." In *Indian Women of Early Mexico*, edited by Susan Schroeder, Stephanie Wood, and Robert Haskett, 255-272. Norman: University of Oklahoma Press, 1997.

———. "Indigenous Rebellions on the Northern Mexican Mission Frontier: From First-Generation to Later Colonial Responses." In *Contested Ground: Comparative Frontiers on the Northern and Southern Edges of the Spanish Empire*, edited by Donna J. Guy and Thomas E. Sheridan, 32-51. Tucson: University of Arizona Press, 1998.

———. "Indigenous Responses to Mission Settlement in Nueva Vizcaya." In *The New Latin American Mission History*, edited by Erick Langer and Robert H. Jackson, 77-108. Lincoln: University of Nebraska Press, 1995.

———. "Magic, Fantasy, Gender, and Power in Nueva Vizcaya." Paper presented at Conference on Social Control on Spain's North American Frontiers, University of California, San Diego, September 2001.

———. "New Spain's Far North: A Changing Historiographical Frontier?" *Latin American Research Review* 25, no. 1 (1990): 226-235.

———. "Rendering Unto Caesar: The Secularization of Jesuit Missions in Mid-Eighteenth Century Durango." PhD diss., University of Arizona, 1981.

de la Teja, Jesús F. *San Antonio de Béxar: A Community on New Spain's Northern Frontier.* Albuquerque: University of New Mexico Press, 1995.

———, and John Wheat. "Béxar: Profile of a Tejano Community, 1820–1832." *Southwestern Historical Quarterly* 89 (July 1985): 1-26.

de la Torre Curiel, José Refugio. "Conquering the Frontier: Contests for Religion, Survival, and Profits in Northwestern Mexico, 1768–1855." PhD diss., University of California, Berkeley, 2005.

de los Dolores Ticareño, Angel. *El colegio de Guadalupe: Lo ideal.* Zacatecas, Mexico: Lejeune, Flores, and Company, 1905.

del Río, Ignacio. *Conquista y aculturación en la California jesuítica.* Mexico City: Universidad Nacional Autónoma de México, 1984.

———. *El regimen jesuítico de la Antigua California.* Mexico City: Universidad Nacional Autónoma de México, 2003.

———. *Todos Santos: una misión Californiana*. Archivo Histórico Pablo L. Martínez, Baja California Sur, Historia 4. Mexico City: Universidad Nacional Autónoma de México, Instituto de Investigaciones Históricas, 1983.

Delanglez, Jean. *The French Jesuits in Lower Louisiana, 1700–1763*. Washington, DC: Catholic University of America, 1935.

Derbes, Anne. *Picturing the Passion in Late Medieval Italy: Narrative Painting, Franciscan Ideologies, and the Levant*. New York: Cambridge University Press, 1996.

Dissanayake, Ellen. "Ritual and Ritualization: Musical Means of Conveying and Shaping Emotion in Humans and Other Animals," In *Music and Manipulation: On the Social Uses and Social Control of Music*, edited by Steven Brown and Ulrik Volgsten, 31-56. New York: Berghahn Books, 2006.

Dittemore, Diane D. "A Comparison of Seri and Western Apache One-Stringed Fiddles." Master's thesis, University of Denver, 1978.

Donohue, John Augustin. *After Kino: Jesuit Missions in Northwestern New Spain*. Rome: Jesuit Historical Institute, 1969.

Drain, Thomas A. *A Sense of Place: Historic Mission Churches of the Southwest*. San Francisco: Chronicle Books, 1994.

Dugmore, C.W. "Canonical Hours." In *The New Westminster Dictionary of Liturgy and Worship*, edited by J.G. Davies, 140-147. Philadelphia: The Westminster Press, 1986.

Dunne, Peter Masten. *Black Robes in Lower California*. Berkeley: University of California Press, 1952.

———. *Early Jesuit Missions in Tarahumara*. Berkeley: University of California Press, 1948.

———. *Pioneer Jesuits in Northern Mexico*. Berkeley: University of California Press, 1944.

Engelhardt, Zephyrin. *Santa Barbara Mission*. San Francisco: James H. Barry Company, 1923.

———. *The Franciscans in Arizona*. Harbor Springs, MI: Holy Childhood Indian School, 1899.

———. "Mission San Juan Bautista: A School of Church Music." Missions and Missionaries of California. Santa Barbara, CA: Schauer Printing Studio, 1931.

Erlmann, Veit. *Music, Modernity, and the Global Imagination: South Africa and the West*. New York: Oxford University Press, 1999.

Escandon, Patricia. "Los problemas de la administración franciscana en las misiones sonorenses, 1768–1800." In *Actas del IV Congreso Internacional sobre los Franciscanos en el Nuevo Mundo*, 277-291. Madrid: Editorial DEIMOS, 1991.

Estrada, Jesús. *Música y músicos de la época virreinal*. Mexico City: Sep/Setentas, 1973.

Evers, Larry, and Felipe S. Molina. *Yaqui Deer Songs: Maso Bwikam, a Native American Poetry*. Tucson: Sun Tracks and University of Arizona Press, 1987.

Ewers, John C. "Symbols of Chiefly Authority in Spanish Louisiana." In *The Spanish in the Mississippi Valley, 1762-1804*, edited by John Francis McDermott, 272-284. Urbana: University of Illinois Press, 1974.

Farnsworth, Paul, and Robert H. Jackson. "Cultural, Economic, and Demographic Change in the Missions of Alta California: The Case of Nuestra Señora de Soledad." In *The New Latin American Mission History*, edited by Erick Langer and Robert H. Jackson, 109-129. Lincoln: University of Nebraska Press, 1995.

Farriss, Nancy M. *Maya Society and Colonial Rule: The Collective Enterprise of Survival*. Princeton, NJ: Princeton University Press, 1984.

Foucault, Michel. *Discipline and Punish: The Birth of the Prison*. Translated by Alan Sheridan. New York: Pantheon Books, 1977.

Frisbie, Charlotte Johnson. *Music and Dance Research of Southwestern United States Indians: Past Trends, Present Activities, and Suggestions for Future Research*. Detroit, MI: Information Coordinators, 1977.

Galán García, Agustín. *El oficio de Indias de los Jesuitas en Sevilla, 1566–1767*. Seville: Fundación Fondo de Cultura de Sevilla, 1995.

Galgano, Robert. *Feast of Souls: Indians and Spaniards in the Seventeenth-Century Missions of Florida and New Mexico*. Albuquerque: University of New Mexico Press, 2005.

Ganson, Barbara. *The Guaraní under Spanish Rule in the Río de la Plata*. Stanford, CA: Stanford University Press, 2003.

García Flóres, Raúl. *¡Puro mitote! La música, el canto y la danza entre los chichimecas del noreste*. Monterrey: Fondo Editorial Nuevo León, 1993.

García Icazbalceta, Joaquín. "Fray Pedro de Gante." *Artes de México* 19, no. 150 (1972): 6-16+.

García Saez, Santiago. "The Use of Song in Class as an Important Stimulus in the Learning of a Language." Paper presented at the Southwest Conference on the Teaching of Foreign Languages, 1994.

Geertz, Clifford. "Centers, Kings, and Charisma: Reflections on the Symbolics of Power." In *Rites of Power: Symbolism, Ritual, and Politics since the Middle Ages*, edited by R. Sean Wilentz, 13-38. Philadelphia: University of Pennsylvania Press, 1985.

Geiger, Maynard, O.F.M. *Franciscan Missionaries in Hispanic California*. San Marino, CA: Huntington Library, 1969.

———. *The Life and Times of Fray Junípero Serra*. Washington, DC: Academy of American Franciscan History, 1959.

Gelineau, J., S.J. "Music and Singing in the Liturgy." In *The Study of Liturgy*, rev. ed., edited by Cheslyn Jones, Geoffrey Wainwright, Edward Yarnold, and Paul Bradshaw, 493-507. New York: Oxford University Press, 1992.

Gerhard, Peter. *A Guide to the Historical Geography of New Spain*. Cambridge: Cambridge University Press, 1972.

———. *The North Frontier of New Spain.* Norman: University of Oklahoma Press, 1993.
Gibson, Charles. *The Aztecs under Spanish Rule.* Stanford, CA: Stanford University Press, 1964.
Gilmore, Kathleen. "The Indians of Mission Rosario: From the Books and from the Ground." In *Archaeological and Historical Perspectives on the Spanish Borderlands West.* Vol. 1 of *Columbian Consequences,* edited by David Hurst Thomas, 231-243. Washington, DC: Smithsonian Institution Press, 1989.
Göllner, Theodore. "Two Polyphonic Passions from California's Mission Period." *Anuario: Yearbook for the Institute for Inter-American Musical Research* 6 (1970): 67-76.
Gómez Canedo, Lino. *Evangelización y conquista: experiencia franciscana en Hispanoamérica.* Mexico City: Editorial Porrúa, 1977.
———. *Primeras exploraciones y poblamiento de Texas.* Monterrey: Instituto Tecnológico y de Estudios Superiores de Monterrey, 1968.
Gonzalbo Aizpuru, Pilar. *La educación popular de los Jesuitas.* Mexico City: Universidad Iberoamericana, 1989.
———. "La influencia de la Compañía de Jesús en la sociedad novohispana del siglo XVI." *Historia Mexicana* 32, no. 2 (1982): 262-281.
González Rodríguez, Luis. "Juan María de Salvatierra y los Seris, 1709–1710." *Estudios de Historia Novohispana* 17 (1997): 229-262.
González Salas, Carlos. *Las misiones franciscanas en la colonia del Nuevo Santander.* Ciudad Victoria, Tamaulipas: Universidad Autónoma de Tamaulipas, 1975.
Gormley, Regina Maria. "The Liturgical Music of the California Missions, 1769–1833." DMA diss., Catholic University of America, 1992.
Gramsci, Antonio. *Prison Notebooks.* Translated by Joseph A. Buttigieg and Antonio Callari. New York: Columbia University Press, 1991.
Griffen, William B. *Indian Assimilation in the Franciscan Areas of Nueva Vizcaya.* Tucson: University of Arizona Press, 1979.
Griffith, Jim. "The Yaquis." *Folk Harp Journal* 23 (1978): 20-21.
Griffiths, Nicholas. *The Cross and the Serpent: Religious Repression and Resurgence in Colonial Peru.* Norman: University of Oklahoma Press, 1995.
Gruzinski, Serge. *The Conquest of Mexico: The Incorporation of Indian Societies into the Western World, 16th–18th Centuries.* Translated by Eileen Corrigan. Cambridge: Polity Press; Oxford, UK, and Cambridge, MA: Blackwell Publishers, 1993.
———. *Painting the Conquest: The Mexican Indians and the European Renaissance.* Translated by Deke Dusinberre. Paris: Flammarion, 1992.
Guest, Francis F. *Fermín Francisco de Lasuén: A Biography.* Washington, DC: Academy of American Franciscan History, 1973.
Guevara-Gil, Armando, and Frank Saloman. "A 'Personal Visit': Colonial Political Ritual and the Making of Indians in the Andes." *Colonial Latin American Review* 3, nos. 1-2 (1994): 3-36.

Gutiérrez, Ramón. *When Jesus Came, the Corn Mothers Went Away: Marriage, Sexuality and Power in New Mexico, 1500–1846.* Stanford, CA: Stanford University Press, 1991.

Gutiérrez Casillas, José. *Diccionario bio-bibliográfica de la Compañía de Jesús en México.* Vol. 15. Mexico City: Editorial Jus, 1974.

Guy, Donna J., and Thomas E. Sheridan, eds.. *Contested Ground: Comparative Frontiers on the Northern and Southern Edges of the Spanish Empire.* Tucson: University of Arizona Press, 1998.

Haas, Lisabeth. *Conquests and Historical Identities in California, 1736–1936.* Berkeley: University of California Press, 1995.

Habig, Marion A. *The Alamo Chain of Missions.* Chicago: Franciscan Herald Press, 1968.

Hackel, Steven W. "Beyond Words: Liturgical Art and Music in the California Missions." Paper presented at *Encuentros*/Encounters 2009: Music of the California Missions, University of California at Riverside, January 30, 2009.

———. *Children of Coyote, Missionaries of Saint Francis: Indian–Spanish Relations in Colonial California, 1769–1850.* Chapel Hill: University of North Carolina Press, 2005.

———. "Sources of Rebellion: Indian Testimony and the Mission San Gabriel Uprising of 1785." *Ethnohistory* 50, no. 4 (Fall 2003): 643-669.

Halpin, Joseph. "Musical Activities and Ceremonies at Mission Santa Clara de Asís." *California Historical Quarterly* 50, no. 1 (1971): 35-42.

Hanawalt, Barbara A., and Kathryn L. Reyerson, eds. *City and Spectacle in Medieval Europe.* Minneapolis: University of Minnesota Press, 1994.

Hanna, Judith. "Dances of Anáhua—For God or Man? An Alternative Way of Thinking about Prehistory." *Dance Research Journal* 7, no. 1 (Autumn 1974): 13-27.

Harper, John. *The Forms and Orders of Western Liturgy from the Tenth to the Eighteenth Century.* Oxford: Clarendon Press, 1991.

Harshbarger, George. "The Mass in G by Ignacio Jerusalem and Its Place in the California Mission Music Repertory." DMA diss., University of Washington, 1985.

Hayburn, Robert F. *Digest of Regulations and Rubrics of Catholic Church Music.* Boston: McLaughlin and Reilly Company, 1960.

———. "Legislation on Sacred Music." In *New Catholic Encyclopedia*, Vol. 10, 129-131. New York: McGraw-Hill Book Company, 1967.

Hefner, Robert W., ed. *Conversion to Christianity: Historical and Anthropological Perspectives on a Great Transformation.* Berkeley: University of California Press, 1993.

Heller, George N. "Music Education in the Valley of Mexico during the Sixteenth Century." PhD diss., University of Michigan, 1973.

Herzog, George. "A Comparison of Pueblo and Pima Musical Styles." *Journal of American Folklore* 49, no. 194 (1936): 283-417.

Hiley, David. *Western Plainchant: A Handbook*. Oxford: Clarendon Press, 1993.
Hill, Jonathan D., ed. *History, Power, and Identity: Ethnogenesis in the Americas, 1492–1992*. Iowa City: University of Iowa Press, 1996.
Hinojosa, Gilberto M., and Anne A. Fox. "Indians and Their Culture in San Fernando de Béxar." In *Tejano Origins in Eighteenth-Century San Antonio*, edited by Gerald E. Poyo and Gilberto M. Hinojosa, 105-120. Austin: University of Texas Press, 1991.
Holden, William Curry. *Studies of the Yaqui Indians of Sonora, Mexico*, vol. 12, no. 1, Scientific Series, No. 2. Lubbock, TX: Texas Technological College Bulletin, 1936.
Hoppin, Richard H. *Medieval Music*. London: W.W. Norton, 1978.
Hsia, R. Po-Chia. "Reformation on the Continent: Approaches Old and New." *Journal of Religious History* 28, no. 2 (June 1994): 162-170.
Hu-DeHart, Evelyn. *Missionaries, Miners and Indians: Spanish Contact and the Yaqui Nation, 1533–1820*. Tucson: University of Arizona Press, 1981.
Huber, Raphael M. *A Documented History of the Franciscan Order*. Milwaukee: Nowiny Publishing Apostolate, 1944.
Hughes, Andrew. *Medieval Manuscripts for Mass and Office: A Guide to Their Organization and Terminology*. Toronto: University of Toronto Press, 1982.
Hughes, Barnabas. "Friars, Hourglasses and Clocks." *Collectanea Franciscana* 53, nos. 3-4 (1984): 265-278.
Hurtado, Albert L. *Intimate Frontiers: Sex, Gender, and Culture in Old California*. Albuquerque: University of New Mexico Press, 1999.
Hüschen, Heinrich. "Franziskaner." In *Die Musik in Geschichte Und Gegenwart*, vol. 4, edited by Friedrich Blume, 823-842. Kassel: Bärenreiter, 1955.
———. "Jesuiten." In *Die Musik in Geschichte Und Gegenwart*, vol. 7, edited by Friedrich Blume, 18-41. Kassel: Bärenreiter, 1955.
Ilari, Bernardo. "Presencia Guaraní en la musica de las misiones." *Revista de Musicología* 16 (1993): 2126-2132.
Jackson, Robert H., ed. *New Views of Borderlands History*. Albuquerque: University of New Mexico Press, 1998.
———. "Visual Representations of Religious Conversion in Spanish American Missions." *Boletín* 25, no. 2 (2008): 5-30.
———, and Edward Castillo. *Indians, Franciscans, and Spanish Colonization: The Impact of the Mission System on California Indians*. Albuquerque: University of New Mexico Press, 1995.
Jacobsen, Jerome V. *Educational Foundations of the Jesuits in Sixteenth-Century New Spain*. Berkeley: University of California Press, 1938.
Jauregui, Jesús, and Carlo Bonfiglioli. *Las danzas de conquista*. Mexico City: Fondo de Cultura Económica, 1996.
Jojola, Theodore. "Introduction: Technology and Native American Culture." *Wicazo Sa Review* 13, no. 2 (Autumn 1998): 5-18.

Jones, Grant D. *Maya Resistance to Spanish Rule: Time and History on a Colonial Frontier*. Albuquerque: University of New Mexico Press, 1989.

Jones, Oakah L., Jr. *Los Paisanos: Spanish Settlers on the Northern Frontier of New Spain*. Norman: University of Oklahoma Press, 1979.

Jourdain, Robert. *Music, the Brain, and Ecstasy: How Music Captures Our Imagination*. New York: Aron Books, 1997.

Kaemmer, John E. *Music in Human Life: Anthropological Perspectives on Music*. Austin: University of Texas Press, 1993.

Keali' Inohomoku, Joann W. "Hopi and Hawaiian Music and Dance: Responses to Cultural Contact." In *Musical Repercussions of 1492: Encounters in Text and Performance*, edited by Carol E. Robertson, 429-450. Washington, DC: Smithsonian Institution Press, 1992.

Kellogg, Susan. *Law and the Transformation of Aztec Culture*. Norman: University of Oklahoma Press, 1995.

Kennedy, John G. *Tarahumara of the Sierra Madre: Beer, Ecology, and Social Organization*. Arlington Heights, IL: AHM Publishing Corporation, 1978.

Kennedy, T. Frank. "An Integrated Perspective: Music and Art in the Jesuit Reductions of Paraguay." In *The Jesuit Tradition in Education and Missions*, edited by Christopher Chapple, 215-229. Scranton, PA: University of Scranton Press, 1993.

———. "Jesuits and Music: Reconsidering the Early Years." *Studi Musicali* 17 (1988): 71-95.

Kennedy, Thomas Frank. "Jesuits and Music: The European Tradition, 1547–1622." PhD diss., University of California, Santa Barbara, 1990.

Kenyon de Pascual, Beryl. "A Further Updated Review of the Dulcians (Bajón and Bajoncillo) and Their Music in Spain." *The Galpin Society Journal* 53 (April 2000): 87-116.

Kerry, Susan Anderson. "Preliminary Observations on Angels in Religious Art in New Spain." *Boletín* 25, no. 2 (2008): 31-48.

Kessell, John L. *Friars, Soldiers, and Reformers: Hispanic Arizona and the Sonora Mission Frontier, 1767–1856*. Tucson: University of Arizona Press, 1976.

———. *Mission of Sorrows: Jesuit Guevavi and the Pimas*. Tucson: University of Arizona Press, 1970.

Klor de Alva, Jorge. "Spiritual Conflict and Accommodation in New Spain: Toward a Typology of Aztec Responses to Christianity." In *The Inca and Aztec States: 1400–1800*, edited by George Collier, Renato Rosaldo, and John Wirth, 345-366. New York: Academic Press, 1982.

Knaut, Andrew L. *The Pueblo Revolt of 1680: Conquest and Resistance in Seventeenth-Century New Mexico*. Norman: University of Oklahoma Press, 1995.

Koegel, John. "Rural Musical Life in the French Villages in Upper Louisiana." In *On Bunker's Hill: Essays on Music in Honor of J. Bunker Clark*, edited by Paul Laird and William Everett, 13-25. Warren, MI: Harmonie Park Press, 2007.

———. "Spanish and French Mission Music in Colonial North America." *Journal of the Royal Musical Association* 126, no. 1 (2001): 1-53.

———. "Spanish and Mexican Dance in Early California." *Ars Musica Denver* 7, no. 1 (1994): 31–56.

Kreitner, Kenneth. "Minstrels in Spanish Churches, 1400–1600." *Early Music* 20, no. 4 (November 1992): 532-546.

Krieger, Daniel. "Music and the Psychology of Colonization in the California Missions, 1780–1834." Paper presented at Encuentros/Encounters 2009, University of California at Riverside, January 30, 2009.

Kroeber, Karl. "Poem, Dream, and the Consuming of Culture." *The Georgia Review* 32 (1978): 266-280.

Kubler, George. *Mexican Architecture of the Sixteenth Century*. New Haven, CT: Yale University Press, 1948.

Kurath, Gertrude, and Samuel Martí. *Dances of Anáhuac: The Choreography and Music of Precortesian Dances*. Chicago: Aldine Publishing Company, 1964.

Kuss, Malena. *Music in Latin America and the Caribbean: An Encyclopedic History*. Austin: University of Texas Press, 2004.

Laird, Paul. *Towards a History of the Spanish Villancico*. Warren, MI: Harmonie Park Press, 1997.

Langer, Erick. "Conclusion." In *The New Latin American Mission History*, edited by Erick Langer and Robert H. Jackson, 189-194. Lincoln: University of Nebraska Press, 1995.

———. "Missions and the Frontier Economy: The Case of the Franciscan Missions among the Chiriguanos, 1845–1893." In *The New Latin American Mission History*, edited by Erick Langer and Robert H. Jackson, 49-76. Lincoln: University of Nebraska Press, 1995.

Lara, Jaime. *City, Temple, Stage: Eschatological Architecture and Liturgical Theatrics in New Spain*. Notre Dame, IN: University of Notre Dame Press, 2004.

Larkin, Brian R. "Liturgy, Devotion, and Religious Reform in Eighteenth-Century Mexico City." *The Americas* 60, no. 4 (April 2004): 493-518.

Lavrín, Asunción. "Women in Colonial Latin America." In *The Oxford History of Mexico*, edited by Michael C. Meyer and William H. Beezley, 245-273. Oxford: Oxford University Press, 2000.

Lázaro Carreter, Fernando. *Teatro Medieval*. Valencia: Castalia, 1958.

Lee, Dorothy Sara. *Native North American Music and Oral Data: A Catalogue of Sound Recordings, 1893-1976*. Bloomington: Indiana University Press, 1979.

———. "Toward an Understanding of Music and Identity in the Social World." In *Discourse in Ethnomusicology II: A Tribute to Alan P. Merriam*, edited by Caroline Card, 1-18. Bloomington, IN: Ethnomusicology Publications Group, 1981.

Le Huray, Peter. *Music and the Reformation in England, 1549–1660*. New York: Oxford University Press, 1967.

Lemmon, Alfred E. "Jesuit Chroniclers and Historians of Colonial Spanish America." *Inter-American Music Review* 10, no. 2 (1989): 119-129.

———. "Jesuits and Music in Mexico." *Archivum Historicum Societatis Iesu* 46 (1977): 191-198.

———. "Preliminary Investigation: Music in the Jesuit Missions of Baja California." *Journal of San Diego History* 25 (1979): 287-297.

Léon Portilla, Miguel. "Face and Heart of the California Missions." In *Historical and Cultural Perspectives on the Peninsula of Baja California: Proceedings of the 19th Annual Conference of the California Mission Studies Association,* edited by Rose Marie Beebe, 1-13. California Mission Studies Association, 2002.

———. "The Norteño Variety of Mexican Culture: An Ethnohistorical Approach." In *Plural Society in the Southwest,* edited by Edward H. Spicer and Raymond H. Thompson, 109-114. New York: Interbook, 1972.

———. *The Texas Missions of the College of Zacatecas in 1749–1750.* Edited by Marion A. Habig. Old Spanish Missions Historical Research Library's Documentary Series, 5. San Antonio, TX: Old Spanish Missions Historical Research Library, 1979.

Levine, Victoria Lindsey. *Writing American Indian Music: Historic Transcriptions, Notations, and Arrangements.* Music of the United States of America, 11. Middleton, WI: A-R Editions, Inc., 2002.

Lewis, Laura A. *Hall of Mirrors: Power, Witchcraft, and Caste in Colonial Mexico.* Durham, NC: Duke University Press, 2003.

Librado, Fernando, John Peabody Harrington, and Travis Hudson. *The Eye of the Flute: Chumash Traditional History and Ritual.* Santa Barbara, CA: Santa Barbara Museum of Natural History, 1977.

Lockhart, James. *The Nahuas after the Conquest: A Social and Cultural History of the Indians of Central Mexico, Sixteenth through Eighteenth Centuries.* Stanford, CA: Stanford University Press, 1992.

———. "Some Nahua Concepts in Postconquest Guise." *History of European Ideas* 6 (1985): 465-482.

Lockwood, Lewis. "Some Observations on the Commission of Cardinals and the Reform of Sacred Music." *Quadrivium* 7 (1966): 39 55.

López-Calo, José. *Historia de la música española.* Madrid: Alianza Música, 1983.

Lowinsky, Edward E. "Music in the Culture of the Renaissance." *Journal of the History of Ideas* 15, no. 4 (October 1954): 509-553.

Lozano, Tomás. *Cantemos al Alba: Origins of Songs, Sounds, and Liturgical Drama of Hispanic New Mexico.* Albuquerque: University of New Mexico Press, 2007.

Madsen, Wanda Jean. "Mexican Mission Music: A Descriptive Analysis and Comparison of Two Seventeenth-Century Chant Books." DMA diss., University of Oklahoma Press, 1984.

Mann, Kristin Dutcher. "Christmas in the Missions of Northern New Spain." *The Americas* 66, no. 3 (January 2010), 131-151.

———. "Music and Popular Religiosity in Northern New Spain." *Catholic Southwest* 12 (2001): 7-27.

———. "The Power of Song in the Missions of Northern New Spain." PhD diss., Northern Arizona University, 2002.

———. "Opus Dei: The Work of God – Franciscan and Jesuit Music in Mexico." In *Religion in New Spain*, edited by Susan Schroeder and Stafford Poole, 266-278. Albuquerque: University of New Mexico Press, 2007.

Martí, Samuel. *Instrumentos Musicales Precortesianos*. Mexico City: Instituto Nacional de Antropología e Historia, 1955.

Martin, Cheryl English. *Governance and Society in Colonial Mexico: Chihuahua in the Eighteenth Century*. Stanford, CA: Stanford University Press, 1996.

———. "Indigenous Peoples." In *The Countryside in Colonial Latin America*, edited by Louisa Schell Hoberman, and Susan Migden Socolow, 167–212. Albuquerque: University of New Mexico Press, 1996.

Mattern, Mark. *Acting in Concert: Music, Community, and Political Action*. New Brunswick, NJ: Rutgers University Press, 1998.

McAndrew, John. *The Open-Air Churches of Sixteenth-Century Mexico: Atrios, Posas, Open Chapels, and Other Studies*. Cambridge, MA: Harvard University Press, 1965.

McCarty, Kieran. "Franciscan Beginnings on the Arizona-Sonora Desert." PhD diss., Catholic University of America, 1973.

———, and Dan S. Matson. "Franciscan Report on the Indians of Nayarit, 1673." *Ethnohistory* 22, no. 3 (Summer 1975): 193-222.

McCloskey, Michael B. *The Formative Years of the Missionary College of Santa Cruz de Querétaro, 1683–1733*. Washington, DC: Academy of American Franciscan History, 1955.

McNett, Charles. "The Chirimía: A Latin American Shawm." *The Galpin Society Journal* 13 (July 1960): 44-51.

Meigs, Peveril. *The Dominican Mission Frontier of Lower California*. Berkeley: University of California Press, 1935.

Merrill, William L. "Conversion and Colonialism in Northern Mexico: The Tarahumara Response to the Jesuit Mission Program, 1601–1767." In *Conversion to Christianity: Historical and Anthropological Perspectives on a Great Transformation*, edited by Robert W. Hefner, 129-163. Berkeley: University of California Press, 1993.

———. "Cultural Creativity and Raiding Bands." In *Violence, Resistance, and Survival in the Americas: Native Americans and the Legacy of Conquest*, edited by William Taylor and Franklin Pease, 124-152. Washington, DC: Smithsonian Institution Press, 1994.

———. "Rarámuri Easter." In *Performing the Renewal of Community: Indigenous Easter Rituals in North Mexico and Southwest United States*, edited by Rosamond B. Spicer and N. Ross Crumrine, 365-421. New York: University Press of America, 1997.

_____. *Rarámuri Souls: Knowledge and Social Process in Northern Mexico.* Washington, DC: Smithsonian Institution Press, 1988.
Mills, Kenneth. *Idolatry and Its Enemies: Colonial Andean Religion and Extirpation, 1640–1750.* Princeton, NJ: Princeton University Press, 1997.
Molina-Molina, Flavio, ed. *Estado de la provincia de Sonora, 1730.* Hermosillo, Mexico: Diócesis de Hermosillo, 1979.
Moll, Jaime. "Música y representaciones en las constituciones sinodales de los Reinos de Castilla de siglo XVI," *Anuario Musical* 30 (1975): 209-243.
Monson, Craig. "The Council of Trent Revisited." *Journal of the American Musicological Society* 55, no. 1 (Spring 2002): 1-37.
Moorman, John R.H. *A History of the Franciscan Order from Its Origins to the Year 1517.* Oxford: Clarendon Press, 1968.
Morales, Francisco. *Ethnic and Social Background of the Franciscan Friars in Seventeenth-Century Mexico.* Washington, DC: Academy of American Franciscan History, 1973.
_____. "Evangelización y culturas indígenas: reflexiones en torno a la actividad misionera de los franciscanos en la Nueva España." *Archivum Franciscanum Historicum* 85, no. 1 (1992): 123-157.
_____. *Franciscan Presence in the Americas: Essays on the Activities of the Franciscan Friars in the Americas, 1492–1900.* Potomac, MD: Academy of American Franciscan History, 1983.
_____. "Mexican Society and the Franciscan Order in a Period of Transition, 1749–1859." *The Americas* 54, no. 3 (January 1998): 323-356.
Moorhead, Max L. *The Presidio: Bastion of the Spanish Borderlands.* Norman: University of Oklahoma Press, 1975.
Moreno Proaño, Agustín. "El influjo de Pedro de Gante en la cultura de Sudamérica." *Artes de México* 19, no. 150 (1972): 93–98+.
Mullen, Robert J. *Architecture and Its Sculpture in Viceregal Mexico.* Austin: University of Texas Press, 1997.
Muriel, Josefina. "La música en las instituciones femeninas existente en el Archivo Histórico del Colegio de San Ignacio de Loyola, Vizcaínas." In *Una Mujer, Un Legado, Una Historia: Homenaje a Josefina Muriel,* 221-226. Mexico City: Universidad Nacional Autónoma de México, 2000.
_____. "Las mujeres en la música del virreinato." In *De la historia: homenaje a Jorge Gurría Lacroix,* 201-206. Mexico: Universidad Nacional Autónoma de México, 1985.
Nava L., E. Fernando. "Música y aspectos afines en los horizontes chichimecos y mesoamericanos." In *Nómadas y sedentarios en el norte de Mexico City: Homenaje a Beatriz Braniff,* edited by Marie-Areti Hers, et al., 57-78. Mexico City: Universidad Nacional Autónoma de México, 2000.
Nawrot, Piotr. *Indígenas y cultura musical de las reducciones jesuíticas.* Cochabamba, Bolivia: Editorial Verbo Divino, 2000.

———. "Vespers Music in the Paraguay Reductions." DMA diss., Catholic University of America, 1993.
Nettl, Bruno. *Folk and Traditional Music of the Western Continents*. Englewood Cliffs, NJ: Prentice-Hall, 1973.
Newcombe, William. *The Indians of Texas: From Prehistoric to Modern Times*. Austin: University of Texas Press, 1972.
Norris, Jim. *After the Year Eighty: The Demise of Franciscan Power in Spanish New Mexico*. Albuquerque: University of New Mexico Press, 2000.
O'Campo, Manuel, S.J. *Historia de la Misíon de la Tarahumara*. Mexico City: Editorial Buena Prensa, 1950.
O'Malley, John W. *The First Jesuits*. Cambridge, MA: Harvard University Press, 1993.
Odloz̆ilík, Otakar. "Czech Missionaries in New Spain." *Hispanic American Historical Review* 25, no. 4 (November 1945): 428-454.
Oldani, Louis J., and Victor R. Yanitelli. "Jesuit Theater in Italy: Its Entrances and Exit." *Italica* 76, no. 1 (Spring 1999): 18-32.
Olmos Aguilera, Miguel. "La herencia jesuita en el arte de los indígenas del noroeste de México." *Frontera Norte* 14, no. 27 (January–June 2002): 201-239.
———. *El sabio de la fiesta: música y mitología en la región cahita-tarahumara*. Mexico City: Instituto Nacional de Antropología e Historia, 1998.
Olsen, Dale A. "Symbol and Function in South American Indian Music." In *Musics of Many Cultures*, edited by Elizabeth May, 363-385. Berkeley: University of California Press, 1980.
Palm, Mary Borgia. *Jesuit Missions in the Illinois Country, 1673-1763*. Cleveland, OH: Sisters of Notre Dame, 1933.
Patch, Robert W. *Maya and Spaniard in Yucatan, 1648–1812*. Stanford, CA: Stanford University Press, 1993.
Pennington, Campbell W. *The Tepehuan of Chihuahua: Their Material Culture*. Salt Lake City: University of Utah Press, 1969.
Peterson, Jeanette Favrot. *The Paradise Garden Murals of Malinalco: Utopia and Empire in Sixteenth-Century Mexico*. Austin: University of Texas Press, 1993.
Phelan, John Leddy. *The Millenial Kingdom of the Franciscans in the New World*, rev. 2nd ed. Berkeley: University of California Press, 1970.
Piaget, Jean. *On the Development of Memory and Identity*. Edited by Eleanor Duckworth. Worcester, MA: Clark University Press, 1968.
Pope, Isabel, and Paul R. Laird. "Villancico." In *New Grove Dictionary of Music and Musicians*, edited by Stanley Sadie, vol. 26, 621-628. London: Macmillan, 2001.
Powers, Karen Vieira. *Andean Journeys: Migration, Ethnogenesis, and the State in Colonial Quito*. Albuquerque: University of New Mexico Press, 1995.
Price, Percival. *Bells and Man*. Oxford: Oxford University Press, 1983.

Pulido Silva, Esperanza. "Mexican Women in Music." *Inter-American Music Review* 4, no. 1 (1983): 120–131.

Queen, Laurinda. "Southwestern Indian Musical Instruments." *The Smoke Signal* 35 (1978): 2–23.

Radding, Cynthia. "The Colonial Pact and Changing Ethnic Frontiers in Highland Sonora, 1740–1840." In *Contested Ground: Comparative Frontiers on the Northern and Southern Edges of the Spanish Empire*, edited by Donna J. Guy and Thomas E. Sheridan, 52-66. Tucson: University of Arizona Press, 1998.

———. "Sonora-Arizona: The Común, Local Governance, and Defiance in Colonial Sonora." In *Choice, Persuasion, and Coercion: Social Control on Spain's North American Frontiers*, edited by Jesús F. de la Teja and Ross Frank, 179-199. Albuquerque: University of New Mexico Press, 2005.

———. *Wandering Peoples: Colonialism, Ethnic Spaces, and Ecological Frontiers in Northwestern Mexico, 1700–1850*. Durham, NC: Duke University Press, 1997.

Rael, Juan B. *The New Mexican Alabado*. Music transcription by Eleanor Hague. Stanford University Publications University Series, Language and Literature, 9, no. 3. Stanford, CA: Stanford University Press, 1951.

Rafael, Vicente L. "Confession, Conversion, and Reciprocity in Early Tagalog Colonial Society." In *Colonialism and Culture*, edited by Nicholas B. Dirks, 65-88. Ann Arbor: University of Michigan Press, 1992.

Ramírez, Susan. *The World Upside Down: Cross-Cultural Contact and Conflict in Sixteenth-Century Peru*. Stanford, CA: Stanford University Press, 1997.

Randel, Don Michael. *New Harvard Dictionary of Music*. Cambridge, MA: Belknap Press, 1996.

Rappaport, Joanne. *The Politics of Memory: Native Historical Interpretation in the Colombian Andes*. Durham, NC: Duke University Press, 1998.

Ray, Mary Dominic, and Joseph H. Engbeck, Jr. *Gloria Dei: The Story of California Mission Music*. Sacramento: State of California Department of Parks and Recreation, 1974.

Reese, Gustave. *Music in the Renaissance*. New York: W.W. Norton and Company, 1959.

Reff, Daniel T. *Disease, Depopulation, and Culture Change in Northwestern New Spain, 1518–1764*. Salt Lake City: University of Utah Press, 1991.

———. "The Jesuit Mission Frontier in Comparative Perspective: The Reductions of the Río de La Plata and the Missions of Northwestern Mexico, 1588–1700." In *Contested Ground: Comparative Frontiers on the Northern and Southern Edges of the Spanish Empire*, edited by Donna J. Guy and Thomas E. Sheridan, 16-31. Tucson: University of Arizona Press, 1998.

Restall, Matthew. *The Maya World: Yucatec Culture and Society, 1550–1850*. Stanford, CA: Stanford University Press, 1997.

Riaño, Juan F. *Critical and Bibliographical Notes on Early Spanish Music*. New York: Da Capo Press, 1971.

Ricard, Robert. *The Spiritual Conquest of Mexico*. Translated by Lesley Byrd Simpson. Berkeley: University of California Press, 1966.
Ricklis, Robert A. *The Karankawa Indians of Texas*. Austin: University of Texas Press, 1996.
Riley, Carroll L. *The Kachina and the Cross: Indians and Spaniards in the Early Southwest*. Salt Lake City: University of Utah Press, 1999.
Ríos, Eduardo Enrique. *Life of Fray Antonio Margil*. Washington, DC: Academy of American Franciscan History, 1959.
Robb, John D. *Hispanic Folk Music of New Mexico and the Southwest: A Self-Portrait of a People*. Norman: University of Oklahoma Press, 1980.
Robertson, Carol E., ed. *Musical Repercussions of 1492: Encounters in Text and Performance*. Washington, DC: Smithsonian Institution Press, 1992.
Robles, Vito Alessio, ed. *Demonstración del vastísimo obispado de la Nueva Vizcaya, 1765*. Mexico City: Editorial Porrúa, 1937.
Robinson, Paschal. "St. Francis of Assisi." *The Catholic Encyclopedia*, vol. 6. New York: Robert Appleton Company, 1909.
Rodriguez, Sylvia. *The Matachines Dance: Ritual Symbolism and Interethnic Relations in the Upper Río Grande Valley*. Albuquerque: University of New Mexico Press, 1996.
Roedl, Bohumír, ed. *Historia de las sublevaciones indias en la tarahumara*. Translated by Simona Binková. Prague: Universidad Carolinga, 1994.
Rolf, Malte. "Constructing a Soviet Time: Bolshevik Festivals and Their Rivals During the First Five-Year Plan: A Study of the Central Black Earth Region." *Kritika: Explorations in Russian and Eurasian History* 1, no. 3 (2000): 447-476.
Romero, Brenda Mae. "The Matachines Music and Dance in San Juan Pueblo and Alcalde, New Mexico: Context and Meanings." DMA diss., University of California, Los Angeles, 1993.
Romero, Raúl R. *Debating the Past: Music, Memory, and Identity in the Andes*. New York: Oxford University Press, 2001.
Rondón, Victor, ed. *Mujeres, negros y niños en la música y sociedad colonial iberoamericana: IV Reunión Científica*. Santa Cruz, Querétaro: Asociación Pro Arte y Cultura, 2002.
Rosewall, Michael Paul. "Sacred Polyphony in New Spain: Performance Issues in the Choral Music of México, 1550–1650." DMA diss., Stanford University, 1995.
Ruecking, Frederick, Jr. "Ceremonies of the Coahuiltecan Indians of Southern Texas and Northeast Mexico." *Texas Journal of Science* 6, no. 3 (1954): 330-339.
Russell, Craig H. *From Serra to Sancho: Music and Pageantry in the California Missions*. New York: Oxford University Press, 2009.
Sadie, Stanley, ed. *New Grove Dictionary of Musical Instruments*, vol. I. London: Macmillan, 1985.

Saeger, James. "*The Mission* and Historical Missions: Film and the Writing of History." *The Americas* 51, no. 3 (1995): 393-415.
———. *The Chaco Mission Frontier: The Guaycuran Experience.* Tucson: University of Arizona Press, 2000.
Samuels, David. *Putting a Song on Top of It: Expression and Identity on the San Carlos Apache Reservation.* Tucson: University of Arizona Press, 2004.
Sanahuja, Pedro. *Historia de la Seráfica Provincia de Cataluña.* Barcelona: Editorial Seráfica, 1956.
Sánchez, Joseph P. *The Río Abajo Frontier, 1540–1692: A History of Early Colonial New Mexico.* Albuquerque: The Albuquerque Museum, 1987.
Sanchez, Nellie van der Grift. *Spanish Arcadia.* San Francisco: Powell Publishing Company, 1929.
Sando, Joe. *Nee Hemish: A History of Jemez Pueblo.* Albuquerque: University of New Mexico Press, 1982.
Sandos, James. *Converting California: Indians and Franciscans in the Missions.* New Haven, CT: Yale University Press, 2004.
———. "Social Control on Spain's North American Frontiers: Choice, Persuasion, and Coercion in Alta California, 1769–1821." Paper presented at Social Control on Spain's North American Frontiers: Choice, Persuasion and Coercion Conference, Meadows Museum of Art, Southern Methodist University, Dallas, TX, April 6, 2002.
———. "Professionalization of Music: Choristers at Mission Santa Clara and the Mystery of Mission San Antonio." Paper presented at Encuentros/Encounters 2009, University of California-Riverside, January 30, 2009.
Santamaría, Francisco Xavier. *Diccionario de mejicanismos.* 2nd ed. Mexico City: Editorial Porrúa, 1974.
Schmidt, Hans. "Franziskaner." *Die Musik in Geschichte Und Gegenwart,* vol. 3, 2nd abbrev. ed. Edited by Ludwig Finscher. Kassel: Bärenreiter, 1994.
Schmutz, Richard. "Jesuit Missionary Methods in Northwestern Mexico." *Journal of the West* 8, no. 1 (1969): 76–89.
Schroeder, Susan. *Chimalpahin and the Kingdom of Chalco.* Tucson: University of Arizona Press, 1991.
———. "Jesuits, Nahuas, and the Good Death Society in Mexico City, 1710–1767." *Hispanic American Historical Review* 80, no. 1 (2000): 43–76.
———, ed. *Native Resistance and the Pax Colonial in New Spain.* Lincoln: University of Nebraska Press, 1998.
———, Stephanie Wood, and Robert Haskett, eds. *Indian Women of Early Mexico.* Norman: University of Oklahoma Press, 1997.
Schroeder, Susan, and Stafford Poole, eds. *Religion in New Spain.* Albuquerque: University of New Mexico Press, 2007.
Schuetz, Mardith K. *The History and Archaeology of Mission San Juan Capistrano, San Antonio, Texas.* Report no. 10. Austin: State Building Commission Archaeological Program, 1968.

Scott, James C. *Domination and the Arts of Resistance: Hidden Transcripts*. New Haven, CT: Yale University Press, 1990.

———. *Weapons of the Weak: Everyday Forms of Peasant Resistance*. New Haven, CT: Yale University Press, 1985.

Seaton, Douglass. *Ideas and Styles in Western Musical Tradition*. Mountain View, CA: Mayfield Publishing Company, 1991.

Seed, Patricia. *Ceremonies of Possession in Europe's Conquest of the New World, 1492–1640*. Cambridge, MA: Cambridge University Press, 1995.

Seeger, Anthony. "Performance and Identity: Problems and Perspectives." In *Musical Repercussions of 1492: Encounters in Text and Performance*, edited by Carol E. Robertson, 451-461. Washington, DC: Smithsonian Institution Press, 1992.

———. *Why Suyá Sing: A Musical Anthropology of an Amazonian People*. Cambridge, MA: Cambridge University Press, 1987.

Shaul, David Leedom. "Language, Music and Dance in the Pimería Alta during the 1700s." Tumacácori, AZ: Tumacácori National Park, 1993.

———. "Mexico." In *The Garland Handbook of Latin American Music*, 2nd ed., edited by Dale A. Olsen and Daniel E. Sheehy, 181-208. New York: Garland Publishing, 2008.

Sheridan, Cecilia. *Anónimos y desterrados: la contienda por el "sitio que llaman de Quauyla," siglos XVI–XVIII*. Mexico City: Miguel Angel Porrúa, 2000.

Sheridan, Thomas E., ed. *Empire of Sand: The Seri Indians and the Struggle for Spanish Sonora, 1645–1803*. Tucson: University of Arizona Press, 1999.

Sheridan, Thomas E. *Where the Dove Calls: The Political Ecology of a Peasant Corporate Community in Northwestern Mexico*. Tucson: University of Arizona Press, 1988.

Sheridan, Thomas E., and Thomas H. Naylor, eds. *Rarámuri: A Tarahumara Colonial Chronicle, 1607–1791*. Flagstaff, AZ: Northland Press, 1979.

Simmons, Marc, ed. and trans. *Indian and Mission Affairs in New Mexico, 1773*. Santa Fe, NM: Stagecoach Press, 1965.

Small, Christopher. *Musicking: The Meanings of Performing and Listening*. Hanover, NH: University Press of New England, 1998.

Smoak, Gregory E. *Ghost Dances and Identity: Prophetic Religion and American Indian Ethnogenesis in the Nineteenth Century*. Berkeley: University of California Press, 2006.

Smolden, William L. *The Music of the Medieval Church Dramas*. London: Oxford University Press, 1980.

Socolow, Susan Migden. *The Women of Colonial Latin America*. New York: Cambridge University Press, 2000.

Sotomayor, Fr. José Francisco, O.F.M. *Historia del Apostólico Colegio de Nuestra Señora de Guadalupe de Zacatecas desde su fundación hasta nuestros dias*. Vol. II. Zacatecas: Mariano R. de Esparza, 1889.

Spalding, Karen. *Huarochirí: An Andean Society under Inca and Spanish Rule.* Stanford, CA: Stanford University Press, 1984.
Spell, Lota. "Music Teaching in New Mexico in the Seventeenth Century." *New Mexico Historical Review* 2 (1927): 27-36.
———. *Music in Texas: A Survey of One Aspect of Cultural Progress.* Austin, TX: AMS Press, 1936.
Spicer, Edward H. *Cycles of Conquest: The Impact of Spain, Mexico, and the United States on the Indians of the Southwest, 1533–1960.* Tucson: University of Arizona Press, 1962.
———. "Types of Contact and Processes of Change." In *Perspectives in American Indian Culture Change*, edited by Edward H. Spicer, 517-544. Chicago: University of Chicago Press, 1961.
———. *The Yaquis: A Cultural History.* Tucson: University of Arizona Press, 1980.
Spicer, Rosamund B., and N. Ross Crumrine, eds. *Performing the Renewal of Community: Indigenous Easter Rituals in North Mexico and the Southwest United States.* Lanham, MD: University Press of America, 1997.
Spiess, Lincoln Bruce. "Benavides and Church Music in New Mexico in the Early Seventeenth Century." *Journal of the American Musicological Society* 17, no. 2 (1964): 144-156.
Spike, Tamara. "To Make Graver This Sin: Conceptions of Purity and Pollution among the Timucua of Spanish Florida." PhD diss., Florida State University, 2006.
Spivak, Gayatri Chakravorty. "Can the Subaltern Speak?" In *Colonial Discourse and Post-Colonial Theory: A Reader*, edited by Patrick Williams and Laura Chrisman, 66-111. New York: Columbia University Press, 1994.
Staats, Susan K. "Fighting in a Different Way: Indigenous Resistance through the Alleluia Religion of Guyana." In *History, Power, and Identity: Ethnogenesis in the Americas, 1492–1992*, edited by Jonathan D. Hill, 161-179. Iowa City: University of Iowa Press, 1996.
Stark, Richard B. "Notes on a Search for Antecedents of New Mexican Alabado Music." In *Hispanic Arts and Ethnohistory in the Southwest*, edited by Marta Weigle, 117-127. Santa Fe, NM: Ancient City Press, 1983.
Steele, Thomas, S.J. *The Alabados of New Mexico.* Albuquerque: University of New Mexico Press, 2005.
Steiner, Ruth, and Kenneth Lily. "Liturgy." In *New Grove Dictionary of Music and Musicians*, vol. 11, edited by Stanley Sadie. London: Macmillan, 1980.
Stern, Steve J. "New Approaches to the Study of Peasant Rebellion and Consciousness: Implications of the Andean Experience." In *Resistance, Rebellion and Consciousness in the Andean Peasant World, 18th to 20th Centuries*, edited by Steve J. Stern, 3-28. Madison: University of Wisconsin Press, 1987.

———. *Peru's Indian Peoples and the Challenge of Spanish Conquest: Huamanga to 1640*. Madison: University of Wisconsin Press, 1982.

Stevens-Arroyo, Anthony M. "The Evolution of Marian Devotionalism within Christianity and the Ibero-Mediterranean Polity." *Journal for the Scientific Study of Religion* 37, no. 1 (March 1998): 50-73.

Stevenson, Robert Murrell. "Ignacio Jerusalem, 1707–1769." *Inter-American Music Review* 16, no. 1 (1997): 57-61.

———. "Mexican Musicology, 1980." *Inter-American Music Review* 3, no. 1 (1980): 65-87.

———. *Music in Aztec and Inca Territory*. Berkeley: University of California Press, 1968.

———. *Music in Mexico: A Historical Survey*. New York: Thomas Y. Crowell Company, 1952.

———. "Written Sources for Indian Music until 1882." *Ethnomusicology* 17 (1973): 6-14.

Summers, William J. "The *Misa Viscaina:* An Eighteenth-Century Musical Odyssey." In *Encomium Musicae: Essays in Memory of Robert Snow*, edited by David Crawford, and assistant editor G. Grayson Wagstaff, 127-141. Hillsdale, NY: Pendragon Press, 2002.

———. "New and Little Known Sources of Hispanic Music From California." *Inter-American Music Review* 11, no. 2 (1991): 13-24.

———. "Orígenes hispanos de la música misional de California." *Revista Musical Chilena* 34, nos. 149-150 (1980): 34-48.

———. "Music of the California Missions: An Inventory and Discussion of Selected Printed Music Books Used in Hispanic California, 1769–1836." *Soundings: Collections of the University Library* 9 (June 1977): 1-26.

———. "Recently Recovered Manuscript Sources of Sacred Polyphonic Music From Spanish California." *Ars Musica Denver* 7, no. 1 (1994): 13-30.

———. "A Reply to 'The Rise and Fall of Indian Music in the California Missions.'" *Latin American Music Review* 3 (1981): 130-135.

———. "Sancho: Alta California's Preeminent Musician." In *Juan Bautista Sancho: Pioneer Composer of California*. Coordinated by Antoni Pizá. Palma, Mallorca: Universitat de les Illes Balears, 2007.

———. "The Spanish Origins of California Mission Music." *Miscellanea Musicologica* 12 (1987): 109-26.

———. "Spanish Music in California: A Reassessment." In *Report of the Twelfth Congress of the International Musicological Society, Berkeley, 1977*, 371-379. Kassel, Germany: American Musicological Society, 1981.

Sweet, David. "The Ibero-American Frontier Mission in Native American History." In *The New Latin American Mission History*, edited by Erick Langer and Robert H. Jackson, 1-48. Lincoln: University of Nebraska Press, 1995.

Tame, David. *The Secret Power of Music: The Transformation of Self and Society through Musical Energy*. Rochester, VT: Destiny Books, 1984.

Tarry, Joe E. "Music in the Educational Philosophy of Martin Luther." *Journal of Research in Music Education* 21, no. 4 (Winter 1973): 355-365.

Taylor, William B. *Landlord and Peasant in Colonial Oaxaca*. Stanford, CA: Stanford University Press, 1972.

———. *Magistrates of the Sacred: Priests and Parishioners in Eighteenth-Century Mexico*. Stanford, CA: Stanford University Press, 1996.

Tiemstra, Suzanne Spicer. *The Choral Music of Latin America: A Guide to Compositions and Research*. New York: Greenwood Press, 1992.

Truitt, Jonathan. "Adopted Pedagogies: Nahua Incorporation of European Music and Theater in Colonial Mexico City," *Americas* 66:3 (January 2010), 311-330.

Turrent, Lourdes. *La Conquista Musical de México*. Mexico City: Fondo de Cultura Económica, 1996.

Twitchell, Ralph Emerson, ed. *The Spanish Archives of New Mexico*, vol. 2. Cedar Rapids, Iowa: Torch Press, 1914.

Underhill, Ruth Murray. *Singing for Power: The Song Magic of the Papago Indians of Southern Arizona*. Tucson: University of Arizona Press, 1993.

van der Veer, Peter. *Religious Nationalism: Hindus and Muslims in India*. Berkeley: University of California Press, 1994.

Van Dijk, Stephen J.P. "The Liturgical Legislation of the Franciscan Rules." *Franciscan Studies* 12 (1952): 176-195, 241-262.

Van Young, Eric. "The New Cultural History Comes to Old Mexico." *Hispanic American Historical Review* 79, no. 2 (1999): 211-247.

Vega, María Luisa, and José de Jesús Vega. *Advanced Education in Hispanic America during the Viceregal Centuries*. Phoenix, AZ: Biblioteca Hispano-Americana de Divulgación, 1986.

Vennum, Thomas, Jr. "Locating the Seri on the Musical Map of Indian North America." *Journal of the Southwest* 34, no. 2 (Autumn 2000): 635–760.

Venziano, Edy. "From One to Two Words: Repetition Patterns on the Way to Structured Speech." *Journal of Child Language* 17, no. 3 (1990): 653-660.

Verlinden, Charles. "Fray Pedro de Gante y su época." *Revista de Historia de América* 101 (1986): 105-131.

Viqueira Albán, Juan Pedro. *¿Relajados o reprimidos? Diversiones públicas y vida social en la ciudad de México durante el Siglo de las Luces*. Mexico City: Fondo de Cultura Económica, 1987.

Voekel, Pamela. *Alone before God: The Religious Origins of Modernity in Mexico*. Durham, NC: Duke University Press, 2002.

von Huebner, Dietmar. "Jesuiten." In *Die Musik in Geschichte Und Gegenwart*, vol. 4, 2nd abbrev. ed. Edited by Ludwig Finscher. Kassel: Bärenreiter, 1994.

Wagstaff, Grayson. "Franciscan Mission Music in California, c. 1770–1830: Chant, Liturgical, and Polyphonic Traditions." *Journal of the Royal Musical Association* 126, no. 1 (2001): 54-82.

Waisman, Leonardo. "¡Viva María! La música para la virgen en las misiones de Chiquitos." *Latin American Music Review* 13, no. 2 (Autumn–Winter 1992): 213-225.

Wallace, Antony. "Revitalization Movements: Some Theoretical Considerations for Their Comparative Study." *American Anthropologist* 58, no. 2 (April 1956): 264-281.

Warkentin, Larry. "The Rise and Fall of Indian Music in the California Missions," *Latin American Music Review* 2, no. 1 (Spring-Summer 1981): 45-65.

Weber, David J., and Jane M. Rausch, eds. *Where Cultures Meet: Frontiers in Latin American History*. Wilmington, DE: Scholarly Resources, 1994.

Wilde, Guillermo. "Toward a Political Anthropology of Mission Sound: Paraguay in the 17th and 18th Centuries." Translated by Eric Ederer. *Music and Politics* 1, no. 2 (Summer 2007): 1-36.

Will de Chaparro, Martina. *Death and Dying in New Mexico*. Albuquerque: University of New Mexico Press, 2007.

Wilson-Dickson, Andrew. *The Story of Christian Music*. Minneapolis, MN: Fortress Press, 1996.

Worth, John E. *The Timucuan Chiefdoms of Spanish Florida*. Vol. 2: *Resistance and Destruction*. Gainesville: University Press of Florida, 1998.

Zambrano, Francisco, comp. *Diccionario bio-bibliografica de la Compañía de Jesús en México*. Vols. 4-6. Mexico City: Editorial Jus, 1961.

———. *Diccionario bio-bibliográfica de la Compañía de Jesús en México*. Vol. 15. Mexico City: Editorial Tradicion, 1977.

Index

Acaxee, 24, 72, 108, 209
accommodation, 2-4, 7-8, 95, 115, 142, 146, 165, 211, 244, 249-251, 256-257, 259
aerophones, 40, 79, 85, 109, 154, 168, 174, 247
alabado, 4, 14, 85, 103, 106, 113, 115, 118, 121-122, 124, 127-128, 130, 138, 152, 161-165, 175, 180, 186-193, 202-207, 213, 228, 249, 255, 260
Angelus, 140, 179, 186, 196-197
antiphons, 4, 46, 49, 63, 76, 103, 165, 206
Apache, 5, 14, 24, 32, 33, 39, 98, 114, 118, 133, 134, 137, 139, 142-143, 146-147, 151, 152, 156
Apalachee, 95, 221
Assinai, 24, 28, 33, 35, 101, 116-117, 240-241
Autos Sacramentales (*see* drama)
Ave Maria, 75, 103, 125, 128, 140, 183, 189, 192, 196-197, 227, 228
Baegert, Jacob, 107, 192, 197, 225, 254
bajón, 79, 85, 110, 144, 154, 156
ball game, 24, 95
Ballejo, fray Francisco, 28-29, 40
baptism, 74-75, 91-92, 95, 97, 99, 102, 117, 146, 148, 162, 168, 199-201, 208, 220-221, 233
bells, 3, 14, 39, 49, 62, 70, 83, 84, 85, 87, 88, 95, 98, 106, 108, 112, 113, 116, 117, 135, 136, 137, 139, 140, 144, 147, 151, 154, 155, 174, 179-181, 186-201, 205-207, 210-211,

215, 218, 221, 232, 234, 237, 251, 257
Benavides, fray Alonso de, 86-88, 189, 197
Bischoff, Xavier, 107, 191
books, liturgical, 46, 49, 54, 82-86, 103, 144, 152, 160, 161, 164, 169, 171, 172, 174, 200, 249, 254
Bourbon reforms, 101, 133, 145, 158, 214, 225, 242, 243
Bucareli, Viceroy Antonio de, 138, 156, 187
Caddo, 30, 116
California, Alta, 8, 14, 22, 36, 127, 131, 134, 136, 144, 158-166, 170-175, 200, 203, 204, 206, 210, 214, 222, 228-230, 233, 246, 248, 249, 255
California, Baja, 14, 22, 26, 38, 104-107, 108, 114, 121, 123, 125, 129, 134-138, 141, 143, 144, 159, 160, 174, 181, 192-196, 199, 201, 205, 207, 210, 228, 229, 236, 238, 240, 247, 251
Calvin, Jean, 45, 49-50, 59, 64
Canonical Hours (*see* Divine Office)
canticle, 46, 50, 52, 83
cantor (*see* also musician), 90, 103, 108, 118, 131, 152, 175, 186-188, 192, 221-222, 226-228, 231, 259
Carancaguases, 118, 152
Cárdenas, fray Joseph, 151-153
catechist, 75, 88, 90, 108, 110, 114, 139, 140, 145, 180, 187, 192-193, 221, 259
catsina (*see* also dance), 94-95, 98, 115, 220, 250

293

ceremony (*see* ritual)
chant (plainchant, plainsong), 4, 5, 43, 45-46, 49, 52-57, 60, 61, 64, 69, 75, 78, 79, 82, 83, 84, 85, 96, 103, 110, 116-117, 121, 127, 130, 141, 160, 161, 166, 171, 174, 176, 213, 215, 224-225, 246-248, 250, 251, 254, 255
chant, figured, 85, 110, 130, 151, 173, 224
Chihuahua, 9, 38, 134, 138, 159, 231
children, 5, 14, 20, 25, 36, 49, 57, 62, 75, 88-90, 96, 101-102, 106, 113, 116-117, 121-122, 130, 137, 140, 145, 156, 161, 183, 186, 190-191, 205, 221, 230, 245
chirimía (*see* also shawm), 78-79, 85, 86, 110, 143-144, 154-155, 199, 254
choir, 5, 45-49, 52, 54, 55, 57, 59, 60, 64, 79, 80, 84-86, 97, 103, 106, 107, 109, 110, 122, 125, 127, 128, 131, 140, 141, 143, 151, 152, 156, 161, 168, 169-173, 175, 187, 189, 190, 220, 221, 225-229, 231, 233, 238, 256, 259
chordophones, 23, 39, 47, 48, 79, 85, 86, 95, 105, 108, 109, 130, 135, 141, 144, 147, 154, 164, 169, 170, 175, 176, 189, 229, 247, 250
Christmas, 46, 51, 58, 76, 96, 130, 140, 148-149, 171, 176, 207, 232, 234, 245, 248-249, 260
Chumash, 22, 167, 169
Cíbola, 73-74
clarines, 85, 215, 216
Coahuila, 14, 22, 116-118, 134, 145-152, 216
Coahuiltecan, 26, 30, 32, 39, 118-119, 146, 147, 149
Cochimí, 26, 36
cofradías (*see* confraternities)
Comanche, 14, 22, 24, 32, 33, 118, 133, 134, 147, 150-151, 152
communication, music and, 3, 6, 10, 13-14, 20-21, 25, 34-40, 46, 52, 56, 64, 69-71, 79, 87-90, 94, 97, 129, 137, 170, 193, 215, 223, 253, 254, 256-257
Communion (*see* also Eucharist), 46, 56, 92, 96, 115, 153, 192, 237
community formation, 3, 12-13, 15, 21, 24-27, 75, 90, 118-125, 256
Compline, 46, 48, 55, 56, 184
confraternities, 48, 57, 127, 226, 239, 256
conquest, 3, 10, 28, 31, 34-35, 69-70, 75, 79, 111, 124, 247
control, 3, 4, 7, 10, 14, 15, 20, 22, 44, 52, 83, 95, 97, 104, 108, 130, 173, 176, 189, 231, 243, 255-257, 259
Cora, 34, 39, 194
corneta, 79, 85
Coronado, Francisco Vasquez de (expedition), 70-74, 88
Corpus Christi, 9, 51, 76, 92, 96, 116, 122, 130, 140, 176, 200, 217, 218, 225, 232, 234-243, 251
costuming, 26, 47, 64, 74, 76, 111, 119, 130, 168, 176, 177, 236, 237, 239-242, 245, 255-256
Council of Trent, 51-52, 59, 64, 80-81, 88, 224, 230, 235, 257
Counter-Reformation, 13, 50-52, 59, 62, 70, 203
Credo, 46, 181, 186
Cucurpe, Los Santos Reyes del, 109, 131, 138-143, 175, 176, 209, 229, 233, 239
Culiacán, 71, 226
cultural hegemony, 10-12, 74, 83, 113, 146, 158, 176, 179-181, 211, 235, 240, 243, 257, 259
dance, 3, 5, 8, 13, 15, 24, 26-41, 47, 48, 50, 64, 70, 74, 76, 79, 80, 82, 83, 86, 87, 90-98, 102-104, 109-115, 118, 119, 123-125, 130-131, 134, 138, 140, 141, 142-145, 146-153, 162, 163, 166-170, 175-177, 180, 183, 193, 195, 198, 208-209, 213-214, 219-220, 224-
de Leon, Alonso, 30, 116, 240
deer, 25, 30-31, 35, 36, 91, 250

devil, 32, 77, 87, 93, 94, 95, 218, 238, 239, 249
discipline, 10, 49, 55, 57, 77, 117, 136, 141, 153, 181-184, 194, 198, 211, 229
disease, 7, 12, 21, 77, 90, 92, 106, 118, 123, 136, 139, 156, 159, 193, 200-201, 211, 223, 231, 233, 257
Divine Office, 46, 50, 53-57, 77, 85, 110, 126, 130, 141, 160, 169, 174, 184, 194, 224, 245
doctrine (doctrina), 2, 3, 5, 11, 14, 43, 44, 46, 50, 61-64, 74-79, 88, 90-92, 103-106, 121-122, 137, 142-143, 157, 163-166, 181-184, 193, 197, 203-207, 237-238
Domínguez, fray Francisco Atanasio, 149-150, 186, 193
Dominicans, 57, 136, 143-144, 173, 191, 199
drama, 43, 44, 46-49, 53, 58, 72, 75, 76, 79, 80, 81, 150, 170, 171, 176, 179, 184, 194, 208, 229, 236, 237, 238, 241-243, 249, 257, 260
drama, Jesuit, 62-64
drinking and drunkenness, 30, 33, 38, 92-93, 148, 150, 219-220, 228, 234
drums, 34, 38, 39, 40, 48, 69, 91, 147, 167, 172, 176, 208, 215, 216, 233
Durán, fray Narciso, 161, 165, 166, 171, 172, 246, 249
Durango cathedral, 168-169
Easter, 70, 76, 140, 148, 149, 207, 232, 234, 235, 238-239, 242
education, 5, 10, 14, 49, 55, 57, 59, 60, 62-63, 69, 74-80, 83, 88-90, 101-104, 106, 114, 116-117, 122, 126-128, 136-140, 157, 160-163, 185-186, 189-191, 225, 254, 257-258
entrada, 13, 65, 69-73, 112, 116, 124, 157, 159, 214-216
Espinosa, fray Felix Isidro de, 30, 33, 55, 116-117, 206
Espíritu Santo de Zuñíga (Texas), 128, 151, 205, 227-228
Esselen, 22, 167

ethnogenesis, 7, 12, 27, 209, 211, 214, 244-246, 249, 251, 258
Eucharist, 45, 47, 50, 80, 96, 202, 216, 235, 240, 241
Eudeves, 30, 109, 131, 138, 139-140, 176, 209, 255
evangelization, and music, 8, 10, 13-14, 44-45, 50, 55, 56, 59, 61, 64, 69-70, 74-77, 80-91, 98, 101-104, 114, 118, 126-130, 185, 186, 190, 203, 206, 218, 221, 232, 256-259
falsobordone, 45, 49, 60
fandango, 148, 149, 162, 229
Florida, 14, 22, 69, 72, 84, 86, 89, 95, 97, 201, 221, 223
flutes, 29, 40, 53, 74, 78, 85, 86, 109, 119, 123, 164, 172, 233, 254
Font, fray Pedro, 148, 160, 204, 213
food, 25-26, 30, 33, 38, 54, 64, 92, 96, 106, 114, 137, 140, 146, 149, 152, 154-156, 168, 182-184, 190, 193, 197, 208, 209, 227, 230, 234, 237, 243, 258
Francis of Assisi, St., 53-54, 57-58, 148
Franciscans, 13-15, 32, 41, 44, 45, 50, 53, 54-59, 61, 65, 70-74, 76, 77, 80, 83, 84, 86-89, 94, 98, 101, 106-108, 112-118, 123, 124, 127-131, 135-138, 142-161, 165, 172, 173, 175, 184-187, 190, 191, 193, 198, 203, 204, 206, 208, 210, 215, 219, 223, 234, 241, 248, 250
Gabrielinos, 165, 166, 224, 228
Galvez expedition, 37, 159
gambling, 148, 219, 234
Gante, fray Pedro de, 75-77, 149, 184
Garcés, fray Francisco, 153, 156-157
García, fray Bartholomé, 146
gift-giving, 64, 70, 71, 74, 87, 88, 97, 112, 117, 153, 158, 165, 208, 215, 221, 227-228, 234, 237, 240, 241, 243, 258
Gilg, Adam, 117, 154
Gloria, 46, 112
gozos, 152, 165

Granados, Bishop José Joaquin, 155-156, 254
Guaraní, 1, 7, 12, 15
Guichí, Agustín, 115-116
guitar, 48, 52, 53, 85, 108, 124, 144, 147, 152, 154, 162, 164, 174
harmony, 5, 45-46, 50, 143, 165, 170
harp, 52, 53, 85, 108, 109, 110, 139, 144, 147, 155, 250
harvest, 24, 26, 28, 30, 35-36, 38, 79, 94, 168, 176, 205, 209, 244, 248
"healing, music and, 13, 23, 30, 33-34, 43, 47, 86, 223, 248, 251
hegemony (*see* cultural hegemony)
Holy Week, 46, 57, 60, 76, 79, 122, 130, 144, 148, 149, 176, 226, 238, 241-243, 251
Hopi, 22, 28, 29, 244
Huicholes, 34, 39
hymns, 4, 9, 12, 27, 43, 48, 50, 54, 55, 63, 64, 73, 76, 83, 84, 91, 92, 102, 103, 107, 113, 121, 123, 126-128, 162, 165, 172, 183, 187, 201-206, 211, 213, 215, 216, 237, 247, 250, 253-256
Ibáñez, fray Florencio. 171
identity, music and, 3-5, 10-14, 24-27, 33, 40, 41-45, 47-50, 52, 56, 64, 69, 70, 90-92, 99, 102, 119, 123-124, 143, 166, 168, 180, 214, 233, 239, 251, 253-259
idiophones (*see* also rattles), 29, 34, 38-39, 111, 119, 143, 149, 167, 176, 195
Ignatius of Loyola, St., 59-63, 124, 127, 233
instrumentalists, 28-29, 34, 46, 48, 49, 75, 80, 109, 110, 131, 139, 169, 173, 174, 177, 180, 221, 233, 240, 259
instruments, musical, 3, 23, 29, 30, 34, 38-40, 47-48, 51-53, 60-64, 73, 77-87, 94, 95, 99, 105, 108-109, 112-113, 126-131, 134, 135, 141, 144, 147, 149, 151, 154-156, 164-167, 169-176, 188, 189, 193, 195, 202, 208, 218, 222, 232-233, 247, 250, 255-259
Introit, 46
Jemez Pueblo, 112, 185-189, 260
Jesuit expulsion 1767, 14, 102, 104, 107, 129, 131, 134-137, 140, 153, 255, 256
Jesuits, 2-5, 10, 13, 15, 33, 40-41, 44, 50, 59-65, 70, 71, 73, 78, 80, 84-92, 96-99, 101, 102, 104, 106-109, 114, 126-131, 134-139, 141, 153, 157-159, 176, 184, 190, 191, 196, 198, 201, 203, 206, 209, 216, 219, 233, 248, 250, 251, 255
Karankawa (*see* Carancaguases)
Kino, Father Francisco Eusebio, 40, 101, 106, 120-121, 221, 233, 236, 249
kiva, 67, 93-94, 98, 113-115, 219
Laguneros, 25, 27, 32, 71
Langsdorff, Georg Heinrich von, 162, 166-167, 170
lauda, 57, 257
Lauds, 46, 48, 55, 56, 169, 183
Lent, 53, 58, 79, 80, 207
litanies, 56, 57, 105, 107, 109, 116, 128, 139-140, 144, 181, 205, 206, 214, 215, 227
liturgy, 4, 13, 14, 43-56, 59, 61, 63, 64, 69, 70, 82, 87, 91, 103, 105, 125, 127-129, 157, 169, 181, 182, 185, 189, 192, 203, 205, 218, 225, 229, 231, 244, 246, 248-250, 255, 256, 259
López de Mendizábal, Bernardo, 94, 124, 236
Loreto Conchó, Nuestra Señora de, 104-107, 124, 127, 136, 143-144, 190-191, 197, 199, 234, 236, 245, 258
Louisiana, 2, 133, 157, 158
Luther, Martin, 49-50, 64, 106
maestro de capilla, 46, 110, 120, 126, 167
Margil, fray Antonio, 14-15, 102, 119-122, 124-127, 153, 163-164, 173, 203-204, 207, 215, 254

Index

Marian devotion, 48, 51, 63, 78, 117, 124, 150, 159, 162-165, 206, 216, 228, 250, 253

Mass, 4-5, 43, 45-46, 48-56, 58-62, 64, 69-73, 75, 77, 78, 81, 84-87, 91, 95-97, 102-103, 105, 106, 109-110, 115-118, 121-125, 128, 130, 137, 138, 140, 141, 144, 148-157, 160-162, 167-169, 172, 174, 175, 176, 182-185, 186-200, 208-209, 214-218, 221-225, 232, 23

matachines (*see* also dance), 4, 31, 111, 140, 149, 208, 229, 243, 250, 260

Matins, 46, 48, 51, 55, 56, 169, 184

Mayo, 30, 92, 111

Mazanet, fray Damián, 116, 240

mestizo, 4, 94, 101, 102, 108, 114, 134, 136, 142-143, 147, 149, 155, 186, 194, 198, 229, 239, 256

Mexican Provincial Councils, 81-82, 110, 133, 150, 196, 225, 230, 236, 257

Middle Ages, 46, 47, 235, 257

minstrels, 46-48, 54, 58

miserere, 79, 238

mitote (*see* also dance), 24, 29, 33, 35, 37-39, 41, 79, 80, 93, 118, 119, 146-147, 149, 193, 229

Montezuma mitote, 79-80, 110-111, 140, 143

Morfi, fray Juan Agustín, 119, 147, 152

moros y cristianos, 80, 110, 150, 208, 229, 236, 250, 257

motet, 85, 130, 174, 176, 248

Motolinía (fray Toribio de Benavente), 77, 86

mourning, 25, 29, 224

music, and healing, 13, 23, 30, 33-34, 43, 86, 146, 223, 248, 251

music, as language, 5, 6, 10, 13, 14, 20, 25, 34-40, 56, 64

music, as mnemonic device, 3, 5, 90, 103, 161, 202, 257

musicians (*see* also instrumentalists, singers), 12, 26, 28, 29, 46-48, 50, 78-82, 85, 103, 110, 131, 134, 143-144, 151, 162, 167-169, 171-173, 177, 180, 187, 193, 199, 208, 221-222, 233, 237, 239, 246, 249, 256

Nahua, 7-9, 32, 37, 74-76, 79-83, 110, 203, 226

Nascimben, Pedro María, 106-107, 128-129, 144-145, 173

Navajo, 22, 87-88, 185

Nentvig, Juan, 35-37, 103, 109, 110, 139-140, 162, 221, 235

neophytes, 10, 58, 75, 91, 102, 117, 122-123, 128, 140, 146-148, 154, 160-163, 165, 169-171, 191-193, 197, 200, 202-205, 206, 210, 220, 224, 233, 235, 238-240, 245, 249

New Mexico, 5, 14, 22, 39, 67, 69, 71-72, 84-86, 89, 94-95, 101, 104, 106, 112-115, 123-124, 130, 134, 147-153, 159, 168, 174, 176, 186-190, 194, 195, 199, 202-203, 206, 208, 216-217, 219, 221-222, 226, 234, 241-242, 245, 250, 255, 260

Nuestra Señora del Pópulo, 154-155

Nuestra Señora del Rosario Mission (Texas), 35, 112, 149-150, 154, 193

Nuestra Señora de Refugio (feast day), 56, 196

Nuestra Señora de Refugio Mission (Texas), 154, 198

Nueva Vizcaya, 2, 6, 8, 12, 14, 22, 69, 84-86, 107-110, 146, 171, 174, 176, 199, 206, 209, 225, 226, 231, 243

Nuevo Santander, 2, 22, 29-30, 39, 173, 198

Och, Joseph, 24-25, 108, 111, 227, 229, 234

Oñate, Juan de, 72, 84, 185

O'odham, 19-21, 28, 29, 33, 40

Opata, 30, 35, 103, 109, 111, 131, 138-143, 162, 176, 209, 255

organ, 38, 46, 49, 51-53, 56, 59, 61, 78, 79, 81, 85, 86, 105, 110, 144, 161, 169, 174, 176, 181, 189

Ortiz Zapata, Father Juan, 85, 140

painting, 26, 76-77, 113, 163-165, 174, 200

pantomine, 43, 79, 83, 150, 209, 234
Papago (*see* O'odham)
pastorelas, 96, 171
patriarchy, 5, 12, 231
Pecos, 67, 112, 115, 222
penitentes, 150, 242
Pentecost, 58, 207, 232
Pérez de Ribas, Andrés, 25, 27, 32, 78-80, 84, 85, 91, 198, 200, 207, 208, 216, 219, 226, 228
peyote, 30, 33, 118, 146
Pfefferkorn, Ignaz, 30, 109, 139-140, 228
Pima, 19, 25, 29, 35, 36, 38, 39, 108, 117, 137, 139, 140-143, 145, 155, 227
Pimentel, fray Mariano López, 159, 253
pitahaya, 26, 38, 208, 248
polygamy, 86, 92, 97, 152
polyphony, 46, 51, 58, 78, 85, 130, 152, 161, 164, 166, 175, 225
possession, rites of, 70, 72, 112, 116, 160, 199, 213, 214-218, 240
power, music and, 11, 15, 20, 28-34, 92-95, 116-117, 179-182, 193, 195, 198, 201, 251, 253, 254, 257, 259, 260
processions, 44, 48, 50, 51, 53, 57, 64, 79, 91, 96, 97, 105, 117, 119, 122, 140, 143, 148, 150, 153, 161, 162, 176, 193, 207, 210-211, 216-221, 227, 234, 236-246, 248, 252, 253, 258
Provincias Internas, 133-134, 193, 198
psalms, 4, 43, 46, 50, 57, 103, 110, 125, 217, 224
Psalmodia Christiana, 10, 82-83
psalterio, 108, 109, 139
Pueblo Revolt 1680, 94-95, 98, 101, 112-114, 185, 222
Puebloans, 5, 24, 27, 38, 74, 94-95, 98, 112-115, 186, 208, 219
Puríssima Concepción (mission, Texas), 149, 198, 233
Querétaro, Colegio de Santa Cruz de, 55, 56, 116, 117, 119, 150, 153, 156, 160, 191-192, 203, 204

rattles, 29, 30, 34, 38, 39, 111, 119, 143, 149, 167, 176, 250
rebellion (*see* also resistance), 3-4, 7, 11, 14, 70, 93-99, 101, 103, 108, 113-114, 118, 139, 141, 154, 167, 168, 185, 188, 190, 194, 199, 201, 216, 222, 223, 226, 243, 244, 246, 249, 255, 259
Reformation, 13, 31, 44-45, 49-50, 61
Renaissance, 45-49, 52, 57, 58, 75, 176, 216
repetition, 3, 5, 24, 25, 46, 62, 76, 90, 102, 105, 113, 134, 152, 180-183, 202, 205-206, 218, 223
resistance, 7-8, 11, 60, 190, 192, 203, 248, 258, 261
Reyes, fray Antonio de los, 136-138, 141, 205, 206
rhythm, 5, 20, 30, 33-34, 40, 46, 51, 61, 75, 79, 80, 83, 90, 149, 164-166, 180, 182, 190, 197, 247-249, 255
ritual , 4, 5, 9, 10, 13, 14, 21, 23, 24, 26, 29, 30, 31, 33-41, 43, 47, 70-72, 74-76, 79-80, 87, 91, 95, 112-119, 135, 136, 146, 155, 158, 160, 166, 168, 170, 180, 199, 209, 213-215, 218-220, 223, 224, 232, 235, 241, 243, 245, 249-251, 258, 259
rosary, 87, 107, 128-129, 135, 138, 140, 144, 147, 150, 161, 187, 192, 193, 200, 204, 205, 240, 248, 258
routines, daily, 10, 14, 55-56, 62, 89, 103, 106, 116, 125, 127, 130, 136, 137, 145, 151-157, 160-162, 165, 179, 181-196, 200, 205-207, 210-211, 228, 257
Rubí, Marquis de, 146, 147, 153, 227
Ruíz, fray Joaquín de Jesús, 185, 187-190, 202
Salvatierra, Juan María de, 14, 15, 102, 104, 119-128, 173, 190, 199, 254
Salve Regina, 56, 75, 78, 85, 88, 103, 109, 128, 138, 139, 152, 157, 161, 165, 180, 186, 189, 192, 206, 227, 228, 248, 255
San Agustín de Isleta, 114, 185-188

INDEX 299

San Antonio de Béjar (villa), 118-119, 146-147, 149, 151-152, 198, 229, 233, 236, 243
San Antonio de Padua, 160, 161, 168, 169
San Bernardino de Candela, 118
San Buenaventura (Alta California), 167, 169
San Carlos Borromeo de Monterrey, 160-161, 165, 167, 200, 215, 228
San Diego (Alta California), 38, 162, 166, 172
San Fernando (colegio), 159, 170, 172
San Francisco Xavier Arivechi, 85, 89, 111
San Francisco Xavier de Cumuripa, 93, 136
San Gregorio, Colegio de, 78, 80, 85, 110, 226
San Ignacio Tórim, 91-92, 219, 237
San José (Alta California), 161, 164-166, 169-172, 214, 215, 233
San José de Tumacacori, 35, 137
San José y San Miguel de Aguayo, 119, 126, 129, 146-147
San Juan Bautista (Alta California), 29-30, 36, 161-162, 164, 169, 172, 210, 215, 248
San Juan Bautista (Coahuila), 118, 148, 152
San Xavier del Bac, 153, 156
Santa Barbara, 160-162, 168-169, 176
Santa Clara de Asís (Alta California), 160-161, 168-169, 222, 229, 238
Santa María Baserac, 142
Santa María de las Parras, 85, 130, 174, 244, 248
Santa María Mulegé, 106-107, 128, 144
Santa María, fray Vicente de, 30-33, 165
Satevó, San Francisco Xavier de, 110, 222
Scott, James (weapons of the weak), 11, 246
Sequences, 47, 49, 51
Seri, 23, 25, 28, 29, 38, 39, 40, 108, 134, 137, 143, 154-156, 251, 254

Serra, fray Junípero, 124, 125, 159-160, 164, 200, 204, 218, 229
shamans, 28, 29, 33, 36, 71, 92, 96, 97, 98, 108, 113, 146, 223-224
shawms (*see* also chirimía), 48, 78
Sinaloa, 2, 22, 32, 38, 40, 91, 104, 107-112, 134, 137, 200, 237
soldiers, 3, 31, 69, 71, 72, 91, 97, 101, 102, 104, 105, 108, 109, 111, 112, 113, 117, 118, 122, 134, 140, 141, 143, 148, 150, 153, 157, 160, 162, 200, 205, 214, 215, 216, 224, 236, 238-241, 255-256
Solis, fray Gaspar José de, 35, 37
songs, devotional, 4, 14, 48, 50, 52, 54, 55, 57-58, 63, 73, 76, 84, 85, 87-90, 96, 99, 102-105, 107, 109, 118, 122, 127-130, 138-139, 147, 152, 157, 160-161, 163-166, 169, 172-175, 179, 181, 202-203, 206, 208, 215-219, 223-224, 227-228, 240-243, 247-251, 254-259
Sonora, 14, 22-25, 30, 36, 38, 101, 106-111, 114, 134-142, 155-156, 159, 170, 203, 209, 210, 216, 226-227, 231, 234, 251
Spain, 47, 53, 60, 62, 75, 80, 82, 83, 101, 106, 119, 127, 169, 171, 202, 225, 229, 236, 242, 253
Spicer, Edward, 23, 185, 203, 218, 250
syncretism, 4, 70, 82, 91, 99, 110-111, 214, 241, 247-249, 259
Tamaral, Nicolás, 105-106, 190, 192
Tamaron y Romeral, Bishop Pedro, 114-115, 225, 241
tambourine, 48, 53
Tapis, Estevan de, 162-164
Tarahumara, 29, 31, 35, 38, 39, 72, 108, 110-111, 137, 155, 170, 198, 201, 210, 219, 222, 250, 251
Te Deum Laudamus, 50, 117, 124, 160, 214, 215
temastián (*see* catechist)
Tepehuan, 30, 34, 39, 72, 96, 108, 171, 216, 246
Tepozotlán, 79, 120

Tesuque, 94, 113, 206
Tewa, 27, 87-88, 113
Texas, 14, 22, 32, 35, 37, 39, 101, 106, 116-119, 122, 123, 129, 134, 145-154, 157, 159, 163, 173, 175, 203, 204, 215-217, 226, 236, 240
time. restructuring, 5, 10, 14, 41, 49, 179-211, 251, 256, 260
Timucua, 36, 97-98, 223
Tobosos, 37, 118
Torim (*see* San Ignacio Tórim)
Trent, Council of, 51-52, 59, 64, 88, 224, 230, 235, 257
tropes, 46, 47, 49, 51
trumpet, 48, 53, 69, 72, 85, 87, 88, 172, 199, 233, 234, 253
trumpet, shell, 36, 40
Ugarte, Pedro de, 123, 179, 199, 245
Vargas, don Diego de, 112, 185, 199
vecinos, 108, 109, 137, 148
Vespers, 46, 48, 53, 55, 56, 60, 61, 63, 85, 128, 130, 140, 150, 175, 184, 189, 192, 196, 216, 234
Vetancurt, fray Agustín 56, 57, 76, 77
villancico, 50, 51, 75, 226

violin, 1, 29-30, 108-111, 139, 141, 144, 147, 151-152, 154, 155, 162, 164, 169, 172, 174, 233, 250, 258
visita, 88-89, 128, 139, 227
War, and music (*see* also rebellion, revolt), 2-3, 5, 23-24, 28, 29, 31-32, 88, 98, 112-113, 155, 216, 224, 245
whistle, 30, 36, 40, 234
women, 5, 12, 25, 26, 27, 29, 30, 31, 33, 36, 37, 52, 58, 71, 76, 91, 104, 106, 115, 138, 139, 152, 155, 157, 162, 165-167, 186-190, 197, 205, 214, 221, 223, 224-232, 246, 250, 251, 259
Xarames (*see* also Coahuiltecans), 117, 146
Xixime, 29, 32, 72, 209
Yaqui, 21, 24, 29-32, 34, 36, 38, 39, 72, 84, 91, 92, 105, 108, 111, 139, 144, 155, 196, 198, 201, 218, 219, 250
Yuma, 39, 134, 156-157, 246
Zacatecas, 56, 75, 120, 122, 137, 138, 154, 203-204, 217
Zuni, 22, 39, 73